Yugoslavia

A World Bank Country Economic Report

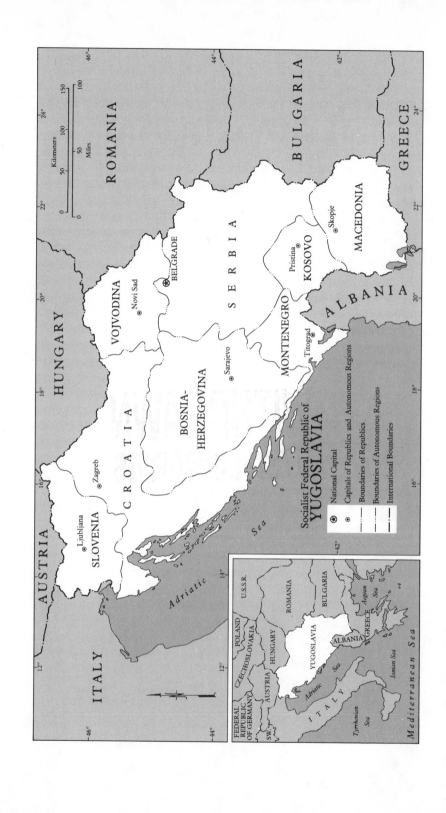

Socialist Federal Republic of
YUGOSLAVIA

⊕ National Capital
◉ Capitals of Republics and Autonomous Regions
······ Boundaries of Republics
–··–··– Boundaries of Autonomous Regions
——— International Boundaries

AUSTRIA

HUNGARY

ROMANIA

Kilometers
0 50 100 150
0 50 100
Miles

ITALY

SLOVENIA
⊙ Ljubljana

CROATIA
⊙ Zagreb

VOJVODINA
⊙ Novi Sad

BELGRADE ⊕

BOSNIA-
HERZEGOVINA
⊙ Sarajevo

SERBIA

MONTENEGRO
Titograd ◉

KOSOVO
Pristina ◉

MACEDONIA
◉ Skopje

ALBANIA

BULGARIA

GREECE

Adriatic

Sea

FEDERAL
REPUBLIC
OF GERMANY
SW.
POLAND
CZECHOSLOVAKIA
AUSTRIA
HUNGARY
ROMANIA
U.S.S.R.
BULGARIA
YUGOSLAVIA
ALBANIA
ITALY
Adriatic
Sea
GREECE
Aegean
Sea
Ionian Sea
Tyrrhenian
Sea
Mediterranean Sea

Yugoslavia

Self-management Socialism
and the
Challenges of Development

*Report of a mission sent to Yugoslavia
by the World Bank*

Martin Schrenk, Cyrus Ardalan,
and Nawal A. El Tatawy

Coordinating Authors

Published for the World Bank
The Johns Hopkins University Press
Baltimore and London

Copyright © 1979 by
The International Bank
for Reconstruction and Development   THE WORLD BANK
1818 H Street, N.W., Washington, D.C. 20433, U.S.A.
All rights reserved
Manufactured in the United States of America

Library of Congress Cataloging in Publication Data

Schrenk, Martin, 1928–
    Yugoslavia, self-management socialism and the
challenges of development.

    (A World Bank country economic report)
    Includes index.
    1. Yugoslavia—Economic policy—1945–
    2. Yugoslavia—Economic conditions—1945–
    I. Ardalan, Cyrus, 1950–   joint author.
    II. El Tatawy, Nawal A., 1942–   joint author.
    III. International Bank for Reconstruction and Develop-
ment. IV. Title. V. Series.
    HC407.Y83   330.9'497'02   79-84316
    ISBN 0-8018-2263-7
    ISBN 0-8018-2278-5 pbk.

Foreword

THIS IS THE EIGHTEENTH IN THE CURRENT SERIES of World Bank country economic reports, all of which are listed on the following page. They are published, in response to a desire expressed by scholars and practitioners in the field of economic and social development, to facilitate research and the interchange of knowledge.

The Bank regularly prepares economic reports on borrowing countries in support of its own operations. These surveys provide a basis for discussion with governments and for decisions on Bank policy and operations. Many governments use the reports as an aid to their economic planning, as do consortia and consultative groups of governments and institutions providing assistance in development. All Bank country reports are published subject to the agreement of —and several have been published by—the governments concerned.

HOLLIS B. CHENERY
Vice President for Development Policy
The World Bank

Washington, D.C.
September 1979

Contents

Figures and Tables

Acronyms and Initials

BOAL	Basic organization of associated labor
COAL	Contractual organization of associated labor
CKD	Completely knocked down
COMINFORM	Communist Information Bureau
EEC	European Economic Community
GDP	Gross domestic product
GMP	Gross material product
GNP	Gross national product
GNS	Gross national savings
ICOR	Incremental capital-output ratio
IMF	International Monetary Fund
ISIC	International standard industrial classification
LCY	League of Communists of Yugoslavia
LDC	Less developed country
NBY	National Bank of Yugoslavia
OECD	Organization for Economic Cooperation and Development
SITC	Standard international trade classification

Currency Equivalents

Before January 23, 1971

U.S.$1.00 = Din12.5

Between January 23, 1971 and December 22, 1971

U.S.$1.00 = Din15.0

Between December 22, 1971 and July 12, 1972

U.S.$1.00 = Din17.0

Since July 12, 1972

The dinar has been floating.

On December 31, 1978

U.S.$1.00 = Din18.6

All dollar figures in this report
are current U.S. dollars.

Preface

THIS IS THE WORLD BANK'S second country economic report on Yugoslavia. The first, *Yugoslavia: Development with Decentralization*, published by The Johns Hopkins University Press in 1974, reviewed the institutional setting and economic performance under the decentralized system established after the economic reforms of 1965. Those reforms emphasized the autonomy of enterprises and embraced the competitive market as the moving force and regulator of economic development. The focus of this report is a new phase in Yugoslavia's development, a phase that gradually emerged in the 1970s in response to external economic challenges and the successes and failures of the 1965 reforms. The new phase was formally initiated by the constitutional amendments of 1971; its essence is defined in the constitution of 1974; its consolidation still is in progress.

Three sets of objectives were adopted in preparing this report. The first was to trace the institutional changes of the 1970s to underlying sociopolitical conditions and to sketch the main features of the present framework for economic management. The second was to review the economic goals of the five-year plan for 1976–80 and to assess the prospects of and the constraints on meeting those goals. The third was to analyze in some detail the six central issues of economic development that Yugoslavia has faced over the years.

The report is arranged in two parts. Part one introduces the main institutional features of Yugoslavia's system of economic management and analyzes the country's economic problems and prospects. Part two presents the more detailed analysis of fundamental issues of economic development; its principal conclusions are incorporated in part one. For readers interested only in a sweeping overview, we recommend chapters one, two, and five. For those interested only in gaining insights about the Yugoslav system, we recommend chapters one through four.

Chapters one and two sketch the social, political, and economic

xv

trends up to 1975; they set the stage for the subsequent description
and discussion of the basic elements of "the Yugoslav system" in the
second half of the 1970s—the centerpiece of part one. Chapter three
sets out the principal premises underlying self-management socialism
and the translation of those premises into institutional arrangements
and instruments for macroeconomic and microeconomic management. Chapter four presents and discusses the Yugoslav perception
of the two central institutional issues of economic management: the
role of the market and the role of planning, particularly the novel
concept of "self-management planning." Because the transition from
the old system to the new is still in progress, chapters three and four
do not attempt to provide a definitive description of the present
state of affairs. By necessity their focus is on the direction of the
changes and on the promises and limitations of those changes for the
efficient management of the economy. Consequently these chapters
present, in addition to objective facts, the hypotheses derived by the
authors from diverse evidence, which is in turn imbued with economic and noneconomic considerations. Chapter five summarizes
the objectives of the five-year plan for 1976–80 and the mission's
assessment of Yugoslavia's development prospects over that period.
The six chapters constituting part two can be considered as self-
contained essays on the respective issues—stabilization, resource
mobilization, resource allocation, the balance of payments, employment, and regional development. A technical note at the end of
chapter eight describes the input-output model that was extensively
used for the analysis.

This report is based on the findings of a mission that visited Yugoslavia in November 1976. Members of this mission were Martin
Schrenk, chief; Cyrus Ardalan, general economist; Charles Chittle,
foreign trade consultant; Kathleen Jordan, input-output specialist;
Boris Blazic-Metzner, national accounts specialist; Nawal A. El
Tatawy, general economist; and Kosara Gavrilovic, interpreter and
translator. Yuji Kubo of the Bank's staff worked with the mission in
preparing the input-output analysis. William Dunn, a faculty member of the Graduate School of Public and International Affairs at
the University of Pittsburgh, wrote the chapter on social and
political development. Bruce Ross-Larson edited the manuscript for
publication. Florence Robinson indexed the text, Harry Einhorn
corrected proofs of the text and tables, the Graphics Unit of the
World Bank's Art and Design Section prepared the charts, Larry
A. Bowring prepared the map, Carol Crosby Black designed the

cover, and Brian J. Svikhart managed the design and production of the book.

We are grateful for the assistance provided to us by the Yugoslav government, particularly the Federal Secretariat for Finance and the Federal Institute for Planning. Without that assistance we would not have been able to piece together a composite interpretation of the new system of economic management. We naturally assume responsibility for any conceptual ambiguities and factual errors—ambiguities and errors that perhaps are unavoidable given the pace of institutional evolution in Yugoslavia.

MARTIN SCHRENK
CYRUS ARDALAN
NAWAL A. EL TATAWY

Yugoslavia

Overview

Yugoslavia embarked on a unique path of development in 1950, when it began its attempt to establish a new social and economic order based on a system of workers' self-management, a system to be characterized by social ownership and workers' control of the means of production. The motivation underlying this decision was complex. Workers' self-management was perceived to be an embodiment of socialism as envisaged by Marx. But the Yugoslav interpretation went beyond nationalization, which merely replaces capitalist domination with managerial and bureaucratic domination. The Yugoslav interpretation also went beyond the concept of workers' participation, which implies some sharing of decisionmaking power by workers and by the owners of the means of production or their appointed representatives. And in contrast with the mainstream of Marxist-Leninist theory and practice, the "withering away of the state" was not expected to occur incidentally and in some distant future as the final element of the progression from capitalism to socialism to communism. This goal was to be pursued purposefully and at once, to be promoted whenever workable substitutes for state functions could be designed in the realm of the "association of free producers." Such a perception of the state engendered decentralization and destatization as persistent features of the evolutionary momentum of self-management socialism.

Transcending both private capitalism and state capitalism, self-management socialism was to institute direct democracy in economic matters, with decisionmaking power as the exclusive prerogative of individuals directly affected by decisions, and with individuals directly exercising their power without the intervention of autonomous intermediaries. As a system of economic management, self-management socialism was to create an institutional environment that would provide workers with control over their workplaces and the economy. Self-management socialism was also to provide a way to deal with the ethnic pluralism of Yugoslav society and enable differ-

3

ent regional interests to be voiced, considered, and harmonized. Through maximum devolution of policymaking from the federal government to the republics and communes, the system could accommodate the diverse needs and aspirations of the various nationalities Yugoslavia comprises. Yugoslavia's development in the postwar period is the story of how these principles have shaped its ability to attain basic objectives and cope with inherited economic problems.

Since 1950 Yugoslavia has continually extended and refined workers' self-management as the institutional framework for decisionmaking on all social and economic matters. The country has had a predilection for innovating and testing novel organizations and systemic relations. Its innovativeness has been characterized by a blend of pragmatism and flexibility and by an irreverence for institutions and policies that fail to meet expectations. Few premises, apart from the commitment to the Marxist dictum of social ownership of the means of production, appear to have been inviolable. Few have withstood the march of time. Although many changes were deliberate responses to diverse—and not always compatible—social, economic, and political issues, an underlying rationale is discernible throughout the entire period. Understanding that rationale is crucial to understanding the continuity of the system's development.

The 1950–65 period was marked by gradual liberalization of the economy, continuing decentralization of decisionmaking, and growing reliance on the market. These trends culminated in the economic reforms of 1965, when Yugoslavia opened its economy to the outside world, adopted a rational price structure and unified exchange rates, and began to use the market as the principal mechanism for resource allocation. Enterprises and banks became the primary decisionmakers in the economy. The drive for decentralization and destatization stripped the state of many functions it previously performed, including fiscal policy and planning. With the number of instruments of economic policy correspondingly reduced, economic management was significantly weakened. The consequences of these changes could be observed in the inflationary pressures that developed and the stop-go policy cycles that ensued. The momentum of economic growth flagged; import dependency increased; balance-of-payments difficulties recurred. In addition, there were growing problems associated with creating enough work opportunities in the modern sector. Some of these developments were inevitable consequences of the changes in priorities and the new directions of the economy. Although the economic performance continued to be satisfactory, it became increasingly difficult to attain prescribed objectives.

The 1965 reforms also engendered an array of social and political tendencies that were soon regarded to be inconsistent with the premises of self-management socialism. Self-management increasingly became equated with the autonomy of enterprise management. Professional managers, particularly in large diversified enterprises, acquired such an overpowering position in decisionmaking that self-management lost much of its practical meaning. The egalitarian power structure originally envisioned was gradually transformed into an inherently elitist and technocratic power structure. Concurrently the autonomy of enterprises induced monopolistic business practices and led to the collusion of management and workers in sharing the monopoly rents of enterprises. Such tendencies threatened the socialist principles of solidarity and equity.

In the early 1970s the Yugoslavs began a critical review of the economic system. A series of constitutional amendments related to economic management were passed in 1971. Consolidating these changes, a new vision of the system of economic decisionmaking was put forward in the 1974 constitution. It transformed all of the principal legislation affecting the economy. A number of measures considerably increased and strengthened macroeconomic management. The most important of these was the introduction of an elaborate and novel system of planning. Under this new system the participation of all economic agents—nongovernment and government—is mandatory and nonhierarchical. Each agent prepares its own plan on the basis of a predetermined and standardized set of indicators that describe prevailing conditions and future expectations. The coordination of these diverse plans involves a series of successive adjustments, or compromises, among the agents. This iterative process is based on mandatory and unrestricted exchanges of information. Social planning, which emanates from the federation, the republics, and the communes, provides the basic framework. It encounters self-management planning, which emanates from economic organizations. The process is not necessarily designed to resolve all conflicts, but to compel planning agents to view their development objectives at different levels of aggregation. Harmonization of social and self-management planning is thus intended to ensure consistency between national, regional, or local considerations and the goals and objectives of enterprises.

The recent constitutional and legislative changes introduced social compacts and self-management agreements as basic instruments of economic management: social compacts establish the obligations of economic organizations with respect to such broad issues as prices, incomes, employment, and the allocation of foreign exchange; self-management agreements are contracts that cover almost all transactions within and between enterprises. Based on the widespread participation and consent of all affected parties, they establish a coordinated framework for action that is consistent with the principles of workers' self-management. These instruments, once agreed upon and signed, have the force of law. The constitution also introduced important changes in the structure of the economy by breaking up enterprises into separate autonomous units called basic organizations of associated labor (BOALS). This organizational decentralization is intended to broaden the control of workers by reducing the size and complexity of the self-managed units and by increasing the discretion of workers over the use of income generated in these units.

The need for more conscious direction of the economy, though increasingly apparent in the early 1970s, became essential after 1973. The events of 1973 and 1974 had a sudden and significant effect on Yugoslavia's economic situation: the rate of inflation, fueled by rising prices of imports of raw materials, approached 30 percent; the balance of payments sharply deteriorated. This deterioration also had a significant effect on Yugoslavia's medium-term outlook. Perhaps most important, the ensuing international recession reversed the prospects for migration by Yugoslav workers, and this inhibited the growth of an important source of foreign exchange. External migration had been a key factor allowing the size of the agricultural labor force to decline rapidly between 1965 and 1973. After 1973, however, external migration virtually ceased, and large numbers of workers returned to Yugoslavia, putting considerable pressure on the social sector to create additional employment opportunities.

The social plan for 1976–80 is the institutional response to issues regarded to be crucial for long-term development: generating employment, stabilizing the economy, reducing regional disparities, correcting structural weaknesses in the balance of payments, and efficiently mobilizing and allocating investment resources—issues that affect all countries. For Yugoslavia, given the changes in external conditions in 1973 and 1974, employment and the balance of payments are most important in the medium term; regional disparities, which have been and will continue to be large, can be resolved only in the long term. To resolve problems associated with the balance of payments, Yugoslavia has opted for import substitution. Particular emphasis is being placed on sectors producing raw materials and intermediate goods. Production in these sectors lagged after 1965 and, despite good opportunities for local production, import dependency increased most. Ensuring greater self-sufficiency in these sectors will consequently require restructuring the economy. To resolve problems associated with employment, Yugoslavia is encouraging the development of labor-intensive and small-scale industries. In addition, the five-year plan places considerable emphasis on transferring resources from the more developed regions to the less developed regions—transferring not only financial resources, as in the past, but managerial and technological resources under new arrangements for joint ventures. Fostering the economic growth of less developed regions in this way should increase the opportunities for social sector employment and begin to make some inroads against regional disparities.

The strategies adopted to confront these issues are basically sound. But the targets—for drastically reducing the growth rate of imports, for maintaining a high growth rate of exports, for increasing the investment in basic industries, and for achieving an economic growth rate of 7 percent a year—may be rather ambitious. The sharp reduction in import dependency may not be feasible in the medium term, and that would affect the country's ability to reach other targets in the plan. Because Yugoslavia has imposed upon itself a prudent and cautious program for external borrowing, and because the import bill may be larger than anticipated, the economic growth rate may be reduced to the range of 5.5 to 6 percent a year—a rate which would still be respectable, given the problems associated with efforts to pursue simultaneously the growth of the economy, the unity of the nation, and the further democratization of work and politics.

Part One

The Self-managed Economy

One

Social and Political Development

THE YUGOSLAV STATE was founded in 1918 on the ruins of the Austro-Hungarian Empire and its bordering territories. The Kingdom of the Serbs, Croats, and Slovenes was superimposed on a society having a diverse ethnic, political, and religious structure that evolved during centuries of domination by competing eastern and western forces. The regions constituting what now is Yugoslavia had for centuries straddled the fluid military border between the two powers of the Balkans: the Austro-Hungarian Empire to the north and west, and the Ottoman Empire to the south and east; the one Catholic, the other Islamic. This constellation of power kept those regions in the backwater of the two slowly disintegrating empires and isolated them almost completely from the social and economic development of Western Europe. Montenegro and Serbia, which then included most of present-day Macedonia and Kosovo, were the only constituent units of the monarchy that attained independent statehood before the First World War. Croatia, Slovenia, and Bosnia-Herzegovina had been territories of the Austro-Hungarian Empire. Proclaimed a constitutional monarchy in 1921, the Kingdom of the Serbs, Croats, and Slovenes proved incapable of maintaining popular support and political unity, the prerequisites for sustained social and economic development. In response to recurrent political clashes, King Alexander suspended the constitution in 1929 and announced the formation of the Kingdom of Yugoslavia, which persisted in a variety of forms until the invasion by Axis forces in April 1941.

On the eve of the Second World War, Yugoslavia was one of the most politically fragile and economically backward countries in Europe. The country had no traditions of modern political democracy. The interwar regime, in addition to its inability to command broad popular support and unite the country, failed to achieve significant improvements in the standard of living of the population.[1] Between 1926 and 1939 the average annual growth rate of national income was 2.1 percent, which barely exceeded the country's population growth rate. There were vast regional differences in income, employment, and literacy along the northwest-southeast axis from Slovenia to Macedonia. The industrial sector, dominated by foreign business interests, employed only 2.5 workers for every 1,000 inhabitants and accounted for 15 percent of national income. In contrast, the agricultural sector, based predominantly on the use of wooden ploughs and other traditional technology, contributed more than 55 percent of national income. The distribution of landholdings was highly inequitable: more than two-thirds of households owned plots of less than 5 hectares. Large reserves of rural unemployed manpower, combined with limited opportunities for industrial employment, contributed to rising unemployment. In short, the nascent system of foreign-dominated industrial capitalism "destroyed the social and economic system that the peasantry had developed through a centuries-old process of adaptation, without replacing it with another which would have enabled the peasantry to improve its economic lot."[2]

Yugoslavia's economic problems were intensified by the Second World War, which in four years canceled the few economic and social gains achieved during twenty years of monarchical rule. Direct losses of national wealth have been estimated at more than $9 billion.[3] Almost 300,000 farms, and more than a third of equipment and plants, were destroyed. All mines sustained extensive damage. Systems of public transport and communication were rendered inoperable. Most coastal and oceangoing vessels were sunk. More than a fifth of all dwellings were unhabitable, leaving 3.3 million persons homeless. About 1.7 million Yugoslavs, or 11 percent of the prewar population, lost their lives.

Many of the conditions that had maintained Yugoslavia in a state

1. See Federal Statistical Office, *Yugoslavia: Thirty Years after Liberation and the Victory over Fascism, 1945–1975* (Belgrade: Federal Statistical Office, 1976), pp. 9–20.
   2. Jozo Tomasevic, *Peasants, Politics, and Economic Change in Yugoslavia* (Stanford: Stanford University Press, 1955), p. 213.
   3. Estimated in 1938 prices the losses represented 17 percent of the losses sustained by the eighteen Allied countries fighting in the war. Federal Statistical Office, *Yugoslavia: Thirty Years after Liberation*, p. 11.

of economic backwardness created a social structure that was highly receptive to the evolution of new forms of social and political organization during and after the war. A rigid class structure had not developed. Industrialization, moving at a slow pace for more than a century, had not fostered the growth of powerful social strata whose interests might threaten those of the postwar political leadership. In 1939 a mere 1.3 percent of the population had completed secondary education; 0.15 percent had completed university education. Postwar Yugoslavia therefore inherited a fluid social structure which provided conditions for the accession to power of an all-Yugoslav movement committed to a common vision of social and economic progress.

Postwar Societal Transformation

In the years following the Second World War, Yugoslav society underwent a transformation whose consequences extended to most spheres of social, political, and economic life. Demographic trends, together with rapid urbanization and industrialization, contributed to marked improvements in the standard of living and shaped the evolution of a distinctive new social structure. Changes in the structure of Yugoslav society in turn created a series of new problems stemming from efforts to pursue simultaneously the goals of economic growth, national unity, and the democratization of work and politics.

Yugoslavia experienced a genuine social revolution between 1941 and 1947, a period marked by the extremely rapid upward social mobility of participants in the national war of liberation. Immediately after the war former partizans and surviving members of the prewar communist party filled positions in government and the economy. By moving directly into positions of power and responsibility, thousands of young peasants and workers advanced from the bottom of the prewar social structure to the middle and upper levels of the new society. After 1950 social mobility gradually decelerated; by the 1960s it no longer involved decisive jumps from lower to higher positions of status. In short, Yugoslav society began to reflect the values of an increasingly urban, educated, and industrial population whose opportunities for mobility had become more limited.

For a society in which the rights associated with private ownership of the means of production have been abolished, in which the power is shared by workers and managers, in which the principal nationalities are treated equally, and in which the political leadership is united by common wartime experiences and shared values, occupational function has become the main source of social differentiation.[4] There nevertheless are other bases of social differentiation, and income is among them. In Yugoslavia a balance is sought in promoting both productivity and equity by having workers remunerated in accord with their labor and by generally restricting incomes to that same labor.

Although postwar Yugoslavia contains strata whose relative position in the social structure is shaped by differences in political power, wealth, and prestige, these differences are minimal and largely uncorrelated. Thus the differences in occupational function, together with those based on nationality, culture, and language, contribute to a complex system of functionally differentiated groups with similar interests. In turn, membership in these groups overlaps with that of various social strata, including political and economic leaders, the intelligentsia, white-collar personnel, production workers, and the peasantry. These groups and strata have neither stable nor mutually reinforcing boundaries. They are continually crossing, conflicting, and periodically uniting in the course of rapid social, economic, and political development.[5]

The transformation of postwar society has not only shaped a new social structure that combines inherited institutions with those developed in the postwar era; it has brought significant gains in social welfare. Key indicators of social development suggest a standard of living that equals or exceeds that of countries at a similar level of economic development. Per capita income in current prices increased from less than $100 immediately after the war to almost $1,600 in 1975. In addition, a growing portion of the social product was placed at the disposal of workers. Indicators for health, education, and housing also reflect continuous social development for the country as a whole, notwithstanding substantial interregional differences in income and welfare. By the mid-1970s about half the population of more than 21 million lived in urban areas; less than 40 percent of all inhabitants were classified as agricultural. Today's population, in contrast with that of prewar Yugoslavia, is youthful, industrial, and urban.

4. Allen H. Barton, "Determinants of Leadership Attitudes in a Socialist Society," in *Yugoslav Opinion-Making Elites*, eds. Allen H. Barton and others (New York: Praeger, 1973), p. 230.
5. Radomir Lukic, "Yugoslav Social Structure and the Formation of Public Opinion," in *Yugoslav Opinion-Making Elites*, p. 71.

Evolution of Government and Politics

The evolution of Yugoslav government and politics after 1945 is closely related to the country's inheritance setting and postwar societal transformation. Three major constitutional reforms in 1953, 1963, and 1974 formalized social, political, and economic changes of preceding periods; each established new institutions that often departed significantly from prevailing practice. The successive constitutional reforms, calling for a periodic transformation of the political system, have also been characterized by a lag between formally announced principles and their implementation in the conduct of government and politics. The postwar evolution of government and politics has therefore been deliberate. But it has also been creative, insofar as conflicts between theory and practice have frequently led to the development of new ideas and institutions. That evolution can be viewed in four principal periods: 1945–49, 1950–64, 1965–70, and from 1971 onward.[6]

After elections were held to choose between a monarchy and republic, the first of Yugoslavia's postwar constitutions was adopted in 1946. That constitution, modeled after the Soviet constitution of 1936, was federal in form and provided for six equal and formally autonomous republics—Serbia, Croatia, Slovenia, Bosnia-Herzegovina, Macedonia, and Montenegro—and two autonomous provinces attached to Serbia—Vojvodina and Kosovo-Metohija.[7] Formal recognition of the various nationalities, which had been one of the principles of the prewar communist party, was combined with roughly proportional representation of the principal nationalities in top government and political posts. The structure of government also closely resembled that of the Soviet Union, with a bicameral parliament, presidium, council of ministers, and federal planning and control commissions. Although the parliament was legally supreme, the council of ministers made most government decisions.

6. See Dusan Bilandzic, "Savez Komunista Jugoslavije i demokratizacija revolucionarne diktature [The League of Communists of Yugoslavia and the Democratization of the Revolutionary Dictatorship]," in *Dijalektika odnosa izmedju radnicke klase i njene revolucionarne avangarde* [*The Dialectics of Relations between the Working Class and its Revolutionary Avant-garde*], 2 vols. (Portorez: Marxist Center of the Central Committee, League of Communists, Slovenia, 1977), vol. 2, pp. 1–26.
7. A constitutional amendment in 1968 changed the name of Kosovo-Metohija to Kosovo.

The formal hierarchical structure of government, planning, and administration, despite its symbolic and ideological importance, was an imperfect reflection of social and political processes in the 1945–49 period. The 1946 constitution and the five-year plan for 1947–52 were much less important as blueprints for the future than as formal recognitions of changes already carried out during and immediately after the war. The foundations of postwar government and politics had been well established by 1942, when the leaders of the partizan movement created a political structure for postwar Yugoslavia: the Anti-Fascist Council of National Liberation of Yugoslavia. That organization, which included a national liberation committee linked to a broad network of partizan units across the country, provided a degree of political cohesiveness that made it possible, even before the end of the war, to implement programs of reconstruction and nationalization. In 1944–45 the governmental machinery was reorganized, the transport system reestablished, the economy partially rehabilitated, and a variety of social welfare and public health programs put into operation. By 1946 three-fourths of the war damage had been repaired and, significantly, more than 80 percent of the arable land was distributed among some 70,000 peasants and veterans. By 1947 the state sector had nationalized all industries at the federal and republican levels and 70 percent of industries at local levels.[8]

The formal structure of government, planning, and administration failed to resonate with the social and political realities of the period for another reason. The war of liberation was in large part an independent effort that depended for its success on indigenous resources, not on outside military and technical assistance from western allies and the Soviet Union. When Yugoslavia was expelled in 1948 from the Communist Information Bureau (COMINFORM), a new international agency led by the Soviet Union and composed of the communist parties of Eastern and Western Europe, it was in large part in response to the independent course of action Yugoslavia followed during and after the war.[9] Although the structure of government and politics closely resembled that of the Soviet Union, the Soviet model

8. See Boris Kidric, *On the Construction of Socialist Economy in FPRY* (Belgrade: Office of Information, 1948); and George W. Hoffman and Fred Warner Neal, *Yugoslavia and the New Communism* (New York: Twentieth Century Fund, 1962), pp. 95–96.

9. See Royal Institute of International Affairs, *The Soviet-Yugoslav Dispute* (London: Oxford University Press, 1948); and Robert Bass and Elizabeth Marbury (eds.), *The Soviet-Yugoslav Controversy, 1948–1958: A Documentary Record* (New York: Prospect Books, 1959).

was voluntarily adopted and not imposed from the outside. Thus the decision to formally emulate the Soviet model was as voluntary as the subsequent decision to formally reject it, a decision considerably hastened by Yugoslavia's departure from COMINFORM.

The significance of the 1945–49 period cannot be fully appreciated without understanding the effect of inherited institutions and the early postwar societal transformation on the structure and practice of government and politics. The successful implementation of programs of reconstruction and nationalization was a direct consequence of rapid political development during the war; the partizan movement was in turn based upon a minimally stratified and essentially egalitarian peasant society.[10] As already mentioned, the new political system not only was well in place by 1943; it was fundamentally different from the formal Soviet model adopted in 1946.[11] The social processes underlying formal centralized administrative management therefore evidenced few of the characteristics normally associated with bureaucratic hierarchies.

The beginning of the second period in postwar societal development (1950–64) can be assigned to the passage in 1950 of the law on the management of government economic enterprises and economic associations by workers' collectives. That law, which followed the establishment of workers' councils in 215 selected enterprises in late 1949, was the first of successive institutional innovations in the postwar period. Workers' self-management, later guaranteed under the 1953 constitution, was more than a new form of industrial management designed to improve the efficiency of enterprises; it was a new form of social and political organization that provided rights to control the results and conditions of work. The motivation to establish workers' councils therefore was not solely or even primarily economic, given that the existing system of centralized planning for investment and production was promoting rapid industrialization and economic development, a record of success that would likely have continued well into the late 1950s. Nor was the establishment of workers' self-management merely a product of philosophical or

---

10. See Josip Zupanov, "Egalitarianism and Industrialism," in *Workers' Self-Management and Organizational Power in Yugoslavia*, eds. Josip Obradovic and William N. Dunn (Pittsburgh: University Center for International Studies, University of Pittsburgh, 1978), pp. 60–96.

11. In 1950 President Tito would observe: "We had too many illusions and were too uncritical in taking and replanting in Yugoslavia everything that was being done in the Soviet Union." Josip Broz Tito, *Workers Manage Factories in Yugoslavia* (Belgrade: Jugostampa, 1950), pp. 10–11.

ideological concerns with industrial democracy and the humanization of work, issues which would become salient only in later periods.[12] The primary motivation for establishing workers' self-management grew out of the need to resolve dissatisfaction with an emerging administrative class that conflicted with the ideals of a revolutionary movement whose conception of postwar politics was essentially populist and egalitarian.

The superimposition of a centralized system of planning and administration on nonhierarchical social processes created wide discrepancies between popular expectations and the performance of political and economic institutions. When combined with the economic dislocation that followed Yugoslavia's departure from COMINFORM, the inherent conflicts between centralized administrative management and a revolutionary social structure produced a widespread drive to find new solutions. The constitutional legislation of 1953, although officially modifying the 1946 constitution, created reforms of such scope that it amounted to a new constitution. The 1953 constitution, seeking to establish a "socialist democracy," strengthened the system of self-management in industry, extended certain self-management rights to social activities, and added a chamber of producers to the federal and republican assemblies. This constitution also devolved greater power to local governmental units. Federal and republican governments held only those powers and rights expressly specified in the constitution; all other power devolved on communes, local committees, workers' councils, and other institutions of direct democracy. The identity and equality of republics was also guaranteed by the same principles of federalism contained in the 1946 constitution, notwithstanding the withdrawal from republics of formal legal sovereignty and rights of secession.

The constitution of 1963, extending rights of self-management to all work organizations under the label of "social self-management," was primarily an effort to resolve technical difficulties associated with the formal retention of many elements of the 1946 constitution and to synthesize and codify new laws and practices that had multiplied since 1953. Although there were certain institutional innovations, including a federal court empowered to rule on the constitutionality of administrative practices and review questions of conflict between republican and federal laws, the 1963 constitution essentially was a consolidation of developments that began in 1950. Throughout

---

12. See Deborah Milenkovitch, *Plan and Market in Yugoslav Economic Thought* (New Haven: Yale University Press, 1971), pp. 62–77.

the 1950–64 period, power was slowly shifted from the federation to republics, local governments, and enterprises as a system formally guaranteeing the rights of producers to manage their workplaces replaced a formal system of centralized administrative management.

Efforts were again made in 1965–70 to transform the structure of government and politics. Federal policymaking was significantly altered under the economic reforms of 1965. Although representing a decisive movement toward the autonomy of republics and communes, the reforms contributed to a weakening of macroeconomic policy and created difficulties in economic management and coordination. Social and political values were increasingly differentiated along regional and ethnic lines, and value conflicts were sharpened by variations in growth rates, per capita incomes, and wage differences between republics and communes.[13] As an ethnically differentiated or pluralistic society, Yugoslavia has traditionally had to deal with the fact that policies involving the redistribution of goods and services are typically met with protest by some constituent units. All forms of redistribution, whether they are directly political, tend to be perceived by contending groups as changes in relative power and advantage. A number of these factors contributed to the politicization of economic issues in the 1965–70 period.

Conflicts also emerged between local communal bodies and enterprises situated in their territory. Communes frequently sought to ensure that economic activities were concentrated in their own territory, chiefly as a means of generating tax revenue and creating employment. That policy ran directly counter to the goal of establishing a unified market economy. Although enterprises and sociopolitical organizations—the League of Communists, the Socialist Alliance, and the Trade Unions—were generally committed to a broad policy of economic integration and a unified market, communal governments tended until 1970 to oppose decisions that did not further their own financial interests. In addition, participation in communal decision-making often was centralized, with the presidents of communal assemblies and administrative staffs exerting a preponderate share of

13. See M. George Zaninovich, "Party and Non-Party Attitudes on Social Change," in *Political Leadership in Eastern Europe and the Soviet Union*, ed. R. Barry Farrell (Chicago: Aldine, 1970), pp. 294–334; Philip E. Jacob, "The Limits of Value Consensus; Implications for Integration in Four Countries," *International Studies Quarterly*, vol. 15, no. 2 (June 1971), pp. 203–20; and Gary K. Bertsch, "A Cross-National Analysis of the Community-Building Process in Yugoslavia," *Comparative Political Studies*, vol. 4, no. 4 (January 1972), pp. 438–60.

influence on decisions about municipal budgeting, town planning, housing construction, educational finance, and the election of enterprise directors. Moreover enterprise decisionmaking often suffered from bureaucratic and technocratic tendencies, a pattern intensified by the increasing complexity of economic problems confronting decentralized firms and their managers. As a result, the influence of the sociopolitical organizations, each of which sought to promote a value system supportive of a self-managed society, was not as strong as was felt to be necessary.[14]

The introduction of new institutions of self-management since 1971 represents a fundamental departure from traditional conceptions of government and politics and a synthesis of experiences acquired in preceding historical periods. These institutions are based on the recognition that centralization and decentralization are equally unsatisfactory routes to a self-managed society. Self-management socialism therefore is not a continuation of the decentralization found in the 1965–70 period; much less is it an effort to reimpose central governmental and political controls by returning to practices of the 1950–64 period and earlier years. Self-management socialism, seeking to transcend contradictory principles and practices of these earlier periods, is a genuinely new and creative response to challenges of social, political, and economic development in the postwar period.

The formal institutions of self-management are contained in the 1974 constitution and 1976 laws on associated labor and social planning.[15] These documents are again syntheses of previous legal and institutional changes, including a constitutional amendment that in 1971 established the principle of agreement among planning parties and provided veto powers, which republics have since exercised on several occasions. The formulation and implementation of policies

14. See Zivan Tanic, "Cognitive Apperception of Self-Management," in *Participation and Self-Management*, 12 vols. (Zagreb: Institute for Social Research, University of Zagreb, 1972), vol. 1, pp. 139–49; Misha D. Jezernik, "Changes in the Hierarchy of Motivational Factors in Slovenian Industry," *Journal of Social Issues*, vol. 24 (1968), pp. 103–14; Veljko Rus, "Influence Structure in Yugoslav Enterprises," *Industrial Relations*, vol. 9, no. 2 (February 1970), pp. 148–60; and Ichak Adizes, *Industrial Democracy: Yugoslav Style* (New York: Free Press, 1971), pp. 197–231.

15. See *The Constitution of the Socialist Federal Republic of Yugoslavia, 1974* and Federal Assembly, *The Associated Labour Act* (Ljubljana: Dopisna Delavska Univerza, 1976). For a discussion of the law on social planning by one of the principal architects of workers' self-management and the 1974 constitution see Edvard Kardelj, *The System of Planning in a Society of Self-Management* (Belgrade: Socialist Thought and Practice, 1976).

of national scope and significance is therefore based on nonhierarchical governmental processes. Concurrently the League of Communists, the Trade Unions, and the Socialist Alliance—remobilized after the ninth party congress in 1969—constitute a systemwide integrative mechanism that has effectively responded to problems of political fragmentation and economic dislocation prevalent in 1965–70. These sociopolitical organizations have focused on efforts to establish new forms of direct democracy in local communes and self-managed enterprises.

The institutional nucleus of self-management in the sociopolitical sphere is the local commune; its counterpart in the economic sphere is the basic organization of associated labor (BOAL). Local communes are being transformed from traditional decentralized instruments of state power and government policy into self-regulating communities of citizens and producers. Under the 1974 constitution, changes in the role and functions of the commune are seen not as a means of redistributing power among different levels of government, as in previous periods, but as a way to integrate and coordinate the actions of consumers, citizens, and producers. Self-management socialism reflects a concern with the supersession of traditional governmental and political structures as forms of mediation between associated producers and the results of their labor. Moreover politics, in contrast with its past role, is to be a direct function of associated labor, that is, of collectives of individuals united as consumers, citizens, and producers.[16] The institutions of self-management, like their predecessors in earlier periods, thus are not social, political, or economic, but all of these at once. The success of self-management therefore does not depend solely or even primarily on economic factors. It depends on historically discontinuous and interdependent social, political, and economic processes. Consequently the further evolution of self-management socialism, and the responses of the system to developmental challenges, will continue to be products of Yugoslavia's inheritance and the revolutionary transformation of society that began in 1941.

16. See Rudi Supek, "Participation and Industrial Democracy," in *Workers' Self-Management and Organizational Power in Yugoslavia*, pp. 35–59.

Two

Economic Management
and Performance to 1975

INSTITUTIONAL CHANGES in postwar Yugoslavia constitute an evolutionary process, not a set of unrelated responses. Moreover the evolutionary process has been dialectical: institutional changes have impinged on the performance of the economy; that performance has in turn prompted further institutional changes. By 1975 the country had adopted four new constitutions, each foreshadowing a new constellation of methods for organizing and managing the economy.[1] Also by 1975 there had been five medium-term plans. They encompassed three broad philosophies of planning: central planning for the 1947–52 period; planning by basic proportions for the 1956–61 period; and, for want of a better label, indicative planning for the 1965–75 period. The 1974 constitution introduced yet a fourth broad philosophy: self-management planning for the period from 1976 onward.

In the years immediately following the Second World War, Yugoslavia relied on a system of economic management closely patterned after the Soviet blueprint. According to the 1946 constitution the state was to "direct economic life and development

1. New constitutions were adopted in 1946, 1953, 1963, and 1974. For detailed descriptions of the evolution of the system between 1945 and 1975 see Branko Horvat, *The Yugoslav Economic System* (White Plains, N.Y.: International Arts and Science Press, 1976); Deborah Milenkovitch, *Plan and Market in Yugoslav Economic Thought* (New Haven: Yale University Press, 1971); idem, "The Case of Yugoslavia," *American Economic Review*, vol. 67, no. 1 (February 1977), pp. 55–60; Vinod Dubey and others, *Yugoslavia: Development with Decentralization* (Baltimore: Johns Hopkins University Press for the World Bank, 1975).

through a general economic plan," establishing what subsequently was referred to as statism or administrative socialism.[2] The Federal Planning Commission was set up in 1946; the first five-year plan was issued in 1947. It was excessively rigid, stifling virtually all initiative outside strict administrative lines of command. All decisions were to emanate from the Federal Planning Commission with little discretion or feedback from production units. The annual plans drawn up in conjunction with the five-year plan included provisions for ten-day plans and directly controlled production of some 13,000 commodities; one annual plan weighed 3,300 pounds. The basic objectives were to overcome the country's economic and technical backwardness; growth in consumption had a low priority.

A decisive turnabout occurred in 1948 when Yugoslavia broke with COMINFORM: treaties were unilaterally abrogated; development loans were canceled; established trade links were severed. This state of economic warfare had serious repercussions on the economic development of Yugoslavia: there was a once-and-for-all loss of the equivalent of five years' growth during a period in which the momentum of economic growth picked up strongly in most European countries. The break coincided with a critical reflection upon the premises of the system; by 1950 a new body of thought started to emerge. Unrestricted state ownership and control was denounced as "state capitalism" and as engendering rigid hierarchical structures, not the liberation of workers. The decision was made to abandon the Soviet model of central planning and to initiate a search for a new system of economic management that would be uniquely Yugoslav.[3]

The Evolution of Self-management

As political premises were being redefined in the late 1940s, a return to the original tenets of Marxism led to the conceptualization of two guiding principles for the evolution of the system: "self-management" by the producers; and "socialist commodity pro-

2. *The Constitution of the Federal Peoples' Republic of Yugoslavia*, 1946, article 15.
3. A drought and the failure of the collectivization of agriculture may also have contributed to the decision. On strictly economic grounds, however, the five-year plan for 1947–52 cannot be judged as either a failure or a success. See Milenkovitch, *Plan and Market in Yugoslav Economic Thought*, pp. 62–77 and Fred Singleton, *Twentieth-Century Yugoslavia* (New York: Columbia University Press, 1976), pp. 124–32.

duction."[4] The 1950 law on the management of government enterprises and economic associations by workers' collectives introduced
the principle of self-management to the system. It was the first step
in providing workers with participation in the management of their
work units. In practice, however, workers' councils remained for
some time subordinate to managers, who as a rule were appointed
by and responsible to the state. The principle of socialist commodity production was propagated in Yugoslavia as a model of
decentralized market socialism. It provided the ideological rationale for embracing market relations. By 1953 the new principles
had firmly taken root. The 1953 constitution, in contrast with the
1946 constitution, stated that social ownership of the means of production and the self-government of working people were to constitute the basis of Yugoslavia's social and political system.[5]

The changes of the early 1950s ensured that workers had growing influence in the day-to-day operation of their workplaces.
Nevertheless the conventional macroeconomic policy instruments,
such as central planning, price and income policies, and fiscal and
monetary policies, remained firmly in the hands of the state. The
respective spheres of competence of workers and the state in economic affairs were well defined, at least in practice. In Yugoslav
eyes, however, this clarity was achieved only by depriving workers'
self-management of much of its substance. Giving workers autonomy
in managing their affairs could not be reconciled with continuing to
state control of resource mobilization and allocation.

Yugoslavia adopted a new system of planning in 1956. The 1951
law on the planned management of the economy foreshadowed its
adoption. Under that law the Federal Planning Commission became
the Federal Planning Bureau, and "state planning" became "social
planning" with increased consultation and participation. Central
planning was to be the planning of basic proportions: notably the
rate of accumulation, the distribution of investment resources

---

4. Many terms in Yugoslav parlance have connotations not always conveyed
by literal translation. When those connotations are not apparent from the context in which such terms are first used, they are indicated by synonyms or
brief definitions. A glossary at the back of this volume consolidates definitions
of these terms; it also incorporates definitions of Marxian principles, insofar as
those principles relate to the Yugoslav economic system, and descriptions of
instruments and organizations of economic management in Yugoslavia.

5. *The Constitution of the Socialist Federal Republic of Yugoslavia*, 1953,
article 4.

through the federal General Investment Fund, and the share of collective consumption. These basic proportions were then used by the Federal Planning Bureau to forecast sectoral growth rates. Such "fundamental" planning was the responsibility of the state; enterprises were to have plans based on these basic proportions and market signals. To facilitate the use of the market, steps were taken to create a unified price structure and adopt a more realistic exchange rate. The introduction of the new planning system coincided with increased emphasis on the growth of consumption. Yugoslavia's economic performance under the plan for 1957–61 was successful in relation to the objectives set: all objectives were achieved in four years.

The success of the second five-year plan brought with it a drive for further changes in the system of economic management. The notion of self-management, initially very general, had slowly been filtering from the realm of vision into practice. The scope of central decisionmaking had gradually declined; the autonomy of enterprises had increased. In resource mobilization and allocation the former continued to dominate; in day-to-day operations the latter gradually gained ground. By 1960 practical questions about the respective roles of enterprises and the state, of the market and the plan, had become increasingly focal issues. In 1961 three reform measures were introduced to increase considerably the role of the market. Yugoslavia opened its economy to world markets, reorganized its financial system, and relaxed controls for the determination of wages. The preparation of reform measures nevertheless was insufficient; their implementation, too hasty.

The ensuing conditions increasingly necessitated ad hoc policy measures, first to raise the level of economic activity, then to control inflation. Although annual planning continued, the medium-term plan for 1961–65 had to be abandoned in 1963. The economic difficulties of the period instigated a national debate over whether the solution lay in further liberalization or in a return to greater central control. Parallel to these discussions, and to the attempt to arrive at a viable consensus, a new constitution was promulgated in 1963. A seven-year plan for 1964–70 was prepared as well, but it had to be abandoned when major economic reforms further liberalized the system in 1965. Thus, between 1961 and 1965, there was no effective medium-term plan. The changes to the system, their repercussions on the economy, and the need for short-term management precluded any attempt at medium-term planning.

This phase in the evolution of the system—a phase of reducing the control of state agencies over enterprise decisionmaking— apparently had two objectives: to give substance to the principle of workers' self-management; and to increase concurrently the efficiency of the system and the quality of goods. One significant change of the period was the abandoning of the federal General Investment Fund between 1963 and 1965. This partly reflected an economic decision to encourage a more rational allocation of investment resources. But to a large extent this may have been a reflection of the increasing difficulty of achieving a consensus on the sectoral distribution of investable funds and on national objectives in general.[6] Furthermore it was difficult to reconcile the system of investment planning with the increasing emphasis on workers' self-management and the use of the market.

The debate about the economic system concluded with a clear choice in favor of liberalization. This led to the issuance of a series of new reform measures during 1964 and 1965, measures constituting what frequently are referred to as the 1965 economic reforms.[7] They included:

- Transferring a large part of the federal government's responsibilities to republics.
- Increasingly integrating the economy with the international division of labor by replacing a complex system of multiple exchange rates with a realistic unified exchange rate and by introducing a considerable degree of import liberalization.
- Transferring responsibility for resource mobilization and allocation from the state to economic enterprises and banks.
- Correcting massive price distortions, curtailing the system of price subsidies, and increasing the autonomy of enterprises in price formation.
- Extending enterprise autonomy to include the distribution of enterprise income to capital accumulation and the personal incomes of workers.

There were three basic objectives underlying these measures: reducing the role of the federation (decentralization) and the state

---

6. See Milenkovitch, *Plan and Market in Yugoslav Economic Thought*, passim.
7. See Dubey and others, *Yugoslavia: Development with Decentralization*, pp. 38–40.

(destatization) to the maximum possible degree; introducing strong incentives for improving the efficiency of enterprises and the quality of output; and spreading the fruits of increased capacity and improved productivity to the population by raising the rate of aggregate consumption.

The reforms initiated a phase in Yugoslavia's economic management referred to as "market socialism." That phase combined laissez-faire elements and residual state interference, which by this time largely originated from republics, not the center. The operation of the market was to be enhanced by realigning prices, abandoning multiple exchange rates, and generally liberalizing foreign trade. Previously enterprises had the right to manage their affairs, subject to the state's influence in determining their role in the economy. Under the 1965 reforms, enterprises were to manage their affairs independent of the state and be subject principally to the impersonal forces of the marketplace. Most of the changes associated with the reforms were amended to the 1963 constitution during 1967 and 1968.

Throughout the period after the break with COMINFORM, the basic trend was toward a gradual increase in the autonomy of individual work units. The constitutional changes and amendments attempted to give more substance to workers' self-management by reducing the control exercised by state organs on enterprise decision-making. The 1965 reforms reflected the culmination of this basic trend. Planning in Yugoslavia became essentially indicative. Plans were to provide forecasts, establish a basis for rational decision-making by enterprises, and set forth the objectives to be pursued by government through nonadministrative instruments. The social plans prepared by the federal and republican planning institutes were indicative in the sense that they did not impose legal or mandatory obligations on enterprises and banks in the social sector. The only compulsory aspect of social plans was that, when accepted, they became directives for sociopolitical communities, the Yugoslav term for political units.

The basic premise of the indicative system of management was that enterprises, by maximizing their income, would further the general interest. Two elements were required to make that system operate efficiently: appropriate market signals, and measures to ensure macroeconomic stability. With the exception of the Federal Fund for the less developed republics, investment decisionmaking was relegated to the market through the establishment of self-managed all-purpose banks.[8] This new system of economic management did not live up to Yugoslav expectations: the economic performance was disappointing; emerging social and political developments threatened the legitimacy of workers' self-management and socialism.

After 1965 the economy exhibited considerable cyclical behavior, with periodic balance-of-payments difficulties, stop-go policies, and growing inflationary pressure. Although it is difficult to speculate about causes, an important factor seems to have been the combination of an imperfect market with instruments of economic policy that were inadequate to facilitate the smooth management of the economy. The 1965 reforms significantly weakened macroeconomic management by reducing the number of macroeconomic policy instruments. Under destatization, some of the state's policy instruments were effectively dismantled—notably those for fiscal policy, resource allocation, and the compulsory coordination and implementation of plans. Policymaking was regionalized, but there was no attempt to introduce alternative mechanisms for coordinating diverse economic objectives.[9] The policy instruments that still were intact, such as those for incomes and prices, were perceived to run counter to the spirit of self-management. They consequently were half-heartedly and erratically applied. In effect, the determination to strengthen self-management at the microeconomic level greatly reduced the scope for the short-term management at the macroeconomic level and for the pursuit of longer term objectives.

The greatly expanded role of the market also affected the performance of the economy after 1965. Under the new system, prices were realigned, and many were freed. Investment decisions were left to enterprises and their confreres, the banks. Imports were liberalized, and exchange rates were adjusted. The greater reliance on the market had many benefits, but the market alone was not sufficient as a coordinating mechanism. The Yugoslav institutional framework created serious distortions which hampered the effective operation of the market. The mobility of investable funds was

8. Variously called the Federal Fund for the Accelerated Development of the Less Developed Republics and the Autonomous Province of Kosovo, the Fund for Financing the Accelerated Development of the Underdeveloped Regions, or the Federal Fund for Less Developed Regions, that fund will be referred to simply as the Federal Fund. Created in 1965, it is the only federal fund.

9. Chambers of the economy, which are equivalent to chambers of commerce, and sociopolitical organizations were intended to perform some coordinating functions; they were not successful.

limited and, in practice, highly regionalized; the influence of enterprises in preempting funds for investment was disparate.

The ramifications of the 1965 reforms were more than strictly economic; the reforms also engendered an array of social and political tendencies that were regarded to be inconsistent with the premises of the Yugoslav system. Although self-management was to be promoted by the autonomy of enterprises, it increasingly became equated with the autonomy of enterprise management. Professional managers, particularly in large diversified enterprises, acquired such an overpowering position in decisionmaking that self-management lost much of its practical meaning for the amorphous collectives of workers. This gradual transformation, from the egalitarian power structure originally envisioned to an inherently elitist and technocratic power structure, was for some years fostered by a law permitting workers' councils to cede their management rights to professional managers. The autonomy of enterprises also precluded their direct coordination—with presumed adverse effects on economic efficiency. It induced monopolistic business practices and led to the collusion of management and workers in sharing the monopoly rents of enterprises. Such tendencies, toward what is known in Yugoslav parlance as "group ownership," threatened the socialist principles of solidarity and equity.

Large trading enterprises, particularly those in foreign trade, became profit centers of the economy, not least because of an oligopolistic market structure. Although such enterprises were restricted in the distribution of profits to their staff, or perhaps because of this restriction, they generated substantial liquid resources that were outside social control and that could be channeled to further profitable investment. Trade enterprises used these resources to expand into quasi conglomerates by merging with financially unviable producing enterprises. They also forced producing enterprises into positions of permanent dependency under arrangements for revolving credit or contracts for preferential delivery. This growing concentration of control—over what in theory were socially owned financial resources in the trade sector—was regarded to be a violation of the principle of self-management. Workers at other stages of production were being deprived of part of their contribution to the total value of output—to the "surplus value" in Marxian terminology—and their right to participate in its allocation. The concentration of resources and power was also deemed to be economically undesirable, insofar as trade enterprises were especially prone to the maximization of profit in the short run, not to balanced growth in the long run.

Similarly the growing control of banks over investable resources was regarded to be equivalent to the appropriation of surplus value by these intermediaries. Banks were formally governed by their founders—the enterprises and sociopolitical communities that supplied risk-bearing permanent deposits in exchange for voting rights in the supervisory organs of banks. But actual decisions on the operation of banks shifted to a considerable degree to the managements of banks. The basis for their growing autonomy was what frequently is referred to in Yugoslavia as "anonymous financial capital," that is, fungible financial resources exclusively controlled and rationed by banks.[10] The absence of a consensus among founders, the collusion of bank managements with big enterprises, the nonequilibrium interest rates, and the control of information by bank managements gave those managing bodies growing power over the course of economic development outside social control. Although it is not clear whether this arrangement improved or impeded allocative efficiency, the political implications were considered to be unacceptable for a socialist system based on Marxian premises. The decisions about the use of the surplus value no longer rested with its producers—the workers of the producing enterprises —but were usurped by autonomous intermediaries.

The constitutional amendments of 1971 and the new constitution of 1974 were designed to remedy these shortcomings. The changes in the system give full expression to the effort to reestablish ex ante coordination. This effort reflects three considerations: macroeconomic management is necessary to achieve short-term economic stability; some form of long-term perspective is necessary at the country's current level of development; and neither macroeconomic management nor the determination of long-term perspectives is to revive state control. Consequently workers' self-management is to extend from the microeconomic to the macroeconomic sphere and relate to such diverse areas as prices, incomes, employment, the use of foreign exchange, and the allocation of investment funds. The constitutional changes also introduced institutional arrangements and provisions that are specifically aimed, whether explicitly or implicitly, at preventing the corrosion of socialism and self-management

10. These fungible resources originated from remrants of state capital administered by banks, permanent deposits of founders, private savings, and the expansion of the money supply.

by group-ownership tendencies and bureaucratic, technocratic, and managerial encroachment.[11] The dual motivation—economic and political—must therefore be kept in mind in any assessment of the recent changes.

The Performance of the Economy

Yugoslavia's economic objectives in the postwar era have included the traditional ones: rapid growth, income equality, integration with the world economy, and the transformation of a preponderantly agrarian economy into a modern diversified economy. Although the country's economic performance was severely constrained by the structural readjustments that the break with the COMINFORM required until 1954, the economy developed rapidly in subsequent years. Between 1954 and 1975 annual growth in real gross material product (GMP) averaged 7.2 percent (table 2.1).[12] During this same period the annual rate of population growth was low and declining; it averaged 1.1 percent. As a result, gross national product (GNP) per capita reached US$1,600 in current prices by 1976.[13] In addition, the economy succeeded in mobilizing a large share of domestic resources for investment. Domestic saving rates averaged about 30 percent of gross domestic product (GDP) in earlier years. That sacrifice permitted rapid growth, which in turn facilitated large gains in personal incomes throughout the period. Real personal incomes in the modern social sector rose by an average of 5.2 percent a year.

11. The conventional theory of the Yugoslav-type firm, as expounded by Ward, Vanek, Domar, Meade, and others, postulates the maximization of personal income per present worker as the enterprise objective function. That objective function is identical with "group ownership," which the Yugoslavs now reject. Whatever empirical relevance the postulate may have had immediately after the 1965 reforms, it has vanished as a result of the new legal provisions and a new consensus on the code of responsible behavior of enterprises. It therefore is not surprising that many predictions of the conventional theory—such as low rates of accumulation and investment, low rates of employment growth, and high rates of productivity growth—are refuted by the statistical facts.

12. Gross material product is the value added in market prices of sectors producing goods and sectors increasing the value of goods by contributing to their production and distribution. It does not include services directly rendered to individuals: housing, social services, and government.

13. World Bank, *1976 World Bank Atlas* (Washington, D.C., 1977). According to preliminary figures, income per capita rose to $1,960 in 1977. Idem, *1978 World Bank Atlas* (Washington, D.C., 1979).

Table 2.1. *Growth Rates of Macroeconomic Indicators, 1954–75*
(percent)

Indicator	Average annual rate of growth		
	1954–64	1965–75	1954–75
Gross material product[a]	8.6	6.4	7.2
Gross industrial output[b]	12.3	7.7	9.5
Industrial employment[b]	6.8	3.3	4.3
Productivity of industrial labor	5.5	4.3	5.0
Employment[b]	6.2	3.0	3.7
Real personal incomes[b]	5.3	4.0	5.2
Inflation[c]	1.5	10.4	5.8
Commodity exports	11.9	6.2	9.0
Commodity imports	11.4	10.1	9.8
Fixed assets[a]	9.2	8.0	8.6

Note: Growth rates are based on least-squares estimates. All estimated growth rates are significant at the 99 percent level of confidence. Growth rates for subperiods are statistically different at the 95 percent level of confidence for all indicators.

Sources: Federal Institute of Statistics, *Statistical Yearbook of Yugoslavia,* 1977 and earlier years.
a. In constant 1972 prices.
b. In the social sector.
c. Industrial producer prices.

The growth of real incomes was accompanied by significant structural changes in the economy. Employment in the social sector increased by 3.7 percent a year between 1954 and 1975. That sector absorbed large transfers of labor from the private sector, which is dominated by small, traditional, individually owned farms.[14] As a result, the share of the labor force employed in the private agricultural sector declined from 66 percent in 1953 to 33 percent in 1975. Over the same period, the share of GMP attributable to the private agricultural sector declined from 32 percent to 12 percent.[15] As the importance of that sector declined, a highly diversified industrial structure developed.

These domestic changes were achieved in an environment of

14. Not all productive enterprises in Yugoslavia are socially owned. Although the social sector predominates in nonagricultural activities, about 90 percent of agricultural land is held by families and is characterized by low productivity.
15. Based on GMP figures in constant 1972 prices. Federal Institute of Statistics, *Statistical Bulletin,* no. 909 (Belgrade, July 1975); *Statistical Bulletin,* no. 1017 (Belgrade, January 1977).

growing integration with the world economy. Although balance-of-payments difficulties constrained growth from time to time, export performance was impressive. Between 1954 and 1975 exports in constant 1972 prices increased by 9 percent a year. By 1975 exports and imports were respectively equal to 18 percent and 24 percent of GNP—a high level of foreign trade for a country of Yugoslavia's size and income.[16] That growing integration with the international economy, in addition to providing additional resources for growth, acted as a spur to efficiency and competitiveness and resulted in significant improvements in the quality of Yugoslav goods and services.

The performance of Yugoslavia's economy in the postwar era has thus been impressive, but there appears to have been some deterioration after the 1965 reforms (see table 2.1). Clearly there were significant declines in the growth rates of output, employment, personal incomes, and commodity exports. Because imports continued to grow rapidly, there was a sharp rise in the trade deficit. The rate of inflation, moderate before 1965, also rose rapidly. In addition, investment had the tendency to elicit smaller increments of output.

Some of these developments were inevitable consequences of changes in external conditions; others were the results of changes after 1965 in the relative weights given to various economic objectives. For example, the decline in the rates of growth of output and employment in part reflected one objective of the 1965 reforms: distributing a greater portion of income to consumption. Similarly the growing inflow of remittances from Yugoslavs working abroad allowed the trade account to deteriorate to the extent that it did during the 1965–75 period. The deterioration in many macroeconomic indicators conceals the considerable improvements realized during this period in the quality and price of domestic goods and services. These improvements were induced by the increased competition that followed the liberalization of the foreign trade regime in 1965. In some instances, they may not have been directly reflected in the growth of output. Furthermore some of the changes are elusive because of the statistical difficulties of comparing data under a system of multiple exchange rates with those under a more realistic and unified exchange rate.

The performance of the economy after 1965 not only reflected new policy priorities; it also reflected increasing difficulty in attain-

16. Based on World Bank estimates of GNP in constant 1972 prices.

ing these objectives. Although many internal and external factors contributed to these difficulties, the system of economic management during this period was the root cause of many problems. As discussed earlier, the economic model after 1965 had weaknesses. Mainly these stemmed from 'attempts to reconcile two divergent objectives: to develop an effective system of workers' self-management; and to retain macroeconomic instruments adequate to manage the development of the economy. This conflict was accentuated by a policy of relying on a market mechanism fraught with imperfections. But even if the market had been allowed to operate efficiently, relying solely on the market would have been difficult. The reason is that market prices can be misleading signals in an economy undergoing rapid structural changes which call for a medium-term perspective and development strategy. Many of the negative economic trends after 1965 can thus be attributed to weaknesses in macroeconomic policymaking and to the performance of the market. The adverse effect of the reforms is particularly evident in inflation, resource allocation, and the balance of payments. The effect on employment and regional development is less evident.

Inflation

After the mid-1960s the Yugoslav economy was subjected to considerable inflationary pressure. Part of this pressure arose because of difficulties in reconciling the demands on resources for investment and consumption; part because of the inflationary bias built into the system. Until the early 1960s prices were fairly tightly controlled by the state. Consequently the degree of price stability was high. With the liberalization of prices, economic growth was increasingly accompanied by high and rising rates of inflation.

Before 1973 the principal causes of inflation were domestic. The 1965 reforms sought to shift the distribution of income toward consumption, but the lack of any mechanism to balance conflicting claims on resources resulted in significant upward pressure on prices. The economic system's inflationary bias added to this pressure. The response of wages to labor market conditions was much stronger in the upward than in the downward direction.[17] The basis of price

---

17. The term *wages* is used in this context as shorthand for personal incomes, which are allocated from enterprise income. Wages, in the common meaning of contractual claims to a fixed payment per unit of time, were abolished in the 1960s.

formation in many instances was cost, not demand. Thus the nominal wage increases—from inflationary expectations, labor market conditions, productivity increases, and attempts to prevent widening wage differences between enterprises and sectors—were quickly translated into price pressure.

Attempts to dampen price increases met with only limited success. The reforms withdrew too many policy instruments; market imperfections weakened those remaining. The use of fiscal policy for demand management became extremely cumbersome, and government was reluctant to rely on mandatory policies for prices and incomes. Monetary policy became the principal, often the only, policy instrument available. It had significant shortcomings. The use of monetary policy to accomplish other objectives, notably the selective credit policy to influence resource allocation, weakened its anti-inflationary impact. This weakening was particularly evident in the difficulties encountered in neutralizing the effect of changes in Yugoslavia's international liquidity on its domestic money supply. In addition, institutional factors often frustrated changes in monetary policy. Enterprises could escape the effects of restrictions in the money supply by building up involuntary credits among themselves. The practice was aggravated and sustained because enterprises were rarely forced into liquidation.

Balance of payments

Three factors influenced Yugoslavia's balance of payments during this period: the growing dependence on imports, the lagging rate of export growth, and the increasing reliance on workers' remittances from abroad to finance the widening trade gap. Greater dependence on imports was partly a natural outcome of the liberalization of trade and partly a policy response to the increased foreign exchange that workers' remittances made available. That dependence was concentrated in intermediate and capital goods. As a result, restricting imports in times of balance-of-payments difficulty directly affected the country's growth rate by reducing industrial production and investment, not consumption. Given the inadequacy of short-term economic management, which might have alleviated the need to restrict imports, continuous growth was interrupted by a series of stop-go policies. The slower growth of commodity exports after 1965 was largely the outcome of the mix of export commodities and export markets. The emphasis was on products and markets that had relatively low growth, and little was done to change that emphasis. Workers' remittances, the principal source of increased foreign exchange earnings, were vulnerable to external factors over which domestic policy had only limited control. They thus were a precarious base for Yugoslavia's balance of payments.

Resource mobilization and allocation

The decentralization of decisionmaking, as well as the intended redistribution of income in favor of personal incomes, changed the pattern of saving. The domestic saving rate, well above 30 percent before 1965, declined to about 25 percent. Although the large inflow of workers' remittances sustained the national saving rate at about 28 percent, excessive demand in relation to available resources characterized the market for investable funds during this period. Many factors contributed to this demand: interest rates were low; the cost of labor was high; enterprises had little reason to fear risk-taking, because bankruptcy was rarely enforced; and social infrastructure development made large demands on investable resources.

If an appropriate mechanism had been available to ration investable funds, excess demand alone would not have led to misallocation and inefficiency. When the state investment funds were abandoned in 1965 and an essentially indicative planning framework was adopted, the coordination of competing investment demands was left to the enterprises and banks.[18] The emerging quasi capital market nevertheless had severe limitations. Banks, often founded by the large enterprises in a republic, were strongly influenced by their founders. Consequently the scope of capital markets tended to be regional, not national. Moreover many different criteria were used in parallel to assess projects for funding, and this made a rational choice among alternatives impossible. Ad hoc coalitions of enterprises and intervention by the state often led to compromises that were not based on the economic merits of projects; large trading enterprises often operated as autonomous financiers. As a result of shortcomings in resource allocation, there was a tendency in the post-1965 period toward duplication and excess capacity in some sectors and toward bottlenecks of capacity in others. The incremental capital-output ratio generally rose, and there was a shift to a more capital-intensive growth path. Neither effect was desirable or intended.

18. The only exception was the Federal Fund.

Employment

The performance of the Yugoslav economy in generating modern social sector employment has been mixed. Employment in the social sector grew less rapidly after 1965 than before, but this does not appear to have been the result of a deterioration in the capacity of the economy to generate employment. As enterprises attempted to rationalize production and increase labor productivity between 1965 and 1967, there was a once-and-for-all decline in employment. After 1968 the decline in employment growth mirrored the decline in the economy's growth rate. In fact, employment-output elasticities before 1965 and after 1968 were quite similar, but capital-labor ratios did rise after 1965.

Employment has always been one of Yugoslavia's most pressing problems. Although the 1965 reforms did not directly impede attempts to solve this problem, they did not contribute to a solution, either. One effect of the reforms was the large transfer of labor out of the traditional agricultural sector. The widening income differences between those employed in the social sector and those in the private agricultural sectors induced that transfer.[19] Interregional migration tended to be limited, however, and this led to vastly different labor market conditions in the various regions.[20]

With the conditions for external migration considerably liberalized in 1965, migration abroad became almost as important as the social sector in absorbing labor. That migration particularly benefited the more developed regions and, as a rule, the more skilled workers. In many instances, it accentuated disparities. Although external migration brought significant gains, the social cost became increasingly apparent as more workers left. Given the recent changes in the attitude of host countries, it has become evident that external migration cannot be sustained as a vent for surplus labor.

Incentives were lacking to develop alternate forms of modern employment within the private agricultural sector or new forms of

19. Income differences sharply increased immediately after the 1965 reforms, but the increases were gradually redressed.

20. *Labor market* is used here as shorthand for labor supply and demand. It does not denote a marketplace where labor is sold, which would run counter to the philosophical premises of the Yugoslav system and which was in effect abolished with the replacement of fixed wages for a variable labor force by variable personal incomes for a fixed labor force. Throughout this volume the term *region* refers to the republics and autonomous provinces.

modern sector employment, such as small-scale, labor-intensive activities in the private or social sector. This lack placed the burden of job creation on established enterprises in the social sector. Thus, despite large annual transfers of labor from the private agricultural sector to the social sector and abroad, the rate of open unemployment began to increase appreciably by the early 1970s—an increase which reflected significant disequilibria in the labor market. Growth alone could not be expected to cope with the employment problem, and it became imperative to enunciate and implement a comprehensive employment strategy.

Regional disparities

Regional differences in incomes have been, and still are, one of Yugoslavia's key economic problems. In contrast with the general emphasis placed on destatization, the 1965 reforms established for the first time a federal agency specifically charged with transferring funds to the less developed republics: the Federal Fund transfers financial resources to less developed regions by providing low-interest, long-term credits. Although that fund has been important in stemming, and recently in slightly reducing, the disparities between regions, the outcome of the coordinated approach has been less than satisfactory. The availability and favorable terms of credits, along with uniform income levels in the social sector, have encouraged capital-intensive development. Consequently their most abundant resource—labor—has not been fully used. Furthermore the purely financial transfer of resources, though a necessary condition for development, has not proven to be a sufficient condition. There has been only a limited transfer of technical and managerial know-how—a crucial ingredient of development—to the less developed regions. As a result, industrial growth, though rapid, has been concentrated in large enterprises: it has often been highly capital-intensive; its effect on incomes has been fairly limited; its economic benefits have been localized.

External events of 1973–74

The diverse problems that persisted in the wake of the 1965 reforms were sharpened by events of 1973 and 1974. Fueled by external inflation, domestic producer prices rose by 13 percent in 1973 and 30 percent in 1974. Rising oil prices and the ensuing recession in Europe adversely affected Yugoslavia's balance of payments.

The current account surplus of US$464 million in 1973 shifted to a record deficit of nearly US$1.2 billion in 1974. The employment situation, already unfavorable, was exacerbated by returning migrants. In 1974 and 1975 about 150,000 workers returned to Yugoslavia—a figure 30 percent higher than the natural increase in the labor force during these two years. The new conditions for the employment of Yugoslav workers abroad have also had significant adverse effects on prospects for the growth of workers' remittances. Consequently significant structural changes are now required to enable the economy to adjust to the increased burden of petroleum imports and to the uncertain future of workers' remittances.

Three

The Premises and Instruments of Self-management

THE NEW CONSTITUTION AND SUBSEQUENT LEGISLATION embody the attempts by Yugoslavia to design macroeconomic instruments compatible with the principle of self-management and to reaffirm the political and philosophical legitimacy of claims to self-management and socialism.[1] These changes are the results of disillusionment with the outcome of the 1965 economic reforms and years of debate about long-term goals for social and economic development. They affect the instruments and organizational arrangements for managing the economy. The underlying premises are not new. Self-management has long been regarded as the institutional framework most compatible with direct democracy in political and economic affairs. The influence of the state in economic decisionmaking has been steadily reduced since the 1950s. The party and other sociopolitical organizations have for years been assigned the task of promoting social and political integration. What is new is that the premises now are more clearly conceptualized. They also are more forcefully and consistently embodied in the instruments and organizations of economic management.

The 1965 reforms emphasized the autonomy of enterprises by

1. Milenkovitch offers a similar interpretation of the constitutional changes as attempts to design macroeconomic instruments compatible with the principles of self-management and to transfer the power of economic decisionmaking from the technocratic and managerial elite back to the workers' collectives. She stresses the extension of the influence of the party and trade unions in filling the power vacuum left first by the discredited state bureaucracy and more recently by the curtailment of the technocratic and managerial elite. Deborah Milenkovitch, "The Case of Yugoslavia," *American Economic Review*, vol. 67, no. 1 (February 1977), pp. 55–60.

shifting much decisionmaking power from state organs to enterprise management. The recent changes took this one step further by establishing the basic organization of associated labor (BOAL) as the principal decisionmaking unit.[2] BOALS are the building blocks of all other economic organizations, from enterprises to such larger entities as composite organizations of associated labor. Thus the principle of decentralization—first applied in the political sphere by assigning decisionmaking power to the smallest units competent to deal with a particular issue—now is firmly imposed on the economic sphere. The expected result, just as for political decentralization, is that workers will dominate the decisionmaking in these smaller and more homogeneous units and, by extension, the decisionmaking in all other economic organizations. This greater participation should in turn increase the accountability of managers and provide more effective controls against the emergence of unwanted power structures. A second major departure, the diminution of the importance of banks and trade enterprises, resolves what was felt to be an uncomfortable compromise between Marxian principles and capitalist practices. Banks no longer have the status of enterprises. They are special organizations, comparable to credit unions, serving the needs of enterprises that constitute them; in their decisions about policy and allocation, they are subject to the decisions of their members. Trade enterprises now have a status comparable to agents supplying services for an agreed share of the receipts.[3]

Of the new legal instruments, social compacts and self-management agreements are most important. Social compacts on such broad issues as prices, incomes, and employment establish the obligations of economic organizations. Enterprises participate in their negotiation and, in the absence of explicit dissent, are obliged to adhere to them. The compacts thus replace the traditional policy instruments

2. It is important to bear in mind that many instruments and institutions codified in the 1974 constitution were introduced by the constitutional amendments of 1971. The new constitution consolidates these earlier changes and provides a comprehensive and consistent vision of the new economic system.

3. The Associated Labour Act of 1976, referred to in this volume as the law on associated labor, gives the most detailed account of the premises and ground rules governing economic and social relations. Frequently referred to as the "constitution of the economy," it is indispensable for understanding the Yugoslav system in the 1970s. Despite its being a formidable compendium of 671 articles, it is not a lawyers' law, but a manual that guides decisionmakers by delineating the rights, obligations, and procedures of self-management. Secretariat of Information of the Yugoslavia Assembly, *The Associated Labour Act* (Ljubljana: Dopisna Delavska Universza, 1977).

that were discredited because of their association with the state and their inherent conflict with self-management. Self-management agreements are contracts, usually medium in term, between BOALS and enterprises. They cover almost all transactions and arrangements, such as deliveries, the pooling of investment resources, and the computation of transfer prices and personal incomes. The agreements thus regulate many transactions that are regulated by the market mechanism in a market economy or by government prescription and obligatory targets in a planned economy.[4]

Premises of Self-management Socialism

It is not the intention here to describe and analyze in detail the philosophical and political premises underlying the Yugoslav perception of self-management socialism or to trace them to their origins in Marxian thought and Yugoslav history. To introduce the role of those premises in the Yugoslav response to the challenges of development, it suffices to sketch the three that are most important for the analysis in this volume: the principle of self-management in economic matters; the role of the state in self-management; and the role of sociopolitical organizations in achieving a broad social consensus by integrating special economic interests.

Self-management in economic matters

The basic sociopolitical premise, applying to political and economic matters, is self-management. As was mentioned in the overview, democracy is to be direct: decisionmaking power is assigned to individuals directly affected by the decisions; those individuals control the decisionmaking process directly without autonomous intermediaries. As was also mentioned in the overview, direct decisionmaking power distinguishes self-management from the concepts of participation and codetermination, which imply that decisionmaking power is shared with management or the state. This direct control applies to all social and economic relations: to citizens

4. The effect of the recent changes on the market and planning is the subject of chapter four.

in their sociopolitical communities, to workers in the organization in which they work, and to consumers of goods and services.[5] In each sphere different institutional arrangements have been devised to organize and regulate self-management. Although social ownership of the means of production is the basis of self-management, new hybrid forms of social and private ownership and control are now emerging.[6] To some degree they enable the extension of self-management to the private sector.

To achieve a practical and efficient form of self-management, two conditions must be fulfilled. First, the decisionmakers have to be organized in relatively small collectives, within which the members have fairly homogeneous views and interests and are able to develop some form of communication on matters of common concern. In the social and political spheres, the communes are the basic collectives for decisionmaking. In the economic sphere the BOALS—the smallest operating units producing a marketable output—fulfill this same function. The fundamental position of BOALS inheres in two legal provisions: every major decision of a larger legal entity comprising a group of BOALS must be agreed upon by all constituent BOALS; every BOAL has the right to split off from broader organizational units, so long as that separation does not endanger the survival of remaining BOALS. These provisions affirm that consensus is the preferred basis for decisionmaking.

The second condition is that the mechanisms instituted have to enable these smallest decisionmaking units to communicate and coordinate their interests and intentions in larger organizations without violating the principle of direct control. To that end, workers or citizens at the lowest level of organization elect a dele-

---

5. As was noted in chapter two, many terms in Yugoslav parlance, particularly those relating to elements of the sociopolitical system, have specific legal, economic, and political connotations not conveyed by literal translation (see the glossary). For example, sociopolitical communities are territorial political units: communes, republics, and the federation; the Yugoslavs also distinguish between workers in the social sector and working people in the private sector. In this volume only the term *workers* is used.

6. The discussions associated with the constitutional changes iterated the decisive differences between "social ownership" and both "state ownership" and "group ownership." The Yugoslav concept of social ownership is that society entrusts the control of assets to the workers using those assets. Society also obliges workers to use the assets for their own benefit and the benefit of society and excludes the earning of income from sources other than that generated by labor.

gation to represent them at the next wider level of organization, where another delegation is formed to represent that wider level in a still wider group. This stepwise election of delegates continues up to the federal level. But in contrast with elected representatives in a system of parliamentary democracy, delegates are obliged to solicit the views of their constituency on every matter pending decision, to express those views in the decisionmaking body to which they are delegated, and to report back to their constituency. If delegates lose the confidence of their constituency, they can be recalled any time. Furthermore delegates are expected to share the socioeconomic background of their constituents. They are also expected to return to their previous working and living environments and their previous social and economic positions after their regular terms expire. Thus representation and decisionmaking work from the bottom up, not from the top down.

Subsidiary to self-management is the principle of equality, which rules out the weighting of voting rights in instances in which majority voting is not precluded by the principle of unanimity. For example, delegations of each republic have the same weight in the federal assembly, regardless of the size of the population they represent; delegations of different BOALS in an enterprise have an equal voice, but not necessarily an equal number of delegates, regardless of size or any financial yardstick; member organizations of a bank are equal, regardless of the volume of their deposits or credits.

Adherence to the principles of self-management and equality leads to the general rule that decisions should be by consensus. Exemptions from this rule are made if attempts to reach a consensus lead to excessive delays or deadlocks that are detrimental to third parties or society as a whole. To prevent such occurrences, the constitution, the law, and the by-laws of organizations specify the application of other mechanisms. In some instances decisions are left to majority voting, such as the decisions in a BOAL. In other instances a temporary ruling can be imposed until a consensus is reached. For example, the Presidency of the federation can promulgate a law if the delegations of republics cannot agree in the Federal Assembly; or the Federal Executive Council can, with concurrence of the Presidency, adopt measures even if the corresponding organs of republican governments have not agreed. In still other instances detailed guidelines can be stipulated. For example, the assemblies of sociopolitical communities can impose decisions on enterprises if those enterprises do not settle specific matters among themselves by a certain date.

The role of the state

The state in its widest meaning—parliament, government, administration, and budgets—is organized in three layers of sociopolitical communities: the communes, the republics and autonomous provinces, and the federation (figure 3.1).[7] Each layer of the state has its own assembly in which delegates and delegations represent the citizens and workers. The assemblies of communes and republics have three chambers; the Federal Assembly has two. In the republican assemblies, a chamber of associated labor comprises delegates representing workers, a chamber of communes comprises delegates nominated by the assemblies of communes, and a sociopolitical chamber comprises delegates nominated by sociopolitical organizations. In the Federal Assembly, the Chamber of Republics and Autonomous Provinces comprises delegations from each republican assembly, and the Federal Chamber comprises delegates nominated by the Socialist Alliance and elected by the assemblies of communes.

In contrast with the system of parliamentary democracy, the assemblies in Yugoslavia hold both legislative and executive power. The executive councils they elect constitute the "government" in the narrow sense. Those councils are responsible for advising their assembly on decisions that need to be taken and implementing the decisions that are taken. For matters requiring particularly close cooperation among republics and the federation, members of the executive councils establish joint interrepublican or federal committees. Executive councils discharge their duties through secretariats, federal committees, and such specialized institutions as planning institutes and statistical offices, which report to individual members of executive councils.

Under the self-management principle the state's functions are decentralized to the largest possible degree: legislative and executive

---

7. Yugoslavia has 510 communes ranging in population from fewer than 10,000 persons to more than 100,000; the average population of communes is about 40,000 persons. The largest of Yugoslavia's six republics, Serbia, incorporates two regions having the status of autonomous provinces: Kosovo and Vojvodina. It thus has three sociopolitical communities at the republican level. Despite differences in the size of delegations from republics and autonomous provinces to the Federal Chamber, the delegations of the autonomous provinces in most respects have equal status with those of republics. Consequently, when the terms *republic* and *region* are used in this volume, they refer equally to the autonomous provinces.

Figure 3.1. *Assemblies of Sociopolitical Communities*

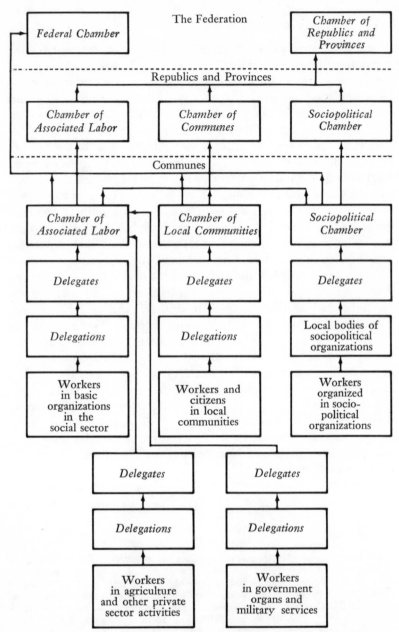

Source: Adapted from Zlatija Dukic-Veljovic, "The Assembly of the Socialist Federal Republic of Yugoslavia," *Yugoslav Survey*, vol. 18, no. 1 (February

power is assigned to the lowest level sociopolitical community that can autonomously take action without disrupting or endangering consistency. The fiscal system provides an example: each republic, in addition to having considerable discretion in raising taxes, has its own budget. For matters of economic policy, however, the federation has primary responsibility for relations with other countries and monetary policy. The maintenance of the "unity of the Yugoslav market" is the joint responsibility of the federation and the republics. The creation and coordination of economic enterprises is in the realm of the republics or communes, depending on the activity. Certain activities, singled out by the republics as being of special importance, are coordinated at the federal level with the active participation of the republics. For all other activities, planning is conducted by the republics, and sometimes only by the communes.

The state also is removed from the management of economic and socioeconomic matters, again to the largest possible degree. It is restricted to establishing a consensus on broad objectives and policy guidelines, carrying out administrative measures, monitoring the implementation of plans and development, and resolving conflicts, mainly but not exclusively in planning, that cannot otherwise be reconciled. Even in policy formulation, the state is restricted to issues that, in the interest of society, cannot be left to self-managed nonstate coordinating bodies or mechanisms, such as chambers of the economy and communities of interest. The involvement of the state in policy matters is usually regulated through social compacts. These compacts restrict the scope for discretionary intervention by the state and generally require some form of prior agreement with the nonstate coordinating bodies, which are parties to the compacts.

The restricted role of the state can also be described by the functions from which it is clearly excluded. The state has no managerial or administrative control over such social services as education, health, and social security; nor does it regularly finance those services through its budgets. The revenue of the state is largely restricted to the resources necessary for financing "general consumption," that is, current expenditure for the classical state functions, such as administration and defense. It also extends to some minor social transfers and to compensation for organizations whose ability to earn adequate income is impeded by collective action. Because society, not the state, owns the means of production, the state is excluded from mobilizing and allocating investment resources, which are controlled by workers through self-managed enterprises and other organizations. In addition, the state generally does not intervene in the transactions among enterprises and organizations. An exception is the direct control of prices for such key items as the tariffs for railways and energy. In these instances, however, the state must provide compensation if prices are not appropriate for producers.

A strong antistatist streak thus is prominent in the Yugoslav system. Because additional functions of the state are to be absorbed gradually by self-managed coordinating bodies or directly by large integrated complexes, further reductions in the role of the state are likely.

The role of sociopolitical organizations

The sociopolitical organizations include the League of Communists of Yugoslavia (LCY), the Socialist Alliance, the Trade Unions, the Youth Federation, and the Association of Veterans. The new constitution explicitly defines their roles. They nominate delegates to the sociopolitical chambers of the republican assemblies. Those chambers have two functions: integrating society by eliminating any bias toward special interests from the positions adopted by the other two chambers; dealing specifically and exclusively with matters affecting the political system and its evolution. Because all three chambers of republican assemblies nominate the republican delegations to the federal Chamber of Republics and Autonomous Provinces, sociopolitical organizations have direct representation in the Federal Assembly as well. At the level of communes, the Socialist Alliance nominates candidates for the first chamber of the Federal Assembly.

The Socialist Alliance is a broadly based organization comprising all citizens who accept the principles of socialism. Its membership in 1972 included about 95 percent of the adult population. In addition to nominating candidates for the assemblies of sociopolitical communities, the Alliance is a forum for the discussion of current political, social, and economic issues. It also provides a means for feedback between citizens and the assemblies of sociopolitical communities, including the initiation of action by the assemblies.

The League of Communists of Yugoslavia (LCY), with a membership of about 15 percent of the adult population, is a tightly knit Marxian organization. After a period of increasing regionalization and gradual withdrawal from political participation during the late 1960s, the LCY reasserted itself in the 1970s as the unified source of political guidance and as the "organized force of socialist consciousness." It spearheads political development and identifies the principal objectives of social and economic development. Prime examples of the involvement of the LCY in economic matters are resolutions of its tenth congress in 1974: one resolution set out the objectives of the five-year plan for 1976–80; another stipulated the reduction of inflation as the principal short-term policy objective. LCY resolutions have no legal force. But because of the Marxist-Leninist principle of democratic centralism, the resolutions oblige LCY members to act in accord with the resolutions in the decision-making of their work organization or community.[8] Thus LCY resolutions are likely to affect the economic and political debate and to find their way into concrete legislative or executive decisions. The LCY not only focuses on broad policy issues; it also attends to matters for which the regular decisionmaking process does not function. An example is the direct involvement of the LCY in matters of transport policy at the end of 1976, specifically in attempting to resolve the unfavorable financial position of railway enterprises. The LCY bases its resolutions on extensive internal discussions and the analytical work of permanent special commissions.

The membership of unions is about equal to total employment in the social sector. The outstanding function of unions is to initiate self-management in organizations by arranging for the nomination of candidates for election to self-managed bodies and to guide the decisionmaking of those bodies. The unions also initiate self-management agreements among BOALS in larger enterprises and among enterprises in sectors for the distribution of income and for other matters affecting the position of workers.

Instruments and Organizations of Self-management

To organize economic relations in accord with the principle of self-management, Yugoslavia introduced two legal instruments: social compacts and self-management agreements. Social compacts

8. In essence, discussions are unrestrained before resolutions are adopted, but the determination to act in accord with resolutions is expected to be unwavering after they are adopted. The principle of democratic centralism and its application to the most politically active segment of society constitute the basis of a strong cohesive force in decisionmaking at all levels. This cohesiveness enables decisions to be made on important issues in an otherwise unstructured setting.

are concluded by the assemblies of sociopolitical communities and, in many instances, by trade unions, chambers of the economy, and associations of enterprises. Self-management agreements are concluded by such organizations as BOALS, enterprises, and banks (table 3.1). Certain provisions are common to both instruments: the procedures for their conclusion are public; they are published after conclusion; the parties to them generally are equal and have no weighted voting rights; they are valid only for parties who sign them directly or through some authorized intermediary, such as a chamber of the economy; adherence to them is either legally mandatory, as for social compacts, or is all but ensured by financial penalties for noncompliance, as for self-management agreements.

, Social compacts regulate rights and obligations affecting broader economic issues and policies: the priorities of social plans; the principles and criteria of policies for prices, employment, and foreign trade; and the functional distribution of income between personal incomes and capital accumulation. Frequently the social compacts lay down obligatory provisions and ground rules for specific self-management agreements that are subsequently concluded. Sociopolitical communities in many instances initiate the conclusion of social compacts. In other instances sociopolitical communities can adopt regulations that oblige organizations to conclude social compacts. Although their legal format makes social compacts appear to be tantamount to civil—that is, microeconomic—contracts, they often set out macroeconomic policies. In these instances they take the place of policy measures that in most other countries would be regulated either by law or traditional economic policies and carried out by government agencies without the direct participation of affected parties. Once concluded, social compacts have, for practical purposes, the force of law. They cannot be abrogated before the specified time of expiry, unless that abrogation is agreed upon by all parties to the compact.[9]

Self-management agreements regulate almost all relations in, among, and between economic organizations: the formation of BOALS, enterprises, and banks; the distribution of jointly earned income among BOALS in an enterprise or among enterprises integrated in reproduction entities; the delivery contracts and principles

---

9. The law on associated labor states, without specifying sanctions for noncompliance, that "the parties to social compacts shall be held socially and politically responsible in the event they shall not carry out their obligations." *Associated Labour Act*, article 558.

Table 3.1. *Composition and Functions*
of Self-managed Organizations

Organization	Composition	Function
Basic organization of associated labor (BOAL)	All workers who join in an "association of labor"	Atomizes economic decision-making to the smallest technically distinguishable unit producing a marketable output
Enterprise	BOALS	Links associated BOALS that jointly realize income in an "association of labor and resources"
Association	Enterprises in a branch	Forum for discussing common matters, horizontal coordination, and decisions binding consenting members
Chamber of the economy	All associations	Forum for discussing common matters and for broad vertical coordination
Reproduction entity	Vertically linked enterprises	Integrates medium-term plans for output and capacity; not a legal entity
Composite organization of associated labor	Vertically or horizontally linked enterprises	Integrates medium-term plans for output and capacity; a legal entity
Community of interest	Enterprises and other social sector organizations	Links suppliers and users of social or productive services for the joint regulation of supply, demand, and financing
Cooperative	Individuals in the private sector	Links private individuals for joint production in agriculture, crafts, and productive services
Contractual organization of associated labor (COAL)	Individuals and workers	Links private workers and owner-operators with social resources in hybrid private and social enterprise
Bank	Enterprises and BOALS as depositors and borrowers	Work community for pooling the resources of members for financing the investment of members

Source: Compiled by the authors.

for establishing transfer prices among associated BOALS or enterprises; the criteria for distributing the net income of BOALS between personal incomes and accumulation; the use of generated investment resources in BOALS and the pooling of those resources in enterprises or reproduction entities. They do not regulate current sales and purchases outside the realm of "sharing of income and risk," which is discussed below. Depending upon the subject matter, self-management agreements may be concluded for a specific period of time or for a specific purpose regardless of time. In many instances the five-year plan period determines the time horizon.

Parties to self-management agreements may default on their obligations only because of changes in priorities or conditions beyond their control. Such defaults nevertheless are severely penalized by provisions for financial compensation to other parties to the agreement. In addition, any deliberate or negligent breach of a self-management agreement would apparently stigmatize the defaulting organization and reduce its ability to enter into other agreements. That ability may, in an environment where long-term agreements are the rule, be essential for survival. It thus seems that all signatories will generally adhere to self-management agreements, unless there is a consensus to dissolve or change an agreement.

The right to codify mutual relations in self-management agreements, if unrestrained, could lead to monopolistic or oligopolistic arrangements. The 1976 law on associated labor clearly acknowledges this danger and contains it by two provisions: self-management agreements must be published before they are implemented; adversely affected organizations, sociopolitical communities, and trade unions may raise objections. Such an objection obliges all parties to reexamine the agreement. If objections are not subsequently withdrawn, the disputed agreement can be submitted to special courts for compulsory arbitration. These courts also settle all other disputes arising from self-management agreements.

Self-managed BOALs and enterprises

Each technical unit producing a marketable output, regardless of whether that output is marketed or transferred to another BOAL in the same enterprise, is to form a separate BOAL.[10] Most enter-

---

10. In Yugoslav political and legal terminology a "work organization" is equivalent to an "enterprise," the term used throughout this volume.

prises are constituted by several BOALS. For example, an integrated textile mill would probably be divided into a BOAL each for spinning, weaving, finishing, final processing, and retail outlets. The law does not specify any minimum or maximum size for BOALS; they can have a few dozen workers or more than a thousand.

The importance of this stratification for decisionmaking can be gleaned from several key provisions. To be valid, the plan of each enterprise or broader legal entity must be accepted by all constituent BOALS. "Income before distribution" is separately computed for each BOAL on the basis of internal prices determined by self-management agreements between BOALS, by the business success of the whole enterprise, and by the contribution of each BOAL.[11] Within the frame established by social compacts and self-management agreements, BOALS decide the distribution of generated income into personal income and accumulation. Within that same frame, BOALS decide the use of accumulation for investment. Generated investment resources can be made available to any other organization—whether to BOALS in the enterprise or to other enterprises—but must be returned to the BOAL from which they originated, unless they are ceded by self-management agreements. In addition, BOALS have the right to separate from the enterprise, after settling their obligations, and to form an autonomous enterprise or join another enterprise, unless the breakaway would endanger the survival of remaining BOALS.

The definition of the BOAL is fairly straightforward; that of the enterprise is less sharply drawn. According to the 1976 law on associated labor, an enterprise comprises workers "linked by a common working interest" or "directly linked by a unified process."[12] Regular generation of joint income by BOALS establishes that common interest. But in contrast with BOALS, which are indivisible and conceptually "permanent," the enterprise is an "association" that can change its composition and orientation according to the needs of the market and the preferences of its members. For example, an enterprise traditionally specializing in agricultural machinery could enter the manufacture of tractors in conjunction with a group of BOALS engaged in the manufacture of diesel engines and mechanical and hydraulic gears, but exclude from the association a BOAL engaged in forging and oriented to customers outside the new activity.

11. Income before distribution is equal to sales minus purchases from other organizations, statutory depreciation, and various contractual and legal obligations. The computation of income is described more fully in chapter seven.
12. *Associated Labour Act*, article 346.

BOALS functionally linked in an enterprise are "pooling labor and resources" to improve their individual capacities to earn income. The "joint income" created is shared among participating BOALS. BOALS associated in an enterprise thus share risks, gains, and losses. The association and the provisions for the cooperation of associated organizations are regulated by self-management agreements. These provisions cover purposes and objectives, delivery relations, the determination of internal prices, the computation and distribution of income, the use of windfall gains and sharing of windfall losses, the harmonization of plans, the establishment of coordinating bodies, and the duration of association.

The "pooling of resources" by BOALS and enterprises—that is, the joint self-financing of investment—usually is integral to any association.[13] It can take two forms: joint pooling with shared income and risk, and pooling through a conventional credit relationship. In joint pooling, BOALS or enterprises make resources available to other BOALS or enterprises, either with the right to share in the income and associated risk, or with the provision for such other benefits as delivery commitments and price arrangements. The right to share in the income from pooled resources nevertheless must be limited either to the amount of the contributed resources, regardless of the time, or to the period over which income can be shared, regardless of the amount transmitted.[14] Joint pooling thus establishes a temporary but renewable financial partnership between the participating BOALS or enterprises; they share in the risks, gains, and losses according to some formula agreed upon before they enter that partnership. The other form of pooling, credits with fixed contractual terms for repayment and interest, can be extended directly from one BOAL or enterprise to another and indirectly through earmarked deposits in banks. Nevertheless the text of the law and other documents leaves little doubt that joint pooling is to be preferred because of its being more compatible with self-management. The pooling of resources has two decisive features. First, the pooling arrangements cannot infringe upon the right of BOALS to retain ultimate control over the resources they generate. Although BOALS may temporarily share that control with another BOAL or enterprise, the re-

---

13. In this context, "resources" are equivalent to financial resources for investment.

14. Additional compensation may be specified as well. The law permits repayment in accord with "revalued" fixed assets—that is, some form of indexed repayment to correct for the effects of inflation.

sources they provide under pooling arrangements must be returned, plus or minus some amount that reflects the sharing of risk and income. Second, the pooling arrangements cannot permanently establish control of one BOAL over another—that is, one BOAL cannot supply funds in exchange for a permanent flow of income from investment, as would occur in equity-type financial arrangements.

The right to self-management is associated with special responsibilities of workers. The most obvious example is the computation of remuneration. Workers do not receive wages or salaries—that is, contractual payments regardless of the result of their work. They receive only some share of the income of the BOAL in which they work.[15] Workers thus participate, through the personal income they receive, in the success or failure of the organization whose affairs they control. That participation is not unlimited. If personal incomes temporarily fall below a certain limit for reasons other than mismanagement or gross inefficiency, an interenterprise "solidarity fund," tantamount to insurance, provides the difference. Similarly the enterprise revenue that arises from exceptionally favorable conditions is excluded from enterprise income and consequently from distributions to personal income.[16] In addition, the distribution of income of BOALS is largely predetermined by social compacts and self-management agreements. Furthermore the law on associated labor explicitly states that the workers are responsible for the rational and efficient management of the social resources at their disposal, a responsibility that includes the obligation to renew those resources and ensure their expansion.[17] Conversely, if workers fail to fulfill that responsibility for reasons within their control or that of their elected management organ, they bear the consequences. Workers can be dismissed, however, only in instances of criminal behavior or severe misconduct. If the services of workers are no longer needed, they cannot be laid off. The BOAL, the enterprise, or the solidarity fund of a broader arrangement must provide them with equivalent substitute employment. The combination of the provision that all workers share in the residual income earned and the exclusion of dismissal in cases other than gross misconduct leads to a peculiar pattern of adjusting to business fluctuations: enterprises do not adjust by changing the number of workers receiving

15. Income here is defined as in note 11.
16. *Constitution of the Socialist Federal Republic of Yugoslavia*, 1974, article 18.
17. *Associated Labour Act*, article 19.

a defined wage; they change the levels of income of the unchanged work force.

The internal workings of self-management deserve elaboration. For BOALS and enterprises, the law stipulates the organization of management in three layers: workers' councils, executive organs, and management organs. Workers' councils, the most important organs of decisionmaking, comprise delegates elected by secret ballot from within the working community and from a list of candidates prepared by the unions.[18] They accept the organization's plan and financial statements; they formulate policies on business and the distribution of income; they elect, discharge, and control the executive and managerial organs. The executive organs perform specific functions in the domain of the workers' council; its members are elected from among the delegates of the workers' councils. The management organ can be a single business manager or a managing board of unspecified size. In either case, the position has to be publicly advertised and the choice among applicants is jointly made by the workers' council, the assembly of the commune, and the union organization of the work unit. The normal term of delegates to workers' councils and executive organs is two years, with the possibility of one re-election. The regular term of the management organ is four years, with the possibility of reappointment.

The management organ has a dual responsibility to the organization and society. First, it is responsible for carrying out the decisions of the workers' council and for handling the day-to-day affairs of the organization according to its plan and business policy and according to procedures laid down in the self-management agreement establishing the organization. The law on associated labor specifies that the management organ has the right to give directives to workers for specific tasks necessary to implement the organization's plan and business policy, but is excluded from personnel management in its broadest sense. The management organ thus has the right to suggest disciplinary measures, but not to hire and fire workers, take disciplinary action, determine the internal distribution of income, or make appointments to management positions at the middle and lower levels. Second, if the workers' council or executive organ makes decisions or requests actions that violate legal provisions, social compacts, or self-management agreements, the

---

18. In BOALS or enterprises having fewer than thirty workers, all workers perform the functions of the workers' council.

management organ has the duty to warn against implementation. If the organization insists on proceeding with implementation, the management organ must refrain from participating and inform the competent agency of the appropriate sociopolitical community of the violation.[19] Notwithstanding the terms of its appointment, the management organ is subject to recall at any time—for negligence, incompetence, legal misconduct, or the failure to maintain cordial relations with other bodies. Proceedings for dismissal can be initiated either by the workers' council, the assembly of the commune, or the trade union. The final decisions are open to appeal, compensation, or both.

Composite organizations and reproduction entities

The definition of the BOAL—as a technically distinguishable unit producing a marketable output—could in principle have led to the economy's atomization into as many autonomous units as there are BOALS and to the regulation of their mutual relations through a market mechanism.[20] But that route was rejected in favor of various legal or contractual forms of association. Two reasons apparently led to this different form of organizing economic relations. First, the creation of an atomized competitive structure can be socially divisive because it strengthens the propensity toward "group ownership" and undermines the socialist principle of solidarity. Second, such an atomized structure would make all but impossible the planning that is considered essential for the efficiency of the economic system. Thus a clear choice was made for what is referred to in Yugoslavia as "integration."

Integration is not a new term; nor is its promotion new. During the late 1960s, the agglomeration of enterprises into diversified quasi conglomerates was a general phenomenon. Integration was supported by some tangible microeconomic benefits, such as the distribution of financial risks and control over supply or demand. Sometimes it was propelled by the belief that bigger is better; sometimes by the vigor of strong management. The creation of BOALS, and the accompanying shift of decisionmaking power from enterprise management

---

19. This obligation of the management organ, backed up by provisions for civil and criminal penalties, apparently is a powerful means for controlling violations of the legal and contractual obligations of enterprises.

20. According to unofficial estimates, about 46,000 BOALS were registered in 1976.

to BOALS after 1971, put an end to this momentum of frequently indiscriminate growth. Integration is again being promoted, but the emphasis now is for integration along functional lines.

Integration can be accomplished in composite organizations of associated labor or in reproduction entities. The law on associated labor defines the composite organization as a legal entity comprising several enterprises that are either vertically or horizontally linked in the chain of production. Horizontal linkage would increase specialization or enable the achievement of greater economies of scale among enterprises engaged in the manufacture of similar products. In contrast with the composite organization, the reproduction entity is not a defined legal form. The term refers to a group of enterprises that are vertically linked by forward or backward delivery relationships and have formalized their long-term relations in self-management agreements on association.[21]

All the aspects of association of BOALS in an enterprise apply to reproduction entities, including the creation of common management organs. The only distinct difference is that for the association of enterprises in a reproduction entity, the individual members can simultaneously be members of several such entities. There seems to be no significant economic difference between a vertically organized composite organization and a reproduction entity. Nevertheless discussions and documents suggest that the reproduction entity is viewed in Yugoslavia as the form in which integration is to be established. In the long run, therefore, the autonomy of enterprises may be reduced by the strengthening of BOALS on one side and reproduction entities on the other. It should also be noted that the recent move toward greater integration in Yugoslavia stresses vertical links; the parallel moves toward greater integration in other socialist countries of Eastern Europe almost exclusively stress horizontal links in associations for different branches of industry.

Integration has decisively changed the position of trade enter-

21. Reproduction entities thus tend to be organized along the rows and columns of input-output tables. They can embrace all stages of production: for example, coal mining, power generation, and power consumption by the metallurgical and chemical industries for electrolytic processing; linkages can even include the delivery of investment goods, such as power generation equipment, and principal inputs for their manufacture, such as ferrous and nonferrous metals. The law on associated labor also specifies legal forms of partial integration, such as "business communities" and "communities for planning and business cooperation." Whatever the fine legal distinctions, they seem to come conceptually close to the reproduction entity and are so constituted.

prises. The new constitution and the law on associated labor put an end to their earlier autonomy. Foreign trade enterprises must now, by prescription, enter into association with production enterprises —an association having all the previously described features of shared income and risk, joint price policy, resource pooling, joint planning, and codification in self-management agreements. It also is strongly suggested that the same relations be established for wholesale and retail trade. For retail trade in consumer goods and services, the intention of the law is that trade enterprises will enter into self-management agreements with organizations representing the consumers on affairs of common concern.

Communities of interest

The community of interest is another institution unique to Yugoslavia. It comprises organizations that supply certain goods or services and those that either use these goods and services or represent final users. The community forms an assembly as a decision-making body in which the parties have an equal weight. The new constitution broadened the scope for setting up communities of interest, which initially were established for such services as health, education, and social insurance. It permits their extension to every product or service for which the market cannot be relied upon to match supply and demand in quantity and quality or establish prices that are appropriate for all affected parties. Mandatory for the social services, they can be set up at the initiative of enterprises and other organizations for any other good or service. In addition, the creation of a community of interest can be made mandatory for certain enterprises and organizations if the assembly of a sociopolitical community regards such action to be in the interest of society. Public statements and recent organizational moves suggest that communities of interest will have an increasing role in the organization of economic affairs, particularly in the organization of such basic goods and services as electric power, water supply, railways, and highways.

Once established by a self-management agreement, a community of interest is an independent legal entity with clearly defined rights and obligations for all parties and the community as a whole. In social activities, and to a large degree in economic activities, the community is responsible for managing supply and demand; it also is responsible for all financial transactions, including the mobilization and allocation of investment resources. These financial transactions can take various forms: the current expenditure of suppliers can be covered by contributions from the consumers as individuals or organized groups, by transfer prices or fees according to goods and services delivered, or by some combination of both.[22] Investment resources can similarly be collected as contributions or as a part of transfer prices; they can also be mobilized as compulsory grants and credits from consumers, or through credits contracted from banks.

Communities of interest in effect supplant the market as a regulating mechanism and the state as a regulatory and administrative agency. They do this by compelling the organized groups of affected parties to search for a direct consensus with little recourse to outside arbitration or the resolution of conflict by political interference. In addition, communities of interest are directly linked to the broader decisionmaking process. Whenever the assemblies of sociopolitical communities discuss and decide legislative or policy matters, the assemblies of the communities of interest affected by those matters become equal partners in political decisionmaking.

Chambers of the economy

It is mandatory that all enterprises belong to the "association" of a particular sector or branch of industry organized at the republican or federal level.[23] These associations in turn constitute the chambers of the economy that comprise all economic activities, again at the republican or federal level. Both institutions perform important functions. First, they serve as a forum for enterprises to formulate common views on matters of economic policy, and as a body to carry out dialogues with the administration and assemblies of sociopolitical communities. Second, they can establish agreements on rules of conduct on special issues—agreements which subsequently

---

22. Because the community of interest is based on the premise that market relations cannot reflect social values of goods and services, transactions within a community are frequently referred to as "free exchanges of labor."

23. Such associations are not related to the associations of BOALS or enterprises discussed in connection with the formation and functioning of enterprises, reproduction entities, and composite organizations of associated labor. Nor are such associations similar to the associations increasingly being established in other socialist countries of Eastern Europe. Those associations not only integrate horizontally linked enterprises into one tightly knit new organization; they also assume many of the powers of the state, such as centralized planning and decisionmaking. In Yugoslavia the associations and chambers of the economy do not have the legal status that would entitle them to engage in any decisionmaking that would be binding for their members, unless they conclude a self-management agreement.

are codified in self-management agreements. Third, they provide the sounding board for their members in the harmonization of their individual plans: the associations primarily for horizontal harmonization within an activity; the chambers of the economy primarily for harmonization of the various stages of production. Fourth, because chambers of the economy are parties to social compacts on major policy matters, they establish the link between their members and sociopolitical communities. The associations and chambers thus perform a number of functions not conducive to direct agreement by the affected parties, such as the harmonization of delivery requirements for subsequent stages of production, or to agreements within or among groups of parties, such as establishing principles for workers' incomes. In most other countries these functions are in the domain of the state. Although chambers appear to be parastatal organs because of their functions and mandatory membership, they are part of the self-managing superstructure of the economy: the state is not a member, nor is it involved in any other way in the proceedings; the chambers cannot autonomously make majority decisions which, by whatever mechanism, are subsequently binding for dissenting members.

Banks

In effect, banks now are service agencies for their members; they pool and exchange the financial resources that their members generate.[24] The change in status is expressed in the draft of the new law on banking: ". . . a banking organization will cease to be an independent banking entity, which concentrates and distributes resources [independent of] organizations of associated labor; instead, it will become a financial association of its members."[25] According to the

24. In this context banks are equivalent to what were designated in the previous banking law as "business banks" having a wide range of functions: holding sight and time deposits from private households and organizations in the social sector, extending credits to citizens and organizations in the social sector, and providing guarantees and credit arrangements for domestic and foreign trade. Under the new law on banking, most of these functions are vested with "basic banks." The other type of bank introduced by the new legislation is the "internal bank." Established in large enterprises or composite organizations of associated labor, they deal exclusively with the BOALS constituting the larger organization. The new banking system is discussed in detail in chapter seven.

25. Federal Assembly, "Proposal for the Adoption of the Law on the Underlying Premises of the Banking System," trans. World Bank (Washington, D.C., 1976; processed), p. 2.

self-management agreements and social compacts they are jointly or individually parties to, the members must reach a consensus among themselves on the use of the available resources and the terms and conditions governing the collection of resources. As organizations, banks have the status of a "work community," not that of an enterprise; they carry out the directions of the members. The gradual reduction of fungible resources and their replacement by earmarking by members are central to this shift in decisionmaking in the financial sphere. The increased responsibility of members accompanies this realignment of control in their favor. Under the new legislation the permanent deposits are abolished. In addition, the community of depositors and borrowers sign a self-management agreement on association in the bank, share in the profits and losses of banking operations, and are fully liable with their assets.[26]

The operational characteristics of the new banking system, and the ways these differ from those of the previous system, have not yet clearly emerged. It seems, however, that control over resources is tighter. The members restrict to a considerable degree the use of resources through the obligations they independently assume in social compacts and self-management agreements. This arrangement probably ties a large portion of available resources to specific activities and projects. The disposition of remaining resources is decided in the context of annual bank plans, which consolidate the capital transactions of the annual financial plans of members. The banks thus are an integral part of planning.

The private sector: individuals, cooperatives, and COALs

Although self-management strictly presupposes social ownership of the means of production, the new constitution guarantees the continued existence of a private sector. The general limits of activities in that sector (there are exceptions) nevertheless are specified: ten hectares of arable land in agriculture; five salaried workers in any other area of activity. In order to relax the constraints these limits impose on the economic viability of private enterprise and to reconcile private ownership with the principle of self-

---

26. Profits from banking operations for distribution would be accidental, not intentional. Because banks, as a work community, do not produce "value," they do not generate any "surplus value," or profit. They consequently are geared in their financial planning to covering operational expenses and building up some statutory reserves.

management, the constitution and the law on associated labor provide for new institutional and legal arrangements. First, private farmers and craftsmen may now form cooperatives, in which the rights of private ownership are maintained. Those rights include a claim to part of the generated income accruing to private ownership and a right to recall the contributed assets upon leaving the cooperative or to receive compensation if their return is impossible or detrimental to the remaining cooperants. The working relations among cooperants thus are analogous to those for workers in a BOAL. Second, private owners, either individually or as a cooperative, may enter into a long-term agreement of association with a social sector enterprise. Such an agreement would entitle them to full participation in the self-management of that organization. Third, the contractual organization of associated labor (COAL) has been devised as an entirely new legal concept to bridge the social and private sectors. It was created to overcome some of the handicaps the private sector has faced; it is designed to provide greater parity in the opportunities available to that sector.

In a COAL individuals pool their financial resources with each other, with socially owned resources, or in both ways. In Slovenia COALS are enterprises in which a private individual contributes 10 percent or more of the initial capital; if more than one person is involved, each individual's contribution must be at least 10 percent. The founders of a COAL work in that COAL but earn, in addition to their wages, income based on their share of the paid-in capital.[27] COALS may employ salaried workers without specific limit. In collaboration with trade unions and chambers of the economy, owners and workers jointly conclude a self-management agreement on the foundation of the COAL—an agreement which specifies the rights and obligations of all parties. The distribution of the net income is in two stages: private individuals and workers receive personal income corresponding to the income in comparable organizations in the social sector; the remainder is then distributed in accord with the shares in ownership. One basic idea of the COAL is that the founders should, over time, be paid back their initial capital. The income from private ownership is accounted against the initial individual participation. Once the initial participation is repaid, the right to further income from ownership ceases. This provision has the effect of transform-

27. The law clearly implies that individuals must be fully active in a COAL to qualify as co-owners; private equity holdings for profit by outsiders are thus excluded. *Associated Labour Act*, articles 303–19.

ing a COAL into a social sector enterprise. Individual owners nevertheless have the right to conclude self-management agreements for the reinvestment of their income.

It is evident from these inventive concepts that a viable and dynamic mixed sector is expected to emerge in a clearly defined framework—a sector which did not previously exist. By drawing the most active segment of the traditional private sector, as well as such new entrants as returning migrant workers into voluntary cooperative arrangements among themselves, and with organizations in the social sector, that mixed sector will fill a major gap in the economic structure. Expectations are high in Yugoslavia that the new arrangements will increase the productivity of the private sector. In the nonagricultural sector, the new institutional forms provide both the opportunities and the incentives for the establishment of small-scale industry sector. That sector would serve two purposes. Largely financed from private resources, it would create opportunities for employment at moderate cost. It would also improve the supply of specialized goods and services. Those goods and services cannot be economically supplied by large-scale industry in the social sector today, and their short supply impedes economic efficiency.[28]

Conclusion

Enterprises now comprising BOALS linked by contractual relations are expected to remain the most important economic organization. The autonomy of BOALS is nevertheless safeguarded by the right of BOALS to join or separate and by the requirement that all major enterprise decisions be approved by all constituent BOALS. The transparency of transactions and the lending among BOALS are expected to reduce opportunities for monopolistic behavior and the accrual of pure economic rent. Furthermore the ability of BOALS to enter into joint pooling could in the long run result in a de facto market for investable resources—a market that would more closely reflect the opportunity costs of investable funds. To overcome the diseconomies of scale that are likely to occur with such atomization of the economy, the constitution recognizes a number of alternative forms of integration. In a manner analogous to the association of BOALS in enterprises, enterprises are also expected to integrate along

28. Yugoslav studies on this subject stress the symbiotic relations between small-scale and large-scale industry and their coexistence in developed countries.

horizontal and vertical lines. The emphasis is expected to be on vertical integration based on interindustry linkages between enterprises. It is hoped in Yugoslavia that the atomistic units which form the foundation of the economy can be brought together on the basis of economic principles to create a more efficient economic structure than one based on historical factors.

Four

Self-management Planning and the Market

THE SYSTEM OF PLANNING in Yugoslavia lost much of its practical relevance during the 1950s and 1960s, particularly after the advent of indicative planning in 1965. Government agencies prepared plans with little input from below; enterprises and banks acted with little regard for the plan; government resorted to ad hoc intervention. The basic dilemma was that planning was still in the domain of the state, and this was in stark contrast with the antistatist direction of the system's evolution. A new perception of planning, in fact a revival of confidence in the need for planning, gradually emerged in the 1970s. Partly in response to structural imbalances, two convictions began to strengthen: ex post coordination through the market mechanism is inherently wasteful; only a high degree of ex ante coordination, or planning, can assure rational use of scarce resources and redress structural imbalances. The new perception of planning is also the result of the conviction that planning and self-management could be reconciled. Indeed the view now is generally held that effective planning must complement self-management if Yugoslavia is to avoid economic chaos.[1]

---

1. For detailed descriptions and analyses of the new system of planning see the following sources. *Law on the Underlying Premises of the System of Social Planning and the Social Plan of Yugoslavia*, 1976; Ljuba Belogrlic and others, *Handbook of Planning: Ideological Premises, Methodology, Regulations* (Belgrade: Federal Institute of Planning, 1976); Tihomir Vlaskalic, "Practice Breaks Ground for Self-Management Planning," *Socialist Thought and Practice*, vol. 15, no. 6 (June 1975), pp. 28–37; Caslav Strahinjic, "Self-Management Agreements and Social Compacts," *Socialist Thought and Practice*, vol. 16, no. 6 (June 1976), pp. 24–47.

The Role of the Market

After the 1965 economic reforms, the Yugoslav economic system increasingly used the market as the general and most efficient mechanism for regulating resource allocation. But the Yugoslav concept of the market never coincided with the market of neoclassical economic theory. The 1974 constitution accepts the market as a constituent element of the economic system, but in a somewhat restricted form that makes it more consistent with the principles of socialism and self-management.

Yugoslavia has never, for philosophical reasons, found the concept of a labor market acceptable—that is the notion of labor as one among several factors of production, with wages reflecting its marginal product and scarcity. According to Marxian theory, that concept postulates that labor is one commodity among others and that workers, by having to sell their labor on the market at its going rate, are turned into objects of the economic domination by the owners of the means of production and subjugated to capital relations. Yugoslavia consequently rejected the concept of "wage labor," with contractual remuneration per unit of time. According to Marxian theory, labor is the sole source of value. Consequently the producers of value—the workers associated in a BOAL—are to maintain control over the creation of value and its disposal. Workers receive as their personal income a share of the residual income of the BOAL or enterprise, after the deduction from gross revenue of all purchased goods and services, depreciation, and dues to society. Society nevertheless has some say in the distribution of the residual incomes.[2] In addition, workers' remuneration differs by skill, region, sector, and even by enterprise within a sector. The various agreements governing the allocation of residual enterprise income to

2. The right of society to participate in the determination of those criteria and limits has three foundations. First, in any given period, workers use the fixed assets, or "past labor," owned and provided by society. Second, workers should be neither rewarded nor penalized for conditions beyond their control. Third, the socialist principle of solidarity requires the maintenance of a balance between equity and incentives to efficiency. The arrangements governing the distribution of residual income on the objective function of the Yugoslav enterprise have given rise to a considerable body of literature on the microeconomic theory of the Yugoslav enterprise.

personal incomes and capital accumulation thus incorporate some supply and demand considerations.

During the 1960s Yugoslavia neither accepted nor explicitly rejected the conventional concept of a capital market: fungible liquid resources voluntarily set aside by organizations or individuals from present income for the generation of future income and deposited with autonomous intermediaries who allocate these resources to other organizations and individuals, with interest rates as equilibrium prices clearing the market. The practice of resource allocation by banks and large diversified enterprises nevertheless approximated such features of a capital market to some degree. In the mid-1970s the practice was rejected on philosophical grounds.[3]

Certain theoretical premises fundamental to Marxian thought underlie this position. Capital is not a separate factor of production; it merely constitutes "past labor," because human labor alone creates value, using and replacing past labor in the process. Consequently the control of workers should extend to the "surplus value," or profit, and to the explicit choice over its ultimate use. Infringement of the control and freedom of choice by managers, banks, or the state constitutes "alienation." Simultaneously such infringement transfers the political power to those having the power to make decisions about the alienated surplus value of society.[4] For the same reasons the decisionmaking power of producers must be direct, explicit, and specific; it cannot be left to the workings of an anonymous market mechanism. For that direct power of resource mobilization and allocation to function in accord with self-management, it must be vested with individual BOALs, the basic units in which workers pool their labor. Any broader decisions—such as those within or among enterprises, with or without the involvement of banks—must accordingly be based on self-management agreements among BOALs. This philosophical premise led to the redefinition of the position of banks.

In Yugoslav thinking, the principle of direct decisionmaking does not lead either to a total fragmentation of resource mobilization and allocation or to a restriction to self-financing as the only acceptable form of management of financial resources. The need for financial

3. See Miladin Korac, "Commodity Production in Socialism—Dilemmas and Development," *Socialist Thought and Practice*, vol. 16, no. 9 (September 1976), pp. 20–21.

4. In Marxian political theory, economic power is, of course, inseparable from political power.

intermediation is acknowledged without reservation. The present position merely sets the ground rules by which intermediation is to take place. The pooling of resources, either through traditional credit relations or through joint pooling codified in self-management agreements, is preferred to anonymous intermediation by banks. It is worth noting that the continued acceptance of traditional credit relations includes the acceptance of interest rates as a permanent feature of the system. The emphasis on direct agreements between lending and borrowing BOALs or enterprises, although apparently antithetical to the notion of having equilibrium interest rates as the mechanism for regulating the supply and demand of investable resources, can result in income relations that reflect the availability or scarcity of those resources. The right of members of banks to determine the borrowing and lending terms in self-management agreements can do the same. If widely practiced, the new institutional setup, which encourages interenterprise investments based on shared income and risk, can also lead to a de facto market for investable resources.

For goods and services, there are four different types of supply-demand relation, each distinguishable by the basis of regulation: communities of interest, self-management agreements, social compacts, or the market. The borderlines between these types are subject to change and, in certain instances, are not clear.

When sociopolitical communities or directly affected enterprises decide that a community of interest is to be established for certain goods and services, a market ceases to exist by definition. Consequently the concept of price does not exist, either. All transactions are categorized as "free exchanges of labor"; suppliers and users directly and jointly determine supply, demand, and all necessary financial arrangements. These goods and services generally are those for which market forces are not expected to operate; if market forces did operate, they would do so ineffectively. Thus such communities of interest apply as a matter of principle, to the provision of social services and public goods and increasingly to a variety of commodities with rising economies of scale, such as railways, electric power, and public utilities./ Self-management agreements regulate the transactions for a large variety of goods and services, either on deliveries among BOALs (in enterprises) or among enterprises (generally in reproduction entities). In Yugoslav terminology the transactions constitute market transactions because an exchange of commodity against payment does take place. But self-management agreements bind the parties to a specific supplier-customer link, to specified prices or criteria of price formation for an extended period, usually five years or longer. Furthermore the parties can choose any mutually agreed basis for determining the transfer prices charged to each other. It is expected that such interlinked enterprises normally would determine the transfer prices by a formula for the sharing of income.[5] Because numerous considerations can enter into their determination, transfer prices may deviate from equilibrium prices by substantial margins or for any period. Such considerations might include calculating prices on a cost-plus basis, transferring income to units that need it, transferring income in return for funds received, equalizing risk and income, and sharing windfall gains and losses.

Given the captive-market relations between parties and the multifaceted determination of prices, these arrangements intentionally exclude two elements considered integral to a perfect market in the neoclassical sense: the reliance on prices as the only information, and the anonymity of purchasers and sellers. In the Yugoslav view, this systematic restriction strictly applies in the short run. If BOALS or enterprises are convinced that the restrictive market relation is to their long-run disadvantage, they are under no obligation to renew a self-management agreement after it expires. They can either renegotiate or dissolve those agreements. In addition, one result of the country's openness to international trade is that there is a substantial amount of information on international prices. That information tends to discourage massive and permanent deviations of transfer prices from international prices. Thus, with some simplification, it could probably be concluded that the establishment of internal markets by self-management agreements reflects an attempt to establish an ex ante market equilibrium for price-delivery relations and other relations in the medium term.

There are, and will remain in the future, a variety of basic or strategic goods and services for which delivery relations are free but prices are controlled—either by social compacts or, if within the competence of sociopolitical communities, by administrative decisions. In the past, suppliers of these goods and services had to ab-

---

5. The law on associated labor sets out only some broad principles for determining the contribution of each BOAL or enterprise to jointly earned income —contributions embodied in transfer prices for work performed. Clear-cut procedures had to await the new law on prices, which had not been passed at the time of writing. The determination of transfer prices in accord with self-management agreements coincides with the "primary distribution of income," a subject discussed in chapter seven.

sorb the burden of prices pegged at too low a level. That practice now is radically different. The 1974 constitution prescribes in such cases that suppliers have a legal claim to compensation, which the sociopolitical community determining the unsatisfactory price level is to provide. The burden of subsidizing artificially low prices thus shifts from suppliers to the sociopolitical communities. The subsidy scheme for railways, which suffer from tariff rates insufficient to cover their operating costs, is an example of such an arrangement. The sociopolitical communities are thus forced to levy extrabudgetary revenue or cut other budgetary expenditure to comply with their obligation for compensation. Because the room for maneuvering is narrow, given the nature of the fiscal system, this arrangement tends to push the incidence of subsidies into the open and to provide strong disincentives for the assumption of such subsidy obligations in other than exceptional cases.[6]

For other goods and services, deliveries and prices are freely determined, with the market working as an equilibrating mechanism in more or less textbook fashion. Much of the recent debate in Yugoslavia denouncing the "blind forces" or "anarchy" of the market referred to this segment of the market and its appropriate share in total transactions. In these discussions many economic distortions—such as rampant inflation, excess capacity in some activities, and underinvestment in others—were traced to overconfidence in the self-regulating forces of the market and to belief in the coincident effects of the invisible hand and the common or social interest. Furthermore a system that rests on isolated ex ante expectations which lead to ex post rewards or penalties for success or failure was increasingly being suspected as causing gross waste, misallocation of investment resources, and structural imbalances.

This critical view of the economic efficiency of the market mechanism is based on two arguments. First, in a medium-sized, semi-industrialized country that has adopted certain socialist premises, the market cannot be made sufficiently perfect to accomplish the efficiency ascribed to it by neoclassical economic theory—a theory which presupposes a different set of political, social, and economic conditions. Second, according to Marxian thought, a laissez-faire market mechanism has built-in destabilizing forces that prevent efficient and stable equilibrium solutions under any circumstances. In addition to these arguments, the efforts of

6. The fiscal system is described in chapter six.

enterprises and individuals to maximize income without regard for the rest of society are seen to be philosophically irreconcilable with the principles of reciprocity and solidarity—principles considered integral to socialism. Current thinking in Yugoslavia seems to be that the first three ways of regulating the relations between suppliers and consumers are in principle preferable to the market mechanism. They consequently should be promoted to the maximum possible degree. Nevertheless those ways would be too cumbersome to introduce and administer for a substantial number of goods and services, particularly nonessential consumer goods.

In sum, the market in Yugoslavia is perceived neither as a neutral mechanism nor as an institution geared at automatically leading to a stable and efficient equilibrium, let alone to a welfare optimum. A balance is being sought between efficiency and the ordering of social relations in accord with philosophical and political principles. In practice, however, the concept of the market will continue to be relevant in the Yugoslav system, but it will be more important for final demand than for factors of production. For final demand the market is accepted as the means to provide most effectively the signals for long-term structural shifts of demand and their translation into investment decisions. Such signals are to be a major input into planning.

Concepts and Procedures of Planning

The new system of planning foreseen in the 1974 constitution and codified in the 1976 law on planning, is radically different from its predecessors (table 4.1). The procedures for the preparation of plans, the methods for the determination of plan objectives, and the instruments of economic policy envisaged for their fulfillment generally are new. Unlike the previous system based on plans prepared by the republican and federal planning institutes, the new system requires the complete and active participation of all decisionmakers. And whereas the previous system was largely indicative—it was mandatory only for sociopolitical communities—self-management planning involves legal obligations binding for all decisionmakers.

The new system is a response to the failure of indicative planning for most decisionmakers. As mentioned earlier, it generally was felt that an economy at Yugoslavia's level of development still required some form of long-term macroeconomic strategy and some form of ex ante coordination. Ex post coordination through the market '

Table 4.1. *Systems of Planning in Postwar Yugoslavia*

	Comment			
Item	Central planning, 1946–50	Planning basic proportions, 1954–61	Indicative planning, 1965–74	Self-management planning, 1975 onward
Period of plan	Short-term	Medium-term	Medium-term	Medium-term
Scope of plan	Entire economy	Macroeconomic aggregates	Macroeconomic aggregates	Entire economy
Coverage of investment by plan	Complete	Complete	Low	High
Coverage of distribution of output	Complete	None	None	High for raw materials and intermediate goods
Level of detail	Specific for all sectors	Aggregative	Highly aggregative	Specific for priority sectors
Extent of participation by enterprises	Low	Low	Low	High
Kind of participation by enterprises	Submission of information	Submission of information	None	Enterprise decisions within broad macroeconomic parameters set by social compacts
Implementation	Compulsory for sociopolitical communities and enterprises	Compulsory for sociopolitical communities and enterprises	Compulsory for sociopolitical communities	Compulsory for sociopolitical communities and enterprises
Means of implementation	Directives	Directives	Manipulation of parameters	Social compacts and self-management agreements; or, if abrogated, social and economic penalties
Planning within enterprises	High	High	Low	High
Planning among enterprises	Low	Low	Low	High

Note: Unless otherwise indicated, planning is that by sociopolitical communities; such planning integrates the planning by enterprises to varying degree.
Source: Adapted from Herbert S. Levine, "On Comparing Planned Economies: A Methodological Inquiry," in *Comparison of Economic Systems,* ed. Alexander Eckstein (Berkeley: University of California Press, 1971), pp. 137–60.

mechanism was felt to be inherently wasteful. Indicative planning and the reliance on the market could have accommodated such a strategy if the instruments of economic policy at the state's disposal had been sufficiently strong and precise. But one principal effect of the evolution toward self-management was the weakening of the conventional instruments of economic policy available to the state. Consequently, with the scope of available instruments considerably reduced, the economy faced the dilemma of having too few instruments to deal with too many objectives. The new planning system, seen as a logical extension of self-management, provides a genuine attempt to develop planning that is based on sound economic principles. Furthermore the mechanism for determining plan objectives attempts to reconcile the pluralistic character of Yugoslav society with the need for coordinated development.

The 1976 law on planning outlines the basic principles of the new system.[7] Although the law provides a detailed catalog of the procedures at various levels of planning, it does not indicate the hierarchy of planning or provide a guide to planning methods. This omission may be deliberate, for planning is seen to be simultaneous and to have no discernible hierarchy.[8]

The basic characteristics of the new system can be summarized as follows:

- Planning must involve all planning agents—that is, all organizations that are affected by the decisions to be made.
- Planning is to be simultaneously carried out by all planning agents at all levels. Microeconomic planning within and among enterprises is referred to as self-management planning. Macroeconomic planning within and among sociopolitical communities is referred to as social planning.
- Planning is continual, with annual assessments of the progress of respective planning agents and with revisions to plans in response to changed circumstances.
- The exchange of information on the plans and the economic situation is obligatory for all planning agents and based on a predetermined list of indicators.[9]

7. *Law on the Underlying Premises of the System of Social Planning and the Social Plan of Yugoslavia,* 1976.

8. Milenkovitch rightly points out that "the mechanisms through which this coordination was to be accomplished were left agonizingly vague in the 1976 Law on Social Planning." Milenkovitch, "The Case of Yugoslavia," p. 58.

9. For a list of indicators by type of economic unit see Belogrlic and others, *Handbook of Planning.*

- Individual plans at all levels must go through a process of harmonization, whereby all affected parties seek to reach agreement on the plans proposed. Fully harmonized plans, as well as all financial dimensions, are then codified in legally binding social compacts and self-management agreements.
- All affected parties must be consulted, and their agreement secured, before they conclude a self-management agreement or social compact.
- Economic activities are divided into two groups: priority and nonpriority. Priority activities have been singled out for their special importance to the development of the economy.[10] Although planning procedures are identical for both types of activity, agreements on individual plans are legally required only for priority activities. Such agreements nevertheless are encouraged for nonpriority activities.
- Laws or decrees bind planning agents to a rigid timetable for planning. In cases of default or unresolvable conflict, the assemblies of sociopolitical communities or bodies of government can issue a temporary ruling.
- The basic plan is the medium-term five-year plan of the federation. There is, in addition, a long-term plan reviewing long-term objectives and structural change.[11]

Planning starts with the passage of a law on the preparation of the plan. This document is equivalent to a social compact at the federal level: it outlines the work program for the plan's preparation; it specifies the plan period and the timetable for the major steps of planning; it provides a list of indicators that must be prepared and a common method that must be adhered to by all units. Simultaneously commencing at all levels, planning is aimed at harmonizing the plans compiled at different levels into a composite medium-term plan or vision of the economy's development. Thus, although social planning and self-management planning initially are

10. Priority activities are officially designated as "activities of special significance for realization of the agreed policy concerning the overall development of the Socialist Federal Republic of Yugoslavia." For the 1976–80 plan period, these priority activities were agreed upon in the early stages of planning and subsequently codified in social compacts.

11. Enterprises and sociopolitical communities prepare annual plans that set out the details for implementing the five-year social plans. The social plan for 1976–80 and the long-term plan for 1976–85 are discussed and assessed in chapter five. Work is in progress on a long-term plan covering the period to 2000.

independent, the purpose of the planning exercise is to fuse them into one consistent master plan.

Although no common and rigorous methodology of self-management planning has emerged, certain features are evident. First, each BOAL or enterprise takes stock of its development during the expiring plan period and determines its starting position. Second, each BOAL or enterprise sets out its assumptions, expectations, and ambitions for the prospective level and composition of output, the corresponding requirements for inputs, and the human and financial resources that are available and required. Third, BOALs and enterprises exchange these initial projections with others—whether forward-linked, backward-linked, or competing—and enter into the harmonization of assumptions, expectations, and ambitions. These encounters occur in ad hoc working groups, but also are more formal in and among associations or in chambers of the economy. Fourth, after a number of rounds of encounters—which gradually adjust assumptions, expectations, and ambitions and establish certain macroeconomic parameters through the parallel process of social planning—the BOALs and enterprises codify their common understanding in self-management agreements. Fifth, the community of workers in each BOAL adopts the final plans of enterprises and BOALs.

As for self-management planning, certain features are evident in social planning. First, the republican and federal planning institutes review and evaluate principal aspects of development during the expiring plan period and identify the problems they need to address in the subsequent period. That assessment is formally submitted to, and discussed by, the communal, republican, and federal assemblies. Second, the planning institutes set out the macroeconomic or aggregate assumptions on external conditions and sketch alternative scenarios of development. The assumptions and scenarios are formally submitted to, and discussed by, the assemblies, which choose from among these scenarios. Third, the sociopolitical communities exchange their tentative social plans and harmonize them in repeated rounds of encounters. Fourth, the trade unions and chambers of the economy extensively review the tentative social plans and, after harmonization, codify them in social compacts. Fifth, the assemblies adopt the final plans of planning institutes.

Harmonization of social and self-management planning is thus intended to ensure consistency between the goals and objectives of enterprises and national consideration. Social (top-down) planning provides a basic framework, which self-management (bottom-up) planning then confronts. The process is not necessarily designed to resolve conflicts, but to compel planning agents to view their development objectives at different levels of aggregation. By so doing, the various enterprises must consider broader objectives, appreciate the tradeoffs, and assume responsibility for decisions taken. To facilitate harmonization, which would become unmanageable if applied literally and if all economic units had to participate, large economic complexes of enterprises are created on the basis of vertical and horizontal linkages.[12] Attempts are then made to coordinate supply and demand within and among complexes. Planning is thus reduced to a system of network planning at different levels.[13] A consensus emerging from harmonization probably constitutes a negotiated solution which is feasible in the sense that all planning agents would be willing to accept it.

Practical Implications of Self-management Planning

Although at first confusing in its complexity, the new system of planning has important positive features. Perhaps most important, the requirement that all economic units participate in planning ensures that all interests are represented and that different views and solutions are considered and discussed. In addition, the compulsory and exhaustive exchange of information among all planning agents will greatly increase the transparency of the economy and enable decisionmaking to be based on a broad range of preferences and production possibilities. These requirements give support to the Yugoslav contention that the process of planning contributes to the achievement of plan objectives. The legally binding programs of action are not imposed from above. Instead they are an outward reflection of the preferences of consumers and producers.

Unlike the market mechanism, which makes uncertain progress toward an equilibrium by trial-and-error, self-management planning attempts to provide an ex ante equilibrium solution. Unlike central planning, it avoids the pitfalls of having to determine prices and inputs with a mathematical model based on exogenous output objectives that either neglect or second-guess consumer sovereignty.

12. See the discussion of reproduction entities, composite organizations of associated labor, and the associations constituting chambers of the economy in chapter three.
13. For example see James Meade, *The Theory of Indicative Planning* (Manchester: Manchester University Press, 1970).

With the horizontal and vertical coordination of planning agents at all levels, self-management planning essentially is an attempt to determine an implicit vector of equilibrium prices and deliveries by the exchange of information and the iterative adjustment of individual plans for mutual consistency.

The sound economic rationale of the new planning procedures, particularly harmonization, can be illustrated by analogy with forward markets. In many respects the procedures of self-management planning resemble the haggling and negotiations in the forward markets for certain raw materials and foreign exchange. Social compacts and self-management agreements on mutual deliveries and on criteria for transfer prices would, in these quasi forward markets, be analogous to forward contracts. Like forward markets, quasi forward markets establish an ex ante equilibrium that fully reflects consumer preferences. In addition, the scope for differences between expectation and result is, at least in theory, reduced to unpredictable forces of nature. In contrast with conventional forward markets, the quasi forward markets have two specific features: they cover a large share of industrial production, not a handful of raw materials; they are for the medium term, not the short term, and in some activities are even for the long term. The extended coverage and time horizon reflects the purpose underlying the quasi forward markets: inducing a rational pattern of investment. In other words the quasi forward markets seek in principle to eliminate market uncertainty and reduce risk by pooling limited knowledge. The potential gain in allocative efficiency over a competitive market system is evident. Capacities needed for structural reasons can be created in time and be approximately tailored to demand, thus eliminating the pitfalls of bottlenecks and excess capacity. Of course, the gains in comparison with a market economy or a centrally planned economy are potential. The degree to which they are realized will depend entirely upon the efficiency and rationality with which planning is organized and carried out. By necessity a good deal of learning by doing must be invested over a long period before that potential can be fully exploited.

Two additional features of the Yugoslav system significantly enhance the capacity of this new system to work effectively: the social ownership of the means of production, and the principles of solidarity and reciprocity. The effective operation of forward markets and contracting is based on many restrictive conditions that in practice will not hold. Important among these conditions are the need for participants to express their true preferences, thereby precluding oligopolistic behavior, and the stipulation that there should be no external, notably public, goods. In Yugoslavia the principles of solidarity and reciprocity preclude, at least in theory, the distribution of windfall gains or pure economic rent to any one enterprise. Furthermore the exhaustive exchange of information in practice restrains oligopolistic behavior.

The new planning system also has positive political aspects. For one thing, planning is now reconciled with the basic premises of workers' self-management. The role of the state is considerably reduced; it now principally acts as an arbiter of last resort and a forum for presenting macroeconomic perspectives of the future. And because the basic premises of the development program are codified in the contractual obligations of enterprises, the shortcomings of policy instruments are less important. For another thing, self-management planning will ameliorate the problems Yugoslavia faces in coordinating the development of regions. The pluralistic character of Yugoslav society has always complicated planning, which traditionally has been based on a monistic view of objectives.[14] The new system of planning provides an opportunity for the representation of all interests and a forum for choosing from among different means and different ends.

In contrast with these potential strengths, the new system of planning has some potential weaknesses.

The full cycle of planning, involving time-consuming iterations within and among numerous planning agents, takes two to three years. The costs of planning, particularly those associated with the absorption of scarce managerial and administrative talent, are thus likely to be high. In addition, because planning is all-embracing and affects production, investment, and income distribution, it leaves economic units with little flexibility. Because the underlying premises of the plans can change at any time before and after the conclusion of contractual agreements, considerable revisions may be necessary in social compacts, self-management agreements, and enterprise plans. Alternatively, specific measures would have to be introduced to increase flexibility—say, for stocks and the phasing of investments—to avoid the arduous task of continual recontracting. The success of the planning system will thus depend in part of how susceptible the economy is to events.

The openness of the Yugoslav economy and the country's de-

---

14. For example see Tony Killick, "The Possibilities of Development Planning," *Oxford Economic Papers*, vol. 28, no. 2 (July 1976), pp. 161–84.

pendence on trade certainly increase the probability of having un-
foreseeable events affect the economy; its large foreign exchange
reserves, access to external sources of capital, and diversified trade
provide a cushion. If circumstances are rapidly changing, however,
the system of planning could face difficulties. Slow reactions associated with the adjustment of contractual obligations could lead
to the misallocation of resources and the need for a complex system
of compensatory fiscal transfers. The Yugoslavs are aware of the
potential inflexibility of the system. They foresee a system of continual planning that is to operate parallel to the medium-term plan
and provide the opportunity to adjust contractual arrangements
through rephasing projects, reordering priorities, or abrogating
agreements and concluding new ones. This process will certainly
add flexibility, but the costs of making adjustments could well be
high because of the time needed to secure agreement among the
parties affected.

Another potential weakness of the new planning system lies in
the different treatment of priority and nonpriority activities. For
priority activities, harmonization is required by law to lead to a program that is agreed upon by a predetermined date and codified in
legally binding obligations. There is no analogous provision for
nonpriority activities: agreement is merely encouraged, insofar as
coordinated programs stand a better chance of implementation than
conflicting ones, but not mandatory. This dual treatment could lead
to anomalies. Because the system of contractual obligation ensures
supply and demand at the negotiated prices for priority sectors, the
price mechanism is nullified in its role as an allocator of resources
between the priority and nonpriority sectors. Consequently, in cases
of shortages, the brunt of the adjustment would fall, at least initially,
on nonpriority activities.

Although an analogy can be drawn between the new system of
planning and a set of procedures that would simulate the operation
of forward markets with forward prices and deliveries, the precise
mechanisms (or rules) for reaching agreements remain undetermined.
Those agreements, it will be recalled, are a key element in the new
system of planning and allocation.

The real issue, then, is the extent to which the process of harmonization will be left to operate. In principle three options exist.
First, harmonization could be made to work as a market, where
individual producers and consumers compete for resources through
a bidding procedure. Something like this was adopted in Yugoslavia
during a brief period in the 1950s, when enterprises bid for in-

vestable resources by offering higher interest rates.[15] That process nevertheless runs counter to the basic philosophical premises of the 1974 constitution: it would imply a capital market in which capital is allocated not by the generators of surplus value, but by an impersonal mechanism which alienates workers from the fruits of their effort. Second, enterprises could agree to the application of analytical techniques, such as cost-benefit analysis, to ensure that funds are allocated to projects promising the highest returns to society.[16] The chambers of the economy, whether federal or republican, could act as forums for such analysis, which appears to be compatible with the philosophical premises of the system and which would provide a sound basis for decisionmaking. The use of cost-benefit analysis nevertheless poses one important question. It presupposes the calculation and application of a consistent set of country parameters, but the calculation of these parameters is not value-free, particularly when issues of income distribution enter in. Thus one prerequisite of the application of cost-benefit analysis would be interrepublican agreements on the value of these parameters. Third, harmonization could be the result of informal compromises among enterprises—compromises based on a variety of economic and other considerations.

Harmonization under the new planning system appears to have been based on informal compromises. To the extent that cost-benefit analysis has been used, it has not been based on a consistent and elaborate methodology. By the same token, however, it seems unlikely that political compromises would be antithetical to the economic viability of projects. The openness of the economy, the role of market-based prices, the new laws on the calculation of income, the interests of enterprises to maximize their income per worker—all these provide strong incentives for economic rationality. It nevertheless is likely that compromises based on political, not economic, criteria have occurred and will continue to occur. The use of a suitable method of cost-benefit analysis cannot avoid such compromises, but it could serve to highlight their costs.

15. See Egon Neuberger, "Yugoslav Investment Auctions," *Quarterly Journal of Economics*, vol. 73, no. 1 (February 1959), pp. 88–115.
16. See chapter eight for a discussion of the absence of a framework for assessing alternatives in the process of resource allocation. It is strongly advocated in that chapter that Yugoslavia introduce some form of cost-benefit analysis.

Five

Medium-term Plans
and Prospects

THE MOST IMPORTANT ECONOMIC CONSEQUENCE of the 1974 constitution is that it extends the principle of workers' self-management to macroeconomic decisionmaking. This change reflects the realization that ad hoc intervention in the economy has been less successful than anticipated and that a consistent framework for macroeconomic management must be agreed upon if short-term economic stability is to be ensured and if longer term aspirations are to be fulfilled. The new constitution provides for the achievement of this objective without transgressing the rights of workers to self-management. Indeed it makes self-management an integral part of economic policy by introducing various macroeconomic instruments that workers are to manage. The new mechanism for self-management planning principally affects the allocation of resources and enables Yugoslavia to address long-term issues. The social compacts and self-management agreements should ensure that broad policies are integrated with the plans of enterprises. In general, the need for selective credit policies will be reduced.

Social compacts on prices and incomes are likely to ease the task of stabilizing the economy by reducing the burden on monetary policy. A social compact on prices reflects a political consensus against inflation and can curb the inflationary spiral. A social compact on incomes can ensure that the growth of personal incomes is in line with the growth in productivity. It can also regulate the distribution of resources to personal incomes and capital accumulation. Measures have also been introduced to prevent the uncontrolled buildup of involuntary credits.

Because social compacts already regulate such diverse areas as the growth of social sector employment, the development of small-scale industry, and the encouragement of growth in the private sector, they are likely to enable Yugoslavia to develop a broad employment strategy. The object of these compacts on employment is twofold: to ensure conscious regulation of the growth of employment opportunities in the social sector and of labor-intensive activities as alternatives to agriculture; and to ensure an explicit recognition of the possible tradeoff between maximizing the growth of worker productivity with that of employment.

The new constitution also introduced significant changes in activities associated with foreign trade. Enterprises are to enter into contractual agreements for sharing the pool of foreign exchange. The guiding principle for these agreements is that foreign exchange resources should be shared on the basis of the contribution of each enterprise toward earning foreign exchange. Linked to the new procedures for distributing foreign exchange is the establishment of communities of interest for economic relations abroad. These communities, to comprise all users and earners of foreign exchange, are being established in each republic. By acting as forums for the distribution of foreign exchange, they should induce enterprises to be more conscious of the implications of their activities for foreign exchange and foster a better method of distribution. It is also expected that a more coordinated and planned approach to foreign borrowing will develop.

Recent Developments

The growth of Yugoslavia's economy has in recent years been closely linked to changes in the balance of payments. The growth rates of gross material product (GMP) were relatively high in 1970 and 1971, when the deficit in the current account was increasing and international reserves were low and declining (table 5.1). In 1972 and 1973 the current account deficit was reversed, but there was a decline in the rate of growth of the economy. In 1974 the effects of rapid economic growth and the fourfold increase in oil prices led to a large deficit in the current account. That deficit continued through 1975. Strong controls slowed down the growth of the economy and in 1976 led to a somewhat unexpected surplus in the current account. The surplus was achieved by depleting stocks of imported commodities and by restricting economic expansion to what, by Yugoslav standards, is a modest rate. Consequently, with the rise in the rate of growth in economic activity in 1977,

Table 5.1. *Selected Indicators of Economic Growth and the Balance of Payments, 1970–77*

Year	Trade balance	Workers' remit- tances	Current account balance	Official reserves in rela- tion to imports (percent)	Real growth in gross material product (percent)	Change in producer prices (percent)
	(millions of dollars)					
1970	−1,195	440	− 330	4	6	9
1971	−1,439	652	− 358	6	8	15
1972	− 990	889	418	19	4	11
1973	−1,658	1,301	464	26	5	13
1974	−3,737	1,511	−1,184	14	9	29
1975	−3,625	1,575	−1,032	10	3	22
1976	−2,489	1,728	150	24	4	6
1977ᵃ	−4,380	1,925	−1,735	18	8	10

Sources: Federal Institute of Statistics, *Statistical Yearbook of Yugoslavia,* 1977; estimates for 1977 are based on figures supplied by the National Bank of Yugoslavia (NBY).
a. Estimates.

there was a sharp reversal in the current account. The deficit for the year is estimated to have been about $1.7 billion.

The external events of 1973 and 1974 had a sudden and significant impact on the Yugoslav economy, but their importance extends beyond short-term cyclical effects. They have also affected Yugoslavia's medium-term outlook, and their legacy is most apparent in two areas. First, the increase in the price of oil permanently boosted the country's import bill by US$600 million, an amount equal to almost 8 percent of total commodity imports in 1974. Second, the international recession reversed the prospects for migration by Yugoslav workers, and that reversal inhibited the growth of an important source of foreign exchange—workers' remittances. Between 1970 and 1973 workers' remittances grew by about 44 percent a year; they accounted for 22 percent of Yugoslavia's foreign exchange earnings in 1973. Between 1973 and 1976, however, workers' remittances grew by only 10 percent a year, a decline that was even more significant because of the higher international rate of inflation after 1973. This slackening rate of foreign exchange earnings, along with the inflated import bill, has made the balance of payments a potentially binding constraint on economic growth.

The decline in external migration naturally affects employment. Between 1969 and 1973 the number of workers absorbed by external migration increased by more than 500,000, nearly twice the national increase in the labor force and almost equal to the increase in social-sector employment during the period (table 5.2). Thus ex-

Table 5.2 *Employment Status of the Labor Force,*
1969, 1973, and 1975
(thousands)

Employment status and sector	1969	1973	1975
Actively employed	8,579	8,801	8,823
Residents	8,007	7,701	7,923
Social sector	3,622	4,222	4,667
Private agriculture	4,095	3,145	2,897
Other private employment	290	334	359
Temporary migrants working abroad	572	1,100	900
Unemployed	198	229	324
Total labor force	8,777	9,030	9,147

Sources: *Statistical Yearbook of Yugoslavia*, various years, and World Bank estimates.

ternal migration was a key factor allowing the size of the agricultural labor force to decline rapidly. Workers in the private sector, traditionally low in productivity, went either abroad or into the modern social sector. After 1973 external migration virtually stopped and many workers returned to Yugoslavia. For the first time since the mid-1960s, the resident labor force began to increase. The net return of workers between 1973 and 1975 equaled the natural increase in the labor force. This return put considerable pressure on the social sector to create additional employment opportunities: despite rapid growth in social-sector employment, migration out of the agricultural sector sharply declined, and open unemployment increased.

The Ten-year Plan for 1976-85

The Yugoslav perception of the long-term objectives and issues of development are set out in a document that will be designated here as the ten-year plan. That plan does not stipulate obligations. It identifies the major development problems that need to be tackled in annual and five-year plans and specifies the direction economic development should be heading.[1] The draft of the ten-year plan was presented to the tenth congress of the League of Communists of Yugoslavia (LCY) in 1974 and formally adopted, giving the document considerable weight. The federal and republican assemblies subsequently discussed the draft, and the Federal Assembly finally adopted it in October 1975 as the principal guide for operational plans.

The ten-year plan identifies six fundamental economic problems that need to be addressed in Yugoslavia.

- *Stabilization.* The economy has suffered from continual fluctuations in the level of economic activity, high and varying rates of inflation, and general price instability. The lack of stability has created uncertainties for enterprise activity and led to many decisions which proved to be detrimental in the long run.
- *Resource mobilization.* There have been severe disproportions and arbitrary fluctuations in the distribution of available resources between final demand—that is, personal, common, and government consumption—and investment and savings.[2]
- *Resource allocation.* Three problems pertaining to resource allocation are prominent. First, there have been misallocations of resources among sectors and a notable lag in the development of raw materials, power, and foodstuffs. Second, there have been general inefficiencies in production—inefficiencies characterized by low profits, low growth of labor productivity, unsatisfactory capacity use in some rapidly expanding sectors and branches, a lack of coordination in the expansion of facilities, and insufficient modernization of facilities. Third, too little attention has been given to indigenous research and development.
- *Employment.* The capacity of the economy to generate employment sharply declined as a result of the 1965 reforms and

---

1. In the first stage of preparation the Federal Institute of Planning commissioned research institutions to conduct about fifty special studies on subjects ranging from macroeconomic models to demand forecasts by sector. In the second stage a consortium of prominent economists condensed the results of the first stage. Then a committee under the auspices of the Federal Institute of Planning drafted and refined the final document. A new long-term plan, covering the period to 2000, is now being prepared. Federal Assembly, "Draft Outline of a Common Policy for Long-Term Development in Yugoslavia (until 1985)," *Yugoslav Survey*, vol. 16, no. 4 (November 1975), pp. 19–90.

2. The problems of resource mobilization and allocation are frequently discussed as the problems of "extended reproduction."

has not sufficiently recovered. The country needs to generate employment in excess of the natural increase of the labor force. The reasons are the reversal of the flow of temporary emigration of workers—which provided an important vent for the otherwise unabsorbable labor force after 1965—and the excess labor force in the rural sector.

• *External economic relations.* Marked by large and increasing deficits in the trade accounts, the balance of payments has reflected a high and increasing degree of import dependency, particularly for raw materials. Because the growth in exports of manufactured goods and agricultural commodities has not sufficiently compensated for the growth in imports, the dependence on workers' remittances and foreign borrowing has grown. All these elements make the balance of payments overly volatile.

• *Regional disparities.* Progress toward reducing the differences in income between regions has been disappointing. The major reasons for this are the lack of adequate spatial planning and the interregional immobility of investment and other resources. In addition, the less developed regions have a disproportionate share of basic industries, which typically are characterized by low efficiency, low profitability, and insufficient resources for investment.

In concluding its critical review of recent development, the ten-year plan makes the following candid assessment of the main roots of the problems.

The emergence and intensity of these problems and contradictions have also been influenced by lack of a nationwide long-term development policy; inconsistency and slowness in the realization of the established policy concerning Yugoslavia's five-year development plans and the execution of decisions and agreements adopted; insufficient synchronization of the instruments of the economic system and measures of economic policy with the aims and tasks of development policy and their insufficient consistency; and uncoordinated decisionmaking on the part of economic and all other agents. As a result, development has taken a somewhat spontaneous course, and primary distribution and accumulation repartition have not been in line with development aims and tasks. The incompleteness and insufficient consistency of the economic system as a whole, the inadequate role played by the market, and [the] absence of a system of self-management planning have all tended to strengthen spontaneity in economic development. For lack of a conscious regulation of the flows of reproduction on a self-management basis and of other systematic solutions, planning has not become an integrally linked system, from basic organizations of associated labor to the Federation, and has not enabled the working class to use it as a successful instrument for enhancing social and economic development. Absence of a long-term development policy has also hindered the creation of conditions for economic stabilization.[3]

The ten-year plan contains an exhaustive set of objectives. These include, in addition to the continuing development of the political and economic system, the conventional objectives: economic growth and stability, improvements in the standard of living, increased labor productivity, growth in employment, integration with the international division of labor, and regional development. Two other objectives are to improve the human environment and to support domestic research and technological development. Although many of the objectives are discussed in detail, the long-term plan does not indicate their relative weight.

Table 5.3. *Targets in the Ten-year Plan for 1976–85*
(percent)

Item	Average annual rate of growth, 1976–85
Total economy	7.0
Industry	9.0
Agriculture	3.5
Employment	3.5
Working-age population	0.9
Labor force	0.6
Exports	9.0
Imports	7.0

Source: Federal Assembly, "Draft Outline of a Common Policy for Long-Term Development in Yugoslavia (until 1985)."

The ten-year plan considers a GMP growth rate of 7 percent a year to be necessary and feasible in the long term (table 5.3). Industry is expected to expand by about 9 percent a year and will

---

3. "Primary distribution" refers to the system of relative prices; "accumulation repartition" to the pattern of investment allocation; "flows of reproduction" to the flow of investment resources. Federal Assembly, "Draft Outline of a Common Policy for Long-Term Development in Yugoslavia (until 1985)," p. 36.

continue to be the principal engine of growth. In the industrial sector, priorities have been assigned to primary and secondary energy, metallurgy, basic chemistry, and some unspecified branches of engineering. Other priority sectors are tourism, primary agriculture, and interregional transport and communication. The intentions are to reduce the country's dependence on imported raw materials and intermediate goods, to create a more stable export basis, and to achieve a more balanced economic structure with an improvement of capacity use. The ten-year plan also sets out some broad targets to be pursued in the annual and five-year plans.

The Five-year Plan for 1976–80

The planning institutes in each republic and autonomous province draw up their own five-year plans; the Federal Institute of Planning consolidates the republican and provincial plans in the national five-year, or social, plan. Based on the findings and emphasis of the ten-year pl n, the five-year plan is the principal operational document. The aggregate targets of that plan are summarized in table 5.4;

Table 5.4. *Targets in the Five-year Plan for 1976–80*
(percent)

Item	Average annual rate of growth, 1976–80
Gross material product	7.0
Personal consumption	6.0
General consumption	6.0
Fixed investment	8.0
Exports	8.0
Imports	4.5
Employment	3.5

Source: Federal Institute of Planning, *Social Plan of Yugoslavia: 1976–80* (Belgrade: Federal Committee for Information, 1976).

the detailed output targets in table 5.5. In addition to the broader objectives of a rapid rate of growth, combined with rapidly increasing personal incomes and a continued emphasis on industrial activities, the targets of the plan reflect a shift in emphasis from sectors producing consumer goods to those producing intermediate and

Table 5.5. *Growth of Output, by Sector and Branch, 1971–75 and Targets for 1976–80*

Sector or branch	Average annual rate of real growth (percent)		Change between periods (percentage points)
	1971–75[a]	1976–80[b]	
Economy[c]	5.9	6.9	1.0
Social sector	6.5	7.5	1.0
Private sector	3.1	3.7	0.6
Industry[d]	7.6	8.0	0.4
Electricity	7.7	10.0	2.3
Coal	2.8	9.5	6.7
Crude petroleum	9.8	6.0	−3.8
Ferrous metallurgy	6.5	11.0	4.5
Nonferrous metallurgy	7.6	11.0	3.6
Metal products	6.3	8.5	2.2
Nonmetallic minerals	4.6	9.0	4.4
Shipbuilding	5.0	9.0	4.0
Electrical machinery	9.0	9.0	0.0
Chemicals	10.5	14.0	3.5
Building material	8.8	9.0	0.2
Wood products	7.6	6.0	−1.6
Paper and paper products	7.5	6.0	−1.5
Textiles	7.3	4.0	−3.3
Leather and footwear	7.9	4.0	−3.9
Rubber products	9.3	4.0	−5.3
Food processing	6.7	7.3	0.6
Printing	4.4	4.0	−0.4
Tobacco	5.8	5.0	−0.8
Agriculture[d]	3.2	4.3	1.1
Social sector	5.9	8.0	2.1
Private sector	2.5	3.1	0.6
Forestry[c]	1.6	2.0	0.4
Construction[c]	3.9	7.5	3.6
Transport and communications[d]	6.3	7.5	1.2
Trade, catering, and tourism[c]	5.7	6.7	1.0
Handicrafts[c]	7.7	7.2	−0.5
Public utilities[c]	n.a.	7.5	n.a.

n.a. Not available.

Sources: Social Plan of Yugoslavia: 1976–80; figures for 1971–75 calculated from *Statistical Yearbook of Yugoslavia*, 1977.

a. In 1972 prices.
b. In 1975 prices.
c. Value added.
d. Gross output.

capital goods. The plan identifies priority sectors that are to receive special encouragement during the plan period and have first claim to investable resources: coal, transport, shipbuilding, agro-industry, basic chemicals, petroleum extraction, mechanical engineering, production of nonmetallic minerals, ferrous and nonferrous metallurgy, and electrical power generation and transmission.

Two beliefs appear to constitute the basis of this strategy. First, it is felt that certain industrial sectors have lagged behind because of unfavorable price relations and the lack of any coordinating mechanism, not because of problems of their economic viability. On economic grounds, there was a case for allocating more resources to these sectors. Furthermore the significant changes in relative prices, stemming from the fourfold increase in the price of oil, were seen to affect the economic viability of projects and require some shifts in the allocation of resources. Second, and more important, there was a realization that, in addition to any inherited distortions or changes necessitated by shifts in relative prices, restructuring the economy became inevitable because of considerations associated with the balance of payments.

Yugoslavia's potential for maintaining a rapid rate of economic growth hinges on the country's ability to mobilize external resources. But the country faces a sharply higher import bill, and the problem of paying for imports is compounded by a perceived erosion of the economy's long-term capacity to earn foreign exchange. How could Yugoslavia respond to these conditions? It could adopt policies designed to increase the capacity to earn foreign exchange and compensate for the deteriorating prospects for workers' remittances—say, by initiating a drive to promote exports. Or it could attempt to reduce its future foreign exchange requirements by reducing its dependence on imports—that is, by initiating import-substitution policies.[4] Or it could do both.

As is apparent in export and import targets, the five-year plan for 1976–80 primarily opted for import substitution. The growth rate of exports, though somewhat higher than the historical rate, is broadly consistent with past experience; the growth rate of imports is considerably below the historical rate. The projected 4.5 percent annual growth in imports, coupled with a 7 percent annual growth in GMP, would imply an average import elasticity of 0.64. That elasticity is about one-third less than the historical elasticity and far

4. Import dependency is measured by the ratio of imports to gross output.

below the elasticity other countries of comparable size and development level are able to achieve. Such a sharp reduction in import elasticity would require a considerable amount of import substitution. Because 90 percent of Yugoslavia's imports are intermediate and capital goods, any significant amount of import substitution would in turn require a considerable restructuring of the economy. Detailed analysis confirms that the industries given priority in the five-year plan are those in which output has tended to lag mainly as a result of growing import dependency.[5] The plan's strategy, then, is to develop import substitutes in those sectors most directly affected by growing import dependency after 1965.

Strictly on a priori grounds, the strategy underlying the plan cannot be faulted. But because the priority sectors tend to be among the more capital-intensive ones, the plan's emphasis may jeopardize the attainment of the country's employment objective. Still, there is some evidence to suggest that the slower growth after 1965 of domestic industries producing intermediate and capital goods was the result of inappropriate pricing policies. Tariffs during the period favored finished goods by providing them with high effective rates of protection. In contrast, the nominal and effective tariffs on raw and intermediate goods were low. This pattern probably contributed to the shift in the pattern of resource allocation away from sectors producing raw and intermediate goods and toward those producing consumer goods. Given the uncertainties surrounding the future prospects of the world economy, emphasis on import substitution is the more prudent strategy. Although Yugoslavia has a diversified export structure, its products are subject to intense competition in international markets or are characterized by the slow growth of demand. Thus import substitution offers a more certain path to achieving an external economic balance; it can also make the domestic economy less vulnerable to externally induced oscillations.

The economic justification for the Yugoslav strategy cannot be readily assessed. Such an assessment would require detailed project data by industry and sector (which are not available) and an evaluation of Yugoslavia's comparative advantage (which is beyond the scope of this analysis). In particular, it would be necessary to compare the cost of saving foreign exchange by developing import substitutes and the cost of earning additional foreign exchange by

5. See the technical note at the end of chapter eight for a discussion of input-output analysis for 1966–72.

promoting exports. This study's assessment of the five-year plan for 1976–80 takes a different tack. Two different macroeconomic models were used to conduct the analysis at an aggregate level. The purposes of the analysis were to determine the internal consistency of the plan, the extent and plausibility of the assumption for import substitution implicit in the plan, and the implications for the broad objectives of the plan, if the implied degree of import substitution is not realized.

Internal consistency and structural change

A static input-output model, similar to the one the Yugoslavs used in their planning exercise, was used to analyze the internal consistency of the plan.[6] Based on the gross output targets, the estimates of the model indicate that the five-year plan appears to overestimate the growth of aggregate final demand. In other words, if interindustry relations are taken into consideration, the targeted growth of output and imports is not sufficient to achieve the targeted growth of consumption, investment, and exports. The targeted growth of at least one component of final demand has to be sacrificed. This implies that if the investment, export, and import rates are maintained, the growth of consumption will be less than expected; alternatively, if all targets are to be achieved, the level of imports must be higher than expected. Assuming that imports are the factor to be adjusted, the implicit growth rate of imports would have to be 6 percent a year, not 4.5 percent as specified in the plan.

The static input-output model was also used to assess the extent and character of import substitution implicit in the plan.[7] What emerges from the analysis is that the plan implies a significant restructuring of imports. The share of the output of priority sectors in their respective domestic markets will have to increase considerably during this period. At the same time, the growth of nonpriority activities, mainly consumer goods, is considerably below the projected growth of consumption. Consequently, if existing pat-

6. See the technical note at the end of chapter eight for a discussion of input-output analysis for 1966–72.

7. Based on historical trends, final demand by sector and industry was estimated by using the plan's estimates of the aggregate growth of consumption and investment. This estimated vector of final demand was then contrasted with the plan's vector of gross output. To ensure consistency between the estimated vector of final demand and the plan's vector of gross output, imports were treated as a residual. By deriving imports in this way, the plan's implicit shifts in import ratios by sector and industry could be analyzed.

terns of demand are to be sustained, the dependence on imported consumer goods will be greater. The decline of import dependency in some industries is particularly noticeable: the import ratio for chemicals would be reduced by 60 to 70 percent; that for ferrous metals by 40 to 50 percent. In other priority sectors the import ratios are to decline by about 20 percent.

Although determining the feasibility of such declines in import ratios requires a more detailed analysis than the one undertaken here, such large reductions raise a number of issues. The new system of planning, based as it is on forward contracting, may provide an effective vehicle for ensuring that incremental domestic production substitutes for imports. Even with this assurance, however, the cost of such a significant reduction of imports might be high for four reasons:

- The provision of domestic intermediate goods of a quality and specification comparable to those imported might be physically impossible in the short run and difficult in the medium run, particularly because of the wide array of intermediate goods affected.
- In certain sectors it might be difficult to achieve import substitution in the short run because of contractual or licensing arrangements between domestic and foreign companies.
- The fall in import ratios implied by this analysis represents only the net substitution of domestic production for imports. If the indirect import content of domestic production is taken into account, a considerably greater amount of gross import substitution must take place.
- The trade gap projected by this study's input-output model is somewhat higher than that indicated in the plan. When imports are residually derived by using the plan's targeted growth rates for consumption, investment, and exports, the estimate of import requirements is about 10 percent higher than the plan specifies for 1980. Thus the import reduction foreseen in the plan must be even larger than these figures indicate. This lower rate of import growth does not appear to be consistent with the plan's aggregate targets; it could be realized only by reducing other components of domestic final demand.

Domestic and foreign exchange requirements

The static input-output model, although useful for checking the consistency of some of the plan's targets, provides little insight into

Table 5.6. *Macroeconomic Indicators, 1971–75 and Simulations based on Targets for 1976–80 and 1980–85*

Indicator	1971–75	1976–80	1980–85
Incremental capital-output ratio	4.2	4.2	4.2
Elasticity of imports[a]	1.0	0.6	1.0
Marginal saving rate (percent)	24.0	21.0	34.0
Investment rate[b] (percent)	29.8	29.2	30.6
Domestic saving rate[b] (percent)	24.0	24.9	27.6
National saving rate[b] (percent)	27.6	27.1	28.4
	Average annual rate of growth (percent)		
Gross domestic product	6.6	7.0	7.2
Investment	5.3	7.2	8.4
Consumption	4.9	6.4	6.3
Imports[c]	5.2	4.5	7.2
Exports[c]	4.8	7.8	8.6

Note: Simulations are based on assumptions and targets in the social plan for 1976–80.

Sources: Statistical Yearbook of Yugoslavia, 1976; figures supplied by the Federal Institute of Planning; *Social Plan of Yugoslavia: 1976–80;* and World Bank estimates.

a. Based on three-year averages.
b. In relation to GDP.
c. Includes goods and nonfactor services.

a number of issues associated with growth. By comparing the characteristics of the economy in 1976 and 1980, the analysis does provide a basis for judging the consistency of the system in those two years. But it does not provide the means for determining whether the economy can attain the level and structure of output projected for the terminal year. Specifically the input-output model does not provide the means for assessing whether the plan's targets can be financed from either domestic or foreign resources.

A two-gap model was used to analyze the implications of the plan for domestic and foreign financing, as well as the links between the two sources.[8] The model first simulated the evolution of the economy, using assumptions close to those in the plan (table 5.6).

8. A similar model was used in Vinod Dubey and others, *Yugoslavia: Development with Decentralization* (Baltimore: Johns Hopkins University Press for the World Bank, 1975), pp. 322–50.

By adjusting certain assumptions—notably those for import elasticity and the overall growth rate—it then contrasted the plan scenario with these alternative possibilities.

PLAN SCENARIO. The first simulation, based on the plan's macroeconomic parameters, indicates that the foreign exchange requirements to finance the plan are considerable. If it is assumed that workers' remittances remain constant in nominal terms and that exports of goods and nonfactor services grow at the average annual rate of 8 percent, foreign exchange earnings will grow by 6 percent a year between 1976 and 1980.[9] The trade gap and the current account deficit will rise throughout the period and call for a significant inflow of foreign exchange on the capital account. Even allowing for the likely inflow of foreign exchange through supplier credits and credits from official sources, there still will be a gap that can be filled only by financial credits obtained in international capital markets. These markets are less certain and more volatile than other sources. Nevertheless, if it is assumed that Yugoslavia will be able to borrow the additional capital required, its debt service ratio should not significantly increase. The main reason is that export earnings are projected to rise rapidly, particularly if the effects of the expected rate of international inflation during the period are taken into account. Furthermore the requirements for financial credits, net of annual repayments of principal, will not be that large. It thus is likely that Yugoslavia will be able to meet the requirements for external financing indicated in the plan.

It also is expected that the availability of domestic resources will not constrain the growth targets of the plan. Historically the incremental capital-output ratio, though volatile, has averaged about 4.0. Even allowing for a somewhat more capital-intensive development under the plan, the incremental capital-output ratio is not expected

---

9. Although the prospects for the growth of workers' remittances are crucial to the development of Yugoslavia's balance of payments, the plan has no estimate of their likely level. To some extent the rise in incomes in host countries will offset the reduced number of workers abroad. In addition, returning workers are likely to repatriate the savings, reported to be substantial, they hold in host countries. The hypothesis in this study is that the offsetting effects are likely to cancel one another, such that remittances remain constant in nominal terms. Since 1973 the tendency has been for remittances to decline in real terms; thus the working assumption of constant nominal remittances seems to be reasonable for the plan period.

to exceed 4.2. The new institutional changes, by avoiding duplication and the waste from inadequate plan preparation and coordination, are likely to have a positive effect on the efficiency of resource allocation. Annual growth of 7 percent in gross domestic product (GDP) and an incremental capital-output ratio of 4.2 would call for a share of investment in GDP of about 29.5 percent. One consequence of the 1974 investment boom was to increase that share to 30.2 percent in 1975; the average for 1971–75 was 29.8 percent. Thus the investment requirements of the plan period do not call for a change in the investment ratio. The average saving rates required to sustain the investment rate during the plan period are 24 to 25 percent for domestic savings and 26 to 27 percent for national savings. Both rates are in line with recent experience and appear to be attainable.

ALTERNATIVE SCENARIOS. The plan's targeted annual growth in exports of goods and nonfactor services is 8 percent, a figure broadly consistent with historical trends, but above the level prevailing after the economic reforms of 1965. Yugoslavia's export structure, with a 90 percent share of manufactured goods in total exports, is highly diversified. Furthermore Yugoslavia's diversified export markets provide opportunities for shifts among markets. The analysis in chapter nine also indicates that a growth of exports of goods and nonfactor services of up to 9 percent is plausible. Thus, for the analysis here, the historical relations between the growth of exports and the growth of foreign markets has been maintained, leading to a secular growth rate of exports of goods and nonfactor services of about 8 percent a year.

As already indicated, however, the plan is based on what appears to be a rather optimistic assumption about the economy's ability to reduce its import requirements. Substantial structural changes are required to achieve this goal. A reduction in import dependency as considerable as that foreseen in the plan will be difficult to achieve in a five-year period, unless Yugoslavia makes sacrifices in the growth and efficiency of its economy. Because of these reservations about the plan's assumption for imports, additional simulations were undertaken to analyze the consequences of adjusting the economy's import requirements upward. This alternative set of simulations concentrates on import elasticity. It still is assumed that Yugoslavia will be able to reduce its import dependency, but at a somewhat slower pace. The import elasticity used in the alternative scenarios for 1976–80 is 0.85, which still is considerably below Yugoslavia's best past performance and is very low by international standards.[10]

Scenario A adjusts the average annual rate of GDP growth from 7 percent for 1967–80 to 5.5 percent. If all other assumptions remain unchanged, the balance of payments in 1980 would be fairly close to that in the plan scenario (table 5.7). But in contrast with

Table 5.7. *Balance of Payments, Alternative Scenarios for 1980 and 1985*
(millions of dollars)

Item	Plan scenario	Scenario A	Scenario B
	1980		
Resource gap	−2,320	−2,470	−2,940
Balance on current account	−1,071	−1,260	−1,780
Medium- and long-term disbursements on capital account	3,179	3,410	3,750
Financial credits	837	960	1,550
Debt service ratio (percent)	15.6	16.3	17.3
	1985		
Resource gap	−2,991	−1,760	−2,440
Balance on current account	−2,369	−1,010	−2,220
Medium- and long-term disbursements on capital account	6,680	4,490	7,070
Financial credits	2,225	570	2,880
Debt service ratio (percent)	16.4	15.3	21.0

Note: The plan scenario is based on assumptions and targets in the plan. Scenario A adjusts the average annual rate of GDP growth to 5.5 percent, from the 7 percent rate specified in the plan. Scenario B adjusts that rate to 6 percent. Scenarios A and B both assume an import elasticity of 0.85 for 1976–80 and unity for 1980–85.
Source: World Bank calculations.

the plan scenario, the balance of payments would considerably improve in the 1980–85 plan period because of the somewhat lower economic growth rate of 6 percent a year during this later period, compared with the plan's long-term growth target of about 7 percent. If the average annual rate of GDP growth is adjusted to 6 percent for

10. The analysis also examined the implications of targets in the five-year and ten-year plans for the 1980–85 period. For this analysis, it is assumed that import elasticity will increase to unity after 1980; this elasticity is in line with the historical value.

1976–80, as in scenario B, the balance of payments rapidly deterio-
rates in both five-year periods, and a sharp rise in external financing
would be required.

In short, if the plan's assumption about reduced import dependency is changed, if a higher and more plausible level of imports
is assumed, and if the external financing requirements of the economy are not to exceed the external borrowing parameter established
by the plan, the overall growth rate must be reduced. An average
annual growth rate of about 5.5 percent for 1976–80, rising to 6
percent in the 1980s, would appear to be the upper limit achievable
within that external borrowing parameter. The somewhat lower
growth rate for 1976–85 seems quite plausible, perhaps even acceptable, because the economy will be adjusting to the poor growth
prospects for workers' remittances and the higher oil import bill.

Labor force and employment prospects

Despite the rapid reduction of the agricultural labor force during
the 1965–75 period, one-third of the active labor force continues
to work in the agricultural sector. The extent of underemployment
in that sector cannot be accurately assessed, but two conditions are
evident: a large portion of the agricultural labor force is engaged
in low-productivity activities; the average income in the agricultural
sector is less than half that in the social sector. In addition to the
problem of underemployment, there has been a tendency for
registered unemployment to rise rapidly in recent years. With
external migration no longer providing a vent for surplus labor, a
crucial question in Yugoslavia will be the extent to which the social
sector can generate sufficient employment opportunities.

LABOR FORCE. Yugoslavia's rate of population growth is expected
to decline gradually between 1976 and 1980. For 1976–80 the projected growth rate of the labor force is slightly lower than that of
the population; for 1980–85 it declines dramatically. This sharp
decline reflects the growing proportion of the population expected
in the marginal age groups, which have lower rates of participation
in the labor force. There still will be considerable differences in
population growth among regions, and differences in the growth of
the labor force are even more pronounced. The projected rates of
labor force growth for 1976–80 vary from 3.3 percent a year in
Kosovo to —0.2 percent in Serbia; those for 1980–85 from 3.4 to
—0.6 percent. Thus regional differences will be sharpened, and

regions already having severe problems of unemployment and under-employment will have the fastest natural rate of increase in the labor force.

In addition to the natural increase in the labor force, the plan foresees two additional sources of labor supply: a return of 250,000 migrant workers; a targeted reduction in registered unemployment of 136,000. If these two factors are added to the demographic increase, the increase required in social sector employment is considerably greater. Table 5.8 brings these elements together and

Table 5.8. *Absorption of Returning Migrant Workers and Reduced Unemployment, by Region, 1976–80*

Region	Annual growth in social sector employment, 1971–75 (percent)	Job-seekers, 1976–80 (thousands)			Required annual growth in social sector employment (percent)
		Returning migrants	Reduced unemployed	Natural increase in labor force	
Less developed regions					
Bosnia-Herzegovina	5.5	54	22	97	4.9
Kosovo	6.7	9	10	52	9.4
Macedonia	5.3	21	22	45	5.1
Montenegro	5.3	3	4	14	4.0
More developed regions					
Croatia	3.7	82	18	47	2.5
Serbia	4.0	43	42	−12	1.2
Slovenia	4.4	19	3	11	1.0
Vojvodina	3.5	19	14	23	2.4
Yugoslavia	4.4	250	136	277	2.9

Source: World Bank estimates.
a. It is assumed that returning migrants go back to their regions of origin and that the reduction of unemployment in each region is proportional to the shares of regions in total unemployment in 1976.

compares the projected growth rates of job-seekers with the growth rate of employment for 1971–75. The figures indicate that opportunities for a continuing decline in the agricultural labor force are likely to be limited for all the less developed regions, particularly Kosovo and Bosnia-Herzegovina. In Kosovo the agricultural labor force is likely to continue to grow, even with fairly optimistic assumptions about the growth of social sector employment and interrepublican migration.

EMPLOYMENT. The plan foresees growth in employment of 3.5 percent a year for the 1976–80 period. Given the experience during 1965–75 and the more rapid growth in output expected during the plan period, it appears that a growth rate of 3.5 percent is somewhat low. By using sectoral employment-ouput elasticities and allowing for the shift in the structure of production, it might be expected that employment will grow at 4.4 percent a year if Yugoslavia achieves the plan's targeted rate of GDP growth. Two points should be noted, however. First, the capital cost per job created during the plan period is expected to rise sharply: for example, the direct capital-labor ratios in priority sectors of industry are twice the average for all industry. Second, if the plan's projection is revised downward by cutting back nonpriority sectors, the effect on employment could be sharp, because nonpriority sectors are considerably more labor-intensive than priority sectors.[11] In addition, if the plan's targets for import substitution cannot be achieved, the economy may grow at a rate lower than foreseen in the plan. Thus annual growth in employment of 3.5 percent a year is a reasonable expectation.

Although the projected growth of social sector employment is attainable, the targeted 5.1 percent annual growth of private nonagricultural employment appears to be somewhat optimistic. An increase in the growth rate of private nonagricultural employment is likely to occur because of the new institutional arrangements and the return of migrant workers. But in 1975 and 1976 alone, the returning migrants saturated the work opportunities in some sectors, notably in catering and road haulage. The new institutional arrangements should encourage private investment in new productive sectors, but their novelty is likely to mitigate any sudden and large increase in employment.

Estimates of the difference between the increments in labor force and job supply indicate that a 2 percent annual reduction in the agricultural labor force is possible during 1976–80.[12] That reduction nevertheless is considerably below the 6 percent annual reduction between 1970 and 1975. At this lower rate, income differences be-

---

11. These issues are discussed in detail in chapter eight.
12. See table 10.19 in chapter ten.

tween the two sectors would narrow only marginally. For the 1976–80 period a growth rate for social sector employment of more than 2.9 percent would result in excess demand for labor and enable a gradual reduction in the agricultural labor force; a growth rate of less than 2.9 percent would result in an increase in either agricultural employment or open unemployment.

Regional disparities

Previous regional policies have supported the less developed regions by transferring financial resources to them. Those transfers, in addition to the efforts of the less developed regions, produced structural changes through industrial growth and established physical and social infrastructure. But despite the progress achieved in GMP growth and social welfare, substantial regional disparities are likely to persist in Yugoslavia for the coming decade, if not longer. Basic conditions in the less developed regions account for the disparities. Their rates of population growth are higher. Their problems of labor force absorption, arising from previous population dynamics, are greater. Their intraregional disparities, given the large proportion of their population engaged in private agriculture, are broader. Their industrial operations are concentrated in sectors characterized by high ratios of capital to output and labor and low levels of profitability. They also suffer more from institutional weaknesses and infrastructure deficiencies. As a result, the ten-year development plan lists the reduction of such differences as a national priority, and one objective of the five-year plan for 1976–80 is for the less developed regions to achieve rates of growth that exceed the national average.

POLICIES TO REDRESS REGIONAL DISPARITIES. New legislation provides for a somewhat larger flow of financial resources to the less developed regions through the two federal transfer mechanisms: the Federal Fund, and federal budgetary grants. Social sector enterprises finance the Federal Fund: almost 2 percent of the GMP of each region's social sector is collected in obligatory loans from the undistributed profits of enterprises. The fund provides concessionary loans, with a grant element of about 40 to 50 percent, to the less developed regions to raise their investment potential in productive activities.[13]

---

13. The distinction between productive and nonproductive activities, or what the Yugoslavs term economic and noneconomic activities, is central to Marxian

Grants from the federal budget amount to about 1 percent of GMP and support social services in poorer areas. For the 1976–80 period, resources from the Federal Fund will account for about 20 percent of productive investment in all four less developed regions and about 75 percent in Kosovo. Together with budgetary grants, they will amount to about 10 percent of their GMP. The gross contributions to these transfers by the more developed regions are equivalent to about 3 percent of their GMP and about 10 percent of their potential for productive investment. Their contributions thus represent a substantial sacrifice in future GMP forgone. The ratio of investment to GMP in the less developed regions is 38 percent on average and about 50 percent in Montenegro and Kosovo; the corresponding ratio in the more developed regions is 27 percent. Those high ratios suggest that the limits of absorptive capacity are probably being approached, if not reached, in the less developed regions, with the inevitable loss of efficiency in using the financial resources available.

Continuing transfers are necessary but not sufficient for reducing disparities. Yugoslavia recognizes that the less developed regions, because of the growing complexity of their economies, require technical and managerial know-how as much as financial support. A new provision of the Federal Fund stipulates that one-fifth of the obligatory contributions of enterprises can be transferred to the less developed regions through the joint pooling of resources. This is an important, though still limited, attempt to share technical and managerial expertise among regions. The new provisions for inter-enterprise cooperation codified in social compacts and self-manage-

---

economics and is followed here for analytical purposes. Adam Smith introduced the distinction to classical economics. He classified as nonproductive that labor which does not produce a physically tangible output, directly contribute to its production, or yield a surplus for future reinvestment. That classification embraces most services in present-day economies. According to Yugoslav statistical conventions, which are close to those of other socialist countries embracing Marxian premises, the principal nonproductive activities are health, education, administration, defense, banking, and housing. This distinction is important for national accounts, which do not include nonproductive services in the aggregate measure of output, the measure commonly referred to as GMP. The GNP and GDP figures in this report have been estimated by the World Bank on the basis of official Yugoslav data on GMP and additional statistical information on the excluded services.

The distinction between productive and nonproductive activities is also important in connection with the recent institutional changes. BOALS and enterprises by definition are productive; work communities for such general services as accounting and planning within enterprises and banks are nonproductive, which accounts for their legally subordinate and economically dependent status in relation to BOALS and enterprises.

ment agreements have a similar orientation. These agreements emphasize the vertical and horizontal integration of production units both interregionally and intraregionally, especially for priority sectors. They also emphasize arrangements based on the sharing of risk and income among enterprises. But transferring technical and managerial know-how invariably is more difficult and time consuming than transferring financial resources. Furthermore the more capital-intensive priority activities, such as energy and basic metallurgy, are located in the less developed regions. Efforts to realize growth targets in these areas could thus reinforce the unfavorable industrial structure and somewhat dilute the efforts of less developed regions to diversify.

PROSPECTS FOR INTERREGIONAL MIGRATION. Given the labor surplus in less developed regions and the emerging labor shortages in some of the more developed regions, interregional migration would appear to be the logical solution. These imbalances, in addition to the opportunities for employment abroad, have led to some migration in the past: for example, a quarter of the resident labor force of Slovenia is not Slovene. The ten-year plan thus stresses the desirability of stepping up internal migration. But future interregional migration is not likely to be on a much larger scale than in the past. In the shorter run the constraint will be pressure in the more developed regions to provide employment for their own surplus agricultural labor force and for migrant workers returning from abroad. In the longer run there are several strong social constraints. For temporary migration there are personal hardships associated with the separation of families. For permanent migration the material and social costs of settling workers and their families in new localities are high. Added to these considerations are the sensitivities arising from Yugoslavia's ethnic and cultural diversity. Furthermore the most mobile workers generally are young, well educated, and well trained. Their migration could lead to a major drain of human resources and intensify the institutional weaknesses of the less developed regions. Because of these constraints, supplementing the transfer of financial resources with transfers of technical know-how is crucial to redressing regional disparities.

LONG-TERM ISSUES OF REGIONAL DEVELOPMENT. Yugoslavia's regional disparities constitute a complex problem requiring comprehensive efforts for its resolution. Three interrelated issues of regional development are important today and likely to impinge on Yugoslavia throughout the 1980s: reducing differences in income between regions, reorienting the industrial structure in individual regions, and generating productive employment in all regions.

In the five-year plan the targeted rate of GMP growth is higher for the less developed regions than for the nation. But if their higher rates of population growth are sustained, as seems likely, the effects of economic growth on income per capita will be diluted. As the figures in table 5.9 show, the targets for reducing interregional

Table 5.9. *Gross Material Product per Capita, by Region, 1975 and Targets for 1976–80*

	1975		1976–80	1980
Region	Average annual rate of population growth (percent)	Gross material product per capita (Yugoslavia = 100)	Average annual rate of GMP growth (percent)	Gross material product per capita (Yugoslavia = 100)
Less developed regions	1.6	62	8.2	64
Bosnia-Herzegovina	1.3	69	8.2	72
Kosovo	2.8	33	9.5	34
Macedonia	1.5	69	8.0	71
Montenegro	1.3	70	8.3	73
More developed regions	0.6	121	6.7	121
Croatia	0.4	124	6.5	124
Serbia	0.7	92	7.0	94
Slovenia	0.7	201	6.1	195
Vojvodina	0.3	121	7.1	126
Yugoslavia	0.9	100	6.9	100

Sources: Figures supplied by the Federal Institute of Planning; *Social Plan of Yugoslavia: 1976–80*; *Statistical Yearbook of Yugoslavia*, 1976.

income disparities are modest indeed. For the less developed regions the average GMP per capita is to rise from 62 percent of the Yugoslav average in 1975 to 64 percent in 1980. Moreover extrapolating the growth rates of GMP and population for 1976–80 raises the average GMP per capita in the less developed regions from 51 percent of that in the more developed regions in 1975 to a mere 57 percent in 2000. For Kosovo, the most severe case, the average income would rise only from 27 percent of that in the more developed regions to 31 percent. True, the assumption of unchanged growth rates implies an improbable scenario. For example, growth rates of GMP in the more developed regions will slow down once the labor force reserves are exhausted, and the demographic parameter has a declining trend for three of the less developed regions. But the extrapolations dramatically highlight the limitations to the current momentum. Only substantial changes in policies and conditions could induce a breakthrough during the 1980s. The solution of the problem requires a skillful mix of demographic policies, transfers of know-how and finance, and changes in the industrial structures in all regions.

The long-term development of the less developed regions and the reduction of regional disparities may well hinge upon a more nearly optimal pattern of regional industrial specialization. For a variety of reasons, the patterns of specialization are inconsistent with the human resource endowments of the regions: many traditional labor-intensive industries are concentrated in the more developed regions. The efforts of less developed regions to diversify their industrial production have also created duplication and excess capacity. A more efficient use of national resources would call for corrective measures that shift the industrial structure in the more developed regions toward industries more intensive in capital and skills and leave the activities intensive in labor to the less developed regions. This fundamental adjustment of the interregional division of labor, painful and complex as it might be, is in the long-term interest of all regions. Because of the hardships and costs of adjustment to certain enterprises and regions, particularly in the context of the decentralized decisionmaking that self-management implies, the process is not likely to be enthusiastically initiated. It may involve transferring an established enterprise from one region to another or even shutting it down; in other cases it may require reaching interregional agreements on the location of new facilities. Because all regions would realize long-term benefits from restructuring the industrial patterns, there may be a need for a mechanism for compensation at the federal or republican level to smooth the adjustment costs for individual enterprises.

Yugoslavia's employment outlook, as discussed earlier, is no indication of the rate at which employment opportunities will develop in the various regions. Because detailed projections of sectoral output are not available for all regions, the effects of structural shifts in the economy cannot be readily ascertained for each region. The analysis in chapter ten nevertheless indicates that the plan's assumptions for growth would permit some reduction in the agricultural labor force in most less developed regions. The exception is Kosovo, which cannot be expected to absorb the increments to its labor force, even under optimistic assumptions and even if the plan's growth targets are achieved. For other regions, the employment situation may be somewhat less favorable than that analysis implies. One reason is that the growth rates for the economy and for individual regions appear to be optimistic, given the planned investment outlays. Another reason is that a high share of industries in the less developed regions have low labor-output ratios. The plan's emphasis on basic industries is likely to affect adversely the capacity of these regions to generate employment. Taking these factors into account, the opportunities for migration out of the agricultural sector are likely to be fairly limited, except in Slovenia and Serbia.

Conclusion

Given the significant changes to the system of economic management, the medium-term prospects of Yugoslavia are difficult to assess. One principal objective of these changes is to strengthen macroeconomic management. The new planning system provides a novel mechanism for coordinating decisionmaking in the allocation of resources. Similarly the use of social compacts in other policy areas will induce various interest groups to consider economic issues in a broader perspective and to appreciate the tradeoffs involved in coordinating diverse objectives. The instruments adopted have many positive features and bear considerable promise. What is significant in these changes is that the shortcomings of the previous system of economic management have been correctly diagnosed and a set of measures consistent with meeting these deficiencies has been adopted. Although other policy measures could be envisaged, the current measures provide a tenable and workable response to acknowledged problems. They are, in addition, compatible with many of Yugoslavia's social and political objectives. The application of these instruments is also likely to raise important practical issues that will need to be resolved. There undoubtedly will be further changes as the new policy instruments are elaborated upon or, where necessary, modified.

Part Two

Six Issues

Six

Stabilization

THE ECONOMIC REFORMS of 1965 set the stage for Yugoslavia's development in the 1966–75 period. Although the rate of economic growth continued to be high by international standards, the institutional decentralization and market orientation of the reforms caused imbalances in the supply and demand for commodities and financial resources. Moreover certain problems, which appeared manageable in the short term, persisted longer than expected. Fluctuating rates of economic growth, rising rates of inflation, and recurring periods of enterprise illiquidity and balance-of-payments difficulties—all characterized the development path during this period. By the mid-1970s, when international inflation pushed the rate of price increases and the deficit in the balance of payments to record levels, stabilization became the primary objective of economic policies.[1] The measures introduced in pursuit of this objective had almost immediate effects. In 1976 the inflation rate, measured by the implicit GMP deflator, declined to about 10 percent from 18 percent in 1975 and 22 percent in 1974. Also in 1976 the current account recorded a modest surplus, compared with deficits of about $1 billion in each of the two preceding years.

What accounted for this turnaround? New laws emanating from the 1974 constitution, which has many provisions designed to pro-

1. In Yugoslav usage the term *stabilization* has a wide connotation that extends to sectoral and structural imbalances. In accord with such usage this chapter, while taking inflation as its central theme, interprets stabilization within a broader context that includes trends of principal economic aggregates and policies. For a discussion of cyclical fluctuations in Yugoslavia, a theme not pursued in this chapter, see Branko Horvat, "Short-term Instability and Long-term Trends in the Yugoslav Economy's Development," *Eastern European Economics*, vol. 14, no. 1 (Fall 1975), pp. 3–31; first appeared in *Ekonomist*, vol. 27, nos. 1–2 (1974), pp. 51–71.

mote long-term stability, must have helped. Political dedication and administrative intervention were more instrumental. It would nevertheless be premature to argue that Yugoslavia has resolved the conditions causing domestic inflation. Requirements remain for a more coherent set of macroeconomic policies. In addition, a continuing political commitment to stabilization as a prime economic objective appears necessary to prevent the recurrence of an inflationary spiral. That commitment is especially important in view of the demonstrated tradeoff between stabilization and economic growth—a tradeoff which in the past has led to frequent policy reversals.

Economic Trends: 1966–76

Yugoslavia has fared well by most economic and social indicators, and in comparison with countries of the Organization for Economic Cooperation and Development (OECD) the Yugoslav economy shows points of strength (table 6.1). Its real GNP growth rate of 7 percent

Table 6.1. *Rates of Saving, Investment, Inflation, and Growth in Gross National Product, Yugoslavia and Selected OECD Countries, 1965–73*
(percent)

	Average annual rate			
Country	Saving[a]	Invest-ment[b]	Inflation	Growth in gross national product
Yugoslavia	28.4	29.5	11.1	7.0
Austria	29.3	29.8	4.4	5.6
Federal Republic of Germany	28.5	26.4	4.6	4.7
France	27.8	27.3	5.2	5.8
Greece	18.8	28.3	3.7	8.1
Italy	22.2	21.1	4.9	4.9
Japan	38.8	37.4	5.4	10.8
Spain	21.4	23.3	6.2	6.2
Switzerland	30.9	28.9	4.3	4.2
Turkey	19.3	20.1	9.6	7.1

Source: World Bank, *World Tables 1976* (Washington, D.C., 1976).
a. Ratio of gross national savings to gross national product.
b. Ratio of gross domestic investment to gross domestic product.

a year in the 1965–73 period was exceeded only by Japan, Greece, and Turkey. Its rates of investment and saving also ranked among the highest. But there was one major economic weakness: an accelerating rate of inflation. Over the 1965–73 period the average rate of inflation was higher in Yugoslavia than in all OECD countries.

In the first years after the reforms, the economic system was still adjusting to structural imbalances in the supply and demand for goods. The imbalances had three basic causes: the change in absolute and relative prices in 1965; the liberalization of foreign trade; and the relegation of income policy to enterprises. In addition to the rise of consumer demand resulting from the planned growth of the share of personal incomes in GMP, a large credit expansion allowed for a rapid increase of investment in fixed assets and inventories.[2] All these factors combined to drive prices higher by the end of the 1960s. Also over the 1966–70 period, imports continued to expand faster than exports, and the balance of trade deteriorated.

In 1971, when government established stabilization as a principal objective, measures were introduced to moderate the expansion of domestic components of demand, influence the distribution of income in favor of a higher saving rate, and improve the balance of payments. The dinar was devalued twice: by 20 percent at the beginning of the year and by a further 18.7 percent at the end of the year.[3] Potential investors in nonproductive activities were required to hold deposits with business banks as a condition for obtaining credit. A law was passed on the recording of liabilities and the means of settling the debts of users of social resources. Another law, intended with the tighter income policy to increase the accumulation potential of enterprises, was passed on the revaluation of fixed assets. Credit and monetary policies were tightened; and prices were frozen in the last quarter of 1971 until February 1972. These stabilization measures moderated the real expansion of the economy, and the average growth of GMP slowed to about 5 percent in 1972–73 from about 9 percent in 1971 (see tables 6.2 and 6.3 and figure 6.1). But they did not check the rise of prices or the nominal increase in consumption or investment demand— all of which continued to accelerate.

2. That expansion occurred after 1967, when monetary policy was unduly restrictive.

3. Before 23 January 1971 the dinar was equal to US$0.08. From 23 January 1971 to 22 December 1971 it was equal to US$0.0667; from 22 December 1971 to 12 July 1973 it was equal to US$0.0589. Since 12 July 1973 the dinar has been floating; on 31 December 1977 it was equal to US$0.0542 cents.

Table 6.2. *Indexes of Aggregate Demand, Foreign Trade, and Money Supply, 1966–75*

Item	1970 (1966 = 100)	1975 (1966 = 100)	1975 (1971 = 100)
Gross material product	159	502	244
Real gross material product	125	168	124
Investment	187	659	266
Consumption	173	542	245
Exports	138	334	225
Imports	183	488	236
Money supply	160	591	323

Note: Real GMP is in 1966 constant prices; all other figures are in current prices.

Sources: Federal Institute of Statistics, *Statistical Yearbook of Yugoslavia*, various years, and National Bank of Yugoslavia, *Annual Report*, various years.

The devaluations were only temporarily effective in stimulating exports and improving the balance of payments. The rise of imports in 1973 again surpassed the rise of exports, and the relatively large surplus for the year resulted from the substantial increase in remittances by workers and receipts from tourism. Because the scope for

Table 6.3. *Prices and Average Workers' Receipts, 1966–76*
(percent)

Year	GMP deflator	Industrial producer prices	Cost of living	Average net nominal personal receipts
		Average annual rate of growth		
1966[a]	15	11	23	38
1967	2	2	7	14
1970	12	9	11	18
1971	19	15	16	23
1972	15	11	17	17
1973	19	13	20	15
1974	22	29	21	28
1975	18	22	24	24
1976	10	6	12	16

Sources: Federal Institute of Statistics, *Index*, 1977, vol. 6, and *Statistical Yearbook of Yugoslavia*, 1976.

a. The increases in 1966 reflect the administrative price adjustments at the end of 1965.

Figure 6.1. *Retail, Industrial, and Agricultural Prices in Yugoslavia, 1952–76*

(1967 = 100)

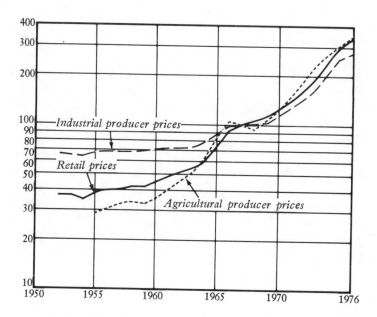

Source: Federal Institute of Statistics, *Statistical Yearbook of Yugoslavia,* 1976.

fiscal policy was marginal, monetary policy, combined with some elements of price control, was the principal instrument for demand management. Given the selective credit policy and the sudden reversal in the balance of payments, monetary policy also proved to be too inflexible. The growth of money supply averaged about 40 percent in 1972 and 1973. As the figures in table 6.3 further illustrate, inflationary pressure was building for the explosion in 1974–75.

Decisions at the highest political levels accorded stabilization the top priority in the mid-1970s. Strong measures were introduced in the second half of 1975 and in 1976 to set the economy on a more even course of development. The strong stand taken by the LCY— that the inflationary fever had reached intolerable proportions and had to be suppressed—apparently was as important as the orthodox measures of fiscal and monetary policy. The results achieved in inflation control and foreign trade were remarkable. In 1976 social product grew by about 14 percent in nominal terms and 4 percent in real terms. As a result of price policy and the slowdown of growth, the rise of industrial producer prices declined to about 6 percent in 1976, compared with 22 percent in 1975 and 29 percent in 1974. The increase in the cost of living declined to 11.6 percent in 1976 from the record rise of 24 percent in 1975. Employment in the social sector continued to grow, at the rate of 3.7 percent in 1976, and facilitated the absorption of workers returning from abroad. Exports expanded by 15 percent in real terms, and imports declined. The deficit in the balance of payments was thus reduced, and the current account recorded a surplus of about $150 million in 1976.

These favorable trends were accompanied, however, by other developments. The rate of GMP growth was relatively low. Real productivity was stagnant. The growth of average personal incomes was relatively high. The number of loss-making enterprises also was relatively high. And monetary expansion, estimated at about 50 percent in 1976, was very rapid. The high demand for money by enterprises to meet new payment regulations dampened the effect of that expansion, which nevertheless carried the danger of fueling inflation after a time lag.

Factors of Instability and Inflation

The household sector became significantly more important after the 1965 economic reforms. The changes to the system, especially the reduction in certain taxes and contributions, allowed workers to control a larger share of enterprise income. This practice in turn supported the intended policy of distributing a higher share of the fruits of growth to the population by changing the pattern of income distribution to favor personal incomes over net enterprise savings. It led to a rapid rise of average personal receipts, which until the early 1970s grew faster than average productivity.[4] Between 1966 and 1971 average personal receipts increased by more than 100 percent in nominal terms and 32 percent in real terms.[5] By comparison, average workers' productivity increased by 84 per-

---

4. The plan for 1966–70 provided for average personal incomes to rise 1.3 times faster than average workers' productivity.
5. See appendix table A.3.

cent in nominal terms and 21 percent in real terms. Workers enjoy-
ing large real increases in personal incomes substantially increased
their consumption expenditure, a pattern that added to the pressure
on prices. The stabilization measures of 1971 and 1972, which aimed
to moderate the rise of personal earnings through social compacts
and self-management agreements on income distribution, brought
the real increase in average personal incomes to a virtual halt.
Nominal consumption expenditure nevertheless continued its rapid
progress for three reasons: the drive to maintain living standards in
the face of rising costs of living; the expansion of total personal
incomes caused by the rapid growth of employment; and the substantial increase of transfer receipts, especially on account of workers' remittances.

The objective to attain high growth of investment and output
accentuated the demand pull. A number of factors caused investment demand to exceed financing capacities under stable conditions.
First, with the large degree of decentralization, and without adequate coordination, enterprises tended to pursue unrealistic production and investment plans that sometimes were not related to
the marketing possibilities. Second, with the constant pressure for
higher wages, the savings potential of enterprises declined. To meet
their ambitious investments in fixed and working assets, they increasingly had to rely on the savings of other sectors, on the expansion of money supply, on external resources from higher import
volumes and foreign borrowing. They also raised their prices. Third,
the system of income computation allowed enterprises to compute
income for distribution on the basis of the value of production,
irrespective of whether they sold goods for cash or unguaranteed
credit or added goods to stocks at unrealistic values. Because personal incomes had first claim to the liquid resources of enterprises,
the share allocated to accumulation may have often been a book-
keeping phenomenon for inefficient producers. Fourth, the practice
of mutual crediting among enterprises, which frequently was involuntary because of the nonrepayment of obligations, led to the
tendency to generate fictitious income. This practice may have had
positive effects by stabilizing production in a self-managed system
that rejects any adjustments to cyclical downswings through laying
off workers. To the extent that the system allowed the perpetuation
and nonrepayment of debts, however, the practice could have had
both distortive and inflationary effects. Inefficient producers could
stay afloat, adding to the rise of average costs and the pressure on
prices. The practice was also translated into higher demands for

new bank credits and for delays in the repayment of past credits.[6] Fifth, the substantially negative real interest rate on borrowed funds may have stimulated the demand for investment credits and additional working capital to carry the inflated stocks.

The deviation in early years between the rise of personal incomes and the rise of productivity exerted pressure on production costs which, unless accompanied by a voluntary reduction of accumulation, could be sustained only if passed on in higher prices. Furthermore the increases in real personal incomes that were justifiable for enterprises achieving productivity increases were emulated by less efficient or even loss-making enterprises, thus perpetuating some inefficiencies and further fueling inflation.

The factors contributing to high inflation in Yugoslavia thus were principally endogenous, but they were aggravated in certain years by external factors. Inflation appears to have been fueled more by consumer demand in the early reform years. It also appears to have spiraled as enterprises tried to realize high levels of investments and the system allowed them to push forward their rising costs in higher prices. The economic system thus maintained high growth at successively higher price levels.

What emerges from the foregoing discussion is that stabilization already was an objective in the early postreform years. The economic and social costs of inflation, which are similar to those in other countries, also mounted with its rising rate. The following perhaps were the principal costs.

First, the expectations of further price increases reinforced the pressure for higher personal remuneration and rapidly rising consumption expenditure. It also reinforced the tendencies for stockpiling, large investments, enterprise illiquidity, and mutual indebtedness. Second, under a system of discriminate price control, price distortions occurred as a result of free price movements for goods not subject to controls and administered price adjustments for other goods. These distortions had repercussions for the profitability of enterprises, their accumulation potential, and allocative efficiency. Third, the unequitable incidence of inflation on recipients of fixed

6. There is some evidence for this effect. In 1971 a decree was passed to convert Din14.5 billion in short-term credits, which had been revolving, to long-term credits for the financing of working assets. In 1973 a similar decree was passed to convert an additional Din18.5 billion to long-term credits. In 1974 Din45.9 billion in long-term credits were transformed into permanent resources of enterprises and sociopolitical communities.

income resulted in periodic adjustments of pensions and payments for social welfare. Similar reasoning applied to the rising costs of social services, and the need to subsidize services extended to the relatively poor segment of the population. Because these services are financed by contributions out of gross personal incomes of the employed, they may have precipitated demands for higher personal incomes and reduced the accumulative potential of enterprises. Fourth, the combination of high inflation and administratively fixed interest rates, resulted in negative yields and costs on financial instruments. This effect may have discouraged financial savings and encouraged borrowing. Fifth, rapid price increases reduced the competitiveness of Yugoslav products abroad, especially in Western European markets. At the same time, those increases made imports more attractive to Yugoslavs and adversely affected the balance of trade. As mentioned earlier, the devaluations of the dinar in 1971 had only a temporary impact; they were overtaken by mounting inflation in subsequent years. The competitiveness of exports in relation to foreign products thus suffered to the extent that exchange rate adjustments did not compensate for domestic price increases in excess of international rates.

Macroeconomic Policies

As noted earlier, the changes of the 1965 economic reforms had some built-in inflationary tendencies. The decentralization of the socioeconomic system also weakened the function of demand management at the macroeconomic level. Price and income determination were liberalized, but price and income policies were lacking. Budgetary functions were regionalized, and the fiscal system was not geared to serve as an instrument of economic policy. The role of demand management therefore rested with monetary policy. But even monetary regulation was often overruled by other economic considerations, and monetary expansion helped to fuel inflation.

Price policy

The price system in Yugoslavia has passed through various degrees of control and liberalization, but has never been totally free of administrative interventions. In addition to the primary objective of equilibrating supply and demand, objectives for production and distribution have often motivated the policy for price formation.

In the decade before the 1965 reforms, and to some extent until now, the price system incorporated five administrative aspects: ceiling prices for a large list of raw materials and intermediate products; prior registration of price increases with the Federal Price Bureau thirty days in advance; control of wholesalers' trade margins by republics and retailers' trade margins by local authorities; temporary price freezes in exceptional circumstances; and, for agriculture, a system of minimum and guaranteed prices for staple food.[7] The measure most relied upon for price control was prior registration. But that measure still left a great leeway for significant price increases through product differentiation.[8] Until 1965 the most rigid price controls applied to raw materials and agricultural products.[9]

As part of the package of economic, financial, and fiscal reforms of 1965, the reform of the price system aimed to align domestic prices with world prices. It resulted in an overall price increase of about 30 percent. Prices of agricultural products rose 43 percent; prices of industrial products 14 percent. In industry, prices of final products increased by 8 percent; those of raw materials and semi-finished products, by 23 percent. Although the objectives were to approximate international relative prices and to allow subsequent price adjustments in response to changing market conditions, this second objective apparently was not vigorously pursued. Prices of many goods and services were again fixed, and a large proportion of producer and retail prices remained under various degrees of social control in subsequent years.[10] This was true for industrial products, major agricultural products, and the tariffs for railways, other transport services, and public utilities. Nevertheless enterprises were in-

---

7. Fixed prices were set for certain essential products, and ceiling prices were set for coal, petroleum, and metallurgical products, which were subject to infrequent but significant changes. Prices were frozen before the price reforms in 1952 and 1965 and at the end of 1971, when they were regarded to be excessive.

8. It has been reported that 25,000 new products were registered in 1964. See Branko Horvat, "Yugoslav Economic Policy in the Post-War Period: Problems, Ideas, Institutional Developments," *American Economic Review*, supplement to vol. 61, no. 3 (June 1971), pp. 71–161.

9. Price differentiation, the tariff structure, and administrative interventions were reported to have had a distorting effect on investment and production in branches having relatively depressed prices. Ibid., pp. 108–13.

10. The height of price liberalization is believed to have been reached in 1971, when producer prices for about 57 percent of industrial output and about 76 percent of commercial turnover were freed. See Dragutin V. Marsenic, "The Price System—Development and Problems," *Yugoslav Survey*, vol. 14, no. 3 (August 1973), pp. 141–54.

creasingly becoming involved in price formation. That involvement was achieved through direct mutual agreements among producers in interlinked production branches and through the associations in chambers of the economy.

There now are essentially four principles of price determination. Market forces determine liberalized prices, which apply to products that do not have a great impact on industrial production or the cost of living. Governments determine prices for some raw materials and intermediary goods by formulas based on international market conditions. Governments determine prices of certain essential goods and services, such as power and railway tariffs and rents, through direct price administration or the conclusion of social compacts. Producers and consumers at different interrelated production levels establish prices on the basis of self-management agreements. This fourth principle encompasses the majority of transactions and underlies the price system now evolving.[11]

Together with the reform objective of price liberalization, which minimizes the direct intervention of the state in price setting, sociopolitical communities were to influence levels of prices and demand through various economic measures, such as those associated with monetary, fiscal, income, and foreign trade policies. These policies in most cases were ineffective in controlling price increases and abating inflationary tendencies. Several other factors may also have contributed to this inability to effectively restrain the price spiral. First, a long-term development strategy for the system of price formation and the goals for stabilization were lacking. Second, the criteria to be applied to agreements on prices by enterprises or sociopolitical communities were insufficiently defined. Third, the ability of enterprises to pass forward price increases generally resulted in agreements that involved higher prices. Fourth, the practice of linking the taxes and contributions of enterprises to personal incomes translated into higher production costs and ultimately into higher prices. Fifth, the attempt to correct for price distortions through periodic but significant adjustments of administered prices, and through catching up by free prices, may have also precipitated the upward movement of all prices.

The success in halting inflation in 1976 nevertheless attests to the capacity of the system to deal effectively with price increases—

11. The new law on prices was still being prepared at the time of writing. Intensely debated, its final version may have a major effect.

once this objective is accorded high priority. As will be discussed below, the price policy has recently been broadened to encompass a broader institutional framework than price determination alone.

Fiscal policy

Decentralization and destatization affected the system of public finance.[12] The first involved the transfer of budgetary functions from the federation to lower sociopolitical communities. The second involved the transfer of some functions from the budgets of sociopolitical communities to public funds and then to self-managed communities of interest. The changing structure of budgetary and extrabudgetary resources indicates that the ability to manage demand, as reflected in budgets, declined (table 6.4). This was true

Table 6.4. *Structure of Budgetary and Extrabudgetary Receipts, 1966–75*
(percent)

Item	1966–70	1971–75
Total receipts	100.0	100.0
Budgetary receipts[a]	55.3	44.1
Receipts of communities of interest	29.7	44.6
Receipts of funds	14.9	11.2
Ratio of total receipts to gross material product	38.5	38.4

Source: Appendix table A.5.
a. Includes receipts for education up to 1971, which are included under the receipts of communities of interest for subsequent years.

despite the stable share of public resources in GMP over the 1966–75 period. An analysis of the outstanding characteristics of the present system of public finance further demonstrates the reduced discretionary power of the state and the reduced effectiveness of fiscal policy in influencing total domestic demand. Multiple institutions, stratified revenue sources, and inflexible budgetary expenditure characterize that system.

Under decentralization, there are thousands of fiscal and parafiscal institutions. Of total budgetary resources, the federal budget now accounts for about 60 percent, republican and provincial budgets for another 18 percent, and the more than 500 city and

12. In this volume the term *public finance* comprises all of the budgetary and extrabudgetary items appearing in table 6.4.

communal budgets for the remainder. Similar multiplicity applies to communities of interest. The 1974 constitution makes obligatory the establishment of self-managed communities of interest for social services: health, education, science, culture, and social welfare. Republics and provinces have enacted laws to regulate the establishment of these communities at the republican, provincial, and communal levels.

The system of taxes, contributing 90 percent of budgetary revenue, is the basic fiscal instrument (table 6.5). It essentially consists

Table 6.5. *Composition of Revenue in Consolidated Budgets of Sociopolitical Communities, 1974*
(percent)

Item	Total	Federation	Republics and provinces	Cities and communes
Total revenue	100.0	100.0	100.0	100.0
Current revenue	93.5	100.0	75.4	90.4
Tax revenue	89.1	95.7	69.7	87.0
Net income and profit taxes	11.1	—	21.6	33.9
Property taxes	1.7	—	—	8.1
General turnover and excise taxes	44.5	46.2	44.3	39.7
Customs duties	30.1	49.5	—	—
Other taxes	1.7	—	3.8	5.3
Nontax revenue	4.4	4.3	5.7	2.4
Subsidies	6.5	—	24.6	9.6
Total revenue (billions of dinars)	71.95	43.76	13.08	15.12

— Not applicable.
Source: Data supplied by the Federal Secretariat for Finance.

of customs duties, income taxes, and turnover taxes collected at different budgetary levels.[13] The basic sources of federal revenue are customs duties and contributions from republics and provinces, neither of which is prone to demand management. The tariff struc-

13. Income taxes comprise taxes on income of enterprises, the personal incomes of workers in the social sector, income from activities in the private sector, income from real estate, and so on.

ture is determined in accord with foreign trade policy, and receipts from customs duties basically are a function of imports. The contributions of republics and provinces to the federal budget—funded out of receipts from turnover and excise taxes—are fixed in advance and based on projections of GMP growth. It would be difficult to obtain additional contributions from this source because of the negotiations involved and the repercussions on the resources of sociopolitical communities. Income taxes are no longer collected at federal level. Taxes on enterprise income are the revenue of republics; taxes on personal incomes are increasingly being reduced from the republican and provincial budgets to communal budgets. The rates of personal income tax, essentially fixed at those lower levels and mainly based on considerations of revenue, are quite diverse. The rates for turnover taxes, constituted by federal, republican, provincial, and communal components, are fixed at the respective sociopolitical level. Uniformity is greater for the rates of turnover taxes than for the rates of income tax.

The composition of budgetary expenditure also indicates the budgetary inflexibility (table 6.6). For the federation, national defense and public administration account for about 50 percent of total expenditure; subsidies to support the lower level sociopolitical communities, for another 15 percent. Expenditure on interventions in the economy—that is, on subsidies to enterprises for prices that were fixed at levels too low to enable the recovery of costs—has accounted for about 20 to 25 percent of federal budgetary expenditure in recent years. Although implying some residual role in demand management, this expenditure is expected to be eliminated by provisions of the new law on the financing of the federation. For sociopolitical communities at lower levels, expenditure on administration accounts for 27 percent of republican and provincial expenditure and 55 percent of communal expenditures. The bulk of the remaining expenditure is in the form of grants for current and investment expenditure—grants that supplement the resources of communities of interest for social services in the less developed communes.

The potential for demand management through the budgets of self-managed communities of interest for social activities is almost nonexistent. Those budgets are basically financed by contributions levied on personal incomes and on the income of enterprises before distribution. Rates are agreed upon each year by the suppliers and users of services through mutual consultation at the assembly of the community. Although the contributions represent de facto taxes

Table 6.6. *Composition of Expenditure in Consolidated Budgets of Sociopolitical Communities, 1974*
(percent)

Item	Total	Federation	Republics and provinces	Cities and communes
Total expenditure	100.0	100.0	100.0	100.0
Current expenditure	62.5	58.9	54.8	80.8
Public administration	18.6	4.7	27.3	55.1
National defense	29.1	46.0	0.4	1.3
Social activities	13.3	8.2	27.1	16.8
Housing and communal activities	1.5	—	—	7.6
Investment	5.0	1.0	15.3	8.4
Nonproductive	3.9	1.0	9.2	8.2
Productive	1.1	—	6.0	0.2
Subsidies	29.0	38.1	26.0	2.9
Productive activities	14.6	23.3	—	—
Nonproductive activities	14.4	14.8	26.0	2.9
Other expenditure[a]	3.5	2.0	3.9	7.9
Total expenditure (billions of dinars)	72.50	45.35	12.91	14.24

— Not applicable.
Source: Same as for table 6.5.
a. Includes current budgetary reserves.

from the payer's point of view, there is little scope for anticyclical policy elements or demand management. The idea of communities of interests is that affected parties settle all financial matters directly with each other and in accord with possibilities and needs in the specified field. There nevertheless is increasing articulation of the need to keep the rise of contributions more in line with the financial potential of enterprises and the growth of the economy.

Income policy

Income policy in the Yugoslav economic system does not primarily aim, as the term seems to imply, at short-term management of the levels of personal income and personal consumption. Instead it aims at the manner in which the distribution of enterprise income between personal income and accumulation affects the longer-term saving rate of the economy.[14] Its outcome nevertheless affects the patterns of expenditure and stabilization. A principal objective of the 1965 economic reforms was to strengthen workers' control over income distribution, which is a cornerstone of the principles of workers' self-management. Under the same principles, however, the prerogative of individual workers is not absolute, but subject to a certain degree of social participation.[15] Society thus sets out some ground rules for income distribution through agreements on income policy. Because of the redistribution of enterprise income in favor of personal incomes after the 1965 reforms, the social regulation of income policy was somewhat tightened in the early 1970s to prevent the rate of enterprise saving from further decline.[16] Additional ground rules were recently laid down in the law on associated labor; social compacts and self-management agreements are to be concluded for more specific criteria.

Monetary policy

With the attenuation, compartmentalization, and rigidity of fiscal policy, and without a strong element of demand management in income policy, monetary policy has had to bear the burden of demand management. The National Bank of Yugoslavia (NBY) and the national banks of the republics and provinces—whose regionalized structure was formalized by a 1972 law—constitute the central banking system and carry out the traditional central banking functions: monetary management, issuing currency, regulating bank liquidity, managing foreign exchange, and lending to the federal government.[17] Monetary policy for a given year is defined in the

14. See chapter seven for details on the distribution of enterprise income.
15. This provision for social participation stems from the view that the success or failure of an enterprise is not exclusively the result of the contribution of the collective of workers, but that it also reflects social, economic, and historical factors beyond the control of the enterprise, such as its access to capital, market position, and level of technological development.
16. See chapter seven for an analysis of enterprise saving.
17. The governor of the NBY is chairman of the NBY's nine-man board of governors; governors of the republican and provincial national banks are the other members of that board.

annual resolutions; the NBY proposes monetary targets, which the Federal Assembly and the Federal Executive Council agree upon. The NBY and the national banks of the republics and provinces are responsible for policy implementation. The NBY relies on quarterly and annual flow-of-funds analyses to determine the increases in the volume of bank credits deemed necessary to realize the envisaged growth of money supply in a given period. The expansion of the money supply is in turn defined on the basis of the projected growth in real and nominal GMP and other variables determining the demand for money.

Yugoslavia has various instruments of monetary control: a legal minimum reserve ratio; an obligatory liquidity ratio; the purchase and sale of short-term securities and foreign exchange; the granting and rediscounting of credits to business banks; the exceptional specification of a ceiling on the expansion of credits by business banks; and political suasion.[18] Despite these instruments, the deviations between the projected and realized monetary expansion have in most years been large, resulting in higher inflation rates than foreseen. The inflexibility of monetary policy and its ineffectiveness in controlling total demand or checking price acceleration is better understood by analyzing the growth and major determinants of money supply.

The growth of money supply, which recorded an average increase of 29 percent during 1970–75 compared with 12 percent during 1965–70, demonstrates the rapid monetary expansion in recent years (table 6.7). There are three major determinants of money supply in Yugoslavia: short-term credits of business banks; money transferred to nonmonetary liabilities of business banks, mainly savings and obligatory deposits; and purchase or sale of foreign exchange by business banks.[19] The expansion of money supply in

18. Sociopolitical organizations constitute one series of levers for political suasion. Many managers of BOALS and enterprises and many of the elected functionaries of self-management belong to the LCY. Because of the principle of democratic centralism, they are bound to represent the positions adopted by the LCY. Sociopolitical communities also exert political leverage. The selection and renewal of terms of the senior managers of BOALS and enterprises require a vote of confidence by both the communal assembly and the local congress of the trade union. Those congresses see their mandate as extending beyond the representation of the interests of workers in organizations to general political considerations.

19. Business banks in Yugoslavia are active in commercial lending and investment. Under the latest legislative changes they are termed "basic banks."

Table 6.7. *Principal Determinants of Money Supply,*
1965, 1970, 1973, and 1975
(billions of dinars)

Item	End-year position			
	1965	*1970*	*1973*	*1975*
Short-term bank credits	39.1	73.4	294.7	456.8
Transfer of money to non-monetary liabilities of banks	−17.6	−34.3	−217.2	−310.7
Adding or withdrawing money for foreign exchange transactions	−1.8	−2.6	5.3	−8.3
Other	3.1	1.9	...	...
Money supply	22.8	38.4	82.8	137.8

... Zero or negligible.
Sources: NBY, various issues.

any given year thus depends on the relative magnitudes of factors causing additions or withdrawals of money.[20]

Credits granted by business banks are the basic channel for the creation of money. The capacity of business banks to expand such credits is a function of three factors: the volume of primary issues of money by the NBY and the national banks of the republics and provinces, the legal minimum reserve ratio and the other deposits of business banks held with national banks, and the net sale of foreign exchange by the NBY. Although all three in principle are subject to regulation by the national banking system, the increasing importance of the selective credit policy has constrained the effectiveness of credit and monetary policy in practice. Under this selective credit policy, the national banks channel credits to the business banks for financing certain priority activities, including agricultural production, export production, and the production and sale of domestic equipment. The obligation to fulfill the need for such financing nevertheless limits the downward flexibility of credits when there are surpluses in the balance of payments, as in 1972, 1973, and 1976, and when there is need for emergency credits to areas affected by natural disasters, as in 1970 for earthquakes and floods in Bosnia-Herzegovina and Serbia, or for greater financing of the federation, as in recent years.

20. See Dimitrije Dimitrijevic, "Money Supply, 1966–75," *Yugoslav Survey,* vol. 17, no. 3 (August 1976), pp. 87–90.

The transfer of money to nonmonetary deposits of more than one year's maturity and to other nonmonetary liabilities of business banks has been the main channel for withdrawing money. Despite the rapid growth of these withdrawals, they have been insufficient to neutralize the large expansion of credits in recent years. The balance-of-payments position has a negative impact on money supply when there is a deficit and money is withdrawn through the sale of foreign exchange by the business and national banks. That position has a positive impact when there is a surplus and money is added through the purchase of foreign exchange. The year-to-year variability of money supply therefore is sensitive to developments in foreign trade and exchange. For example, in years of unexpected surpluses, such as 1972 and 1973 as well as the second half of 1975 and 1976, the annual growth of money supply soared to 40 percent or more.

The NBY has tested the statistical relations between changes in money supply and changes in domestic demand and prices for the 1964–72 period. Results indicate that changes in money supply explained 55 percent of the same-month increase in fixed-asset investments and 43 percent of the same-month increase in total demand. For prices, same-month changes in money supply explained 27 percent of the rise of prices; with a time lag of fifteen months, changes in money supply explained 58 percent of price increases.[21] A clear association therefore appears to exist between increases in money supply on one hand and expanding domestic demand and rising prices on the other.

The New Legislative and Institutional Framework

A number of important laws, measures, and institutional changes were introduced during 1974–76 to ensure the greater financial discipline of enterprises and curb the excessive investment not supported by financial ability or market potential.

Two laws were enacted in mid-1975 to ensure that new investments are in accord with national and regional priorities and to avoid unjustified investments, financing shortfalls, and the duplication of facilities. One required prospective investors to register all new projects at the republican and provincial chambers of the

21. See Dimitrijevic, "Money Supply, 1966–75," p. 85.

economy and to supply evidence on the adequacy of financing arrangements. It also required prospective investors to register at the federal chamber all projects having a total cost exceeding Din30 million. Repealed in mid-1977, the law was an intermediary measure pending full implementation of the new planning system, which required the harmonization of all investment decisions. The second law, on the revaluation of fixed assets, provides for regular updating of the value of fixed assets on which the legal depreciation rate applies. This measure is to ensure that the accumulation of funds is sufficient for capital replacement.

The law on securing payments among users of public resources was enacted at the end of 1975. It has two basic purposes: dealing with the massive growth of interenterprise indebtedness, which perpetuates inefficiencies and enables the massive buildup of stocks; and encouraging the eventual liquidation of inefficient producers. That indebtedness amounted to Din263 billion at the end of 1975 and represented about 60 percent of social sector GMP for the year. The law provided for three phases of settlement of outstanding accounts. In contrast with earlier similar legislation, the law is being more strictly enforced. By the end of 1976, 600 enterprises were reportedly subjected to sanctions, and about 300 were undergoing liquidation; liquidated units are essentially integrated into more efficient enterprises.

The Federal Assembly adopted the law on income computation in 1976 to stop the practices of distributing personal incomes and initiating investment programs on the basis of partly fictitious income that arises from unmarketable production or uncollectable debts. The law sets out three requirements for establishing the income available for distribution: that goods be delivered and services be performed; that invoices be prepared; and that payments be made by legally accepted instruments, that is, by cash, check, or a guaranteed promissory note with a ninety-day maturity. Estimates indicate that by the end of 1976 more than a third of the payments were by promissory notes, which were increasingly being discounted by business banks and forming the foundation for money creation.

The high priority accorded to checking inflation in the annual economic resolutions for 1975 and 1976 was further codified and spelled out in social compacts on the implementation of price policy concluded by the federal government with the republican and provincial governments. The compact for 1975 set out in detail the margins for price increases allowable in 1975—margins that were to be lower than those of the previous year. The compact for 1976, unlike those for previous years, did not define bounds for permissible price increases, but it did express the firm determination to keep them significantly lower than those in 1975. The reason for not defining those bounds was to avoid their being taken as permissible benchmarks. The compact also spelled out the measures to secure sufficient supplies of essential products at relatively stable prices: the measures included imports, reserve stocking and sale in case of shortages, subsidies and bonuses, changes of turnover taxes and customs duties, and investment in retail trading and warehouse storage.

The Federal Assembly enacted a new law on the national banks in 1976 to sanction the regional decentralization of the national banking system. It introduced few changes in organization, instruments, or functions. The main substantive changes related to the liquidity business banks are to maintain and the criteria for issuing money. It also reduced the maximum legal reserve requirement from 30 percent to 25 percent. The expansion of money supply is to be more closely tied to the needs of the economy. The rediscounting of promissory notes issued by enterprises and discounted with business banks is gradually to replace selective credit expansion. Priorities in discounting will be for activities of special interest: export, agricultural production, the sale of domestic equipment, imports from developing countries, and financing commodity reserves. The social plan also emphasizes the objective of maintaining the growth of money supply within the agreed limits of monetary policy.

It has been argued that the trends associated with decentralization and destatization have left little scope for demand management through fiscal policy. Provisions in the social plan and annual resolutions call for the growth of budgetary expenditure (general consumption) at lower rates than the growth of GMP and for limiting the deficit financing of general social needs to the minimum possible. For expenditure on social services (collective consumption) the plan recommends a growth rate below that of GMP so as not to overburden the resources of enterprises. For taxation the plan envisages the use of tax exemptions as an incentive for promoting such activities as research, investments in less developed regions and priority sectors, and contractual associations of private producers. The taxes on property and other private sources of income are to be higher. In addition, a recent agreement on common elements of fiscal policy sets up the framework for better harmonization of tax structures. Within the decentralized framework of the public finance system, the residual role for demand management through fiscal policy is through turnover taxes. Global and selective variation of the rates of turnover tax is articulated as an instrument for affecting supply and demand conditions. But whereas selective changes could possibly affect the demand or supply of particular products, a global increase in rates could affect total demand only if the additional revenue generated does not translate into higher budgetary expenditure, or if a rise in other taxes to maintain local receipts does not compensate for a decline in revenue arising from lower rates.

Important institutional changes accompanied these laws and measures. The Federal Secretariat for Markets and Prices and the Federal Secretariat for Current Economic Movements have become more active in the stabilization effort and in laying down the foundation for more stable conditions for price formation. That involvement reflects the priority accorded to stabilization at the highest political levels.

The Federal Secretariat for Markets and Prices was set up in 1973. Its main function is to influence the market through indirect measures and only exceptionally through direct price-setting. An inspectorate in the secretariat has the function of following up and controlling the implementation of policies agreed upon. The secretariat assists enterprises by setting up criteria and mechanisms for price formation and by guarding against monopolistic and distortive practices. In this connection, it encourages mutual price agreements among producing, consuming, and trading entities which are backward and forward linked. These agreements aim, in addition, to insulate the economy against short-term fluctuations and ensure equitable income generation at various stages of interrelated production.

The Secretariat for Current Economic Movements was established in 1971 as a specialized unit of the Federal Executive Council. Its main duties are to follow up and assess short-term forecasts including surveys of business expectations. In carrying out its tasks, the secretariat has established strong links with economic institutes in the country and abroad. In its work on inflation and stabilization, the secretariat emphasizes the importance of nurturing social consciousness of the need to curb inflation. Through dialogues with associations of enterprises, it also seeks to break the propensity for price increases intended to maintain or even increase revenue in the face of rising costs. The secretariat, in association with the Federal Institute of Planning, is also responsible for preparing the annual resolutions. Starting in 1977 these resolutions set priorities for the actions of sociopolitical communities and enterprises in relation to the implementation of the five-year plan.

The new legislative and institutional measures, although unique in their combination, fall individually into patterns familiar in other countries. A less formal, but no less important element, has been introduced as well: political and social suasion. Whereas enterprises some years ago could in most cases get away with raising prices as long as they did not violate any laws or contracts, strong psychological barriers now inhibit such market behavior—barriers that were created after the LCY took a determined stand in 1974 against unjustified upward price adjustments and spiraling inflation.

Prospects for Stabilization

Given the decentralization of the fiscal system, demand management will continue to be a function of price, monetary, and income policies. As noted in the preceding section, the new legislative and institutional framework imposes greater financial discipline on enterprises through the laws on income computation and the financing of investment. That framework also provides for price and monetary policies that are more effective in pursuing the goal of stabilization without violating the principle of self-management.

For price policy the continued involvement of federal secretariats —in price formation, in following up and forecasting short-term trends, and in their dialogues with enterprises—is important for establishing social consciousness about the desirability of checking inflation and achieving more stable rates of growth. The social compact on prices is a principal instrument reflecting the political consensus on the price targets for a given year. The direct and indirect involvement of sociopolitical communities as cosigners of that compact is likely to remain important until the social awareness and the practice of greater price stability, as reflected in self-management agreements, is better embedded in the system.

For monetary policy the new provisions for using the promissory notes issued by enterprises as the basis and main instrument of money creation should link the increases in money supply to the growth of the economy. The impact of that policy on inflation, however, relates more to monetary expansion. As noted earlier, the monetary and credit targets for given quarters and years are worked out on the basis of sophisticated analysis and projections by the NBY, which has numerous instruments of monetary control. But the selective credit policy, the need for supplementing the federal budget and other financing, and the unexpected shifts in the balance of payments have often compromised objectives for the growth of money supply. Insofar as new laws provide for greater flexibility and discretion by the national banking system in monetary regulation, the control of the volume of credits of business banks is to assume greater importance. But if monetary expansion is to remain within target limits consistent with stabilization, the selective expansion of credit, based on discounting and rediscounting of promissory notes issued by enterprises, may under some circumstances have either to be restrained or to be used to replace other credits. Implementation of the new law on financing the federal budget would also limit the capacity of governments to finance deficits by increasing the money supply. There is, in addition, need for a mechanism to absorb excess liquidity associated with temporary surpluses in the balance of payments.

For income policy the new law on income computation establishes a sound and realistic foundation for determining the enterprise income that is available for distribution. The new law on the revaluation of fixed assets also assures more sufficient allowances for depreciation. For the allocation of enterprise income to personal incomes and accumulation, the social plan for 1976–80 calls for linking the growth of average personal incomes to the growth of average productivity. The details are to be worked out in social compacts at the republican and provincial levels and in self-management agreements by enterprises. As will be discussed in chapter seven, the new framework, once fully implemented, could broadly define the growth of personal incomes and the growth of consumption expenditure. Given the investment requirements for the plan period, it is important to maintain the growth of total demand in line with domestic production and a manageable deficit in the balance of trade.

In summary: political dedication and the strict enforcement of legislative and supportive measures in 1976 succeeded in containing inflation. This favorable outcome was nevertheless accompanied by such developments as rapid monetary expansion and the deviation between the growth of personal remuneration and real productivity. Both carry the danger of fueling further inflation. Data for 1977 indicate that GMP growth is higher, but they also reveal a higher price trend and a substantial deficit in the current account. There consequently are doubts about whether inflation has been permanently curbed. It appears likely, however, that the new measures will prevent recurrence of such excessive instability as that registered during 1973–75.

Seven

Resource Mobilization

THE DEVELOPMENT OF FINANCIAL SUPERSTRUCTURE in Yugoslavia reflects the institutional changes of the mid-1960s: the gradual disengagement of the state from the economy, especially from investment; the decentralization of the public finance system from the federal budget to regional sociopolitical communities and self-managed communities of interest; and the strengthening of self-management principles, whereby enterprises became the main decisionmakers for investment and income distribution. These changes had a definite effect on the growth of the financial system and the patterns of investment and financing.

Despite the rapid growth of gross savings and investment, there was some decline of their shares in GMP during the postreform period (table 7.1).[1] That decline was most noticeable in the years immediately following the reform. The reason is that a basic objective was to redistribute national income in favor of personal incomes so as to improve living standards and stimulate productivity. As a result, the share of net personal incomes in the GMP of the social sector rose from 30 percent in 1961–65 to 36 percent in 1966–70. The growth of personal and public consumption also surpassed the growth of GMP by about 10 percent between 1966 and 1970; it almost matched the growth of GMP after 1970 and led to some moderation of the saving rate, which nevertheless remained high by international standards (see table 6.1). When the saving performance in these periods is viewed in the framework of national accounts, the

---

1. Gross savings and gross investment, including that of the foreign sector, are equal. Consequently the sectoral imbalances become important for analysis.

Table 7.1. *Rates of Saving and Investment, 1961–75*
(percent)

Ratio	1961–65	1966–70	1971–75
Gross savings (and investment) to gross material product[a]	42.6	37.0	39.1
Gross national savings to gross national product	32.6	28.7	27.1
Gross domestic investment to gross national product	33.7	29.7	28.4
Foreign financing to gross national product	1.1	1.0	1.3
Gross savings (and investment) (billions of dinars)	109.7	223.5	649.8

Sources: NBY, *Annual Report*, various years; NBY, *Quarterly Bulletin*, July 1975 and July 1976; World Bank estimates.
a. Based on flow-of-funds accounts, which differ somewhat from national accounts, gross savings (and investment) includes the foreign sector. See appendix table A.6.

ratios of gross national savings (GNS) to GNP are consistently lower than the gross saving rates just mentioned.[2]

Four factors were most important in maintaining the national saving and investment rates from further slippage after the initial effects of income redistribution were felt in the postreform period: the rapid growth of workers' remittances and private foreign-exchange savings with Yugoslav banks; the measures taken in 1971–72 to tighten the income policy, which increased social sector savings; the somewhat greater reliance on foreign sources of financing; and the rapid monetary expansion, which accommodated extensive borrowing for short-term investment by enterprises and fueled in-

2. Reasons for those lower ratios are the following: GNS includes net factor income from abroad, but excludes foreign financing; the GNP base is broader than the GMP base because it includes an estimate of value added in nonproductive activities; the estimate of GNP entails an adjustment for inventory valuation, which for GMP biases the investment and saving rates upward by a factor equal to the inflation rate.
The analysis in this chapter essentially relies on four sets of data: the flow-of-funds accounts and other data published by the NBY in quarterly and annual reports; the national accounts and other data published by the Federal Institute of Statistics in annual statistical yearbooks; consolidated data on public finance prepared by the Federal Secretariat for Finance; and the social plan for 1976–80 and background data prepared by the Federal Institute of Planning. Because of differences of definitions, classifications, and adjustments, certain discrepancies arise for some aggregates. Use has therefore been made of each set of data wherever it contributed most to the analysis.

Table 7.2. *Gross Savings and Financial Savings,*
by Sector, 1961–75
(percent)

Sector	1961–65	1966–70	1971–75
	Gross savings		
Socialist enterprises	47.4	49.5	51.5
Federal government	−9.7	−2.1	−4.9
Other sociopolitical communities	8.4	5.7	4.3
Other social sector organizations	10.5	8.0	10.3
Investment loan funds	27.1	14.9	3.5
Households	9.5	25.7	31.2
Unclassified	4.3	−4.7	0.2
Rest of the world	2.5	3.0	3.9
Total	100.0	100.0	100.0
Total (billions of dinars)	109.7	223.5	649.8
	Financial savings		
Socialist enterprises	−71.3	−75.7	−75.6
Federal government	−28.3	−8.4	−24.4
Other sociopolitical communities	−0.4	4.3	0.4
Other social sector organizations	10.9	9.5	15.4
Investment loan funds	67.2	49.4	14.7
Households	5.0	26.6	53.2
Unclassified	10.8	−15.9	0.1
Rest of the world	6.1	10.2	16.2
Total	0.0	0.0	0.0
Total (billions of dinars)	44.2	67.6	155.5

Note: Financial savings are the difference between gross savings and gross
investment in fixed and working assets as recorded in the accounts of the Social
Accounting Service and as appear in the flow-of-funds accounts of the NBY.
Sources: Same as for table 7.1.

flationary pressure. That pressure eroded the purchasing power of
individuals and led to some forced saving.

As a result of the decentralization and destatization of the system,
the sectoral composition of savings and investment changed: enterprises and households assumed greater importance in resource mobilization; the importance of public investment funds correspondingly
declined (table 7.2).[3] These changes are particularly evident in sec-

3. The analysis here relies on flow-of-funds accounts, which give the necessary sectoral breakdown and are largely consistent for the entire period.

toral financial surpluses and deficits, which reflect the difference between the gross savings and investment of each sector and give rise to financial intermediation. Despite a large increase in financial savings, their ratio to gross savings considerably declined from 38.2 percent in 1961–65 to 30.2 percent in 1966–70 and 23.9 percent in 1971–75. This trend nevertheless is misleading as an indication of the need for financial intermediation: the dwindling role of public investment funds accounted for it, and those funds constituted intermediation only in a very narrow sense. The significant shift in the net financial position of sectors responsible for voluntary savings and investment better exemplifies the need for financial intermediation and the concomitant growth of the financial mechanism.

Social sector enterprises accounted for more than 50 percent of savings and about 70 percent of investment. They also accounted for about 75 percent of total financial deficits and were the major deficit sector. Because of the reduced fiscal burden on enterprises, a larger share of the income they generated was left at their disposal—a share manifested in the rise in their self-financing ratio in the postreform period.[4] A growing financial deficit nevertheless developed along with the large rise of investment. Coupled with the decline of direct financing of enterprises from budgetary and other public funds, this deficit increased the reliance of enterprises on funds channeled through the banking system from the surplus sectors, mainly households.

What about the other sectors? The significant sectoral decline of the federal government's financial deficit from 1961–65 to 1966–70 was reversed in 1971–75. This reversal was more the result of the budgetary constraints than of an expansion of investment activities. Regional governments, on the other hand, returned to balance in 1971–75, after realizing a modest financial surplus in 1966–70. As already mentioned, decentralization and destatization greatly diminished the role of public investment funds in the direct financing of enterprise investments.[5] Their combined financial surplus declined from 67 percent of total surpluses in 1961–65 to about 15 percent in

4. Enterprises were burdened less by taxes and by contributions to budgets and public investment funds. On the basis of flow-of-funds data, the ratio of gross savings to gross investment of enterprises increased from an average of 58 percent in 1961–65 to 72 percent in 1966–75.

5. After 1966 the principal public funds remaining were the Federal Fund, similar funds for the regional development of republics and provinces, a fund for financing and insuring exports, joint reserve funds of enterprises, and the resources of sociopolitical communities earmarked for productive investment.

1971–75. The financial position of other social sector organizations, remained almost stable, accounting for 10 to 15 percent of total surpluses.[6] The increased financial surpluses of the rest-of-the-world sector reflected a somewhat higher reliance on external financing. The change for the household sector, which includes private producers, was most significant: its financial surplus rose from 5 percent of the total in 1961–65 to more than 50 percent in 1971–75. This dichotomy between financial deficits of social sector enterprises and savings by households increased the need for financial intermediation and spurred the rapid development of the financial system.

Financial Institutions

The financial sector of Yugoslavia comprises the NBY, the national banks of republics and provinces, business banks, savings institutions, investment funds, and insurance institutions. Banks conduct both commercial and investment activities; savings institutions basically collect post office savings, which then are deposited with business banks. As noted earlier, the decentralization of decision-making, the redistribution of income, and the concomitant rise in the share of autonomous savings by nonstate units all shifted the emphasis in the financial sector from public investment funds to banks. Measures associated with the reform involved the transfer of a large proportion of assets of these and other funds, such as that for housing, to banks; the increasing complexity of the economy and expansion of branch networks led to a multiplication of bank assets. On a consolidated basis net of transactions within the financial sector, the share in GMP of the assets of financial institutions increased from 136 percent in 1965 to 149 percent in 1970 and then declined to 123 percent in 1975.

The banking system has passed through various stages of dispersion and integration; it now accounts for almost 65 percent of the assets of financial institutions. Under socialist self-management principles, banks are not independent profit-making institutions; nor are they instruments of state organs. Instead they are to form an integral part of the economy and service its financial needs. Whereas major head-

---

6. These organizations include self-managed communities of interest—except those for education, which are grouped in the sector of other sociopolitical communities—as well as such organizations in nonproductive activities as banks and insurance institutions.

way was made after 1965 in enlarging the base for financial intermediation, some shortcomings have either persisted or emerged to
limit the efficiency of the banking system. Recent laws concerning
the role and activities of banks are still being implemented. They
tend to correct for past deficiencies, but are intended more to mini-
mize "anonymous financial capital," by strongly encouraging depositors to earmark deposits for specific purposes and recipients, and
to reduce the financial autonomy of banks.

Business banks

The 1965 and 1971 laws on banking and credit altered the structure of business banks and broadened their functions in investment
and financial intermediation. Those laws encouraged the integration
of commercial banks and abolished the territorial limitation on their
activities.[7] The laws also strengthened the role of enterprises in the
management of banks to rectify the earlier predominance of political
and administrative influences. As the system developed, business
banks operated as mixed banks performing all investment and commercial banking functions. The earlier differentiation between short-
term and long-term operations in separate balance sheets was
eliminated; banks were allowed to transform the term structure of
their resources, subject to the maintenance of legal reserve requirements.[8]

Most founding organizations were large net borrowers, and their
interests dominated the policy of business banks. This had two major
consequences. First, with enterprises as the major deficit sector and
with no representation of nonenterprise depositors, the policy of
banks was biased in favor of borrowers. The objective of banks was
regarded to be "the maximization of lending at the lowest possible
cost." Because the interest-rate structure remained rather inflexible,
real rates became significantly negative in years of high inflation.[9]

7. The number of independent banks gradually declined from 225 (with
405 branches) at the end of 1965 to 36 (with 900 offices) in 1975. Although
the most recent law on banking envisions some restructuring of business banks
along functional lines, the fragmentation of the banking system is unlikely.
8. Legal reserve requirements were differentiated by the term. In 1971 the
legal maximum on sight deposits was reduced from 35 percent to 30 percent;
the rate on savings deposits was maintained at 3 percent.
9. Interest rates were outside the domain of credit and monetary policies
and not subject to the approval of the national bank. The national bank inter-
vened only in the determination of rates to be charged on its credits to business banks. Selective credits and other credits out of primary issues, except
those for bank illiquidity, were generally granted at concessional terms.

This pattern possibly encouraged the demand for credits and discouraged greater financial savings. Second, although the 1965 banking law eliminated statutory territorial limitations on banks' operations, the constituencies and operations of business banks generally remained regional. One implication of this regionalization was that founders, belonging to a given region, often were susceptible to pressure from local sociopolitical communities. That pressure constrained the development of a fully consistent credit program and the scrutiny of credit requests on the basis of economic criteria. Another implication was that banks tended to operate within regional boundaries, thus hampering the interregional mobility of financial resources.

The effectiveness of business banks in mobilizing resources and satisfying the demands for credits can be gleaned from the trends of their balance sheets (table 7.3). For liabilities the banks clearly were

Table 7.3. *Structure of Resources of Business Banks at Year-end, 1965, 1970, and 1975*
(percent)

Item	1965	1970	1975
Short-term liabilities	33.3	39.0	51.1
Gold and foreign exchange	1.5	4.7	8.8
Short-term deposits	18.6	21.8	30.5
Credits from national banks	12.2	10.4	5.0
Credits from business banks and other short-term credits	1.1	2.1	6.8
Long-term liabilities	66.7	61.0	48.9
Gold and foreign exchange	—[a]	2.8	8.3
Time deposits	2.7	13.1	8.8
Credits from sociopolitical communities	25.9	19.9	15.1
Resources for financing housing and communal activities	...	9.3	7.2
Credits from banks[b]	7.2	5.2	4.4
Bank funds[c]	30.9	10.7	5.1
Total resources (billions of dinars)	120.7	191.8	491.7

... Zero or negligible.
Sources: NBY, *Annual Report*, various years.
a. Included under short-term liabilities.
b. Excludes resources transferred for the permanent use of enterprises and sociopolitical communities.
c. Includes founders' funds, reserve funds, and other bank funds.

less successful in mobilizing long-term resources than short-term resources, especially in the first half of the 1970s. The exception was foreign exchange savings, which earn a relatively high rate of interest, are denominated in foreign currencies, and thus provide a hedge against domestic inflation. The core of investment resources, 31 percent of total resources in 1965, initially provided through the contribution to bank funds thus was not subsequently maintained through an increase of other long-term resources. Credits from sociopolitical communities also accounted for a declining, though still significant, share of the banks' long-term resources. That share reflected their residual leverage on bank policy. Demand deposits, essentially held by enterprises, increasingly accounted for the bulk of short-term resources. Although the rapid growth of those deposits reflected the spread of banking habits and financial intermediation, the practice of holding deposits as a condition for borrowing was another factor in that growth. For assets the increase in the share of short-term assets between 1965 and 1975 was similarly notable, mainly because of the increase in short-term credits to enterprises (table 7.4).[10] Investment in social sector housing and communal activities, the resources for which were initially transferred from various funds in 1966, maintained a constant share of about 10 percent.

Although a breakdown of bank credits shows that the enterprises consistently accounted for the largest share of credit expansion, business banks were unable to satisfy the demand for credits (table 7.5). The magnitude of the problem of liquidity is illustrated by the massive buildup of interenterprise indebtedness in trade credits, which were largely involuntary because payment obligations were not met. The total value of those credits increased from Din25 billion in 1965, when they accounted for 24 percent of the financial instruments of nonfinancial sectors, to Din263 billion in 1975, when they accounted for almost 40 percent. In 1975 trade credits were equivalent to almost 62 percent of the social product and 25 percent of the gross value of production in the social sector.

Lacking internally mobilized resources, the banking system tried to meet these needs with credits extended by national banks. Although the regulation of money supply was the main preoccupation of the national banking system, the selective provision of credit to

10. The conversion of credit terms in the first half of the 1970s somewhat blurs the comparison of trends for short-term and long-term assets.

Table 7.4. *Structure of Assets of Business Banks at Year-end, 1965, 1970, and 1975*
(percent)

Item	1965	1970	1975
Short-term assets	27.9	37.0	43.6
Gold and foreign exchange	1.4	1.5	3.5
Short-term credits	17.2	27.0	26.9
Deposits with national banks	8.6	6.9	7.3
Other short-term claims	0.7	1.6	5.9
Long-term assets	72.1	63.0	56.4
Gold and foreign exchange	—a	1.8	3.8
Long-term credits to clients	44.7	43.5	38.4
Claims on Yugoslav banks	25.7	3.5	2.3
Investment in housing and communal activities	...	10.9	9.9
Other long-term assets	1.7	3.3	2.0
Total assets (billions of dinars)	120.7	191.8	491.7

... Zero or negligible.
Sources: NBY, *Annual Report*, various years.
a. Included under short-term assets.

business banks—for financing certain activities in agriculture and export production—assumed almost equal importance. Because the achievement of the second objective often frustrated the goal of stabilization by limiting the effectiveness of monetary policy, national banks were more active in the financing of enterprises than is conventional.

To reduce the debt burden of enterprises and enhance their self-financing ability, laws were passed to transform the credit structure

Table 7.5 *Distribution of Bank Credits at Year-end, by Sector, 1970 and 1975*
(percent)

Sector	1970	1975
Socialist enterprises	78.0	78.8
Federal government	8.4	9.0
Other social sector organizations	5.9	5.7
Households	7.7	8.5
Total (billions of dinars)	31.8	96.8

Source: Appendix table A.7.

by converting Din25.6 billion in 1971 and 1973 from short-term to long-term credits at very concessional terms. The conversions first involved the credit relations between the NBY and business banks, then the relations between business banks and enterprises. The national banks of republics and provinces converted additional amounts.[11] In 1974 credits of Din26.6 billion and Din19.4 billion were respectively transferred to the permanent resources of enterprises and sociopolitical communities and used by enterprises to finance priority projects in their territories. In line with the antistatist position that sociopolitical communities should refrain from any role in productive activities, these resources were eventually ceded to enterprises for their permanent use.

Other financial intermediaries

The importance of public investment funds, as mentioned earlier, gradually declined: the general investment funds and other funds were abolished; the contributions that alimented these funds were reduced and finally discontinued in 1971. Nevertheless the remaining federal and republican investment funds are important for their designated purposes: accelerating the development of less developed regions in the federation and of less developed communes in the regions. Social sector enterprises in all republics and provinces finance the Federal Fund by making obligatory loans from their undistributed profits. The loans total about 2 percent of the value added in each republic and are distributed to the less developed regions on the basis of agreed-upon shares. Since the 1965 reforms, public investment funds have become media for collecting and channeling resources, not bodies for decisionmaking. About 50 percent of their resources were channeled through business banks in 1975, compared with 8.4 percent in 1962 (table 7.6). Their share in the assets of financial institutions also declined to about 16 percent on an aggregate basis and 8 percent on a consolidated basis.

Insurance institutions remained unimportant in view of the comprehensive social insurance for pensions, health, unemployment, and child welfare. Although their assets almost doubled in recent years, they still account for only about 3 percent of the assets of financial institutions. Bank deposits are about the only option they have for

11. See Radoslav Vuksanovic, "Credit and Monetary Trends, 1969–73," *Yugoslav Survey*, vol. 15, no. 2 (May 1974), pp. 41–54.

Table 7.6. *Balance Sheet of Investment Loan Funds
at Year-end, Selected Years, 1962–75*
(percent)

Item	1962	1965	1970	1975
Credits to socialist enterprises	47.2	28.5	33.5	31.3
Credits to banks	8.4	17.3	44.8	53.7
Other investments[a]	44.4	54.2	21.7	15.0
Resources of the federation	33.3	5.0	45.3	8.7
Resources of the Federal Fund	—	5.6	11.0	20.9
Resources of other sociopolitical communities	22.2	82.7	25.3	58.0
Fund for export financing and insurance	—	—	2.1	5.4
Other liabilities[b]	44.5	6.7	16.3	7.0

— Not applicable.
Sources: NBY, *Annual Report*, various years.
a. Includes claims on banks for commissioned transactions.
b. Resources for commissioned transactions.

investing their resources. Because the social security system in Yugoslavia is based on balancing disbursements and receipts, which accrue to communities of interest from contributions levied on personal and net enterprise income, surpluses arise only accidentally. It thus does not constitute an intermediary for savings.

The 1971 and 1972 laws on securities expanded the scope for sociopolitical communities, communities of interest, enterprises, and other social sector organizations to issue bonds denominated in dinars and foreign currencies. Nevertheless the most prevalent issues were bonds having maturities of one to two years to finance the deficit in the federal budget. Between 1961 and 1975 the bond issues denominated in dinars totaled Din24 billion; of these bonds 23 percent were for investment. The major issues for investment were for highways, power plants, the port of Bar, the Belgrade-Bar railway, and the reconstruction of Skopje after the 1963 earthquake. Returns were about equal to those paid on bank deposits of comparable term. Because their issue was usually accompanied by high-level political campaigns, they were fully subscribed by individuals and social sector entities. Only two bond issues were denominated in foreign currencies between 1961 and 1975: one for DM15 million in 1970 by a factory producing motors and tractors; the other for US$50 million in 1975 by NBY on behalf of the federation.

Enterprise Savings

The decisions of social sector enterprises and BOALS on the net income available for distribution and its distribution between personal incomes and accumulation are major determinants of the resources mobilized in Yugoslavia. (Recall that enterprises account for about 70 percent of investment and 50 percent of savings.) Enterprise income is computed and distributed at three levels: primary, secondary, and tertiary (table 7.7).

Primary distribution refers to the determination of enterprise income on the basis of prevailing prices.[12] For given production conditions, sales and input prices and principles of income computation determine the total revenue and material costs of enterprises. To the extent that the self-management agreements on transfer prices and the administrative intervention in price-setting or self-management agreements have affected the sales revenue and material costs of various organizations, they have also affected the income and ultimately the savings potential of those organizations. Legal depreciation is deducted as part of primary income distribution: to safeguard social capital from being consumed in production, a statutory minimum depreciation rate applies to the year-end value of the enterprises stock of fixed assets. Secondary distribution refers to the distribution of income between the enterprise or BOAL and society—that is, the proportion of enterprise income that goes to taxes, contributions, and legal and contractual obligations. It thus determines the fiscal and parafiscal burden on enterprise income and the share of income available for tertiary distribution. It also determines the resources of sociopolitical communities and communities of interest. Tertiary distribution refers to internal distribution of the residual—that is, the division of net enterprise income into personal incomes and accumulation, which is a proxy for net enterprise savings. Decisionmaking at this level of distribution is in the realm of what frequently is referred to as income policy.

In the Yugoslav framework of social ownership of the means of production, the principle has generally been upheld that the capital resources entrusted to enterprises must be conserved and increased for "extended reproduction," that is, net investment. There thus

12. The new law on prices was still being prepared at the time of writing.

Table 7.7. *Scheme for the Computation and Distribution of Enterprise Income*

Level of distribution	Computation	Composition or definition
Primary	ENTER Gross income	Calculated according to the new law on income computation on the basis of realized income—that is, sales for which payment has been made in cash or by promissory note.
	MINUS Material and other production costs	
	EQUALS Gross value added	Also referred to as social product or GMP, it represents the gross value added in commodity production and in productive services—that is, it is comparable to GNP less the value added in housing, social and financial services, and public administration.
	MINUS Depreciation	Allocations for depreciation of enterprise fixed assets; the legal minimum rate applied to the year-end value of fixed assets. Enterprises are free to allocate more of their net income for depreciation, but allowances above the legal requirements as a rule are not exempt from taxation.
Secondary	EQUALS Enterprise income	
	MINUS Contractual obligations	Payments for banking services, interest on loans, insurance premiums, membership dues, and other similar obligations.
	MINUS Statutory and legal obligations	Turnover taxes, contributions to communities of interest for social services decreed by law, contributions to communal activities for water and roads, and other statutory obligations.

Table 7.7 (*continued*)

Level of distri- bution	Computation	Composition or definition
Tertiary	EQUALS Net enterprise income	
	DISTRIBUTE TO	
	Taxes on personal income	Withheld from gross personal income
	Net personal incomes	Take-home pay of workers after deduction of personal income taxes. In principle, monthly payments to workers are made as advances, and quarterly and yearly adjustments correct for actual work conditions and receipts.
	Contributions on account of personal income	Payments made to social service communities of interest levied on the basis of personal income. As a rule these contributions are proportional and collected at the source.
	AND TO	
	Reserve funds	An enterprise reserve fund is to ensure liquidity and a joint reserve fund at the level of the republic is to ensure the maintenance of minimum personal incomes. Contributions to these funds are set by law at a certain percentage of enterprise income.
	Business funds	The amount enterprises set aside to build up financial assets (quasi equity) under their permanent control.
	Collective consumption funds	Allocations for additional benefits to the work collective of enterprises—contributions for housing funds, day care centers, recreation, and nutrition are examples.

Source: Adapted from official documents.

are two aspects to accumulation: one is to ensure the replacement of social capital; the other is to realize an adequate return on capital. Statutory minimum depreciation, to which enterprises may add, takes care of the first. The second has proven more difficult to specify, and various direct and indirect solutions have been sought. In prereform years enterprises were charged a tax on the amount of social capital they used at a rate of 6 percent for the use of social capital. Reduced to 4 percent in 1965, this rate was finally abolished in 1971.[13] In postreform years the net accumulation has been largely determined as a residual after the allocations made to personal incomes. That determination has been in accord with the changing rules of the income policy, as regulated by social compacts and self-management agreements. To allow some differentiation by labor skill and productivity and at the same time to avoid unjustified allocations to workers for the higher productivity associated with greater capital-intensity, the income policy incorporated a complex adjustment system. The basis for total personal incomes paid out by enterprises was "net enterprise income per standardized worker."[14] Enterprises realizing higher net income per standardized worker could pay higher average personal incomes, but were required to allocate a greater part of their net income to accumulation. Although seemingly rigorous, the system still allowed enterprises scope for maneuvering through skill definition.

As a result of the reduced fiscal burden on enterprises, the proportion of GMP at their disposal was higher after the reform than before it: 61 percent for 1966–75, compared with 54 percent for 1960–65. This increase enabled the realization of higher personal incomes and greater accumulation. Allocations to personal incomes increased somewhat more than total net income immediately after the reform; the ratio of gross enterprise savings to their GMP declined from 29 percent in 1966 to 21 percent in 1969 (see appendix table A.9). In an effort to prevent further slippage of the saving rate in the early 1970s, the republics and provinces concluded vari-

13. Proceeds from interest payments and repayments of principal were fed into the federal General Investment Fund. For details see Branko Horvat, *The Yugoslav Economic System* (White Plains, N.Y.: International Arts and Sciences Press, 1977), pp. 218–24.

14. The standardized work force of an enterprise was determined by first reducing each skill category into equivalent units of unskilled labor on the basis of skill coefficients and then aggregating those units. See Vinod Dubey and others, *Yugoslavia: Development with Decentralization* (Baltimore: Johns Hopkins University Press for the World Bank, 1975), pp. 237–39.

ous compacts to establish a more appropriate ratio for distribution
to personal incomes and net accumulation. The share in GMP of
gross enterprise savings subsequently rose; that of net personal incomes accordingly declined (table 7.8). With the increasing emphasis on the right of self-managed BOALS and enterprises to decide
on income distribution, the income policy became less rigorous,
although not necessarily less effective, than when initially introduced.
The gross saving rates in table 7.8 exaggerate the voluntary and

Table 7.8. *Distribution of Gross Material Product
of Economic Organizations
in the Social Sector, 1966–75*
(percent of GMP)

Item	1966–70	1971–75
Social product[a]	100.0	100.0
Depreciation	10.4	11.3
Net social product	89.6	88.7
Fiscal and parafiscal contributions	39.6	39.0
Net personal incomes	36.2	34.7
Allocations to fund	14.0	15.0
Residual enterprise income[b]	60.5	61.0
Gross enterprise savings[c]	24.3	26.3
Inventory valuation adjustment	4.4	9.6
Adjusted gross savings[d]	20.8	18.4

Source: Calculated from appendix table A.9.
a. Gross value added or GMP for productive activities.
b. Equal to depreciation, net personal incomes, and allocations to funds.
c. Equal to depreciation and allocations to funds.
d. Adjusted for inventory overvaluation.

actual saving performance of enterprises on two counts. First, the
gross saving rate was kept from proportional decline—especially
in the early postreform years—by statutory depreciation and the
periodic revaluation of fixed assets.[15] The net accumulation of many
enterprises probably was negligible or negative. Second, the gross
saving rates inflate actual savings because of the overvaluation of

15. Before the new law on the revaluation of fixed assets became effective
in 1976, fixed assets were revalued every five years; the last time was in 1971.
Between 1972 and 1975 depreciation was computed by adjusting the unadjusted
book values of 1971 for inflation in the intervening years.

inventories. When corrected for this factor, the adjusted gross saving rates are lower.[16]

A similar complication arises for investment: a large part of the increase in total investment was a reflection of the buildup of overvalued inventories. The ratio of investment in inventories to total investment rose from 24 percent in 1966–70 to 35 percent in 1971–75. Those ratios are significantly lower when adjusted for overevaluation. Compared with the earlier period, depreciation allowances covered a higher proportion of gross investment in fixed assets during 1971–75; net investment, or capacity expansion, accounted for a correspondingly smaller share. Adjusting savings and investment for inventory overvaluations, and notwithstanding significant year-to-year variations, the self-financing rate of enterprises also was slightly lower in the later years (table 7.9).

To meet their financial deficits—that is, the balances between gross savings and the expenditure on investment—enterprises primarily relied on credits from business banks. As table 7.5 shows, the enterprise sector accounted for 77 percent of credits outstanding at the end of 1975. The higher share of their short-term borrowing is consistent with their higher investment in working assets and their repeated problems of illiquidity. These shares nevertheless understate the true proportions because of the credit conversion. This heavy reliance on business banks for financing explains both the importance of banks as financial intermediaries and the new legal and institutional arrangements to reduce their autonomy.

Household Savings

As noted earlier, the household sector in the postreform period became increasingly important in resource mobilization, especially in generating surpluses of financial savings. The share of households in gross savings increased from about 10 percent in 1961–65 to 26 percent in 1966–70 and 31 percent in 1971–75. The increase in the share of households in financial savings from 5 percent in 1961–65 to

---

16. In Yugoslav statistics, inventories are valued at year-end prices. Under the inflationary conditions and stockpiling in the first half of the 1970s, the method inflated the value of investment in working assets and consequently the figures for investment and savings. The adjustment made by World Bank staff essentially corrects the inventory valuation by the difference between year-end and midyear prices. See appendix tables A.8 and A.9.

Table 7.9. *Gross Investment in Productive Activities
and Self-financing Rate of Economic Organizations
in the Social Sector, 1966–75*
(billions of dinars)

Item	1966–70	1971–75
Total investment in fixed assets	125.0	320.3
Depreciation[a]	49.6	156.7
Net investment in fixed assets	75.3	163.6
Inventory		
Unadjusted	40.0	171.3
Adjusted[b]	17.9	41.7
Total investment in fixed and working assets		
Unadjusted	165.1	491.6
Adjusted[b]	142.9	362.0
Adjusted gross savings	95.5	231.1
Self-financing rate[c] (percent)	66.8	63.8

Sources: Federal Institute of Statistics, *Statistical Yearbook of Yugoslavia,* various years.
   a. The distinction between depreciation and net investment is not clear-cut. The reason is that enterprises can take allowances higher than the legal minimum when they replace capital with more advanced technology to improve the capacity and quality of production.
   b. Adjusted for inventory overvaluation.
   c. The ratio of adjusted gross savings to adjusted gross investment.

53 percent in 1971–75 further demonstrates the significance of that sector's financial position. Those savings could be channeled to investments by the deficit sectors, mainly enterprises (see table 7.2).

   In accord with objectives for the distribution of income in the postreform years, household receipts increased at a faster rate than GMP in 1966–70 and at a comparable rate after 1970 (table 7.10). The growth of transfer receipts exceeded the growth of personal income receipts. The share of transfers greatly increased after 1970, largely because of the rising share of foreign exchange remittances by Yugoslav workers employed abroad. Receipts from this source rose from less than Din1 billion in 1965 to Din30 billion in 1975. Concomitant with these developments, the household saving rate, or average propensity to save out of total receipts, rose from about 15 percent in 1966–70 to 18 percent in 1971–75 (table 7.11). Physical

Table 7.10. *Household Receipts, 1966–75*
(percent)

Item	1966–70	1971–75
Nominal growth rate of gross material product	15	26
Growth rate of household receipts	18	26
Composition of household receipts		
Personal incomes from work	81	73
Transfers and other receipts	19	27
Transfers from abroad	4	10

Sources: Statistical Yearbook of Yugoslavia, various years; NBY, *Annual Report*, various issues.

investment, basically in housing by individuals and equipment by private producers, accounted for the largest share of gross savings over the entire period, but that share declined in 1971–75. The rising preference for financial savings and investment was consistent with the trend of rising foreign exchange savings, which earn relatively high interest rates and which holders prefer to dinar-denominated deposits.

Table 7.11. *Household Savings and Investment, 1966–75*
(percent)

Ratio	1966–70	1971–75
Gross savings to total receipts	14.5	18.3
Gross dinar savings to total receipts	13.4	14.6
Gross foreign exchange savings to total receipts	1.1	3.7
Gross investment to gross savings	68.3	59.1
Financial savings to total receipts	4.6	7.5
Financial savings to gross savings	31.5	40.8

Sources: NBY, *Annual Report*, various years; NBY, *Quarterly Bulletin*, various issues.

The financial return on different household assets—that is, the interest rates paid on various deposits—remained inflexible in the face of mounting inflation.[17] This inflexibility resulted in negative

17. The members of the Association of Yugoslav Banks agree upon the interest rate for dinar deposits; the rate for long-term deposits is 10 percent. The policy of business banks has been to maintain the same rates even under inflationary conditions.

real interest rates on dinar savings in the first half of the 1970s. There nevertheless was growth and change in the portfolio of household financial savings: the ratio of savings held in cash declined; the dinar assets held with banks—representing the difference between sight, savings, and time deposits and consumer credits from banks and enterprises for the sale of goods—increased. Four factors accounted for these developments: the expansion of the banking network; the growing practice of paying personal incomes and remuneration for services into current and savings accounts with banks; the practice of banks to grant consumer credits to customers holding deposits with them; and the volume of consumer credits allowed under the credit policies in different years.[18] Another notable trend was the more than doubling of the share of foreign exchange deposits (table 7.12). Interest of up to 12 percent is paid

Table 7.12. *Portfolio of Household Financial Savings, 1966–75*
(percent)

Item	1966–70	1971–75
Money: currency and demand deposits	54.0	32.8
Net position of dinar assets	9.5	13.8
Net position of foreign exchange assets held with Yugoslav banks	17.0	38.1
Net position of foreign exchange assets held with foreign banks	19.5	15.3

Sources: Same as for table 7.11.

on these deposits in foreign exchange, providing a hedge against domestic inflation and guaranteeing liquidity and transferability. The growth of remittances and the efforts to mobilize foreign exchange savings were therefore important in raising the savings of households and sustaining the national saving rate over the decade.

Resource Mobilization under the Social Plan for 1976–80

As noted in chapter six, the rates of saving and output growth in Yugoslavia have been relatively high by international standards. The twin objectives of growth and stabilization and the constraints

---

18. See Radoslav Vuksanovic and Miodrag Nikolic, "Monetary Assets and Credits of Households, 1970–73," *Yugoslav Survey*, vol. 16, no. 1 (February 1975), pp. 129–36.

on foreign borrowing nevertheless underscore the need for successful domestic resource mobilization, According to the current plan,
social product is to grow at the average annual rate of 6.9 percent
a year in 1976–80, compared with 5.9 percent a year in the previous
plan period; the share of foreign borrowing in total resources is to
remain constant at 3.5 percent (table 7.13). Investment is projected to grow at a faster rate than personal and general consumption; the share of investment in productive activities is to record
the fastest growth. These targets have two major, and interdependent, implications. First, given the unchanged rate of net foreign

Table 7.13. *Formation and Distribution of Total Resources,*
1971–75 and Projections for 1976–80

Item	Cumulative resources (billions of dinars)		Average annual rate of growth (percent)		Structure (percent)	
	1971–75	1976–80	1971–75	1976–80	1971–75	1976–80
Available resources						
Total resources	2,448.4	3,328.0	5.7	6.5	100.0	100.0
Social product	2,366.4	3,207.0	3.6	6.9	96.6	96.4
Balance of foreign transactions	82.0	121.0	—	—	3.4	3.6
Uses of resources						
Standard of living[a]	1,624.6	2,135.1	5.7	6.3	66.4	64.2
Personal consumption	1,268.4	1,643.2	5.3	6.0	51.8	49.4
Social standard	356.2	491.9	7.1	7.2	14.6	14.8
Nonproductive investment	269.8	385.5	8.4	7.5	11.0	11.6
General consumption[b]	146.0	189.9	5.0	6.0	6.0	5.7
Productive investment	589.2	860.3	6.0	7.5	24.1	25.9
Fixed assets	404.7	608.0	6.2	8.5	16.5	18.3
Working assets	184.5	252.3	5.4	5.0	7.6	7.6
Increase in re- serves and other	88.6	142.7	—	—	3.5	4.3

Source: Reconstructed from various tables in Federal Institute of Planning,
"Analytical Basis for the Documents of the Social Plan of Yugoslavia for the
1976–80 Period" (Belgrade, 1976; processed).
— Not applicable.
a. Includes nonproductive investment.
b. Current expenditure of state organizations.

borrowing, the domestic saving rate has to be stepped up if the higher gross investment rate—42 percent compared with 39 percent during the preceding plan period—is to be realized during 1976–80. Second, the growth rates of investment and GMP have to be sufficiently high to generate the targeted employment growth of 3.5 percent a year and allow for some increase in average real personal incomes without impairing the saving rate.

According to the plan, the direct financing of investments by enterprises and households will further increase; that of nonproductive organizations in the social sector, mainly communities of interest and sociopolitical communities, will significantly decline (table 7.14). The share of foreign financing will remain about the same.

Table 7.14. *Direct Financing of Investment, by Sector, 1971–75 and Projections for 1976–80*
(percent)

Item	1971–75	1976–80
Total resources for investment by social and private sectors in fixed and working assets	100.0	100.0
Enterprises	56.3	58.2
Depreciation allowances	22.3	23.0
Business fund	26.0	27.4
Housing and other	8.0	7.8
Nonproductive organizations in the social sector	14.3	9.2
Households	20.0	23.0
Foreign financing	9.4	9.6

Note: Figures in this table relate more to the structure of investment and are not strictly comparable to those in table 7.2; they nevertheless are illustrative.
Source: Same as for table 7.13.

Prospects for enterprise savings

The social plan for 1976–80 and the new legislative and institutional setup are to provide the framework for ensuring that enterprise savings are sufficient. In that framework the saving rate of enterprises could be increased in three basic ways: reducing fiscal and parafiscal burdens; increasing the allocation for the depreciation of fixed assets; and raising, within socially acceptable bounds, the rate of net accumulation.

Despite continuing reference to the need for reducing the burden of public finance, the share in GMP of the revenue of budgets, communities of interest, and public funds remained almost stable at about 38 percent during 1965–75. The social plan for 1976–80 again states the need to keep the growth of public expenditure (collective and general consumption) below the growth of GMP and thus to enhance the share of income remaining with enterprises. Naturally this decision will affect the revenue of these institutions, the quantity and quality of the services they provide, and the share of investments they account for. The replacement in appropriate instances of sociopolitical communities by communities of interest, in which contributing enterprises have direct decisionmaking powers, could lead to greater cost consciousness.

Because legal depreciation charges are a principal component of gross enterprise savings, the 1976 law on the revaluation of fixed assets could be important for maintaining a high saving rate. The law provides for annual revaluations of fixed assets in accord with the principle of identical replacement. A complex set of life-span benchmarks is being prepared for the computation of minimum depreciation rates; these benchmarks, together with the complex set of inflators introduced a few years ago, will enable realistic assessments.

For accumulation it will be difficult to achieve a higher rate than that in the preceding plan period, unless the growth rates of GMP and income are sufficiently high to allow acceptable growth in real personal incomes as well. Another problem is that enterprise saving rates are indirectly determined—either as a residual of enterprise income after distribution to personal incomes according to self-management agreements or by giving the financing obligations in self-management agreements first claim to enterprise income. Consequently the enterprise saving rates, whether microeconomic or macroeconomic, are almost impossible to determine ex ante. An alternative, more direct and possibly geared more to efficiency, would have been to stipulate that a minimum accumulation rate be applied to the resources (value of assets) entrusted by society to the organization. Ideally the rate could be equivalent, for example, to the opportunity cost of capital, however defined. Because it would be constitutionally unacceptable to return to the practice of collecting these charges in public investment funds, they could, in a manner similar to depreciation, be left at the disposal of enterprises, but be earmarked for investment in accord with agreements.

The 1974 constitution also introduced new legal provisions that allow taxing away enterprise income arising from exceptionally favored circumstances, or monopoly positions, and from windfalls.[19] The proceeds from these taxes can be left with the generating enterprise for reinvestment, or they can be reallocated elsewhere. In exceptional circumstances and to secure sufficient financing of certain priority projects, an obligatory loan can also be levied on enterprise income and designated for a particular purpose.

Prospects for private savings

In addition to the growth of personal incomes, the rise of workers' remittances was a major factor underlying the rapid expansion of household savings. By the end of 1975 private foreign exchange savings held with Yugoslav banks were Din37 billion, the equivalent of about US$2.1 billion. In 1971–75 the increase of these deposits accounted for more than a third of household financial savings. With the expected return of temporary migrant workers, greater emphasis must be placed on attracting the repatriation of savings held abroad and on mobilizing private savings in general.[20] The social plan for 1976–80 recognizes this need—it foresees some deceleration of transfers from abroad in real terms—and envisages measures to stimulate private saving, and particularly private investment.

For private sector investment the plan spells out measures for promoting investment in housing construction by residents, returning workers, and the families of workers still abroad. These measures include access to bank credits earmarked from private deposits, to complement individual savings used for this purpose, and exemptions or reductions of turnover taxes and customs duties on some construction material and equipment. The plan also emphasizes the need to encourage productive investment in the private sector within the new legal framework for private sector enterprises and cooperatives.

For the mobilization of household financial savings, the relatively high return on foreign exchange deposits continues to be an important incentive for saving. Because the motivation for household dinar savings is varied and complex, including variants of income considerations, the interest rate paid on these savings is one among

19. *The Constitution of the Socialist Federal Republic of Yugoslavia*, 1974, article 18.
20. Estimates of savings held abroad differ greatly; they range from US$0.8 billion to US$2.6 billion for those in West Germany alone.

many factors that could influence the private saving rate.[21] The low inflation rate in 1976 and the continued emphasis on stabilization over the plan period could improve the relative real return on private deposits and possibly have a positive effect on saving. Although the level of the real interest elasticity of private savings is a matter of speculation, it is likely to be positive. Consequently an argument can be made for preventing real interest rates from again becoming negative.

In addition to possibly discouraging financial savings, interest rates affect income distribution in a way not generally perceived. The level of nominal interest rates in isolation is not indicative of the size and direction of income transfers. Whereas positive real rates of interest would generate income not earned through work to the depositors, the converse is true for the negative real interest rates, which thus entail a transfer of unearned income from depositors to borrowers. A novel method of enlisting the participation of private savers in self-managed financial intermediation is established in the new banking law, which provides for depositor representation in councils of business banks. Nevertheless these councils have only advisory functions, pertaining to the policy for lending private deposits, but not to that for the terms of deposits and loans. Thus, the policy of business banks for interest rates is not likely to change unless other savings institutions mentioned in the law are allowed to follow an independent interest-rate policy and lend directly to potential borrowers.[22] In their competition for funds, business banks would be induced to follow suit.

Because of the comprehensive coverage by health and social insurance, the scope for resource mobilization by insurance is likely to remain limited. The potential appears to be greater for the floating of bonds by sociopolitical communities, communities of interest, and enterprises. Early in the period of the current plan, Serbia floated Din4 billion in public bonds for highway construction and river regulation; Croatia floated Din4.2 billion in bonds for highway construction; Bosnia-Herzegovina floated a public loan of Din1.4 billion for highway construction; Vojvodina floated a public loan of Din2 billion for energy projects; Slovenia and Macedonia each floated

21. Those considerations include the Keynesian concept of absolute income and Duesenberry's, Modigliani's, and Friedman's concepts of relative and permanent income.
22. The status of the other savings institutions was not clear at the time of writing; it seemed probable that they would be treated in a separate new law.

Din1 billion in bonds. The plan foresees a significant role for public bonds in supplementing resource mobilization and assuring the financing of projects of national and regional interest.

In addition to the financial return, which recently has been about 10 percent for five-year maturities, bonds issued by sociopolitical communities entitle holders to other benefits. The bonds may be used as collateral for investment credits, payments of contributions and taxes to the issuing bodies, or to constitute up to 30 percent of the reserves held by enterprises and other social sector organizations. These bonds also appeal to patriotic and social sentiments. All the issues just noted were oversubscribed; sales exceeded the initial targets by 35 to 70 percent. Less clear, however, is whether these bonds constitute a net increase of total private savings or merely a change in the mix of financial assets held by households.

New functions of banks

The law on banking promulgated in January 1978 introduces organizational and functional changes which are likely to affect resource mobilization and financial intermediation by banks and savings institutions. It reduces the autonomy of banks, increases the service function of banks in the direct pooling of resources among BOALS and enterprises, and aims to abolish "anonymous financial capital" by the earmarking of deposits by user and use. It also excludes sociopolitical communities from membership in banking organizations—an exclusion which largely curtails the influence of sociopolitical communities on bank policies. Because the banking system and banking procedures are still being adjusted, the following discussion is conjectural.

According to the provisions of the new law, banks are to be organized in a three-tier system of "internal banks," "basic banks," and "associated banks." That system also incorporates specialized financial organizations and other savings institutions.

An internal bank can be established by self-management agreements of BOALS, enterprises, communities of interest, or other social legal entities (but not sociopolitical communities) that are mutually linked in production and trade or in earning and sharing income. It can perform all banking transactions for its members, but does not accept sight deposits or approve credits on their basis. It consequently does not create money and is not subject to monetary regulation. Internal banks had previously appeared in some complex organizations of associated labor to service their internal financial transactions. Although setting up internal banks is not mandatory, they are likely to develop as the forum and foundation for agreements on the pooling of resources within and between enterprises. Basic and associated banks form the core of the banking system. They replace the business banks and perform all commercial and investment operations. Basic banks can be established by self-management agreements of BOALS, enterprises, communities of interest, other social legal entities (but not sociopolitical communities), and internal banks. Unless otherwise specified, members of basic banks assume unlimited liability for their bank's obligations. Associated banks are formed by business banks to finance large investment undertakings and to represent them in negotiating and concluding foreign business transactions. In contrast with the provisions for business banks, in which founders had decisionmaking power weighted by their contribution to the founders' fund, the new law does not specify a minimum number of members or a minimum contribution to banks' funds by individual members. Nor does it link membership to depositors. Members are all organizations that regularly carry out financial transactions of any kind through the bank and share in the liability agreement; all members have equal voting power in the assemblies of banks.

Alternative arrangements exist for the territorial and functional reorganization of business banks. For example, if a business bank has branches throughout a region or the country, the head office could become an associated bank and the branches basic banks. Enterprises that initially founded the branches of business banks could become members of basic banks, either directly or through their newly established internal banks. Branches of business banks could associate interregionally along functional lines, thus facilitating greater interregional pooling of resources.

Another change associated with the new banking law is that banks participate in planning. Banks—internal, basic, and associated—are required to prepare annual and five-year plans. These plans are integrated with the planning framework, because bank plans have to be accepted by the members and consolidated with their plans. Members in turn must consolidate their plans with the social plan. The plans of banks are thus to be harmonized with the social compacts and self-management agreements to which its members are parties. What effect is this likely to have? To the extent that the financing of priority activities is specified in the social compacts and self-management agreements of bank members, these activities would have first access to the members' own resources and priority access to banks' resources. The arrangement could assure more timely and effective financing of these activities. But if there are shortfalls of financial resources, activities that are less codified in agreements would have to bear the brunt of adjustment—an effect which could have repercussions on the targets for sectoral growth and employment.

The latest legislative changes are also likely to affect the structure of financial flows. In line with the new regulations on securing payments and computing income, the volume of interenterprise crediting should decline and a larger volume of transactions will be made with banks through the discounting of promissory notes. Banks would remain the basic intermediary for mobilizing household savings and channeling the surplus for investment by enterprises. The emphasis of the new banking law on internal banks in the direct pooling of resources among enterprises and the designation of enterprise deposits by purpose, while sharply reducing the decisionmaking power of banks for credit allocation, the functions of banks as autonomous intermediaries, may or may not affect the volume of resources channeled through banks. Because internal banks are likely to be members of basic banks, surplus funds other than those needed for immediate current or investment transactions would still be held as deposits with basic banks. Surplus funds nevertheless will increasingly be designated by purpose.

The importance of banks as financial institutions has not changed: in the continuing decentralization of decisionmaking, they remain indispensable for mobilization and intermediation of resources. The new law tries, however, to eliminate anonymity in financial relations and establish a more direct link between the providers and the users of resources, between those with financial surpluses and those with deficits.

The new system can be seen to integrate physical and economic relations with monetary and credit relations. The efficiency of the system will nevertheless depend on the success and efficiency of integrating the economy. The banking system, despite its more restricted role, can provide an important catalytic function. It arranges for the pooling of resources first in an internal bank, then more broadly through basic banks, and then globally through associated banks. Depending on the degree to which banks are incorporated in planning, they may also, because of their technical expertise, make an important contribution to the rational intermediation of resources.

Eight

Allocation of Investment Resources

THE CAPITAL STOCK in Yugoslavia was heavily concentrated in 1952, when the country was still trying to cope with the physical damage of the Second World War and the economic disruptions associated with the break with COMINFORM (table 8.1). Slovenia and Croatia accounted for about half of the capital stock of the country; Serbia for almost a quarter. By 1974 the average capital stock per capita had tripled, and the differences in endowment between regions were narrower. Sizable interregional investment flows thus occurred during the period in favor of the less developed regions. Nevertheless the differences among regions still were very large.[1]

Before the 1965 economic reforms investment mobilization and allocation largely were centrally determined. Fiscal resources were collected from enterprises for the federal General Investment Fund and some other regional or special purpose investment funds. The resources were passed on as direct grants to investing enterprises or as credits by banks, which administered the resources of the General Investment Fund. In practice, however, the federal plan and, to less degree, the republican plans determined allocation. The role of enterprises in allocative decisions was similarly limited because of the instrumentality of the resources of the General Investment Fund in total financing and the obligatory provisions of plans. Enterprises nevertheless were increasingly supplementing those grants and credits with self-generated resources.

Yugoslavia abolished the federal investment funds in 1963 and the corresponding republican funds in 1964. Debt-service payments

---

1. The issues associated with regional disparities are discussed in detail in chapter eleven.

Table 8.1. *Capital Stock in Productive Activities
of the Social Sector, 1952 and 1974*

Region	1952		1974	
	Share in total capital stock (percent)	Average capital stock per capita (Yugoslavia = 100)	Share in total capital stock (percent)	Average capital stock per capita (Yugoslavia = 100)
Less developed regions	19.0	61	25.6	71
Bosnia-Herzegovina	12.7	77	13.6	73
Kosovo	1.8	37	2.9	44
Macedonia	3.7	49	6.4	78
Montenegro	0.8	33	2.7	103
More developed regions	80.9	118	74.5	116
Croatia	28.5	123	26.4	124
Serbia	23.4	89	22.5	89
Slovenia	20.7	233	16.0	192
Vojvodina	8.3	82	9.6	103

Note: Capital stock is equal to fixed assets at purchase value in 1966 prices.
Sources: Federal Institute of Statistics, *Studies, Analyses, and Reviews*, no. 62 (Belgrade, 1973); idem, *Statistical Yearbook of Yugoslavia*, 1972 and 1976; idem, *Statistical Bulletin*, no. 954 (December 1975).

continued for credits previously extended to enterprises, but were directly channeled to the banks. The assets and liabilities of what then was called "state capital" became part of the banks' balance sheets. But the state, particularly the republics, for several years maintained a large degree of control by stipulating the specific purposes for which banks could use the debt-service payments on state capital. In 1970 about half of the investable resources available still were under this indirect control of the state.[2] After that year state capital was gradually dissipated by transferring the assets either to enterprises, canceling debt-service obligations, or to some republican funds with narrowly defined special purposes.

Thus, during the decade after the economic reforms, three major agents jointly determined allocation: enterprises, banks, and the

2. See Dubey and others, *Yugoslavia: Development with Decentralization*, p. 234.

state. Their respective weight in allocative decisions shifted over time in line with the goal of increased decentralization and destatization. Enterprises and banks gradually gained influence. The state retained an initially considerable but steadily diminishing influence.

After the abolition of centrally established targets for investment, enterprises became the sole initiators of investment projects. They were affected in their initiatives by considerations of cost and return and ultimately by market signals. Well-established enterprises gained influence in allocative decisionmaking because of their growing self-financing ability and their capacity to contract foreign loans. Enterprises also gained influence through their representation, as founders, on the boards of banks. Formally the banks were not autonomous institutions: they could only act in accord with the decisions of their founder enterprises. In practice, the managements of banks gained increasing influence in allocative decisions through their control over the information system and their opportunity to mediate among competing requests of individual founder enterprises for credits from fungible resources—that is, resources not earmarked for specific purposes. The share of fungible resources in the total investable resources of banks was growing for four reasons: the de facto transfer of previous state funds to the banks; the requirement that founders provide permanent paid-in participation in the bank; the rapid rise of private savings; and the discontinuation of the practice under which the state handed down investment decisions.

Governments also were cofounders of banks. Although their voting rights were limited by law to 10 percent, their practical leverage probably was larger than expressed by voting rights. Governments could marshall a considerable persuasive leverage. Furthermore, the use of selective credits—which initially were short-term credits from the NBY to commercial banks for onlending, but which repeatedly were converted from short-term to long-term credits and ultimately to the permanent funds of enterprises—gave the state the potential to determine the use of new resources. In addition, the specifications in plans for certain major projects provided grounds for governments to urge the implementation of those projects. Last, the republican governments increasingly came under local pressure to do something for certain communes—pressure which they passed on to banks for the provision of special credits from available resources. Thus, while the republican governments continued to exert some influence on resource allocation, the influence of the federal government became minimal.

These changes in the weights of decisionmaking agents naturally affected the broad pattern of allocation. Their effect is particularly evident in a comparison of three subperiods having distinctly different sets of policies: the 1962–64 subperiod before the economic reforms; the 1967–69 subperiod after the economic reforms; and the 1972–74 subperiod before the recent systemic changes and the distortions originating from the balance-of-payments crisis in 1974–75 (table 8.2). Over these three subperiods the investment rate con-

Table 8.2. *Allocation of Investment in Fixed Assets, 1962–74*
(percent)

Item	1962–64	1967–69	1972–74
Productive investment	64.0	72.6	67.8
Social sector	61.8	68.4	61.3
Private sector	2.1	4.2	6.5
Nonproductive investment	36.0	27.4	32.2
Social sector	28.5	13.0	14.9
Private sector	7.5	14.5	17.3
Housing and communal services	30.0	21.8	23.6
Total investment	100.0	100.0	100.0
Social sector	90.3	81.3	76.1
Private sector	9.7	18.7	23.9
Share of fixed investment in GMP	34.4	30.5	28.9
Share of fixed investment in GNP	31.0	26.8	25.8

Note: Figures are three-year averages in 1966 prices.
Source: Appendix table A.15.

tinuously dropped, but it still was at a remarkably high level by international standards throughout the period. The decline of nonproductive investment, such as that in housing and social services, caused this downward trend, at least through the 1967–69 subperiod. The continuing high shares of productive investment were sustained in 1967–69 by a growing concentration of the social sector on productive investment.[3] This concentration left a rapidly rising share of non-

3. As was noted in chapter five, the distinction between productive and nonproductive activities, or what the Yugoslavs term economic and noneconomic activities, is central to Marxian economics and is followed here for analytical purposes. According to Yugoslav statistical conventions, the principal nonproductive activities are health, education, administration, defense, banking, and housing. This distinction is important for national accounts, which do not include nonproductive services in the aggregate measure of output, the measure commonly referred to as GMP.

productive investment, mainly that in housing, to the private sector. During the 1972–74 subperiod, however, the private sector also increased its share in productive investment—to about 11 percent, from 3 percent in 1962–64. Tying these trends together was the continuous rise of the investment of the private sector to about a quarter of the total by 1972–74. The objectives of the economic reforms of 1965 thus were clearly reflected in the trends of investment. A growing share of GMP was distributed to households, but a corresponding slack of total investment was largely avoided because of the growing portion of household resources directed toward savings and investment.

High investment shares led to an impressive buildup of capital stock. Total fixed assets for productive activities in the social sector —the only sector for which complete data are available—increased at an average annual rate of 8.5 percent a year in constant prices between 1952 and 1974, or at about the same rate as the output (GMP) of that sector (see appendix table A.15). Because of the similarity of those growth rates, the average capital-output ratio was fairly stable. Beginning at 2.6, it declined to 2.2 in 1964 and rose to 2.5 in 1974.

Efficiency of Resource Allocation

Measuring the efficiency of resource allocation is notoriously impracticable.[4] Furthermore in no country is resource allocation exclusively determined by considerations of efficiency. It always reflects noneconomic objectives as well, thus impeding intercountry comparisons even if accurate measurement were possible. To assess allocative efficiency in broad terms, some aggregate indicators can be used. One frequently used crude indicator is the aggregate incremental capital-output ratio (ICOR)—that is, the ratio of the gross investment in fixed assets and stocks to the increase in GDP. Yugoslavia's ICOR for the 1961–75 period was 5.4. Annual ICORS oscillated by wide margins around the secular ICOR, mostly because of fluctuations in the growth rate of GDP. Although no trend was discernible for the period up to 1967, the average annual ICOR tended to stabilize at a somewhat lower level of about 4.2 thereafter—

---

4. The term *efficiency* is loosely used in this discussion, either in relation to the growth of output resulting from investment or to some ratio of surplus to capital stock or investment.

that is, after the adjustment to the economic reform and before the balance-of-payments crisis in 1974.

Table 8.3 compares Yugoslavia's ICOR and per capita GNP with those of a sample of other countries having diversified economic structures. The data show that a positive correlation between ICORS and levels

Table 8.3. *Aggregate Incremental Capital-Output Ratio and Gross Domestic Product per Capita, Yugoslavia and Selected Countries*

Country	Incremental capital-output ratio[a]	Gross domestic product per capita[b] (dollars)
Middle-income and high-income LDCs		
Yugoslavia	4.2	1,010
Chile	8.8	720
Ireland	4.5	2,150
Argentina	4.0	1,640
Spain	3.4	1,710
Greece	3.3	1,870
Colombia	3.2	440
Mexico	3.1	890
Turkey	2.9	600
Portugal	2.8	1,410
Korea	2.2	400
Brazil	1.4	760
Developed OECD countries		
Sweden	7.9	5,910
Norway	6.6	4,660
United Kingdom	6.5	3,060
Switzerland	6.5	6,100
Federal Republic of Germany	5.0	5,320
Netherlands	4.8	4,330
United States	4.8	6,200
Denmark	4.7	5,210
France	4.6	4,540
Italy	4.6	2,450
Japan	3.7	3,630

Sources: World Bank, *1975 World Bank Atlas* (Washington, D.C., 1976); idem, *World Tables* (Washington, D.C., 1976).
a. Average for 1968–73.
b. Calculated in accord with the method used in World Bank atlases; figures are for 1973.

of development does exist, but is fairly weak. Yugoslavia's ICOR was close to the upper range for the sample of higher income developing countries.

The aggregate ICOR nevertheless is a poor indicator of the efficiency of investment allocation: it encompasses a great number of structural factors, such as natural resource endowment and the development of basic infrastructure; it encompasses investment in such social infrastructure as housing, health, and education; it also encompasses various short-term factors, such as operating efficiency and capacity use. The structural factors affect the composition of the country's total investment program by sector and branch. Sectoral and branch ICORS automatically are high for investment components that for technological reasons are inherently capital-intensive or have a long gestation period before measurably affecting economic development. They also are high for components primarily undertaken for social, not economic, reasons. Both types of component figure heavily in Yugoslavia's pattern of total investment. For the 1962–74 period 32 percent of total investment in fixed assets was allocated to nonproductive investment, which essentially is for social infrastructure. An additional 13 percent was allocated to transport and communications. In no year did the combined share of these categories in total investment fall below 42 percent.[5]

A better indicator of allocative efficiency than the aggregate ICOR is a series of sectoral ICORS for activities that yield direct and fairly quick returns to investment. From the limited cross-country data that is available, ICORS based on gross investment in fixed assets have been computed for a bundle of productive activities in Yugoslavia and selected countries (table 8.4). The activities comprise ISIC groups 1–4: agriculture, mining, manufacturing, and electricity, gas, and water.[6] Because these partial ICORS still pertain to large aggregates and combine the effects of structural and short-term factors specific to individual countries, they do not permit a clear-cut ranking of countries by allocative efficiency. The figures nevertheless refute the

---

5. A simple example can illustrate the sensitivity of the aggregate ICOR to the sectoral composition of total investment. If a third of total investment were for social infrastructure, the improvement of which would not enter GDP, an aggregate ICOR of 4.2 would imply an ICOR of 2.8 for the remaining two-thirds of investment.

6. Differences between the international standard industrial classification (ISIC) and the Yugoslav classification of industry preclude any further statistical breakdown.

Table 8.4. *Incremental Capital-Output Ratio for Productive Activities, Yugoslavia and Selected Countries, Averages for 1968–73*

Country	Incremental capital-output ratio
Yugoslavia	2.8
Norway	7.5
United Kingdom	6.2
Sweden	5.3
Ireland	4.5
Italy	4.0
Finland	3.6
Netherlands	3.5
Denmark	3.0
Belgium	2.7
Portugal	2.6
Greece	2.3
Republic of Korea	1.5

Sources: United Nations, Statistical Office, *Yearbook of National Accounts Statistics* (New York, 1976); *Statistical Yearbook of Yugoslavia*, 1976.

hypothesis that Yugoslavia was out of line by international standards.[7] Although Yugoslavia faced unresolved problems in achieving an efficient pattern of allocation, the problems do not seem to have created obstacles more severe than those faced by most other countries.

Evidence of substantial interregional differences between the potential and actual allocative efficiency in Yugoslavia is more conclusive. The basis for comparison is the "gross profit rate"—that is, the ratio to fixed assets of depreciation plus additions to various enterprise funds—which can be used as a proxy for the efficiency of

7. Other studies have used different methods to examine the same issue. One study, an econometric analysis based on actual and possible growth rates for seventy countries during the 1965–70 period, indicated that Yugoslavia's annual growth rate was 17 percent less than the rate that would have been possible if "optimal" policies had been pursued. But for that study, there are difficulties of interpretation because of conceptual ambiguities in the input data and the specification of the model. Sateesh K. Singh, *Development Economics: Some Findings* (Lexington, Mass.: Lexington Books, 1975), pp. 200–208.

Table 8.5. *Gross Profit Rate, by Region, 1974*

Region	Gross profit rate (percent)	Gross profit rate (Yugoslavia = 100)
Less developed regions		
Bosnia-Herzegovina	16.6	86
Kosovo	11.2	58
Macedonia	17.6	91
Montenegro	13.3	69
More developed regions		
Croatia	21.5	111
Serbia	18.6	96
Slovenia	21.7	112
Vojvodina	21.0	108
Yugoslavia	19.4	100

Note: The accuracy of absolute rates can be questioned because of conceptual ambiguities. But because there is no evidence that the ambiguities differ between regions, they should not affect the significance of relative differences.
Source: Federal Institute of Statistics, *Statistical Bulletin*, no. 954 (December 1975).

capital stock in a given year (table 8.5). As in the foregoing comparisons, the ratios simultaneously measure the differences of structural and short-term factors. If Slovenia were the benchmark for the efficiency that can be achieved within the framework of institutions and policies in Yugoslavia, the country has considerable reserves for improvement.[8] If the total resources of the country were to be concentrated on regions where efficiency is greatest, the efficiency and growth of the economy would be considerably higher, the ICOR lower. For obvious social and political reasons, however, the policy conclusion drawn from this comparison points in another direction: the causes of lower economic efficiency must be corrected by massive transfers of investment resources from the more developed to

8. For reasons already implied, there is no basis for comparing Slovenia's standard of efficiency with that of other countries. A Yugoslav study, estimating the marginal product of capital in industry by region, found a similar pattern, but even wider differences. Deviations from the country average of 12.7 percent ranged from 17 percent of the average for Kosovo to 125 percent for Slovenia. Vlado Frankovic, *Nagrajevanje Produkcijskih Tvorcev v Jugoslavenski in Slovenski Industriji [Compensation of Production Factors in Yugoslav and Slovenian Industries]* (Ljubljana, 1974; processed in Slovenian).

Table 8.6. *Net Profit Rate, by Sector and Branch, Averages for 1972–74*
(Yugoslavia = 100)

Sector or branch	Net profit rate[a]
High-profit activities	
Forestry	263
Tobacco	238
Trade	219
Printing	216
Textiles	203
Wood products	166
Rubber products	165
Leather goods	156
Chemicals	150
Low-profit activities	
Agriculture	88
Nonmetallic minerals	84
Nonferrous metallurgy	79
Ferrous metallurgy	56
Shipbuilding	49
Coal	44
Electric power	31
Transport	21

Note: See the note to table 8.5. Sectors and branches not shown fall between 88 and 150.

Sources: Statistical Bulletin, nos. 830 (December 1973), 889 (December 1974), and 954 (December 1975).

a. The average net profit rate for Yugoslavia was 8.6 percent during 1972–74.

the less developed regions. To do so probably would sacrifice some growth, at least in the short run.

Intersectoral and interbranch differences of "net profit rates"—the ratios to fixed assets of allocations to enterprise funds—are also significant (table 8.6).[9] Although some instances of high-profit and low-profit activities are special, the differences seem to point to some significant differences in efficiency, both allocative and operative, among activities—differences which depress the efficiency of the

9. The study just cited found similar differences; they ranged from 50 percent to 200 percent of the average for industry.

economy.[10] It can also be hypothesized that the differences between activities reflect not only differences in efficiency, but differences in relative prices.

Given the large differences in profitability between activities, it could be suspected that these differences would, together with the different economic structures of the regions, explain interregional differences in profitability. But the comparison of gross profit rates by sector for the two extreme cases, Slovenia and Kosovo, does not strongly support such a hypothesis (table 8.7). Even this comparison

Table 8.7. *Gross Profit Rate
in Slovenia and Kosovo, by Sector
and Branch, 1974*
(Yugoslavia = 100)

Sector or branch	Slovenia	Kosovo
Industry	110	41
Agriculture	65	42
Forestry	86	61
Construction	169	38
Transport and communications	94	75
Trade	113	87
Handicrafts	132	350
Total	112	58

Source: *Statistical Bulletin*, no. 954 (December 1975).

is incomplete, because the relative weights of sectors in the economy and branches in industry greatly differ from region to region. To illustrate the effect of this structural factor, the distribution of fixed assets for any two regions can be inverted. Applying the actual profit rates by sector and branch for one region to the structure of another region—comparing, say, Slovenia and Kosovo—hardly affects the initial estimates. The average rate for Slovenia would fall only slightly, from 21.7 to 19.6 percent; the average rate for Kosovo would rise only slightly, from 11.2 to 12 percent. Thus regional differences in rates of profitability point to some genuine differences

10. Because enterprises have discretion in choosing between voluntary depreciation above the legal minimum and allocation to funds, the gross profit rate seems in principle to be a superior proxy for efficiency. But because the life span of fixed assets can differ considerably among activities, the net profit rate would appear to be superior for this comparison of sectors and branches.

in the economic performance of regions and to the potential for improving the efficiency of the Yugoslavia economy by improving efficiency in the less developed regions.[11]

Structural Imbalances

Yugoslav documents and public statements concede or allude to deficiencies in resource allocation. But in the critical assessment of the allocative performance since the mid-1960s, the internal discussion in Yugoslavia assigns substantially more weight to the emergence of what frequently are referred to as structural imbalances.[12] In Yugoslav parlance this term covers several closely interrelated tendencies: first, the rapid expansion of activities catering predominantly to final demand, particularly private demand, and the slower expansion of activities supplying raw materials and intermediate goods; second, the growing dependence on imports and the growing reliance upon a volatile export mix, whether in price or quantity; third, the emergence of some excess capacity in many of the most rapidly growing activities, in some instances accompanied by the expansion of parallel production facilities that are suboptimal in size.

The first two tendencies are revealed in a variety of structural coefficients, which can be directly computed from the flows of input-output tables (table 8.8). The changes in ratios show stagnating or falling import shares for final goods—that is, successful import substitution in an era of liberalized imports. In addition, although the share of intermediate goods in total imports increased, the ratios of imports to total demand and to total production rose, as did import dependency. The rise of import dependency is even more clear in trends of the ratios of total import content to the output of sectors and branches (table 8.9). The trends are uniform for almost all sectors and branches; a progressive rise can be observed between

11. It could be argued that the comparison overstates the case, because the output mix in a certain branch, say textiles, can differ between regions. To the extent that the output mix differs between regions, the comparison here only substitutes one problem of efficiency for another. Obviously the more developed regions have greater success than the less developed regions in selecting a profitable mix of output in each branch.

12. The terminology is not clear: the Yugoslav analysis frequently refers to "structural disproportions," which apparently is interchangeably used with "structural imbalances."

Table 8.8. *Structural Coefficients, 1966 and 1972*
(percent)

Coefficient	1966	1972
Domestic production to total demand	89.6	87.6
Imports to total demand	10.4	12.4
Imported to total final demand	8.3	7.5
Imported to total consumption	6.3	4.3
Imported to total investment	17.0	17.0
Imported to total intermediate demand	13.1	18.6
Imported intermediates to total imports	54.4	65.9
Imports to production	11.6	14.1
Exports to production	10.6	11.0
Exports to imports	91.4	77.9

Sources: Federal Institute of Statistics, *Studies, Analyses, and Reviews*, no. 50 (Belgrade 1970); figures supplied by the Federal Institute of Statistics.

1966 and 1972. The sources-of-growth analysis described in the technical note at the end of this chapter supports these observations. Further analysis of the negative import substitution in industry is described in chapter nine.

Those structural changes are consistent with, if not a logical consequence of, the principal objective of the 1965 reforms: opening the Yugoslav economy to external trade by adopting a more realistic and unified exchange system and gradually reducing the quantitative restrictions on trade. The faster growth of imports and exports relative to the growth of final demand reflected the growing integration of the economy with the world economy. Given the rapid growth of foreign exchange earnings from nonfactor services and workers'

Table 8.9. *Import Content of Output, by Sector and Branch, 1966 and 1972*
(percent)

Sector or branch	Total import content		Import content in 1972	
	1966	1972	Direct	Indirect
Building materials	7.6	13.5	6.0	7.5
Chemicals	26.4	36.8	25.0	11.0
Electrical equipment	21.7	31.8	20.1	11.7
Metal products	18.5	27.8	17.4	10.4
Nonferrous metallurgy	21.4	39.0	26.4	12.6
Shipbuilding	31.6	41.3	32.8	8.5
Wood products	9.6	16.9	9.9	7.1

Source: Appendix table A.24.

remittances, the declining coverage of commodity imports by exports was inevitable, unless these earnings were used to add to foreign exchange reserves. Thus the structural changes of the period should not necessarily be considered as resulting in imbalances.

The growing import dependency was, however, exclusively concentrated in intermediate goods. This concentration greatly increased the vulnerability of the economy to external factors. Because consumer goods accounted for a small and declining share of imports, the brunt of any downward adjustment in imports inevitably fell on intermediate goods, with adverse effects for the growth of the economy. Furthermore, after the oil price increase of 1973 and the ensuing recession in Europe, Yugoslavia could no longer sustain its past pattern of development. The reduction of external migration was foreshadowing a period of stagnant workers' remittances. Consequently the thrust of Yugoslavia's development strategy had to change toward restricting the increased import dependency, inducing faster growth in exports, or both. Thus the imbalances, if they can be called that, were inherited from the period before 1974, but amplified by the events of 1973–74.

There is no unambiguous statistical evidence for the third aspect affecting structural imbalances—growing excess capacity and suboptimally sized facilities for parallel production. Data on capacity use in industry do not show a significant deterioration between 1966 and 1974.[13] The importance given in Yugoslavia to this aspect of structural imbalances thus seems to rest on generalizations from conspicuous specific cases.

The identification of structural imbalances is the point of departure of the Yugoslav social plan for 1976–80. Priorities have been assigned to activities having the most obvious imbalances and the physical preconditions to correct those imbalances. What, then, is the link between allocative efficiency, or deficiency, and structural imbalances? It could be hypothesized that imbalances emerged as the response of enterprises to price signals for outputs and inputs, but that the signals pointed in the wrong direction. Estimates of rates of effective protection lend some support to such direct causality; in Yugoslavia, as in other developing countries, those rates have been highest for consumer goods. But because of the lack of conclusive evidence, it is difficult to argue persuasively for or against the posi-

13. Federal Institute of Statistics, *Statistical Yearbook of Yugoslavia*, 1977, p. 198.

tion that a correction of relative prices in isolation would have automatically led to an allocative pattern that would have simultaneously increased efficiency and reduced structural imbalances. As already mentioned, the Yugoslav development policy implicitly rejects the validity of such a hypothesis and focuses on directly correcting structural imbalances.

Unresolved Issues of Resource Allocation

During the 1965–75 period the problems of resource allocation essentially were the result of the excessive demand for investment resources and the deficient mode of rationing available resources under the conditions of rising inflation that ensued in the first half of the 1970s. Many factors contributed to the high level of demand for investment resources: ambitious investment plans, a low aversion to risk, substantial investment in social infrastructure, low real rates of interest, the enterprise objectives to maximize personal incomes, and the incidence of taxes and contributions.[14] The demand for investment credits created severe rationing problems for banks in their attempts to match the demand for, and the supply of, fungible investment resources.

Excessive demand for resources

After the temporary sluggishness during the period of adjustment after the reform, the recovering growth momentum of the economy had two results: enterprise expectations for rapidly expanding demand; ambitious investment plans to meet the expected market potential. Both outcomes were to a large extent reactions to the overly restrictive monetary policy in the years immediately after the reforms. Dynamism was, by its nature, accompanied by a low degree of risk-aversion as well. Enterprises were easily induced to take chances. Even if they ran persistent losses, their survival rarely was at stake. Statutory joint-reserve funds, easy access to additional

---

14. The sequence of presentation of causes is not intended to imply their relative importance; nor is the list complete. Among the causes omitted are the loose rules governing the computation of enterprise income and the expectation that price increases would enable complete financing during project implementation. The discussion in this section also disregards causes of the limited supply of investable resources, a subject already covered in chapter seven, and the effects of relative prices of outputs.

credits for working capital from banks, the prospect of being bailed out by government in times of severe difficulty, and the ability to resort to involuntary supplier credits provided a safety net. In the rare cases of bankruptcy, society was the main loser—of the squandered socially owned assets. Workers faced little risk of extended unemployment, because job-seekers with experience and skill could find alternative employment at home or abroad.

Investment ambitions for nonproductive purposes, mainly for housing and social services, also were high. Such investment significantly declined during the late 1960s from a very high level before the reform, but strongly recovered during the 1970s to about a third of total investment (see table 8.2). The need to improve the standard of living, particularly in areas where deficiencies were perceived to be most intense, maintained the momentum. Because such investment yields immediate benefits to beneficiaries or to investors in private housing, and because the social objective was rapid improvement of the standard of living, banks and enterprises were under considerable social pressure to set aside a substantial part of their total resources for nonproductive investment. Those provisions commensurately reduced the part available for productive investment. Apparently the determination of the socially most desirable shares of productive and nonproductive investment was an unresolved issue.[15]

The cost of borrowing did little to discourage the ambitions for investment. After adjusting for inflation, interest rates turned negative in real terms in 1970 (table 8.10). Although few borrowers could have expected highly negative real interest rates to prevail through the maturity of credits, the assumption perhaps was not uncommon that credits would essentially be free in the long run.[16] This perception tended to increase the total demand for credits by making more projects and more variants of capital-intensive projects appear financially viable than would have been the case if real interest rates had been higher. In a market economy the level of real interest rates should ideally reflect the marginal product of capital. Although the marginal product of capital is notoriously elusive when attempts

15. When excessive nonproductive investment was considered to contribute to the inflationary momentum, deposit requirements were tightened to slow down the investment drive. The measures were strictly temporary, however. They did not affect the principal component of nonproductive investment: private housing construction.

16. A negative real interest rate implies a transfer of income from the depositor to the borrower and makes borrowing an economic proposition, even if the investment outlay can just be recovered in real terms.

Table 8.10. *Real Interest Rate, 1966–76*
(percent)

Item	1966	1967	1968	1969	1970	1971
Interest rate on credit	8	8	10	8	8	8
Rise in index of industrial producer prices	11	2	1	3	9	15
Real interest rate	3	6	9	5	−1	−7

Note: Interest rates are not weighted averages, but prevailing rates reported by banks for long-term nonpreferential credits. There apparently was always some spread around these figures, which are more illustrative than accurate.

Sources: Statistical Yearbook of Yugoslavia, 1976; figures supplied by Yugoslav banks.

are made to estimate it, there is little doubt that Yugoslavia's average real interest rate was substantially below the marginal product of capital for almost every year after 1966.[17]

The objective function of enterprises may also have contributed to excess demand. If a self-managed enterprise were geared in its allocation decisions to maximizing the personal incomes of its work force, it would strive to maximize labor productivity, which normally is positively correlated with capital intensity. To the extent that this maximization could be achieved by a more capital-intensive choice, the enterprise would be tempted to make that choice, provided it would not result in the redundancy of any of the enterprise's work force. This argument relies on there being some scope for technical substitutability of labor and capital resources, either in the choice of alternative outputs or in the choice of alternative techniques for a given output.[18] Thus there may be tendencies to employ more financial resources in equipment—and, as a corollary, to employ fewer workers—than are necessary and justified at a given volume and composition of demand. Under the assumption of the substitutability of factors, access to investment resources at low or negative interest

17. Problems of the technique of estimation and the availability of suitable data are compounded in Yugoslavia by conceptual problems of the appropriate coverage arising from the fragmented "capital market." For example, country-wide or regional rates could be considered, and the private sector or non-productive investment could be included or excluded.

18. Substitutability is the crucial assumption in this context. It can also be argued that the scope for choice in many instances is extremely limited. Usually only one efficient technology is available. Furthermore the maximization of personal incomes of the work force as the guiding criterion is postulated, not empirically supported.

1972	1973	1974	1975	1976	Item
12	12	12	12	12	Interest rate on credit
11	13	29	22	6	Rise in index of industrial producer prices
1	−1	−17	−10	6	Real interest rate

rates would tend to reinforce these tendencies. The reason is that the substitutability of factors permits the distribution of a greater part of the productivity increased by increased capital intensity to workers as higher incomes.[19] The applicability of this model to Yugoslavia is unclear. It probably did not apply to the less developed regions, given their surpluses of labor. Whether it was applicable to the more developed regions is no longer relevant because it implies group-ownership behavior, which now is illegal.

The incidence of taxes and contributions was another factor fueling the demand for investment resources. As was pointed out in chapter seven, most of the heavy burden of taxes and contributions (quasi taxes for financing social services) are charged either on enterprise income before the distribution between personal incomes and accumulation or directly on distributed gross personal incomes. Their burden has been heavy: for example, in 1974 the margin of gross over net personal incomes in productive activities in the social sector was 37 percent; taxes and contributions paid by enterprises were equal to 20 percent of gross personal income. Thus the "gross

19. As Vanek rightly points out, this increase is, in effect, a "rent" portion in the personal income earned from socially owned means of production; it accrues to those who succeed in finding employment in the social sector. In the 1970s, however, enterprises apparently came under some political pressure at the local level to increase employment beyond the level they would otherwise have chosen. This practice probably is one reason for the low growth of productivity; it may in turn have induced enterprises to counteract the effect on personal incomes by searching for even more investment resources. The substance of this assessment is similar to that of "group ownership," which is considered to be an aberration from the socialist principle of solidarity. Jaroslav Vanek, "The Yugoslav Economy Viewed through the Theory of Labor Management," *World Development*, vol. 1, no. 9 (September 1973), pp. 43–45.

labor cost" to the enterprise greatly exceeded net personal incomes.[20] Consequently, if the enterprise were to maximize net personal incomes through its allocative decisions, it would be induced to strive, within the range of choices available, for capital-intensive projects or techniques.[21]

Rationing resources

Banks were swamped with requests, which overloaded the institutional capacity to analyze those requests thoroughly. In addition, there was no consensus on the criteria for assessing the merits of competing requests. The reported use of a large number of criteria, alternatively or in parallel, was evidence of the absence of this consensus. Such criteria ranged from the ratio of accumulation or income generated per unit of investment to the self-financing ratio of the enterprise or its ability to negotiate foreign financing. The latter pair of criteria invariably assigned priority to well-established enterprises, not to new enterprises or to the merits of proposed projects.

A new element was introduced in 1975 with the legal requirement to register all projects having investment costs exceeding Din30 million, or about $1.8 million, with the federal chamber of the economy. The effect of the measure was to block projects for which the sponsoring enterprises could not provide evidence of assured financing. For projects that had questionable economic justification, the chamber was obliged, in addition, to initiate exchanges of information and negotiations among the project sponsor and other affected enterprises, such as competitors, suppliers, or customers. The intention was to find a consensus on the merits of specific projects. Apparently no rigorous analytical criteria were used in these confrontations, and the law was repealed in July 1977. The enactment of the law on planning, which requires the harmonization of investment decisions in self-management agreements and social compacts, was felt to supersede it.

Given this complex situation—excessive demand for limited resources, uncertain relative weights of an abundance of criteria, and diffuse motivations of the parties to decisionmaking—many invest-

20. Yugoslav procedures for accounting reflect the sociopolitical ground rules and do not encompass "labor cost" in the strict sense. For decisionmaking by worker-managed enterprises, these procedures do not invalidate the thrust of the conclusion.

21. As Robinson persuasively points out, the wage bill of enterprises in a Marxian framework is a perfectly rational and just basis for taxation. Joan Robinson, *An Essay on Marxian Economics* (London: MacMillan, 1966), p. *xx*.

ment decisions were to a large degree negotiated. Furthermore, as the absence of firm criteria and rules seems to indicate, most investment decisions probably were negotiated without the use of rigorous analytical techniques for comparing alternatives. In such a situation, an investment pattern that could be considered optimal by strict economic standards would emerge only by accident. Nevertheless the open exchange of views and ambitions among parties that share integrity, professionalism, and mutual trust, as well as some notion of the commonweal, would normally prevent gross misallocation as well. Moreover the fact that decisions were taken demonstrates that the compromises constituted solutions regarded as acceptable to all parties. In a decentralized system, that acceptability is as important as narrow economic rationality.[22]

New System of Resource Allocation

In the period of greater decentralization and enterprise autonomy subsequent to the economic reforms of 1965, any correction of the deficiencies of allocation could not have been in the direction of strengthening central planning. The dismantling of central planning was the purpose of the reforms. A more relevant alternative could have been an evolution of the "socialist market" system toward including a "socialist capital market," thus marrying neoclassical principles with social ownership of the means of production and decentralized decisionmaking.[23] Instead Yugoslavia opted for a different route toward improving allocative efficiency—a route more consistent with its sociopolitical premises and institutional setup.

Procedures of the social plan for 1976–80

The procedures of resource allocation for the 1976–80 period mingle old and new elements.[24] Because they are considered in

22. In every economic system, except in a perfect market economy or perfectly planned economy, the allocative decisions probably are multidimensional and negotiated.

23. For a description of the contours and policy postulates of such a system, see Vanek, "The Yugoslav Economy Viewed through the Theory of Labor Management," pp. 39–56. Vanek nevertheless discounts a piecemeal approach: the parts of his suggested package that appear to be politically viable are not likely to provide for an economically feasible program.

24. This section concentrates on the practical application of the planning model in drawing up the social plan. For a discussion of procedures underlying the new planning system, see chapter four.

Yugoslavia to be transitional procedures, only some hypotheses about their main features can be advanced.

The principal decisions affecting allocation—the selection of the priority activities aimed at correcting structural imbalances—were made at an early stage of planning.[25] Planning for priority activities started with tentative physical targets for output or capacity. Various rounds of harmonization refined the targets until a regional balance was struck for each priority activity as to the size, location, and technical characteristics of major projects to be implemented. Part of the harmonization apparently established the financial dimension of emerging programs. Starting with broad principles about the parties that should contribute to financing the program, and by what criteria, the process went through several refining iterations to develop fairly detailed estimates of the total investment costs and the contributions to be provided by specific contributors. For the physical targets and financial provisions, social compacts were concluded to specify the obligations of all affected sociopolitical communities and enterprises. Subsequently the provisions and obligations of the social compacts were defined in greater detail in self-management agreements among and within enterprises. For example, the financial provisions include arrangements for enterprises to invest in other enterprises without the intermediation of banks—either in conventional credit relationships or in joint pooling. Because harmonization for priority activities was mandatory for all affected parties, the social compacts and self-management agreements virtually assure the implementation of programs, unless assumptions about the internal demand and export potential for output prove to be grossly out of line.

Two aspects of the planning of resource allocation for priority activities are particularly important. First, the social compacts and self-management agreements are not only binding for enterprises signing them; they also are automatically binding for the banks to which those enterprises belong. The reason is that the members of banks decide upon the use of resources available to the bank. Second, priority activities automatically have the first claim to investment resources: investment programs for priority activities are largely predetermined and, after the signing of all social compacts and self-management agreements, mandatory; investment programs for non-priority activities are neither mandatory nor comparably specific.

25. The discussion here pertains to federal priority activities. Essentially the same procedures apply to additional priority activities of each republic.

The portion of firmly preempted resources probably is in excess of half the productive investment that is planned.[26]

For nonpriority activities, harmonization and final allocation apparently proceeded quite differently. This difference follows from two conditions. Although enterprises are obliged to search for complete harmonization of their investment plans, they are not obliged to reach it.[27] And because priority activities preempt a sizable share of total resources, the other activities have to make do with the remainder. Problems of harmonization thus reappear in the need for compromises on the claims to fungible resources at the disposal of banks. The fungible resources probably are a good deal smaller than the portion not preempted by priority activities. The reason is that all enterprises retain under the new legislation the right to determine the use of their accumulation. That right includes the right to commit resources in advance through self-management agreements on the pooling of investment resources. The margin of truly fungible resources may thus be quite small, even though that margin in many instances is critical for project implementation, because complete self-financing is rare.

Because the financial plans of all bank members must be harmonized with that of the bank and thus indirectly with each other, and because the plan of the bank has in turn to be harmonized with those of sociopolitical communities, the compromises are probably struck in the annual plan of the bank. By whatever procedures the compromise across all nonpriority activities is eventually established, this mutual financial harmonization is likely to compel all members of the bank to justify their respective projects to each other. The eventual selection of the recipients of the total available investment resources would then be acceptable to the greatest number of bank

---

26. The five priority activities identified in table 8.12 account for 60 percent of the total. Although some minor parts can fall outside the priorities, other priority activities, such as those in tourism, engineering, and nonmetallic minerals, are included elsewhere. The total program of priority activities is thus reported to be about 65 percent. Nevertheless minor projects in priority activities probably fall outside the first-claim category.

27. An example is the attempt to harmonize the plans for automobile manufacturing, which is not a priority activity. An enterprise manufacturing cars from self-produced or locally purchased components on a moderate scale tried to initiate a joint program with three other enterprises assembling cars from CKD (completely knocked down) sets, which are imported against exports of mass-produced components to the foreign suppliers. No agreement was reached, which may or may not have increased the efficiency of the industry. Each enterprise is now pursuing an independent program of development; that independence may result in some overcapacity and suboptimal layout of plants.

members. For an enterprise to improve the chances for its specific projects, an obvious route would be to search for agreements with other enterprises on mutual financial assistance and for acting in concert with the bank's organs when it comes to supporting requests for financing the uncovered margins.

Given the claims of priority activities over nonpriority activities, the share of truly fungible resources in total resources is likely to decline. Alternatively the self-financing of individual enterprises or of groups of enterprises that agree to pool resources will increase. This self-financing is completely in the spirit of the new constitution. Enterprises are increasingly to rely upon mutual arrangements. Banks are to perform service functions and ration supplementary financing. Anonymous financial capital is gradually to disappear.

Assessment of the new procedures

Because the principal features of the allocation procedures for the 1976–80 period could only be hypothesized, the assessment is conjectural as well. Three of those features seem to be particularly noteworthy.

First, the emphasis on harmonization—which is institutionalized by the law on planning, the law on associated labor, and social compacts and self-management agreements—establishes the greatest possible ex ante transparency. This emphasis implies that all options, their merits and costs, and their underlying assumptions are, in principle, extensively discussed by all affected parties well in advance of implementing action. Extensive discussion thus substantially reduces the scope for ad hoc decisions and gross misallocations. The link between the financial planning of enterprises and that of banks should also reduce the tendency for excessive investment. This tendency in the past manifested itself in the underfinancing of projects. To complete overly ambitious projects, investors tried to increase their output prices, if market conditions permitted, or to stretch out project completion. Three provisions, already discussed in detail, further support the greater discipline imposed on initiating and carrying out investment projects: the new legislation on the computation of enterprise income, the continued requirement to submit evidence of firm financing commitments of all contributing parties before any physical action, and the unlimited liability of members of banks for the financial commitments of their banks.

Resource allocation probably is most efficiently carried out in the relations among BOALS within enterprises or between enterprises connected by agreements for joint pooling. This conclusion rests on two a priori assumptions: efficient decisionmaking through consensus is easier when the number of parties is smaller; the worker-controlled BOALS and enterprises have a fairly clear perception of their objective to maximize the benefits to workers.[28] The allocational alternatives selected would tend to be the ones most efficient with respect to this objective and all the conditions external to the enterprise. They are also the alternatives for which outside financing through banks is eventually being sought.

The second feature is that an overall adjustment, if and when it becomes necessary, would follow a distinct pattern. If the total availability of investment resources falls short of expectations, or if actual investment outlays in priority activities exceed expectations, the burden of adjustment would likely fall on nonpriority activities.[29] Productive investment in nonpriority activities would have to be reduced. Or the share of productive investment would have to be raised at the expense of nonproductive investment. Or the domestic saving rate, foreign borrowing, and total investment would have to be raised more than planned. Or any combination of these adjustments would become necessary. Because the domestic saving rate already is high, a further increase does not appear to be socially feasible, particularly if the economic growth rate falls short of expectations. Adjustment by increased foreign borrowing probably is not feasible either, unless the constraint of the plan for debt service, discussed in chapter five, is dropped. To compress nonproductive investment may also be difficult, given the high share of the private sector in that investment and the need for housing and social infrastructure. Thus any downward adjustment would probably result in

28. As already mentioned, the content of this general objective is subject to speculation. Three particular aspects are not clear: whether it relates only to personal incomes—including fringe benefits, which can at least notionally be expressed in monetary equivalents—or extends to broader benefits to society; whether it is sought in the short term or over some time horizon; and whether it refers strictly to present workers' community or includes those who may join that community in the future.

29. An additional factor is that a large part of investment outlays in priority activities is for technically indivisible projects or for programs having long gestation periods. That aspect leaves little room for alternative adjustments other than stretching out implementation, the least efficient form of adjustment. The remaining alternative is to delay construction of certain projects that would not cause serious bottlenecks.

a reduced investment share for nonpriority productive activities.[30] Such a result would extend past problems of rationing available resources into the future.

The third feature is that harmonization is the crucial step for progressing to a coherent and consistent pattern of allocation. Although the procedural framework is fairly clear—harmonization between specified parties must be accomplished within a determined time frame—it is not clear how the harmonization process actually works or how it is supposed to work. Obviously a broad spectrum of general economic, financial, technical, and political considerations enter into harmonization. But nothing is yet known about the way these considerations are pulled together, evaluated, and translated into a systematic weighing of alternatives. For priority activities, no persuasive evidence could be found for there to have been an exhaustive search of countrywide, least-cost programs for given output targets. Similarly for nonpriority activities no evidence was available for there to have been the application of any rigorous analytical methodology to ensure that allocations from the limited fungible resources of banks to all their members are most conducive to the growth of output and employment. In short, harmonization seems to have succeeded in establishing a rigorous procedural framework. It does not yet seem to include a complementary analytical framework for evaluating alternative options. Thus it still seems to rely heavily on negotiated decisions. As mentioned earlier, negotiated decisions probably are a feature of any real system that does not meet all the requirements for optimality specified by the pure models of either a centrally planned or a market economy. Moreover the negotiations do not automatically lead to poor decisions. The decisions emanating from harmonization will inevitably be subject to certain boundary conditions based on economic factors. This conclusion is the more apposite, given the openness of the Yugoslav economy to foreign trade. Nevertheless negotiated decisions, in the absence of a formal analytical framework for choosing among options, could lead to misallocations, particularly when choices are not clear-cut and market signals do not provide an adequate basis for choice. The adoption of a generally accepted and common ana-

---

30. The argument about the likely effect of downward adjustment would work in the opposite direction if the adjustment were upward. But because the plan's assumptions appear to be on the high side, for a variety of reasons discussed elsewhere in this volume, such an outcome is unlikely.

lytical framework could serve to highlight different assumptions and expectations and provide a basis for comparing alternatives.

Analytical techniques for refining harmonization

The absence of a rigorous method for comparing alternatives is a serious gap in the framework for planning and resource allocation. It could be remedied by the systematic application of cost-benefit analysis.[31] The use of cost-benefit analysis, as an analytical tool supporting rationality in decisionmaking, would not be a substitute for conscious choices by planning agents, but merely a supplement. It could serve as the basis for a systematic comparison of alternatives by organizing all quantifiable considerations into a generally accepted analytical framework. It could extend the transparency of costs and benefits from the level of enterprises to that of society. It could establish a ranking of comparable projects by their contributions to social welfare, within the limitations of any such analytical technique. It would not dictate the eventual choice. For reasons not covered by cost-benefit analysis, planning agents could choose an alternative other than the best alternative determined in the framework of cost-benefit analysis. But the cost of such choices to society—additional social costs, reduced social benefits, or both—would be explicit. This information would sharpen the focus for considerations that cannot be covered by quantitative comparisons, but remain to be settled by qualitative considerations.

Because cost-benefit analysis would neither supplant conscious choices nor lead to financial obligations, there seems to be no fundamental contradiction between its use and the principles of self-management and socialism.[32] On the contrary, it could increase the economic and sociopolitical potential of self-management. In a self-

---

31. Cost-benefit analysis is here used as a generic term. Many variants of cost-benefit analysis are advanced under specific terms, such as economic project evaluation or social project evaluation. Common to all variants is the extension of the focus beyond the narrowly defined financial success of isolated projects by including externalities and using shadow prices, which reflect social, not actual, prices. Also common is the discounting of flows of costs and benefit over the life of projects to the decision point in time—that is, discounting by a rate which in some cases is to reflect the social choice of preference of present over future consumption and in others some social rate of profit.

32. The general use of cost-benefit analysis is reported for several COMECON countries.

managed socialist system, with a dual focus on efficiency and solidarity, the analytical potential of cost-benefit analysis would find an ideal environment. Indeed the scope for cost-benefit analysis can extend beyond the perspective of growth and efficiency to include such social objectives as employment generation and income distribution.

Resource Allocation under the Social Plan for 1976–80

The proportions of aggregate investment under the five-year plan for 1976–80, when compared with estimated investment during the preceding plan period, show little variation (table 8.11). One excep-

Table 8.11. *Structure of Investment, 1971–75 and Targets in the Social Plan for 1976–80*
(percent)

Item	1971–75	1976–80	1976–80 (1971–75 = 100)
Social sector	83.8	83.6	148
Private sector	16.2	16.4	146
Productive investment	68.6	69.0	150
Nonproductive investment	31.4	31.0	143
Fixed assets	78.5	79.8	147
Increase in stocks	21.5	20.2	136
Total investment	100.0	100.0	145
Share of investment in gross material product	37.0	38.8	138

Note: Investment includes the investment in inventories.
Source: Figures supplied by the Federal Institute of Planning.

tion is the higher share of total investment in GMP. The variation is greater for the composition of investment in productive activities, which account for about half of total plan investment (table 8.12). Although the shares of some sectors—notably agriculture, transport, and the private sector—are expected to remain virtually unchanged, those for trade and tourism are expected to decline sharply; that for industry is to rise. The expected changes are most pronounced in the industrial sector. Total investment in two industrial complexes, one for energy and the other for basic chemistry, is

Table 8.12. *Structure of Investment in Fixed Assets*
for Productive Activities, 1971–75 and Targets
in the Social Plan for 1976–80
(percent)

Sector or branch	1971–75	1976–80ᵃ	1976–80 (1971–75 = 100)
Industry	47.3	51.2	163
Energy	11.2	21.7	292
Basic metals	8.7	6.6	113
Basic chemistry	1.7	4.3	381
Other	25.7	18.6	109
Agriculture	9.7	9.5	156
Construction	3.2	3.0	136
Transport and communications	18.5	17.6	151
Trade and tourism	12.0	8.2	103
Handicrafts	1.8	1.6	138
Private sector	7.4	7.4	149
Total	100.0	100.0	150

Source: Appendix table A.16.
a. Figures do not total 100 because of an unallocated reserve.

expected almost to triple, with an aggregate share rising from 13 percent of the total to 26 percent.[33] Investment in basic metallurgy is expected to rise by 13 percent; its share in fixed investment in productive activities is to decline from 9 percent to 7 percent. Investment in all remaining industries is expected to remain at about the same level; consequently their share in total industrial investment is to decline from 54 to 37 percent.

The plan sets out investment and growth targets, from which unlagged ICORS can be derived for comparison with estimates for the preceding plan period (table 8.13). Any assessment of the realism

33. These two sectors are the core of priority activities in industry. Other priority sectors in industry include basic metallurgy and industrial equipment and electronics. Analysis of the sources of growth during the 1966–72 period shows that the sectors now designated as priority activities tended to lag in output growth. They also experienced massive growth of competing imports, which resulted in increased import dependency. The sectors not designated as priority activities did not lag in output growth. Although competing imports also grew rapidly, this growth was the result of demand and technological factors unrelated to the substitution of imports for domestic deliveries. See the technical note at the end of this chapter for a discussion of the sources-of-growth analysis for 1966–72.

Table 8.13 *Growth Rate of Gross Material Product
and Incremental Capital-Output Ratio
for Productive Activities, 1971–75 and Targets
in the Social Plan for 1976–80*

	Average annual rate of GMP growth (percent)		Incremental capital-output ratio	
Sector	1971–75	1976–80	1971–75	1976–80
Social sector	6.8	7.5	3.02	2.93
Industry	8.1	8.0	2.81	3.10
Private sector	3.9	3.7	2.16	2.78
Total economy	6.3	6.9	2.94	2.91

Source: Figures supplied by the Federal Institute of Planning.

of the planned growth rates and investment targets should begin with a comparison with documented past performance. Unfortunately such a straightforward assessment is severely hampered for several reasons. For GMP growth the plan used estimated 1975 figures, which differ considerably from reported 1975 data. The sectoral targets for output growth cover the private and social sectors, but the sectoral targets for investment are for the social sector alone. No estimates of GMP growth by branch, and only a few estimates of investment were available for the industrial sector, which accounts for more than 50 percent total productive investment in the plan and 42 percent of GMP.

Given the deficiencies of the data, the analysis here is based on a narrow, mechanistic approach. It is intended to be indicative, not predictive. By using reported GMP data by sector and branch for 1975, reported GMP growth by sector and branch for 1970–75 in constant 1972 prices, and plan data for investment by sector and branch for the same period, the corresponding implied ICORs of sectors and branches were estimated in constant prices (table 8.14).[34] In the first variant for 1976–80 the ICORs were assumed to remain unchanged. By multiplying those ICORs with the investment targets of the plan, the corresponding output levels and growth rates were

34. Because of the inadequate data, this estimation assumes no time lags in the ICORs. A test using aggregate data from another source indicates that for a time lag between investment and output of one year, the ICOR would be about 5 percent lower; for a time lag of two years, it would be about 10 percent lower. *Statistical Yearbook of Yugoslavia,* 1976.

Table 8.14. *Growth Rate of Gross Material Product and Incremental Capital-Output Ratio, Estimates for 1971–75 and Three Variants for 1976–80*

		1976–80		
Sector	1971–75	First variant	Second variant	Third variant
Average annual rate of growth (percent)				
Social sector	6.4	6.8	6.0	5.8
Basic industries	8.0	15.1	10.4	8.7
Light industries	7.7	6.0	6.0	6.0
Total industries	7.8	9.0	7.4	6.8
Other	5.4	4.9	4.9	4.9
Private sector	3.3	4.1	4.1	4.1
Total	5.8	6.4	5.7	5.5
Incremental capital-output ratio				
Social sector	3.5	3.5	4.0	4.2
Basic industries	5.2	3.6	5.7	7.1
Light industries	2.6	2.6	2.6	2.6
Total industries	3.3	3.1	3.9	4.3
Other	3.8	4.1	4.1	4.1
Private sector	2.7	2.7	2.7	2.7
Total	3.5	3.4	3.9	4.0

Note: The assumptions underlying the computation are described in the text.
Source: Calculated from *Statistical Yearbook of Yugoslavia,* 1976 and figures supplied by the Federal Institute of Planning.

computed. In that variant, however, the ICORS for two branches, petroleum and basic chemicals, were unrealistically low.[35] Consequently in the second and third variants, adjustments were made to

35. In the preceding plan period the ICOR for petroleum was 2.1; that for basic chemicals 2.2. The reasons for the low ratios are not clear. In both instances investment during the preceding period was very low. It is expected to be seven times higher during the current plan period for petroleum and four times higher for basic chemicals. Apparently both branches—for technological reasons they are very capital intensive and slow yielding—grew in the recent past at a moderate pace by improving the use and efficiency of the existing capital stock. The new plan envisions several major new projects.

take this into account. In the second variant the ICORS of those two branches were increased to 3.3, the level of all industry. The corresponding output levels and growth rates were then recomputed. In the third variant the ICORS for those two branches were further raised to 5.1, the level of all basic industries, and the computation was carried out in the same way. Given the technical characteristics of these two branches and the artificially low ICOR of total basic industries, which ICOR reflects to a considerable degree the low ICORS of the two branches in the base period, even the ICOR of the third variant appears to be low.[36]

For the 1971–75 period the computed average growth rates in table 8.14 are about half a percentage point lower than the empirical rates shown in table 8.13. The data basis and a somewhat exaggerated ICOR explain the underestimation. Thus the annual growth rates in the first variant, which is equivalent to the computation for 1971–75, are correspondingly lower than the plan's rate of 6.9 percent. In the second and third variants, which for reasons indicated in the foregoing paragraph appear to be more realistic than the first variant, the differences in growth rates and ICORS are significant. This analysis is incomplete, however, because of the disregard for second-round effects. At lower growth rates, total investment resources will also tend to be lower, unless higher saving rates, reduced nonproductive investment, or higher foreign borrowing make up the shortfall. As indicated earlier, the downward adjustment of total investment would not affect all sectors and branches equally. It would mainly reduce investment in the nonpriority productive activities, which are characterized by low ICORS. Thus, if any downward adjustment becomes necessary, it would raise the average ICOR of the reduced program, thus reducing the growth rate of GMP and available investment resources even further. To illustrate: If a hypothetical 20-percent reduction of planned volume of productive investment were to be absorbed exclusively by nonpriority activities in the social sector and by an identical rate of reduction for each activity, their investment program would need to be slashed by about 60 percent. As a result, the growth rate would, on the basis of the third variant, further drop to a mere 3.7 percent a year. The aggregate ICOR would

36. Excluding those two branches from the ICOR of basic industries further reduces the economic growth rate to 5.3 percent and raises the total ICOR to 4.2.

rise to 4.9 and lead to a third round of downward adjustment.[37] In addition to the implications of an increase in the aggregate ICORS for growth, there are severe implications for employment. The reason is that nonpriority activities not only have lower ICORS than priority activities; they also have lower incremental capital-labor ratios.[38]

The crucial assumption in the model presented here is the intertemporal stability of ICORS by sector and branch, an assumption which can neither be supported nor refuted by a priori considerations or by available empirical evidence. The model nevertheless demonstrates that the plan rests on the assumption of significantly lower ICORS. Put differently, to make the growth and investment targets of the plan mutually consistent, the total ICOR of the third variant must be reduced from 4.0 to 3.2, which is equivalent to a reduction by 20 percent across the board. Although the possibility of such an improvement in allocative efficiency cannot be ruled out, the improvement implied within a short period gives rise to some doubts. That improvement would certainly require new efforts to improve operative and allocative efficiency throughout the economy. Improving the operative efficiency of existing capital stock appears to be the principal remedy foreseen in the plan, as is evidenced by numerous references to using existing capacity more fully and operating it more efficiently.[39]

As stressed before, in the absence of sufficiently detailed information on assumptions and quantitative relations, the calculations are mechanistic and purely illustrative. They are not an attempt to indicate how targets of the plan might be corrected. They merely consider those targets in the light of empirical evidence and some sweeping assumptions distilled from the plan document, particularly on adjustment procedures. They also point to potential problems that may emerge. The simulations indicate that the resolution of struc-

---

37. In addition to these contractionary effects in the productive activities, contraction would occur in nonproductive activities because a reduction of GMP growth in productive activities is likely to reduce the availability of resources for nonproductive activities.

38. The subject of capital-labor ratios is discussed in detail in chapter ten.

39. The assessment of growth prospects in chapter five recognizes the possibility that the ICOR is underestimated, but the quantitative assessment there and in this chapter do not match because of differences in the base and in coverage. In chapter five the base is historical evidence, and the coverage is total investment and GNP; here the base is plan data adjusted in the light of empirical evidence, and the coverage is productive investment and GMP.

tural imbalances may carry a considerable cost: higher savings, lower nonproductive investment, increased borrowings, or growth rates of GMP and employment that are considerably lower than anticipated. To the extent that the allocative and operative efficiency of the system improves and resource mobilization matches actual requirements, these social costs would be reduced. We concur with the Yugoslav assessment that there is considerable scope on both scores and that a number of the recent changes would tend to work in the right direction. Nevertheless the evidence about the potential for such improvement from one plan period to another is inconclusive.

Technical Note. Analysis of the Sources of Growth: 1966–72

A demand version of sources-of-growth analysis is designed to analyze changes in the structure of production by disaggregating those changes and assigning them to changes in various components of demand: final demand, intermediate goods, exports, and imports.[40] Balanced growth—defined as the growth of all sectors at the same rate as the increase in aggregate final demand—is used as the benchmark for measuring structural change. For example, a benchmark output vector for 1972 is obtained by assuming that output levels of all sectors in the initial year, 1966, grew at the same rate as aggregate final demand. This balanced-growth vector of gross output is then compared with that actually observed for 1972. The differences— that is, the deviations from proportional growth—are then explained by disproportionate changes in the components of demand: exports; domestic final demand, which comprises consumption, investment, and the net increase in stocks; import requirements in final demand; import requirements in intermediate demand; and changes in technology. The changes in import ratios within the cells of the inter-industry matrix are measures of the import requirements in intermediate demand; the changes in the technical coefficients of the

40. For rigorous expositions of the analytical framework used in this analysis see Moshe Syrquin, "Sources of Industrial Growth and Change: An Alternative Measure" (paper presented at the August 1976 meeting of the International Econometric Society in Helsinki; processed) and Yuji Kubo and Sherman Robinson, "Sources of Industrial Growth and Structural Change: A Comparative Analysis of Eight Countries" (paper presented at the international conference on input-output techniques sponsored by the United Nations Industrial Development Organization, April 1979, Innsbruck; processed).

interindustry matrix are measures of changes in technology. Thus the analysis highlights the effects of a variety of autonomous factors on the growth of different sectors.

Table 8.15 summarizes the broad features of the growth pattern for 1966–72.[41] If industry is taken as an example, it can be observed that output growth was about Din3.2 billion, or 1.3 percent, higher in 1972 than balanced growth. Changes in domestic final demand led to an increase in output of Din10.1 billion in excess of the proportional growth; exports, an increase of Din7.3 billion; import substitution in final demand, an increase of Din0.2 billion; and technological change, an increase of Din6.6 billion. The effect of negative import substitution—that is, increased import dependency—canceled most of the positive effects. The negative import substitution in intermediate goods amounted to Din21.1 billion.

The analysis also shows that there were major structural changes between sectors over the period. The output in agriculture and forestry respectively were 40 percent and 37 percent lower than the levels under balanced growth; the opposite was true for all other sectors, particularly construction and trade and catering. There consequently was a significant reorientation of output among sectors, with agriculture and forestry growing at a considerably lower rate than if they had expanded in line with the growth in aggregate demand.

The effect of the growth in domestic final demand was mixed. It was strongly positive for industry, construction, public utilities, and trade and catering; for each of these branches it was the most important single factor accounting for the disproportional growth in output. In agriculture, forestry, and handicrafts, the effect was negative; it was particularly pronounced in agriculture, reflecting the low income elasticity of demand for primary foodstuff. The effect on total output of final demand in all sectors combined, though negative, was small. The effect of export growth on sectoral outputs was mixed; it was significant only for industry, for which its strong positive effect indicated that there was a higher-than-proportional growth in exports and that this growth had a positive effect on output of the industrial sector. In aggregate, however, the export effect, though positive, was fairly modest. Import substitution in final

41. Full details of the sources-of-growth analysis for 1966–72 are in World Bank, "Yugoslavia: Self-Management Socialism and the Challenges of Development," report no. 1615a–YU (a restricted circulation document), 6 vols. (Washington, D.C., 1978; processed), vol. 6.

Table 8.15. *Decomposition of the Sources of Growth of Output, 1966–72*

	Gross output in 1972 (billions of dinars)			
Sector	Balanced growth	Actual growth	Deviation	Percentage deviation
Industry	239.4	242.6	3.2	1.3
Agriculture	97.7	69.8	−27.9	−40.0
Forestry	7.1	5.2	− 1.9	−36.8
Construction	52.7	63.8	11.1	17.4
Transport and communications	26.7	27.8	1.1	3.9
Trade and tourism	51.2	64.8	13.6	20.9
Handicrafts	10.6	11.3	0.7	5.8
Communal services	2.1	2.4	0.3	11.7
Other	1.2	1.3	0.1	6.4

... Zero or negligible.

Note: Figures may not reconcile because of rounding. When the figures for deviations are negative—that is when the growth in a sector is less than proportional to the growth in aggregate demand—a positive contribution to the deviation indicates that a factor contributes to reductions in output. The converse is true when the figures for deviations are positive.

demand had a positive, though fairly modest effect on output in all sectors. It nevertheless had a small negative effect on the construction and "other" sectors, which are a small residual item. A detailed breakdown shows that, although the output effect was positive, import substitution for investment goods had a negative effect on all sectors, signifying increased dependence on imports of capital goods. The most striking feature of table 8.15 is the effect on output of import substitution in intermediate goods: it was negative in all sectors, except "other." These output effects cannot be directly translated into changes in sectoral import dependency.[42] The results

42. Although the negative effect on output of import substitution signifies some form of increased import dependency, it does not enable inferences about the extent and incidence of that increase. The reason is that the analysis here covers all direct and indirect effects. To illustrate: It is possible to observe a decline in import dependency in a sector, say forestry, but to observe in the analysis here that output in that sector was adversely affected through import substitution. This outcome may simply be the result of growing import de-

		Import substitution				
		Contribution to deviation (percent)				
Final demand	*Exports*	*Final demand*	*Inter-mediate inputs*	*Tech-nologi-cal change*	*Total*	*Sector*
315	235	6	−660	205	100	Industry
121	12	−7	1	−27	10C	Agriculture
32	−6	2	30	42	100	Forestry
112	−20	−1	−1	10	100	Construction
75	−3	3	−84	109	100	Transport and communication
77	9	1	−5	18	100	Trade and tourism
−43	−18	5	−39	195	100	Handicrafts
96	4	. . .	−14	14	100	Communal services
98	−69	−30	69	32	100	Other

Source: World Bank, "Yugoslavia: Self-Management Socialism and the Challenges of Development," report no. 1615a-YU (a restricted circulation document), 6 vols. (Washington, D.C., 1978; processed), vol. 6.

nevertheless indicate that there was a sharp increase in dependence on imported intermediate goods, the effects of which grossly outweighed the positive effects of export growth.[43]

The technological effect reflects three sets of factors: changes in interdependency among sectors within the interindustry matrix leading to a change in output more rapid than the change in final demand; changes in efficiency affecting intermediate input requirements to produce a unit of intermediate output; and relative price changes, which affect the composition of intermediate inputs used to produce a unit of output. During the 1966–72 period the technological effect was positive, except for forestry, and considerable in a number of sectors. Although it is not possible to determine the specific factors underlying this trend, the most likely cause is the increasing interdependency of the economy.

---

pendency in other sectors, which dependency adversely affects the output of those sectors and, through the interindustry matrix, eventually affects the output of the forestry sector.
43. This conclusion is confirmed by the analysis in chapter nine.

Table 8.16. *Decomposition of the Sources of Growth of Output, for Twenty-nine Sectors and Branches, 1966–72*

Sector or branch	Final demand Con- sump- tion	Invest- ment	Stocks	Ex- ports	Import substi- tution Con- sump- tion
Electricity	258	49	−85	55	13
Coal	10	−6	6	−8	−1
Petroleum	64	11	−19	−30	5
Ferrous metallurgy	−7	−12	7	−2	−2
Nonferrous metallurgy	−6	−4	26	−36	−1
Nonmetal products	−99	−37	39	46	−15
Metal products	−127	−170	88	40	−59
Shipbuilding	27	−153	−8	189	−1
Electrical machinery	125	75	−103	80	27
Chemicals	20	11	−49	38	14
Building materials	43	139	−8	−51	1
Wood manufactures	253	51	−75	−56	0
Paper products	−165	−32	272	−49	−5
Textiles	3	−1	52	−21	−4
Leather goods and footwear	−199	1	18	471	−54
Rubber products	127	35	−74	61	−34
Food manufactures	49	1	−7	13	−2
Printing and publishing	−14	−25	249	−50	−91
Tobacco	−48	0	49	46	−6
Film products	−1	0	64	12	−3
Miscellaneous manufactures	−19	−3	39	−18	47
Agriculture	88	−5	39	12	−12
Forestry	19	−5	18	−5	1
Construction	17	94	0	−20	0
Transport and communication	78	48	−50	−3	7
Trade and catering	75	8	−6	9	1
Handicrafts	−51	44	−36	−18	8
Public utilities	95	12	−10	4	2
Sewage control and waste	−103	−56	257	−69	−13
Total economy	−390	−1,725	2,302	−313	−452
Total industry	511	169	−364	235	41

Note: Figure may not reconcile because of rounding.
Source: World Bank, "Yugoslavia: Self-Management Socialism and the Challenges of Development," vol. 6, tables D.1 and D.2.

Contribution to deviation (percent)

Import substitution			Technological change	Deviation in output (millions of dinars)	Sector or branch
Investment	Stocks	Intermediate inputs			
−3	0	−160	−26	300	Electricity
1	−1	29	71	−1,901	Coal
0	−1	−30	101	1,935	Petroleum
1	2	53	59	−5,480	Ferrous metallurgy
0	−9	116	12	−4,887	Nonferrous metallurgy
1	13	138	13	−422	Nonmetal products
46	17	395	−131	−1,130	Metal products
65	0	−7	−12	385	Shipbuilding
−4	−8	−78	15	661	Electrical machinery
0	−4	−53	124	2,183	Chemicals
−1	−3	−38	18	680	Building materials
−3	−8	−64	1	1,056	Wood manufactures
1	−2	256	−176	−312	Paper products
0	1	36	33	−5,481	Textiles
0	−9	−88	−40	418	Leather goods and footwear
−3	−4	−52	45	154	Rubber products
0	−2	2	46	15,652	Food manufactures
1	−4	70	−37	−98	Printing and publishing
0	20	31	8	−231	Tobacco
0	4	0	25	−178	Film products
0	17	20	16	−132	Miscellaneous manufactures
0	4	1	−27	−27,918	Agriculture
0	1	30	42	−1,926	Forestry
−1	0	−1	10	10,092	Construction
−2	−3	−84	109	1,082	Transport and communication
0	0	−5	18	13,562	Trade and catering
−1	−3	−39	195	665	Handicrafts
0	−1	−14	13	285	Public utilities
8	−25	69	32	−82	Sewage control and waste
58	183	2,234	−1,796	−1,069	Total economy
−15	−19	−661	205	3,171	Total industry

The sharply differing behavior of individual branches is apparent in a detailed breakdown of industry (table 8.16). In five major branches output growth was more than 10 percent below proportional growth: coal, textiles, ferrous metallurgy, nonferrous metallurgy, and nonmetallic products. The main factor in the coal industry was the technological effect, which reflects the shift toward other sources of energy; in all four other branches the increased negative import substitution of intermediate goods was important. The positive effects on output were large in crude petroleum, chemicals, building materials, and food manufacturing, mainly because of the effects of technological change and domestic demand. But once again, despite the more than proportional growth in output, the import substitution effect was highly negative in all these sectors, except in food manufacturing.

Nine

Balance of Payments

INTEGRATION WITH THE WORLD ECONOMY has exposed Yugoslavia to the fortunes of its trading partners and made its economy increasingly vulnerable to external events. The growing importance of foreign trade and recent structural changes in the balance of payments underlie that vulnerability. Three structural changes have been most important: the greater orientation of trade toward market economies, particularly those in Western Europe; the greater prominence of intermediate and capital goods in imports; and the greater reliance on workers' remittances as a principal, but now declining, source of additional foreign exchange. Nevertheless the diversity in the commodity composition and market orientation of exports has moderated, and at times shielded, the economy from the influence of external events. Those effects clearly are evident in the way Yugoslavia has shifted the direction of its trade between its Western European and Eastern European partners.

Between 1962 and 1971 Yugoslavia generally ran moderate deficits in the current account. After surpluses in 1972 and 1973 the deficits reached dramatic proportions in 1974 and 1975. Over most of the period the structure of the current account gradually changed: the relative importance of merchandise exports consistently declined because of the growth of nonfactor services and workers' remittances; the share of merchandise imports was stable (table 9.1). There consequently was a decline of the coverage of merchandise imports by exports. Whereas exports covered 78 percent of merchandise imports in 1966, they covered only 56 percent in 1975. The growth of exports and imports increased the openness and orientation of the economy to foreign trade. Between 1962 and 1974 the share of exports in GNP rose from 15.2 percent to 20.9 percent; the share of imports from 17.8 percent to 27.8 percent (see appendix table A.17).

Table 9.1. *Structure of the Current Account,*
Selected Years, 1962–75
(percent)

Item	1962	1966	1970	1975
Exports				
Merchandise	72	68	56	51
Nonfactor services	20	25	28	27
Workers' remittances	...	3	15	20
Other factor services[a]	8	4	2	3
Imports				
Merchandise	90	86	85	85
Nonfactor services	8	10	11	11
Interest payments	2	4	4	4
Ratio of merchandise exports to merchandise imports	72	78	60	56

... Zero or negligible.
Note: Figures are three-year averages, except those for 1975, which
are averages for 1974–75.
Source: Appendix table A.17.
a. Includes transfers.

The deterioration in the balance of payments in 1974 and 1975 was
a result of three principal factors: the significant shift in the terms of
trade, mainly because of the rise in oil prices; the recession in
Western Europe; and the rapid increase of domestic demand for
imports and exportables. Before 1973 the terms of trade had comparatively little effect on the trade balance. Cumulatively the terms
of trade improved by 6 percent between 1956 and 1973. In 1974,
however, the terms of trade fell by 10 percent; only half of this
decline was recovered by 1976. Changes in trade volumes and prices
highlight these movements (table 9.2).

The recession in OECD countries, the major market for Yugoslav
merchandise exports, was another important external factor in the
long-term growth of commodity exports and their slump in 1974–75.
Between 1966 and 1973 the aggregate GNP of those countries grew by
about 5 percent a year; during the same period they absorbed about
55 percent of Yugoslavia's exports (see appendix table A.20). In
1974 the rate of economic growth in OECD countries dropped to
zero; in 1975 their aggregate GNP fell by 2 percent. As a result Yugoslav exports to OECD countries declined by more than a third in real
terms between 1973 and 1975—a decline that was only partly com-

Table 9.2. *Volume and Prices of Exports and Imports
and Change in the Terms of Trade, 1972–76*
(percent)

| Year | Annual rate of growth | | | | Change in the terms of trade |
	Export volume	Export prices	Import volume	Import prices	
1972	17.3	6.7	−6.2	5.6	1.1
1973	6.8	19.5	16.4	20.0	−0.4
1974	0.9	31.6	14.5	46.1	−10.5
1975	−1.9	9.2	−3.0	4.9	3.9
1976ᵃ	15.0	4.0	−7.0	3.0	1.0

Source: Appendix table A.18.
a. Preliminary estimates.

pensated for by export expansion to centrally planned economies
and less developed countries (LDCS). Import controls aggravated the
decline in OECD demand for Yugoslav exports. The ban that countries of the European Economic Community (EEC) enforced on
beef imports was of particular relevance to Yugoslavia; it reduced
the growth rate of Yugoslav exports by 2 to 3 percentage points.

In 1974 the high rate of domestic growth—GMP grew by about 9
percent—helped to precipitate the large deficit in the current account. With the rapid rise of domestic demand, producers were less
aggressive in seeking export markets because it was easier to sell their
products at home. In addition, bottlenecks in supply strengthened
the demand for imports. These effects were reinforced by a 29 percent rise in producer prices which far exceeded international rates
and spurred stockpiling and speculative importing.

The prospect of continuing deficits in the balance of payments
led in mid-1974 to the introduction of various policies and measures:
tightening the controls on domestic investment credits, increasing
the basic turnover tax and the import surcharge, raising the share of
imports subject to licensing procedures, providing customs rebates
for exporters, allowing the nominal depreciation of the dinar, linking
imports to exports, easing the conditions for export credits, and
tightening the conditions for import credits. These measures, together with the economic recovery in Western Europe, turned the
balance of payments around in 1976 (see appendix tables A.17 and
A.18). The improvement nevertheless had its cost: the growth of
industrial production and GMP began to slacken. More recent trends

indicate the reappearance of deficits. Although such deficits may persist, the new policies and measures should enable more effective management of foreign trade.

Geographical Trade Patterns

Yugoslavia's position as a leading member of the group of nonaligned nations has affected its international economic relations. Yugoslavia holds a special status with respect to the OECD and COMECON, has a trade agreement with the EEC, and now trades with more than a hundred countries. Despite this geographical spread, four countries account for almost half of Yugoslavia's merchandise trade: the Soviet Union, the Federal Republic of Germany, Italy, and the United States. The Soviet Union recently overtook the Federal Republic of Germany as Yugoslavia's most important trading partner. Its share in Yugoslavia's trade rose from 11 percent in 1973 to 15.5 percent in 1975, mainly because of a 150 percent expansion of its imports from Yugoslavia. During the same period, the share of the Federal Republic of Germany declined from 16 percent to 14.9 percent.

Long-term trends of the geographical structure of Yugoslav trade are best observed by aggregating countries into three groups: OECD countries, centrally planned economies, and LDCs. In 1956 about two-thirds of Yugoslavia's exports went to OECD countries; the share of exports to centrally planned economies—a close approximation to exports to COMECON countries—was 23 percent, compared with 1 percent in 1954 and 52 percent in 1948 (table 9.3). The share of the OECD remained fairly stable at somewhat more than half of Yugoslavia's exports during 1967–73. When the economic recession in Western Europe reduced the OECD share to 36 percent in 1975, the shares of exports to the centrally planned economies and LDCs accordingly rose. A quickening pace of economic activity in OECD countries subsequently caused their share in Yugoslav exports to rise to about 42 percent in 1976. The geographical structure of imports has been more stable than that of exports; the most significant change was the relative increase in imports from the LDCs since 1972. The increased participation of LDCs in Yugoslavia's foreign trade, an objective for many years, was achieved after specific export endeavors were undertaken to pay for higher priced oil imports. The lower share of centrally planned economies in Yugoslavia's imports than in exports reflects the philosophy of balanced bilateral trade

Table 9.3. *Geographical Orientation of Trade,*
Selected Years, 1956–76
(percent)

Origin or destination of trade	Share in Yugoslav trade					
	1956	1970	1973	1974	1975	1976
Exports						
OECD countries	65	56	56	47	36	42
Centrally planned economies	23	33	34	47	47	42
Less developed countries	12	11	10	12	17	16
Imports						
OECD countries	66	69	63	61	61	55
Centrally planned economies	23	21	25	23	25	29
Less developed countries	11	10	13	16	14	16

Source: Appendix table A.20.

with those countries and the less competitive selling conditions in their markets, in which quality, design, and technical standards are less rigorous.

The commodity breakdown of trade by region for 1973 reveals that the EEC is the major market for Yugoslav exports of primary products, whereas Eastern Europe and LDCs are the destinations of the largest share of manufactured exports—that is, of groups 5–8 in the standard international trade classification (SITC).[1] This pattern is consistent with the suggestion in the foregoing paragraph that it is easier to enter markets for manufactured goods in Eastern Europe and LDCs than in Western Europe. LDCs tend to account for a lower share of such labor-intensive goods as clothing, footwear, and leather products. For imports the EEC dominated in manufactured goods by supplying more than half the total; centrally planned economies and LDCs had a stronger relative position for raw materials and intermediate goods.

An outgrowth of these diverse relationships is that a sizable part of Yugoslavia's trade is conducted under bilateral clearing arrangements. The balance of payments with the convertible-currency and bilateral-clearing areas considerably differs for such specific balances

1. See OECD, *Statistics of Foreign Trade, 1973* (Paris, 1974), series B.

Table 9.4. *Trade Balances with the Convertible-currency and Bilateral-clearing Areas, 1968, 1971, and 1974*
(millions of dollars)

Balance and area	1968	1971	1974
Trade balance			
Convertible-currency area	−493	−1,113	−3,500
Bilateral-clearing area	−94	−97	−181
Service balance			
Convertible-currency area	379	998	2,368
Bilateral-clearing area	108	115	205
Current account balance			
Convertible-currency area	−115	−115	−1,132
Bilateral-clearing area	15	18	24

Note: Figures for 1968 and 1971 are three-year averages; those for 1974 are two-year averages for 1974–75. Most bilateral trade agreements have provisions for settlement in convertible currency of balances outstanding at the end of a year or specified period.
Source: Appendix table A.18.

as those for trade, services, and the current account (table 9.4). Before 1974 the massive surplus in services largely compensated for the deficit with the convertible-currency area. Workers' remittances, tourism, and construction work abroad were the principal items. But as a result of the recession in Western Europe and the return of many workers, the growth of receipts from workers' remittances and tourism virtually halted in 1975. Yugoslavia's recent balance-of-trade difficulties are thus centered on trade with the EEC; the average deficit in the balance of trade with the EEC during 1974–75 was more than $2 billion a year, or 60 percent of the Yugoslav trade deficit.[2] In contrast, the guiding principle of trade relations with the bilateral-clearing area has been to achieve equilibrium in the current account for each country. In aggregate, Yugoslavia generally had a surplus in its balance of services with its partners in the bilateral-clearing area, and the trade balance has tended to be the adjustment mechanism for balancing the current account over the medium term.[3]

2. Exports to the EEC as a percentage of imports from the EEC fell from 78 percent in 1966 to 29 percent in 1975.
3. To avoid an excessive accumulation of surpluses, it was at times necessary to impose preconditions on exports to the bilateral-clearing area, such as the requirement that the exporter agree to import certain goods from that area or from particular countries.

The large current account deficit with the convertible-currency area points to the heavy net borrowing from that area. The dichotomy between the negative balance in the current account for the convertible-currency area and the artificial balance in that for the bilateral-clearing area is a fundamental dilemma in Yugoslavia's balance of payments. The heavy borrowing in convertible currency eventually has to be serviced in convertible currency, thus preempting a sizable portion of earnings from exports to the convertible-currency area. This requirement may leave Yugoslavia with little choice but to shift import demand to the maximum degree toward trade outside the convertible-currency area, even at some cost in quality or price. Otherwise Yugoslavia would have difficulty preserving its ability to service its debt and finance the necessary imports for which no substitute exists in bilateral trade.

The dichotomy has additional aspects that are more subtle, but no less severe. For example, an export drive directed toward markets in the bilateral-clearing area and fueled by export credits could aggravate the problems of the balance with the convertible-currency area. To the extent that such additional exports incorporate imports purchased in convertible currency, there would be a "leaking through" from one trade area to the other. Trade in chemicals is an example. In 1973 about 53 percent of chemicals exported by Yugoslavia were sold to Eastern European countries, predominantly under bilateral-clearing arrangements. But the production of chemicals is intensive in imports. Input-output computations for 1972 show that 37 percent of all material consumption of the chemical industry was directly or indirectly imported; most of these imports were purchased in convertible currency.

Exports of Goods

Exports, especially industrial exports, have expanded at a pace commensurate with industrial growth (table 9.5). This general pattern in part reflects the Yugoslav policy of simultaneous import substitution and export expansion—a policy that sets Yugoslavia apart from most developing countries. Since 1971, however, the momentum of export growth has slackened. The growth of exports was slower than the growth of GMP; the growth of manufactured exports was slower than the growth of industrial production. Nevertheless manufactured goods, defined as SITC groups 5–8, rose from 29 percent of merchandise exports in 1952 to 80 percent in 1975. Exports

Table 9.5. *Growth of Exports and Production, 1956–75*
(percent)

	Average annual rate of growth				
Item	1956–65	1965–70	1970–75	1965–75	1956–75
Merchandise exports	18.8	5.8	5.1	5.4	8.4
Gross material product[a]	8.8	5.7	5.8	5.8	7.2
Manufactured exports	15.1	6.8	5.5	6.2	10.3
Industrial production[a]	12.2	6.2	8.0	7.1	9.4

Source: *Statistical Yearbook of Yugoslavia*, 1976, tables 102–6, 102–21, 102–22, and 102–23.
a. In 1972 prices.

originating directly from the industrial sector averaged 77 percent of exports during 1956–60 and rose to 89 percent during 1971–75. Examination of the structure of exports by sector of origin reveals growing diversity (table 9.6). The sectors traditionally exporting materials and intermediate goods—especially agriculture, but metallurgy as well—lost greatly. The traditional manufacturing sectors—textiles, shoes, and wood products—held their positions. The new manufacturing sectors—engineering and chemicals—increased their share in total exports from 10 percent in 1956 to 45 percent in 1975.

By using constant-market-shares analysis, the growth of Yugoslavia's exports can be traced to four factors: the growth of world trade, the commodity structure, the market structure, and a residual effect, which at times is imprecisely termed the competitive effect.[4] Various influences may be subsumed under this residual effect, such as changes in relative prices, quality and marketing factors, govern-

---

4. Constant-market-shares analysis adopts as the standard for comparison a constant country share in world export markets over time. The difference between the growth of exports and the hypothetical growth implied by this standard is then disaggregated into commodity, market, and residual effects. Such analysis proceeds from the following identity:

$$E^2 - E^1 = (rE^1 + r_i - r)E^1_i + \sum_i \sum_j (r_{ij} - r_i)E^1_{ij}$$
$$+ \sum_i \sum_j (E^2_{ij} - E^1_{ij} - r_{ij}E^1_{ij}),$$

where E stands for the value of Yugoslav merchandise exports, 1 for the initial year, 2 for the end year, i for the commodity i, j for the market j, and r for the percentage change in world exports between years 1 and 2. The analysis was applied to three time periods (1961–65, 1965–70, and 1970–74), six SITC commodity groups (0 plus 1, 2 plus 4, 3, 5, 6 plus 8, and 7), and nine markets (EEC plus the European Free Trade Association, Sino-Soviet, other Europe, United States, developing Asia, developing America, developing Africa, Japan, and all others).

Table 9.6. *Structure of Exports, by Sector of Origin, 1956, 1965, and 1975*

(percent)

Sector	1956	1965	1975
Agriculture[a]	33.7	25.1	11.6
Metallurgy	21.0	11.3	14.5
Engineering[b]	6.1	27.9	34.3
Textiles, leather, and wood products	20.5	21.1	21.3
Chemicals[c]	4.3	6.7	11.7
Others	14.4	7.9	6.6

Source: Appendix table A.23.
a. Includes forestry and food processing.
b. Includes metal products, ships, and equipment.
c. Includes paper.

ment policies, and different development strategies. For example, the negative residual effect after 1965 may simply reflect the increasing provision of commodities under the post-1965 liberalization of domestic consumption, a factor that did not jeopardize the balance of payments because of the rapid increase of workers' remittances. Such a shift in strategy would not itself imply a change in competitiveness.

During 1961–65 total world exports increased by 39 percent; Yugoslav exports by 91 percent. For this period the world-trade effect—the hypothetical increase in exports that would have occurred if Yugoslavia's exports had expanded at the same rate as world exports—was $223.5 million, the equivalent of 43 percent of Yugoslavia's total export growth of $522.5 million (table 9.7). The residual effect, also reflecting the expansion from a relatively small base, exerted an even stronger influence: it was responsible for 59 percent of export growth. Both the market-distribution effect and the commodity-composition effect were virtually neutral.

In the two postreform periods the growth of Yugoslav exports failed to keep pace with the growth of world exports. The world-trade effect nevertheless exceeded 100 percent during these periods; consequently the other effects deteriorated. In the 1965–70 period Yugoslav exports tended to be concentrated in markets that grew slowly relative to other markets; in the 1970–74 period, in commodities that grew slowly relative to other commodities. The residual effect swung from being large and positive to being small but distinctly negative. As noted earlier, this catch-all residual effect is difficult to interpret; its causation cannot be assessed with precision.

Table 9.7. *Constant-market-shares Analysis of the Growth of Yugoslav Exports, 1961–65, 1965–70, and 1970–74*

Item	1961–65	1965–70	1970–74
	Value in millions of dollars		
Increase in exports	522.5	587.7	2,125.6
Increase attributable to:			
World-trade effect	223.5	736.8	2,814.0
Commodity-composition effect	−10.4	−27.7	−471.0
Market-distribution effect	2.3	−113.0	−45.6
Residual effect	307.1	−8.4	−171.8
	Percentage composition of effects		
Increase in exports	100	100	100
Increase attributable to:			
World-trade effect	43	125	132
Commodity-composition effect	−2	−5	−22
Market-distribution effect	0	−19	−2
Residual effect	59	−1	−8

Sources: Calculated from OECD, *Statistics of Foreign Trade*, various years, series B.

It is clear, however, that the growth of Yugoslav exports lagged behind that of world exports in the postreform years for a variety of reasons. This lag may have been a logical consequence of the rapid growth of consumption, the domestic demand boom, and an inflation rate which in the first half of the 1970s exceeded that of Yugoslavia's principal trading partners. Other factors may have been the restrictive credit policy in the early postreform years, the policy to reduce surplus clearing balances with Eastern Europe, and the discrimination in Western European regional trade blocks. In sum, the negative residual effect points to a need to examine whether the effect is attributable to a decline in competitiveness, as reflected in unit costs in Yugoslavia, or to factors unrelated to competitiveness.

Exports of Services

Exports of services recorded a phenomenal rise from 22 percent of exports of merchandise and services in 1956 to a peak of 51 percent in 1973. This growth mainly reflects three factors: the attractiveness of Yugoslavia to tourists, the migration of Yugoslav workers to factories in Western Europe and resulting inflow of workers' remittances, and the growth of construction activity abroad by Yugoslav enterprises. These exports have been decisive in keeping the growing trade deficit manageable.

Workers' remittances were negligible before 1965; by 1976 they had grown to $1.7 billion. Thus the migrants indirectly financed part of the growth of output and domestic employment. The growth of remittances, in relation to the purchasing power for imports, peaked in 1973, when the number of workers abroad started to fall. Between 1973 and 1976 real remittances declined by about 6 percent. The decline will probably continue and possibly turn into a decline in nominal terms if the absorptive capacity of the countries of destination rapidly falls, if the opportunity for domestic employment rapidly increases, and if the repatriation of accumulated savings held abroad does not accelerate. Estimates of workers' savings held abroad range as high as $2.6 billion, the equivalent of about 150 percent of total remittances in 1976.

Earnings from tourism, predominantly in hard currencies, have been another important source of inflows of foreign exchange. Rising from $81 million in 1965 to $800 million in 1976, their share in exports of services remained at about 20 percent. During 1965–75 tourism receipts grew at an average annual rate of 25 percent in current prices and 15 percent in constant prices using the import deflator. Yugoslav tourism expenditure abroad also grew rapidly in recent years: in 1976 it was equal to two-thirds of earnings from tourism. Net receipts from tourism thus are a volatile item in the balance of payments and could continue to decline.

Construction work abroad has increasingly become an important source of employment and foreign exchange. It started to become significant by the late 1960s; during the 1970s it grew in value at an average annual rate of 20 percent, rising from $250 million in 1970 to $760 million in 1976. It also was unaffected by slack in the growth of most other categories of earning foreign exchange during 1974–75. Growth prospects for this activity appear to be more favorable than those for workers' remittances or earnings from tourism. In the burgeoning economies of Iraq, Libya, and Algeria—the main sites of Yugoslav construction work abroad—Yugoslav enterprises have won large contracts. In addition, construction work abroad stimulates merchandise exports that complement construction and increases the marketing potential for other Yugoslav goods.

Imports of Goods and Services

Merchandise imports grew more rapidly during 1965–75 than 1956–65, but most of the higher growth occurred immediately after the reforms. The growth rate of imports was also significantly above that of exports after 1965. This pattern, together with the slackening of the GMP growth, implies that import dependency increased after the 1965 reforms. It reached a peak in 1974, when imports were equal to 28 percent of GMP. The elasticity of imports in relation to GMP during the 1965–70 period was 2.9, up considerably from 1.1 during 1956–65; it then declined to 1 during 1970–75 (table 9.8). The rise

Table 9.8. *Import Elasticity, 1956–75*

Item	1956–65	1965–70	1970–75	1965–75	1956–75
Average annual rate of real growth of merchandise imports[a] (percent)	9.6	14.3	5.8	10.0	9.8
Average annual rate of real growth of gross material product[a] (percent)	8.8	5.7	5.8	5.8	7.2
Import elasticity .	1.1	2.9	1.0	2.1	1.8

Source: Statistical Yearbook of Yugoslavia, 1976, tables 102–6 and 102–21.
a. Compound growth rates between three-year averages for the border years of the indicated periods.

after 1965 was a reflection of the greater openness of the economy. Its subsequent decline can be traced to adjustments to that openness: import-competing industries faced up to the new competition; economic policies were modified in response to the new situation.

The upward trend in import dependency can also be observed by considering all input-output linkages and examining the import content of the components of output and demand (table 9.9). The import requirements of broad categories rose substantially between 1966 and 1972, especially after 1968. The import dependency of export production experienced the fastest increase; by 1972 the share of imported inputs in industrial exports was about 30 percent. One implication of this level of import dependency is that data on gross earnings of foreign exchange for individual industries do not accu-

Table 9.9. *Total Import Content of Output and Demand, 1966–72*
(percent)

Item	Direct and indirect import content			
	1966	*1968*	*1970*	*1972*
Gross output	11.9	12.5	15.2	16.4
Investment	21.1	26.0	28.5	28.1
Industrial investment	59.1	63.0	66.2	65.4
Private and public consumption	15.2	15.4	16.8	18.4
Exports	15.3	16.8	21.5	23.4
Industrial exports	20.2	22.3	27.5	29.3

Sources: Figures for 1966, 1968, 1970, and 1972 were respectively calculated from Federal Institute of Statistics, *Studies, Analyses, and Reviews,* nos. 50 (Belgrade, 1970), 57 (Belgrade, 1971), 71 (Belgrade, 1975), and 80-81 (Belgrade, 1976).

rately indicate the contribution of those industries. Import content for fifteen of nineteen branches increased between 1966 and 1968; eighteen sectors became more dependent on imported inputs between 1968 and 1972 (see appendix table A.24). Among the sectors highly intensive in imports were ferrous metals, metal products, electrical machinery, chemicals, rubber products, and leather and footwear. Because these sectors were all favored by policies for import substitution, the policies can be seen to have been self-defeating to some degree.

To explore the behavior and underlying factors of imports, a sources-of-growth analysis was conducted for imports by sector.[5] Imports in 1972 were compared with imports that would have resulted if imports in each sector had grown at the same rate as the growth in aggregate final demand during the 1966–72 period. Deviations of actual growth from balanced growth can then be explained by changes in the composition of final demand, exports, imports, and intermediate demand. The results for a broad, nine-sector breakdown confirm, with the exception of agriculture, that the actual growth of imports during the period exceeded balanced growth (table 9.10). Given annual fluctuations because of weather conditions, that exception is not significant. Imports during the period were 18 percent higher than they would have been under balanced growth; if agriculture is ignored, 26 percent higher. The reduced import dependency for the nonindustrial sectors as a whole was

5. See the technical note at the end of chapter eight.

Table 9.10. *Decomposition of the Sources of Growth of Imports, 1966–72*

		Imports in 1972 (millions of dinars)		
Sector	Balanced growth[a]	Actual growth	Deviation	Percentage deviation
Industry	44,629	60,750	16,121	26.5
Agriculture	9,941	5,538	−4,403	−79.5
Forestry	214	443	229	51.7
Construction	...	81	81	100.0
Transport and communications	1,141	1,461	320	21.9
Trade and catering	347	480	133	27.7
Handicrafts	...	7	7	100.0
Other	507	318	−189	−59.3
Total	56,779	69,078	12,586	18.2

... Zero or negligible.
Note: Figures may not reconcile because of rounding.
Sources: Appendix table A.19 and World Bank, "Yugoslavia: Self-Management Socialism and the Challenges of Development," report no. 1615a-YU (a restricted circulation document), 6 vols. (Washington, D.C., 1978; processed), vol. 6.

entirely attributable to agriculture; import dependency in the industrial sector increased by nearly 27 percent over the period.

Except in agriculture and forestry, demand expansion contributed to the disproportionately high growth in imports. In agriculture half of the relatively slower growth in imports was the result of the relative decline in the growth of final demand. Export expansion had mixed results, but most effects were fairly small. The principal factor underlying the growth of import dependency in most sectors was the direct substitution of imports for domestic inputs, which substitution increased sectoral import coefficients. Increases in import ratios in final demand generally were modest. The exceptions were agriculture and construction, but neither exception was particularly important, because of the large annual fluctuations in agriculture and the small size of imports in construction. Thus, despite the rapid growth of incomes after 1966, domestic production for final demand was sufficiently rapid to stabilize the relative importance of imports

Contribution to deviation (percent)						
		Import substitution				
Final de-mand	Ex-ports	Final de-mand	Inter-mediate inputs	Tech-nology	Total	Sector
16	8	2	59	16	100	Industry
53	−2	50	−4	2	100	Agriculture
−3	2	10	143	−52	100	Forestry
19	…	82	…	…	100	Construction
13	−1	1	57	30	100	Transport and communications
11	…	1	−8	97	100	Trade and catering
3	…	…	50	47	100	Handicrafts
1	−3	23	117	−37	100	Other
2	11	−15	80	22	100	Total

a. Assumes that all sectors grow proportionally to the growth in aggregate final demand during 1966–72.

in final demand. For intermediate goods, however, the situation was quite different. For all major sectors the principal factor under-lying the disproportionate growth of imports was the increased de-pendence on imports of intermediate goods. In aggregate, such im-ports accounted for 80 percent of the disproportionate increase of imports; 96 percent of that increase occurred in the industrial sector.

The relatively rapid growth of imports of raw materials and semi-manufactures after 1966 can also be seen in an examination of import categories by end use in constant prices. Imported inputs grew by 11 percent a year between 1966 and 1976 (table 9.11). Imports of con-sumer goods, in contrast, grew at an average annual rate of 3 percent during the 1966–76 period. This slower growth was essentially the result of the compression of imports by about 30 percent after 1974.

Another way of addressing the question of import dependency is to examine for various categories of commodities the ratio of imports to total supply (see appendix table A.25). The ratios almost uni-formly show a rise of import shares up to 1972. By 1975, however, the shares appreciably declined, reflecting measures taken to improve the

Table 9.11. *Index of Imports, by End Use, 1966–76*
(1972 = 100)

End use	1966	1968	1970	1972	1974	1976	Average annual rate of growth (percent)
Raw materials and semi-manufactures	52	59	94	100	131	143	10.7
Capital goods	80	97	111	100	140	204	9.8
Consumer goods	78	80	95	100	135	108	3.3

Note: Figures were calculated from current-price imports deflated by the appropriate index of import prices.
Sources: *Statistical Yearbook of Yugoslavia*, various years.

balance of payments.[6] The data also suggest that the greatest scope for import substitution is in coal and petroleum, ferrous metals, non-metallic minerals, metal products, chemicals, rubber, and electrical machinery. Imports of these seven sectors accounted for 74 percent of total merchandise imports in 1975. But reducing imports will be limited by the country's insufficient endowment of natural resources and the high requirements of these seven industries for imported inputs.

Capital Inflows and External Debt

Because of deficits in its balance of payments, Yugoslavia has borrowed relatively large amounts of capital. After the break with COMINFORM, Yugoslavia received substantial aid from the United States. That aid, mostly grants or highly concessional contributions, amounted to about $2 billion for the 1949–61 period. As it tapered off in the 1960s to an average of about $65 million a year, commercial sources in Western European countries became principal suppliers of foreign capital to Yugoslavia. Medium-term capital, mostly supplier and financial credits, has been the dominant source since the second half of the 1960s. Accordingly the share of long-

6. The figures in appendix table A.25 are based on information in *Statistical Yearbook of Yugoslavia*, 1976; they are not strictly comparable to those for other years, which were derived from input-output tables.

term official flows continued to decline in the 1970s. The World Bank is now the principal single source of official long-term capital to Yugoslavia.

Since the 1965 reforms the system of external borrowing and debt management has mainly been based on market forces. Administrative controls have been minimal; the activities of the federal government as a contractor or guarantor of external debt has consistently declined. The initiative to borrow was completely left to enterprises, which now are free to negotiate loans directly with foreign creditors. Transactions must nevertheless be made through the banks, of which borrowing enterprises are members. Twenty banks are authorized to carry out foreign exchange operations on behalf of enterprises. Banks can also contract debt on their own account to maintain liquidity, but such borrowing is limited. Enterprises are obliged to inform the authorized banks of any intention to contract for debt. In this application the enterprise is to give details on the proposed size, terms, purpose, and creditor of the loan. The authorized bank reviews this application and submits it to the republican offices of the NBY. If the borrower satisfies the regulations for foreign borrowing, the NBY automatically registers the loan, which can then be used.

Structure of external debt

The measures for decentralization under the 1965 reforms had two important implications for the structure of Yugoslavia's external debt: a rapidly declining share of federally guaranteed debt; a growing dependence on commercial sources of credit.

The structure of debt remained fairly stable between 1965 and 1969, with the share of federally guaranteed debt amounting to two-thirds of total debt. But because most commitments for new borrowing were not federally guaranteed, there was a pronounced shift in the structure of debt after 1969. By 1973 more than 50 percent of Yugoslavia's debt was not federally guaranteed; the proportion rose to 61 percent by the end of 1975 (table 9.12).

Although enterprise initiative in borrowing has facilitated the contracting for debt without federal guarantees, most loans carry the guarantees of banks. The legal provisions of these guarantees are unique, because banks in Yugoslavia are founded by enterprises which have unlimited liability toward their bank. The banks, in turn, have unlimited access to foreign exchange from the NBY for the repayment of foreign credits. Once foreign credits are registered, the NBY guarantees the availability of foreign exchange. Thus, although

Table 9.12. *External Debt Outstanding at Year-end,*
1967, 1970, and 1975

Type or source	1967 Millions of dollars	1967 Percentage composition	1970 Millions of dollars	1970 Percentage composition	1975 Millions of dollars	1975 Percentage composition
Disbursed external debt	1,356.3	100.0	2,063.6	100.0	5,765.2	100.0
Public debt[a]	1,171.3	86.4	1,201.1	58.2	2,272.5	39.4
Multilateral sources	188.1	13.9	251.4	12.2	564.4	9.8
World Bank	178.1	13.1	243.7	11.8	559.1	9.7
Government sources	577.0	42.5	636.2	30.8	1,304.2	22.6
Centrally planned economies	72.3	5.3	200.9	9.7	299.4	5.2
Financial institutions, suppliers, and other publicly guaranteed loans	406.2	30.0	313.5	15.2	403.9	7.0
Private debt	185.0	13.6	862.5	41.8	3,492.7	60.6
Disbursed and undisbursed external debt	2,136.9	100.0	2,977.4	100.0	8,543.2	100.0
Public debt	1,801.3	84.3	1,750.4	58.8	3,353.1	39.2
Private debt	335.6	15.7	1,227.0	41.2	5,190.1	60.8

Sources: Debtor Reporting System of the World Bank; Dubey and others, *Yugoslavia: Development with Decentralization*, appendix table 4.2.
a. Includes publicly guaranteed debt.

default is technically possible if the banks and member enterprises face a shortage of dinars, it is unlikely in practice.

The second major change, closely linked to the first, was the growing importance of commercial sources of credit. At the beginning of 1966 multilateral and bilateral official sources accounted for about two-thirds of Yugoslavia's debt outstanding, including undisbursed debt; government sources alone accounted for about half. By 1975 the share of official sources declined to 32 percent;

that of debt to governments to 23 percent. The continuity of this shift is evident in the recent experience in contracting credits. Of all commitments between 1972 and 1974, only 22 percent came from official sources. It is probable that even this figure significantly overstates the availability of credits to Yugoslavia from official sources. Two special loans, unlikely to recur, accounted for nearly half these commitments.

Detailed information on the structure of Yugoslavia's commercial debt is not available. But by combining information from several sources, it is possible to deduce certain conclusions. According to data compiled by the NBY, 63 percent of the debt outstanding at the end of 1974 consisted of supplier credits. The bulk of this debt had been contracted from foreign commercial banks and thus was likely to have the guarantees of national agencies for export credit. Between 1973 and 1975 Yugoslavia contracted for nearly $900 million in publicized Eurocurrency loans, reflecting the importance of that market in satisfying Yugoslavia's residual capital requirements.[7] The remainder of private nonguaranteed debt is principally in bank-to-bank financial credits, generally linked to an export credit. Yugoslavia has not been very successful in floating bonds. Between 1970 and 1975 it was able to raise only $109 million through the bond market.

The burden of external debt

Despite the rapid increase in borrowing in recent years and the sharp reduction in borrowing from official sources, Yugoslavia's capacity to service its debt has not visibly deteriorated. Moreover, in comparison with other developing countries active in the international capital markets, its current indebtedness, although high, is not excessive.

Between 1970 and 1975 Yugoslavia's outstanding and disbursed debt increased from $2.1 billion to $5.8 billion, or at an average annual rate of nearly 23 percent. Of the debt outstanding in 1975, nearly 90 percent had been contracted in convertible currencies. During the same period the net transfer fell sharply as a proportion

---

7. With an estimated gross inflow of about $2 billion between 1973 and 1975, the stock of financial credits, as reported by the NBY, increased by $1.1 billion. Bilateral government loans accounted for $700 million of this gross inflow. Thus publicized Eurocurrency credits alone accounted for 70 percent of the total inflow; in addition, there probably have been unpublicized Eurocurrency credits.

of gross disbursements. But the debt service ratio in recent years does not indicate any significant problems. After a rise in the early 1970s, the ratio declined and remained at about 17 percent in 1974 and 1975 (table 9.13). On a basis net of payments received on account of

Table 9.13. *Burden of External Debt, 1966–75*
(percent)

Item	1966	1970	1971	1972	1973	1974	1975
Gross debt service ratio[a]	13.2	13.4	17.6	19.3	17.6	16.4	17.6
Net debt service ratio[b]	13.0	11.6	15.7	17.5	15.5	14.4	15.6
Ratio of debt service payments to disbursed debt oustanding[c]	20.6	23.2	23.3	18.2	24.0	24.6	24.6
Ratio of debt service payments to gross domestic product	2.7	3.5	4.2	5.4	5.0	4.5	4.4

Sources: Debtor Reporting Service of the World Bank; *Statistical Yearbook of Yugoslavia,* 1976.
a. The ratio of all debt service payments to commodity exports, including nonfactor services and all workers' remittances.
b. Net of all debt service credits.
c. Disbursed only.

Yugoslavia's lending abroad, that ratio is even lower. The value of export credits extended between 1970 and 1975 is estimated to have been about $400 million; the amount outstanding at the end of 1974 was equal to $708 million. Similarly other indicators of indebtedness, such as the ratio of external debt to GDP or exports, do not point to any significant undesirable trends.

These changes in the burden of external debt are hardly surprising, given the rapid growth of the economy in the past decade and the effects of inflation in reducing the real cost of borrowing. Commodity exports grew at an annual rate of 5.4 percent in real terms between 1965 and 1975; earnings from services, notably tourism and workers' remittances, increased even more rapidly. As a result, the average annual growth in foreign exchange earnings was more than 9 percent in constant prices and 19 percent in current prices. During the same period, Yugoslavia's GMP expanded at a rate of 6.3 percent a year in real terms; the industrial sector at a rate of more than 7 percent a year. Furthermore the significant increase in the country's real indebtedness between 1965 and 1972 was followed, after adjusting for the effects of international inflation, by a decline in 1974.

It is important to note that Yugoslavia's increased borrowing, as that in other developing countries, took place in a rapidly expanding international capital market. Yugoslavia's share in that market probably has not undergone any significant change.

Debt management

External debt management in recent years has increasingly operated through affecting the demand for external borrowing by changing the market conditions surrounding the contracting for external debt. The principal policies adopted have regulated the demand for external resources through changes in the aggregate level of economic activity and the cost of external funds. The NBY is responsible for the policy toward foreign borrowing. Regularly reviewing capital requirements and flows, it accordingly adjusts the instruments of debt management. In addition the authorized banks often impose certain conditions on borrowing from abroad: the conditions on terms imposed through gentleman's agreements concluded in the Yugoslav Association of Banks are an example. In principle such decisions are independent of the NBY, but NBY representatives may be present.

During 1965–71 the policies for debt management were rather ineffective. The principal instrument was limiting the contracting for debt by establishing a fixed ratio of borrowings to the foreign exchange holdings, or the potential to earn foreign exchange, of the borrower. Little attention was paid to the terms and volume of borrowing. Consequently some enterprises had temporary difficulties in servicing their debt. In 1971, however, the NBY instituted new procedures for registration and reporting. Those procedures obliged all banks and enterprises to report any planned borrowing from abroad to the NBY and to register that borrowing with the NBY. The NBY could refuse to register a loan if the terms and the amount were felt to be excessive. Commercial banks could not guarantee unregistered loans.

Until April 1972 enterprise borrowing was limited by the foreign exchange resources they obtained from their retention quota and depreciation allowance. Banks had similar limits to their capacity to guarantee loans. In addition, macroeconomic limits, determined principally by the NBY, were imposed on borrowing each year. The regulations changed in April of 1972 with the abolition of all direct controls. In recent years the federal government has not directly imposed restrictions on the volume of loans that the authorized banks can guarantee and enterprises can borrow. Annual limits on guarantees are internally set by the executive boards, and assemblies of banks. In addition, the Social Accounting Service and the Secretariat of Finance regularly inspect the balance sheets of banks. Such inspections considerably restrict a bank's capacity to act irresponsibly in foreign exchange markets.

The principal instrument of debt management now is the dinar deposit, which restricts borrowing by increasing the effective cost of most borrowing from abroad. Dinar deposits are free of interest and payable to the NBY when debt is contracted for. The deposit can be withdrawn only when the loan is fully repaid. The policy is designed to discourage the use of foreign credits for domestic costs and working capital. The requirements for supplier credits (and buyer credits) are considerably lower; they are graduated by maturity to encourage loans with longer maturities. This NBY policy has been reinforced by the gentleman's agreements between the authorized banks in the Yugoslav Association of Banks to contract for loans having maturities of more than five years.

In addition to policies designed to increase the cost of external funds, the country has shown a willingness to restrict economic activity by reducing the growth rate rather than jeopardize its creditworthiness. As mentioned earlier, most of Yugoslavia's imports are capital and intermediate goods; most imports of capital goods are financed through supplier credits. Thus the policies affecting investment and the growth rate have a direct effect on the demand and contracting for supplier credits. Because supplier credits are the principal source of borrowing, a deceleration in the rate of economic growth affects the growth of Yugoslavia's external debt. This relation was evident in 1971 when, following a standby agreement with the International Monetary Fund (IMF), Yugoslavia pursued a contractionary policy that reduced the growth rate of the economy and tightened the control on external borrowing. The modest surplus in the balance of payments in 1972–73 eased the foreign exchange squeeze. In 1974 the growth rate again increased, but with the rise in the price of oil, high international inflation, and the economic recession in Western Europe, the balance of payments sharply deteriorated. After an upsurge of foreign borrowing, stabilization measures were introduced to reduce the growth rate of the economy —measures reflected in a modest balance of payments surplus for 1976.

The effect that the new laws on foreign trade and exchange will have on foreign borrowing is not yet clear. One innovation of the new laws is the establishment of communities of interest for foreign economic relations. These new institutions are to provide forums for projecting and coordinating the receipts and requirements of foreign exchange. They could also project and coordinate borrowing requirements. Although borrowing is still expected to be undertaken at the initiative of enterprises, the new arrangements are likely to encourage greater coordination among borrowers; in particular, Yugoslav borrowers are likely to enter increasingly the international capital markets as consortia.

Changes in Policy

In 1961 a uniform foreign exchange rate replaced the system of import and export coefficients for import and export transactions. As many as thirty-five different coefficients had been used for exports alone, leading to substantial differences in the exchange rate applicable to different foreign transactions.[8] A system of tariffs, import quotas and licenses, export premiums and subsidies, and foreign exchange retention quotas replaced the coefficients in 1961. Export premiums and subsidies reached the equivalent of 45 percent of the value of exports. The devaluation of the dinar in 1965, from 7.5 to 12.5 new dinars to the dollar, nevertheless overstates the effect of the reduction of direct subsidies. The 1965 economic reforms abolished the various measures to promote exports, except the foreign exchange retention quota, which continued to be the principal policy tool for export expansion. But export subsidies soon reappeared in preferential credits, interest subsidies, and tariff rebates.

Yugoslavia devalued the dinar twice in 1971: from 12.5 to 15 dinars to the dollar in January and to 17 dinars in December. Weighted by trade, the total devaluation was about 20 percent. The dinar was devalued by a further 10 percent—a trade-weighted devaluation of about 8 percent—along with the dollar in 1973. Fixed exchange rates were abandoned in mid-1973; the dinar has since been floating under close supervision. Adjusting the nominal changes in the exchange rate for changes in the parity of purchasing power, provides better measures of the attractiveness of exporting, relative to selling

8. In 1960, or just before the introduction of a uniform exchange rate of 750 old dinars to the dollar, the exchange rate ranged from 505 to 1,264 dinars per dollar for exports and 632 to 1,580 dinars per dollar for imports.

Table 9.14. *Nominal and Purchasing-power-parity Exchange Rates, 1966–75*
(dinars per dollar)

	Nominal exchange rate	Purchasing-power-parity exchange rate[a]
1966	12.50	14.71
1970	12.50	15.71
1971	15.17	15.68
1972	17.00	17.00
1973	16.19	16.76
1974	15.19	15.37
1975	17.39	15.74

Sources: IMF, *International Financial Statistics*, various issues; World Bank calculations.

a. The purchasing-power-parity exchange rate is the nominal rate multiplied by the ratio of the index of the unit value of exports in SITC groups 5–8 by principal exporting nations to the index of industrial producer prices in Yugoslavia.

in the domestic market, and of the relative price of imports. A comparison of the two rates indicates that changes in the nominal exchange rate since 1972 have not kept pace with inflation in Yugoslavia (table 9.14).

Commercial policy

The right of enterprises to discretion in the disposition of their foreign exchange earnings has been the principal official device for export promotion since 1965. Until 1972 the proportion of export earnings affected by this provision was an increasing function of the export share of an enterprise's total sales; the maximum proportion was twice the basic rate of 7 percent for export shares above 60 percent. The retention quota also varied by type of export; services, pharmaceuticals, motor vehicles, and certain capital goods received the highest quotas. In 1972 a flat 20 percent share of export sales replaced the progressive rate. Exports of tourism services received a preferential rate of 45 percent; construction work abroad, a rate of 100 percent.

The average tariff rate in Yugoslavia has been moderate in comparison with that in other developing countries. After an increase from 10.5 percent in 1965 to 13.9 percent in 1969, the average rate declined to 9.4 percent in 1975. It rose to 10.1 percent in 1976.

Allowing for additional taxes and surcharges—a 10 percent import surcharge, a 5 percent tax equalization duty, and a 1 percent inspection fee, which were not always applied in full—the average tax on imports amounted to about 14 percent. The tariff structure follows the usual pattern: the rate is increased with the level of processing. Such a tariff structure implies higher effective protection to finished products in relation to those at earlier stages of production, but the effective rates of protection are not high by standards of developing countries.

In addition to the protection accorded by tariffs, some imports are subject to restrictions on access to foreign exchange—restrictions which can be more important as protective devices than tariffs. Before the 1974 reforms were implemented, imports were classified by the degree of import restriction.

- Imports for which foreign exchange is freely available: raw materials, foodstuffs, spare parts, and some consumer goods.
- Imports for which a special license is required for statistical purposes: certain consumer goods.
- Imports for which foreign exchange is available from the global quota, retention quota, depreciation allowance, and credits from abroad: raw materials, semifinished goods, capital goods, and some consumer goods.
- Imports subject to physical or foreign exchange quotas: plastics, machine tools, and agricultural and mineral products.
- Imports subject to licensing: narcotics, armaments, motor vehicles, tractors, fertilizer, natural gas, and railroad rolling stock.

The first two categories can be characterized as liberalized; the third as liberalized but subject to the availability of foreign exchange; the last two as restricted. By classifying imports in this way, the general trend of import policy since the 1965 reform can be shown (table 9.15).

The federal and republican governments and the chambers of the economy have jointly developed a new tariff schedule. The aims of the new schedule are to avoid rising tariff rates and to reduce the maximum rate to 25 percent. It is also intended that changes in the tariff structure will accord greater protection to primary products and less protection to finished goods, including some equipment. The changes are to encourage the expansion of primary production for import substitution or export. An implication of this structural change in nominal tariff rates is that the effective protection on more

Table 9.15. *Structure of Imports, by Category of Restriction, Selected Years, 1967–74*
(percent)

Year	Liberalized	Liberalized but subject to the availability of foreign exchange	Restricted
1967	39	56	5
1968	35	46	19
1972	28	46	26
1973	52	21	27
1974	60	14	26

Source: Figures supplied by the Secretariat for Foreign Trade.

highly finished goods will tend to fall, making their import more attractive. Unless the effect of increased competition is sufficiently positive, the changes also may adversely affect the export of finished goods.

Fiscal and credit policies

In addition to the foreign exchange retention quota, export credits and tax and tariff subsidies are the principal policy instruments for promoting exports. To the extent that an enterprise exports its output, it enjoys preferential rates of turnover tax and enterprise income tax. There also is a policy for drawing back customs duties: the tariffs paid on imports used to produce goods for export can be partly or fully remitted. If an importer exports goods of equal value to imports before or within one year of importing, the Federal Executive Council can reduce or eliminate the tariff on those imports. The federal budget for 1976 contained a provision for $663 million to be paid out for promoting exports by tax refunds. A special subsidy also applies to exports shipped on Yugoslav carriers; it can vary depending on the destination of exports. For example, exports to some LDCs receive greater stimulation.

Two mechanisms have been used for export financing. First, the fund for export financing and insurance finances exports of capital goods, including complete plants, and refinances medium- and long-term credits granted by banks to enterprises exporting equipment and ships or doing construction work abroad.[9] In 1976 gross disbursements were about Din2.5 billion, or about 3 percent of merchandise exports. Most of the financing was for exports of capital goods to developing countries. Second, commercial banks provide financing for short-term export credits under the selective credit policy of the NBY. These credits may also be used to organize production for export and supplies intended for export. The commercial banks discount loans at the appropriate republican national bank. The NBY determines the terms, which are identical for all regions. In 1976 the rediscount rate applied to export credits was about 50 percent of the general rate; commercial banks were charging an interest rate on export credits that was less than half the rate for general loans.

Other policies

In the broad economic context, policies for stabilization and prices have an important bearing on foreign trade. The early postwar emphasis on industrialization resulted in a price policy that favored the production of manufactured goods relative to primary and semimanufactured products. Since 1955, however, the internal terms of trade between agricultural and manufactured goods has been in favor of agriculture (table 9.16). The sharpest rise came in

Table 9.16. *Internal Terms of Trade between Agricultural and Manufactured Goods, 1955–75*

Year	Terms of trade (1955 = 100)	Year	Terms of trade (1965 = 100)
1955	100	1965	100
1960	117	1970	107
1961	130	1971	117
1962	147	1972	130
1963	161	1973	144
1964	189	1974	127
1965	235	1975	118

Note: The terms of trade are calculated from producer prices.
Source: Statistical Yearbook of Yugoslavia, 1976, table 122–1.

9. Established as a government organization in 1967, this fund began operations in 1968. It was reorganized in 1972, when seventeen banks and a hundred enterprises became its founders.

1965, when a price reform was implemented. Agricultural prices rose by 43 percent, in contrast with a 14 percent increase in the prices of manufactures.

Despite the improvement of the agricultural terms of trade, the view that the primary sector has suffered from price policy is widely held in Yugoslavia. To the extent that the prices of primary and semifinished products were initially set too low, the net income and self-financing ability of their producers has been retarded, the expansion of these sectors perhaps constrained. It is difficult, however, to assess the extent to which initial levels were distorted, and not sufficiently compensated for, by shifts of the terms of trade toward agriculture and the effect such distortions may have had on the structures of imports and exports.

The effects of stabilization policy on imports and exports have been more obvious. In 1975 and 1976 Yugoslavia adopted restrictive policies because of accelerating inflation and a rising trade deficit. These policies, described in chapter six, produced dramatic effects on the rate of inflation and the balance of payments. The slowdown in the growth of the domestic economy stimulated exports: producers tried to substitute exports for lost domestic sales.[10] The lower inflation rate increased the competitiveness of Yugoslav products in relation to foreign products. The rapid recovery of economic activity in the first half of 1977, the tendency to replace depleted stocks, and the rise in import prices nevertheless resulted in an expansion of import values that has been significantly faster than that of export values.

The policy permitting foreign direct investment in the Yugoslav economy, introduced in 1967, also has implications for foreign trade. The regulations governing foreign investment are broad, with details to be spelled out in the contract between the foreign and domestic partners. Official approval of a foreign investment agreement is not given unless it is shown that modern production and management techniques will be adopted and that exports will be fostered. A decree enacted in June 1976 iterated the provision concerning the export orientation of the investment, apparently reflecting that the export expansion associated with foreign investment had not lived

10. Because of the legal barriers to laying off workers, the shift toward exports probably is stronger in Yugoslavia than in most other countries. With the elimination of this mechanism for adjustments to demand cycles, the propensity to recover at least some income in foreign trade at less than full cost must be very strong.

up to expectations.[11] A built-in incentive to export is contained in the conditions for profit repatriation, conditions which are subject to the foreign exchange earnings of the enterprise. In 1976, 53 percent of export earnings could be used for the repatriation of profits. To the extent that such investment leads to an increase in economic efficiency, exports will be stimulated and imports discouraged. The conditions for profit repatriation and for the foreign investment project to be approved are also designed to encourage exports. A new law on foreign investment is also expected to make the obligation to export more explicit.

The New Legislative and Institutional Framework

The system of foreign trade and payments has been in a state of transition. New laws designed to bring about conformity to the new constitution were implemented in 1978. The changes increase the participation of BOALS and other economic organizations in planning foreign economic relations, just as in other domains of the economy. Because the foreign exchange system operates within a unified Yugoslav market, policies relating to export promotion, import substitution, exchange rates, foreign exchange reserves, foreign borrowing, and the balance of payments are to be annually determined by the Federal Assembly on the recommendations of the Federal Executive Council and in accord with the five-year plan.[12] BOALS, enterprises, communities of interest, and other organizations are thus required to align their own plans for foreign trade and borrowing with the republican and national plans. A major element in the new system is the law on foreign exchange operations and credit relations with foreign countries.[13] Enacted in March 1977, it changed the method for distributing foreign exchange earnings,

11. Exhaustive information on foreign investment by activity, origin, and location was available only up to the end of 1973. Total foreign participation during 1968–73 accounted for only about 1 percent of productive investment in the social sector. Evidence for that period suggests that the primary orientation of foreign investors was to serve the domestic market. See appendix table A.26.

12. The Federal Executive Council makes semiannual reports to the Federal Assembly on the implementation of policies for foreign exchange and the balance of payments.

13. The implications of the new legislation were not clear at the time of writing.

established communities of interest for foreign economic relations, and introduced a system relating imports to exports.

The new law contains the provision that BOALS or enterprises are to enter self-management agreements to govern the distribution of the foreign exchange earnings of final exporters. The underlying principle is that foreign exchange earnings belong not only to final exporters, but to all producing entities that contribute to the production of exported goods and services. The self-management agreements between final exporters and indirect exporters along the chain of production specify the shares of various producing units in the foreign exchange earnings of direct exporter. The agreements also specify the extent of the claim and the rules concerning its disposal. The share cannot be sold; it can only be disposed of through the pooling of resources under a self-management agreement. Risk-sharing between enterprises, including export-import enterprises, also is significant. This risk-sharing is part of the broad arrangement—mandatory for foreign operations and urged for domestic operations—guiding the operations of trade enterprises: profits and risks of the trading stage are to be shared backward through the chain of production according to rules set out in self-management agreements.

Under the new system the retention quota and the global quota are to disappear. Both have been highly discriminatory in favor of the final exporter. The import of certain goods nevertheless may still be subject to some quotas for volume or value, specified in self-management agreements. Given the absence of price as a rationing device in the foreign exchange market, the sharing of foreign exchange has theoretical appeal. In essence the scheme allocates foreign exchange according to the value added an enterprise directly exports and the value added the same enterprise provides as an input to the exports of other enterprises. To illustrate: the shipbuilding industry has considerable backward linkages but few forward linkages. According to statistics on foreign trade in 1972, shipbuilding exports were Din3.8 billion; the value added the shipbuilding industry directly and indirectly exported was Din1.2 billion. The allocation of foreign exchange according to direct and indirect contributions to the production of exports thus has appeal from the standpoint of equitability. Because the production of some products depends more on imports than the production of others, an additional criterion for the equitable and efficient distribution of foreign exchange could have been related to the import intensity of various industries or enterprises. Under the new system, such considerations as import requirements and import substitution may thus affect decisions on the allocation of foreign exchange.

Republican and federal communities of interest for economic relations with foreign countries coordinate the system of foreign exchange allocation. The republican communities of interest constitute the federal community of interest. These organizations comprise, with the exception of sociopolitical communities, all earners and users of foreign exchange. As part of planning, targets are set for the balance of payments of individual republics—some are to have surpluses, other deficits—and the allowable levels of foreign borrowing. The targets determine how republics pool foreign exchange. The communities of interest then become the forums for deciding how foreign exchange is distributed among the enterprises in each republic.

Passing to enterprises the responsibility for allocating scarce foreign exchange forces them to consider the implications of their activities in the broad economic context. This is seen to be important in ensuring the controlled development of the balance of payments. But the precise way the system is to operate, particularly with respect to the republican targets for the balance of payments, is not yet clear. All planning units make annual projections of foreign trade and payments; individual regions take measures to realize targets and correct deviations that arise. The measures could modify the orientation of development and the policies for credit, taxation, prices, integration, and foreign exchange. Because of the obvious implications and repercussions of policies taken in one region on another, the range of policy variation, constrained by the principle of the unity of the Yugoslav market, must be agreed upon by all regions.[14]

The policy linking imports to exports was implemented in 1975 as a reaction to the deterioration in the balance of payments. Although such a policy is not new—a similar policy was adopted for a brief period in 1967—it appears to be a logical consequence of the new system for foreign exchange. Because large deficits in the balance of trade are projected for the 1976–80 period, the system does not imply that exports are to match imports. The pooling and

---

14. The ability of each republic to formulate commercial policy is limited. But if one region has a more restrictive import policy than others, this difference could lead to attempts by BOALS to import through a region having a less restrictive policy. Consequently methods have to be devised to handle such situations.

allocation of foreign exchange through communities of interest nevertheless encourages enterprises seeking imports to find appropriate markets for exports. By exporting, enterprises would directly benefit from greater access to foreign exchange for imports. For example, a Yugoslav transport enterprise that wants to import equipment from a western country will search for Yugoslav products the foreign supplier is willing to purchase to close the transaction. The foreign supplier can then use the linked imports or, more often than not, merely find a trading company to take over final marketing. This reversion to what essentially is a barter system of international trade has been of increasing worldwide importance.

In Yugoslavia export-import linking was imposed on trade with countries in the convertible-currency area during 1975 and 1976. For each enterprise the average export-import ratio in 1973–74 was to be maintained in the following years. The system did not operate on the basis of individual commodities or countries. It generally linked trade with all western industrialized countries. In some instances the foreign firm marketed the goods tied to its exports to Yugoslavia; in other instances a Yugoslav export-import enterprise arranged to market the products. The share of the value of imports that had to be covered by exports varied by commodity. Imports of consumer goods and automobiles were at the high end of the spectrum with an export obligation equal to imports. Imports of capital goods had the relatively low export obligation of 30 percent. Since the policy was put into effect, the aggregate export-import ratio rose from 50.6 percent in 1974 to 52.9 percent in 1975 and 66 percent in 1976. Although other factors contributed to this rise in exports relative to imports—for example, the slowdown in growth of the domestic economy, the recovery of growth in western economies, and the restrictions on imports—the policy linking imports to exports had a strong effect in 1975–76. The much faster rise of imports than of exports in 1977 nevertheless pointed to a relaxation of that policy.

The reversion to a barter system has drawbacks for efficiency. A likely result of the system is that Yugoslav importers will not always be able to import goods at the lowest price, because the supplier selling at the lowest price may not agree to the import requirement. The additional costs the foreign supplier must bear may also be passed on to the Yugoslav importer and result in a decline in the terms of trade. Nevertheless a flexible system linking imports to exports may, in addition to having positive effects for the balance of payments in the short run, have certain other effects that would be more lasting. The greater exposure of Yugoslav products in foreign markets could have substantial ripple effects over time. The policy also enables Yugoslav producers to tap the marketing skills and networks of multinational corporations.

Under the new system, the instruments of commercial policy—that is, import duties and other import restrictions—are more fully integrated with self-management. All enterprises, through their membership in republican and federal chambers of the economy, participate in policymaking. Initiatives for policy changes may originate in the various councils of the chamber of the economy or in federal organs; they are subject to review and discussion by the chambers. Because enterprises may be members of several councils in a chamber, depending on their interests, and because enterprises are consumers and suppliers, it is expected that decisionmaking will increasingly be based on greater appreciation of the consequences and implications of alternative courses of action. To illustrate: if the textile council proposes to ban imports of textiles, if the furniture council, whose members import cloth for upholstery, considers the ban to be unacceptable, and if the two councils cannot reach agreement on this matter, the issue is considered first by the council for economic relations with foreign countries and then at higher levels. The federal chamber of the economy is represented at all talks on economic matters concerning foreign countries.

A new financial institution with responsibilities in foreign economic relations—the Yugoslav Bank for Economic Cooperation with Foreign Countries—has also been established. Once this bank is fully operational, it will bring several separate institutions dealing with foreign economic relations under a common umbrella. The basic functions of the bank are these: conducting market research and analysis on matters of economic relations with foreign countries, approving export credits and the provision of insurance, screening and approving foreign direct investment, seeking new channels of foreign financing, and authorizing the establishment of joint banks and representative offices of foreign banks.[15]

15. Resources for export insurance originate from insurance premiums and other federal allocations; resources for export financing from pooled resources of enterprises and other organizations, credits from the NBY, allocations by sociopolitical communities, the issuance of securities, and foreign credits.

Prospects for 1976–80

The export target in the social plan for 1976–80 appears to be in line with historical trends and recent developments (table 9.17). The import target, reflecting the emphasis on correcting structural imbalances and reducing import dependency, points either to funda-

Table 9.17. *Growth of Foreign Trade, 1971–75 and Targets in the Social Plan for 1976–80*
(percent)

	1971–75		1976–80
Item	Target	Actual[a]	Target
Gross material product	7.5	5.7	7.0
Exports	12.0	8.1	8.0
Imports	10.0	6.3	4.5
Import elasticity	1.33	1.11	0.64

Sources: *Social Plan of Yugoslavia, 1976–80*; Federal Institute of Statistics, *Index*, 1977, no. 2; *Statistical Yearbook of Yugoslavia*, 1976.

a. Calculated from three-year averages.

mental shifts or to problems of adjustment. Because neither the plan nor the other documents available had information more detailed than the growth rates shown in table 9.17, the analysis here must be crude and conjectural.[16] It is clear, however, that the size of the gap in foreign exchange will determine whether the plan's targets for growth can be achieved.[17]

16. The information available to World Bank staff also does not indicate, except in broad, qualitative terms, what specific assumptions influenced the determination of the targeted growth rates.

17. The plan stipulates that "external indebtedness will not increase relative to the inflow of foreign exchange. . . ." This constraint has been interpreted as implying that the debt service ratio—that is, payments of interest and annuities in relation to total export earnings—is not to increase. Federal Institute of Planning, *Social Plan of Yugoslavia: 1976–80* (Belgrade: Federal Committee of Information, 1976), p. 113.

Imports

The aggregate import elasticity brings into focus the ambitious target for reducing import dependency. The plan's implicit targeted elasticity of 0.64 has first to be judged against past performance.[18] Not only is the targeted elasticity about 60 percent of the level during the previous plan period; it also is far below any level ever achieved in Yugoslavia (see table 9.8). Average import elasticities rose from about 1.1 before the 1965 economic reforms to 2.65 during 1965–69 and then dropped to the prereform level during 1970–75. Given this historical trend, an import elasticity of unity may be normal for Yugoslavia.[19] The temporary peaking above that level was the result of opening up the economy during the ascent of the trend and the subsequent adjustments during the descent of the trend. The targeted elasticity appears immediately plausible from this purely mechanistic perspective only under the assumption that the descending trend will continue during the plan period and accelerate.[20]

To shed additional light on the growth of imports, data for 1966–75 were used to estimate simple import functions for three major import categories: raw materials, capital goods, and consumer goods. Considering raw materials and semimanufactures first, the regression equation using the ordinary least-squares method of estimation is:

$$(1) \qquad \ln MRS = -1.437 + 1.328 \ln IVA,$$
$$(-1.11) \quad (4.66)$$

$$R^2 = 0.90; \text{Durbin-Watson statistic} = 1.81$$

where MRS is the index of imports of raw materials and semimanufactures in constant prices and IVA is the index of industrial

---

18. The import elasticity in the plan is for goods and services; all other elasticities were computed only for goods. This hardly affects the conclusions, because of the small size of imports of services; a large part of those imports, particularly for transport and interest payments, are not compressible and probably have an elasticity that is greater than unity.

19. By "normal" is meant an equilibrium level that could be attained in the absence of external disturbances and internal shifts in policy.

20. The downward trend would have to accelerate because the target of 0.64 is not the final elasticity in 1980, but the average elasticity for the entire period. It should be added that almost all countries have long-term import elasticities which are greater than unity, a factor that raises additional questions about the feasibility of the targeted decline in Yugoslavia.

value added in constant prices. In this and other equations *ln* indicates that data are in natural logarithms.[21] Equation (1) indicates that a 10 percent increase in industrial value added is associated with an approximate 13 percent increase in imports of nondurable producer goods. Given the elasticity coefficient of 1.328 and the forecast of an annual rate of growth in industrial value added of 8 percent during 1976–80, the average growth rate of imports of raw materials and semimanufactures would be 10.6 percent a year.

Imports of capital goods are assumed to be a function of domestic investment in fixed assets. The regression equation using the Cochrane-Orcutt iterative technique of estimation is:

$$(2) \qquad \ln MKG = -0.1253 + 1.07 \ln I,$$
$$(-0.13) \quad (5.22)$$

$$R^2 = 0.82; \text{Durbin-Watson statistic} = 1.81$$

where MKG and I respectively are indexes of capital-goods imports and domestic fixed investment in constant prices. An 8 percent growth rate of investment in fixed assets is targeted for 1976–80. Based on the relation between investment and imports of capital goods during 1966–75, imports of capital goods could be expected to increase at a rate of about 8 percent a year.

Regressing imports of consumer goods on personal consumption expenditures, again using the Cochrane-Orcutt iterative technique, yielded the following equation:

$$(3) \qquad \ln MCG = 0.625 + 0.879 \ln PC,$$
$$(1.33) \quad (8.42)$$

$$R^2 = 0.67; \text{Durbin-Watson statistic} = 2.42$$

where MCG and PC respectively are indexes of imports of consumer goods and personal consumption. Based on the historical data for 1966–75 and the growth projections of the five-year plan for the independent variables in the foregoing equations, merchandise imports would be expected to grow at an average annual rate of about 9.4 percent. That growth implies an import elasticity of about 1.3, which is about twice that targeted in the plan. Although the predictive power of this simplistic statistical approach can be questioned, the results point to the decisive problem ahead: the import substitu-

---

21. The parenthetical values beneath the constant and the coefficient are *t* scores.

tion required to close the gap between the historical and planned growth rates of imports is considerable.[22] Import substitution must be on a very large scale even to come close to the ambitiously low growth rate targeted for imports in the plan. In this context the composition of imports should be kept in mind. In 1976 only 12 percent of imports were consumer goods, which could be compressed without repercussions for growth. Sixty-four percent of imports were raw materials and intermediate goods: part of these imports cannot be substituted; another part can be substituted only if and when domestic capacity is ready unless current production is to be interrupted. The remaining 24 percent were investment goods, for which competing imports can be compressed only selectively over time, unless investment programs are slashed. These comments are not intended to demonstrate that the plan's targets are completely unrealistic; they merely indicate serious doubts, given the paucity of information about the way the targets are to be achieved during the plan period.

Exports

To assess export prospects, total exports were disaggregated into exports of merchandise and nonfactor services. Merchandise exports were in turn broken down into exports to the convertible-currency and bilateral-clearing areas. During the 1966–75 period, exports to these two areas constituted between 87 and 98 percent of annual merchandise exports. The rationale behind this division of exports is that the principles of trade with the two areas are fundamentally different and that exports to the two areas differ with respect to income changes.

It is hypothesized that exports to countries in the convertible-currency area are primarily associated with the GNP of those countries. The estimated equation for exports to the convertible-currency area, based on observations for 1966–75 and using the ordinary least-squares method, is:

(4) $$\ln EC = -5.115 + 2.107 \ln YOECD,$$
$$(-9.62) \quad (17.93)$$

$$R^2 = 0.97; \text{Durbin-Watson statistic} = 2.54$$

---

22. Note 18 in this chapter describes differences in the methods used to estimate elasticity here and in the plan.

where EC is the index of exports to the convertible-currency area in constant 1972 prices and $YOECD$ is the real GNP of OECD countries, which are considered to be a proxy for the countries of the convertible-currency area. The elasticity coefficient indicates that Yugoslav exports to OECD countries increase by 2.1 percent for each 1 percent rise in the GNP of those countries.

For exports to Eastern Europe, the volume of which is negotiated by governments, the assumption is that the size of this bilateral trade is a direct function of the GNP of Eastern Europe. Using the ordinary least-squares method and the GNP of the Soviet Union as a proxy for the national product of the entire region, the estimated regression equation is:

$$(5) \qquad \ln EEE = -1.272 + 1.253 \ln YSU,$$
$$(-1.47) \quad (6.60)$$

$$R^2 = 0.83; \text{ Durbin-Watson statistic} = 1.77$$

where EEE is the index of exports to the Eastern European bilateral-clearing area in constant 1972 prices and YSU is the index of real GNP in the Soviet Union. As might be expected, the elasticity coefficient for exports to the bilateral-clearing area is considerably less than that for exports to OECD countries.

Exports of nonfactor services are assumed to be primarily oriented to western markets and determined by national income—that is, exports of nonfactor services are assumed to be directly associated with the GNP of OECD countries. The regression equation in this case, again using the ordinary least-squares method, is:

$$(6) \qquad \ln ENFS = -1.916 + 1.427 \ln YOECD,$$
$$(-4.65) \quad (15.67)$$

$$R^2 = 0.96; \text{ Durbin-Watson statistic} = 2.11$$

where $ENFS$ is the index of exports of nonfactor services.

The tenth five-year plan of the Soviet Union projects a growth in national product of 24–28 percent for the 1976–80 period.[23] If growth is in the upper part of this range, the annual compound growth rate would be 5 percent. Given an elasticity coefficient of 1.253, the growth rate of exports to the Eastern European bilateral-

---

23. Donald W. Green and others, "An Evaluation of the 10th Five-Year Plan using the SRI-WEFA Econometric Model of the Soviet Union," in U.S. Congress, Joint Economic Committee, *Soviet Economy in a New Perspective*, 94th Cong., 2d sess., 14 October 1976, pp. 301–31.

clearing area would be 6.3 percent a year. The growth of GNP in OECD countries is also forecast to be 5 percent during 1976–80. This rate of growth, given the elasticity coefficients of 2.107 and 1.427, implies that the growth rate of merchandise exports to OECD countries will be 10.5 percent a year; the growth rate of exports of non-factor services, 7.1 percent a year. Exports of factor services mainly are workers' remittances: in real terms they are expected under the best circumstances to remain at the 1975 level during 1976–80.

The estimated growth rates of merchandise exports to the two areas indicate an average annual growth of merchandise exports during 1976–80 of about 9 percent. This forecast is based on the respective shares of these areas in Yugoslav merchandise exports in 1975: 63.6 percent for the convertible-currency area and 36.4 percent for the bilateral-clearing area. This demand model of export growth thus forecasts a rate of expansion for merchandise exports that is higher than the 7 percent rate projected in the Yugoslav social plan for 1976–80. For exports of goods and services, however, the plan's projection of 8 percent exceeds the forecast of 6.6 percent based on the foregoing elasticity coefficients and the structure of exports of goods and services in 1975, when merchandise exports accounted for 50.8 percent of total exports, nonfactor services for 28 percent, and factor services for 21.2 percent. An important element in this forecast is the zero growth rate assumed for exports of factor services.

Summary

The analysis indicates that the gap between the targets of the plan and the projections based on historical data is less for exports than for imports. The export gap may also be easier to close. For example, maintaining a less overvalued rate of foreign exchange could provide a boost to exports. Institutional changes may help steer exports onto a higher course. Less protectionism in the EEC would also speed up the expansion of Yugoslav exports, as would the rapid growth of the oil-producing economies. Optimism on this last point is tempered, however, by the results of a study on trade between developing countries.[24] Yugoslavia's manufactured exports to developing countries were shown to be inversely related to the level of industrialization, measured by the share of manufacturing in GDP, of those countries. This finding implies that the scope for trade with

---

24. Alice H. Amsden, "Trade in Manufactures between Developing Countries," *Economic Journal*, vol. 86, no. 344 (December 1976), pp. 778–90.

these countries declines as they become more industrialized. But the growth in income that accompanies industrialization is a force working in the opposite direction.

For imports the system linking imports to exports may reduce some imports from what they would otherwise be. In addition, foreign investment is being encouraged in industries that have viable prospects for import substitution. The social plan calls for a halving of the share of imports of chemicals in total domestic supplies to between 12.5 and 15 percent. But the extent to which these policies for import substitution will lead to a net reduction in imports is open to question. In many countries, pursuing such policies has proved to be self-defeating because of the implied large increases of imported raw materials, intermediate goods, and capital equipment.

The substitution of imports of raw materials generally is difficult to achieve in the medium term, and in Yugoslavia it could be costly. The agricultural sector perhaps offers the greatest scope for import substitution. In the machinery and equipment sectors, it may also be possible to reduce dependence on imports by providing more ready credit for sales of domestically produced products. On the whole, the plan's targeted 4.5 percent growth rate for imports of goods and services is, according to the foregoing analysis, more consistent with a somewhat slower rate of economic growth than the plan envisions. It also is consistent with the constraints the plan embodies for external indebtedness.[25]

Because foreign exchange is a principal constraint on economic development, an important question arises regarding the most efficient method of increasing its availability. It appears that insufficient attention has been given in Yugoslavia to the real cost of earning or saving a unit of foreign exchange: for example, by import substitution in steel, coal, equipment, and basic chemicals, or by export expansion in electronics, agro-industries products, leather, and footwear. Industries can be ranked according to their share in total imports or their export-import balance. Policy can then be related to these rankings. But a large share of imports or a substantial balance of imports over exports still does not provide much information on the efficiency of import substitution. What is needed is information on the real costs associated with saving or earning foreign exchange on a product-by-product basis—that is, estimates of domestic resource costs that take into account the shadow prices

---

25. See the assessment of the plan scenario in chapter five.

of primary factors and the opportunity cost of alternative lines of production. Only these estimates would provide useful information on the structure of a nation's comparative advantage, information which is required for the rational implementation of policies for import substitution and export expansion.

Ten

Employment

THE LABOR MARKET in Yugoslavia, despite recent declines in the size of the resident active labor force and rapid sectoral shifts in employment use, continues to be characterized by considerable imbalances.[1] Consequently the new economic system has introduced novel instruments and institutional arrangements to encourage a faster rate of growth in modern sector employment. Rapid growth in employment is crucial if returning migrants, the unemployed, and new entrants to the labor force are to be employed. In addition, there will be a continuing need to provide opportunities for migration out of low productivity work in the agricultural sector. Although the new measures bear considerable promise, the character and magnitude of the employment problem preclude rapid solution. This is particularly apparent if the regional dimension of the employment problem is considered. The less developed regions, notably Kosovo, will have large reserves of labor in the agricultural sector well beyond the current plan period.

Characteristics of the Labor Market

The labor market in Yugoslavia has five dominant features. First, it is divided into a modern social sector with high productivity and

1. The term *labor market* is used in this chapter as shorthand for labor supply and demand. It is not used to denote a marketplace for labor transactions, which would be inconsistent with the basic philosophical premises of the Yugoslav system. This chapter also departs from the Yugoslav definition of employment as covering only recipients of personal incomes in the social sector and contractual wages and salaries in the private sector; here all self-employed persons earning income in the private sector are also considered. And just as in other chapters the term *worker* applies to "workers" in the social sector and "working people" in the private sector.

incomes and a traditional, private agricultural sector with low productivity and incomes. Second, employment opportunities differ considerably from one region to another. Third, although external migration absorbed many Yugoslav workers after the 1965 reforms, the recent restrictions on migration in Western European countries have led to a return of Yugoslav workers and exacerbated existing imbalances. Fourth, despite rapid structural changes in the labor market, there are indications that segments of the working-age population have withdrawn from the labor force because of the difficulties in obtaining employment in the modern sector. Fifth, by analyzing input-output tables, a significant decline can be observed in labor requirements for all sectors. Changes in production technology have caused labor-output ratios to fall, a pattern accentuated by a strong shift in final demand away from primary agricultural produce to other commodities requiring fewer labor inputs.

Dualism

The disequilibria in the labor market can be seen more clearly by analyzing the differences in income between the modern and traditional sectors than by attempting to estimate surplus labor in the agricultural sector. Numerous studies have estimated surplus labor in the agricultural sector—that is, labor having a marginal product that is low or zero.[2] Because such estimates for any one year provide little indication of the likely change in the size of the surplus labor force, particularly given the changes in technology and the individual preferences to work, it would seem to be more fruitful to view the country's employment objective as an attempt to redress the income differences by providing opportunities for productive employment.[3] This attempt would facilitate a transfer of workers out of less productive occupations, even though they may have a positive marginal product and are not surplus labor in the strict neoclassical sense. Concurrently it would increase the land-labor ratio and in-

2. Although beset by methodological shortcomings and conceptual difficulties, most of them indicate a surplus of 20 to 30 percent, which World Bank studies of the less developed regions in Yugoslavia confirm.

3. One stated objective is to achieve full employment by 1985. Federal Institute of Planning, "Outline of a Common Policy for Long-Term Development in Yugoslavia (until 1985)," *Yugoslav Survey*, vol. 16, no. 4 (November 1975).

directly foster an increase of incomes in the private agricultural sector.[4]

There have been, and continue to be, significant differences in the average incomes of workers in the traditional and modern sectors. One of the important consequences of the 1965 reforms was to considerably increase these differences. Although income differences have tended to narrow in recent years, principally as a result of the rapid depletion of the labor force in the agricultural sector, registered unemployment has rapidly increased. Thus migration out of the agricultural sector has been accompanied, at least in part, by an increase in the ranks of the registered unemployed, not only by a transfer of workers from low to high productivity employment.

During the 1962–74 period, average incomes in private agriculture ranged from less than a third to less than a half of those in the social sector; they ranged from 41 to 68 percent of those of unskilled workers in the social sector (table 10.1).[5] Personal incomes in private agriculture, relative to those in the social sector, fell sharply after the 1965 reforms. Just before the reforms, incomes in private agriculture were about 40 percent of average earnings in the social sector; by 1968 they had fallen to 30 percent. The principal reason for this deterioration in relative incomes was the threefold increase in nominal personal incomes in the social sector, a result of the rapid rise in productivity immediately after 1965 and the distribution of a larger share of enterprise income to personal incomes. Meanwhile modern sector employment fell, curbing rural-to-urban migration. Thus it is not surprising to observe the large increase in the rate of migration from the agricultural sector after 1968, when more social sector jobs became available and opportunities for external migration increased. Between 1968 and 1974 there was a gradual improvement in relative incomes, principally as a result of the rapid decline in the agricultural labor force. Despite this improvement, differences remain large and are comparable to those before the reforms.

4. Although the maximum size of farm of a private farm family generally is 10 hectares, this limit has not acted as a constraint. In 1971, for example, there were an estimated 2.7 hectares of arable land per active worker in the private sector. In 1969 farms of less than 5 hectares accounted for 47 percent of all cultivable land.

5. These results are consistent with official Yugoslav estimates, which show that wages in the social sector were about three times those in private agriculture in 1971. Miloje Nikolic, "Employment and Temporary Unemployment," *Yugoslav Survey*, vol. 15, no. 2 (May 1974), pp. 1–22.

Table 10.1. *Personal Income in the Social
and Private Agricultural Sectors, 1962–74*

Year	Average annual income per active worker (dinars)			Index of incomes in the private agricultural sector	
	Social sector		Private agricultural sector	(average social-sector worker = 100)	(unskilled social-sector worker = 100)
	Average worker	Unskilled worker			
1962–64	3,552	n.a.	1,400	39	n.a.
1966	8,760	5,928	3,400	39	57
1968	10,740	7,920	3,220	30	41
1970	15,000	9,696	4,720	31	49
1971	18,168	12,468	5,970	33	48
1972	21,120	15,036	7,760	37	52
1973	24,384	17,808	10,410	43	58
1974	30,408	20,076	13,610	45	68

n.a. Not available.

Note: Official estimates of the number of active workers in the private agricultural sector exist only for the census years 1961 and 1971; even these figures have to be adjusted. Consequently the active labor force in agriculture has been estimated by treating the sector as a residual employer of the active labor force. These derived figures were used to obtain the series of indicative figures for personal incomes in private agriculture presented here.

Sources: Figures supplied by the Federal Institute of Statistics; *Statistical Yearbook of Yugoslavia*, various years; and World Bank calculations.

Regional differences

All regions except Slovenia have pockets of low-income private farmers seeking social sector employment. Although such demand for social sector employment has led to considerable rural-to-urban migration within regions, movements of workers between regions have been fairly limited. Consequently employment opportunities have differed considerably between regions, reflecting differences in the relative size of the private agricultural sector and in the demographic characteristics of regions.

The large differences in rates of registered unemployment are an indicator of the differences in employment opportunities (table 10.2). There are three striking features. First, the increase in unemployment rates for Yugoslavia has been a continuous and rapid

Table 10.2. *Rates of Unemployment, by Region, 1971–75*
(percent)

Region	1971	1972	1973	1974	1975	1971–75
Less developed regions						
Bosnia-Herzegovina	5.6	6.2	7.7	9.8	11.5	8.3
Kosovo	18.6	17.8	20.1	20.8	23.5	20.5
Macedonia	17.3	17.0	18.5	19.8	21.2	18.8
Montenegro	6.0	6.6	10.1	12.8	14.7	10.3
More developed regions						
Croatia	4.0	4.3	4.8	4.8	5.6	4.7
Serbia	7.9	8.2	9.9	11.3	12.8	10.1
Slovenia	2.7	2.1	1.8	1.4	1.5	1.8
Vojvodina	6.1	6.7	8.2	8.9	10.8	8.2
Yugoslavia	6.7	7.0	8.1	9.0	10.4	8.3

Source: Ljubica Srdic-Dakovic, "Employment, 1971–75," *Yugoslav Survey*, vol. 17, no. 3 (August 1976) p. 60.

rising from 6.7 percent in 1971 to 10.4 percent in 1975.[6] Second, the differences between regions are large. Although Slovenia has virtually full employment, Kosovo has a registered unemployment rate of about 25 percent. All the less developed regions have unemployment rates that are higher than average. Third, with the exception of Slovenia, which has low and falling unemployment rates, even the more developed regions have fairly high and rising unemployment rates.

The regional aspects of employment can also be seen in the structure of employment (table 10.3). The differences between regions are large, with the share of the social sector ranging from 67 percent in Slovenia to 31 percent in Kosovo. Given the income differences between the social sector and the private agricultural sector, the differences in the share of the labor force in the private sector are important in accounting for differences in the standards of living between regions. They provide a crude indication of the relative size of the "surplus labor" that could be shifted to more productive activities. This structural feature is accentuated by differences in the incomes of private farmers in the various regions: the least developed regions not only have a higher share of private farms; they

6. The unemployment rate is the ratio of registered unemployment to social sector employment plus registered unemployment. In 1971 the ratio of registered unemployment to total labor force was 3 percent; in 1975 it was 5.3 percent.

Table 10.3. *Personal Income in the Social
and Private Agricultural Sectors, by Region, 1971*

Region	Average income per active worker (Yugoslavia = 100)		Percentage of labor force in the social sector
	Private agricultural sector	Social sector	
Less developed regions	85	90	40
Bosnia-Herzegovina	76	95	39
Kosovo	80	83	31
Macedonia	101	83	43
Montenegro	109	87	49
More developed regions	106	104	46
Croatia	120	111	49
Serbia	83	93	37
Slovenia	145	115	67
Vojvodina	171	97	49
Yugoslavia	100	100	44
Yugoslavia (dinars per month)	597	1,514	—

— Not applicable.
Sources: Figures supplied by the Federal Institute of Statistics, and appendix table A.31.

also have lower incomes per worker in the private sector. The differences in private sector incomes tend to be most pronounced in the less developed regions; the interregional spread for the social sector, although following a similar pattern, is narrower. As would be expected, the structural differences between regions are accentuated by the much faster natural increase in population and labor force in the less developed regions. During 1961–71 the average annual rate of population growth in Kosovo was 2.6 percent; that in Vojvodina was 0.5 percent.

Migration and labor mobility

The large differences in earnings between the modern and traditional sectors and between labor market conditions in the various regions led to a rapid movement of the labor force out of the agricultural sector. Thus, while the growth in the labor force between 1961 and 1975 was relatively modest at 0.66 percent a year, the active population in private sector agriculture declined at an average rate of more than 3 percent a year. The rate of decline accelerated to 6 percent a year between 1970 and 1975. As a result, the number of workers leaving the agricultural sector during 1961–75 was more than twice the natural increase in the labor force. During much of this period, external migration provided an important vent for workers seeking nonagricultural employment. But with the restrictions placed on migration by labor-importing countries after 1973, migration out of the agricultural sector became associated with a rapid increase in open unemployment.

Interrepublican migration has been very low in comparison with intrarepublican migration and external migration (table 10.4).[7] Between 1961 and 1971 net interrepublican annual migration amounted to 0.1 percent of the population; there was an outmigration from all the less developed regions, ranging from 0.5 percent in Bosnia-Herzegovina to a marginal outmigration from Macedonia. The average annual external migration was equal to 0.5 percent of the population; the average annual rural-to-urban migration within regions to 0.4 percent. More developed regions, despite being net recipients of interrepublican population flows, tended to have high rural-to-urban migration, a pattern reaffirming the disequilibria even in those regions. As a result, interrepublican migration has been modest and is likely to be so, as long as there are pockets of "surplus

Table 10.4. *Labor Mobility, 1961–71*

Type of migration	Average annual number of migrants	Ratio of migrants to mean population (percent)
Intrarepublican migration	102,500	0.5
Net interrepublican migration	23,950	0.1
Net external migration[a]	71,300	0.4

Source: Dusan Breznik, "Internal Migration," *Yugoslav Survey*, vol. 17, no. 1 (February 1976).
a. For 1963–71.

7. Sectoral shifts in employment do not necessarily imply rural-to-urban migration. One feature of the Yugoslav labor market is the considerable amount of commuting between rural and urban areas.

labor" in search of social sector employment in all regions. Social and cultural differences have also impeded interrepublican mobility.

With the increase in income differences and the decline of employment opportunities in the social sector after 1965, external migration became an important substitute for local employment. It is estimated that the number of workers temporarily employed abroad rose from about 138,000 in 1964 to 400,000 in 1968. But between 1968 and 1973 that number rose by 700,000 to a peak of 1.1 million in 1973. During those same five years the natural increase in the labor force was more than 300,000, the increase in social sector employment was 740,000, and the exodus from the agricultural sector was 1.2 million. Although external migration clearly was important, its regional incidence was uneven. The importance of external migration for the provision of jobs outside the traditional agricultural sector can best be gauged by analyzing the absorption of the incremental labor supply during 1961–75.[8]

The supply and absorption of labor during the 1961–65 period reflects the basic trends in the prereform era. Already during this period the exodus of workers from the private agricultural sector accounted for 60 percent of the incremental labor supply (table 10.5). The social sector could not absorb all of the incremental labor supply, but it did provide more than 70 percent of all employment opportunities. Employment opportunities in the social sector declined slightly during the 1965–68 period. That decline, largely the result of attrition, reflected the objective of the economic reforms to increase labor productivity and the competitiveness of Yugoslav goods. Temporary employment abroad became increasingly important, absorbing some 76 percent of the labor supply. There also was a sharp increase in unemployment during the period; the share of those seeking private nonagricultural employment also rose significantly. In the 1968–73 period the agricultural sector again became the main source of the incremental labor supply. Social sector employment increased, absorbing almost 50 percent of job-seekers. Temporary employment abroad absorbed 46 percent of the labor supply. The 1973–75 period is characterized by the reversal of work

8. The incremental labor supply is defined here as the number of job-seekers during the period under consideration. It thus includes the natural increase in the labor force and the decline in employment in any sector. In practice, this second component essentially is the number of workers leaving the agricultural sector.

Table 10.5. *Incremental Labor Supply and Absorption, 1961–75*
(percent)

Item	1961–65	1965–68	1968–73	1973–75
Labor supply				
Agricultural outflow	62	11	80	42
Demographic increase	38	56	20	21
Other[a]	0	33	0	36
Labor absorption				
Social sector	73	0	48	78
Private nonagriculture	4	9	4	5
Net external migration	18	76	46	0
Unemployment	5	15	3	17
Mean annual incremental labor supply as proportion of the mean annual labor force	1.7	1.1	3.5	3.0

Source: Appendix table A.27.

a. Other sources of labor supply were the decline in social sector employment during 1965–68 and the returning migrants during 1973–75.

opportunities in Western Europe and the net return of workers. Social sector employment rose rapidly, but not enough to absorb the incremental labor supply. Unemployment absorbed about 17 percent of the incremental labor supply during the period.

The effects of the curtailment of external migration on open unemployment were significant. After an initial rise in the rate of registered unemployed after the 1965 reforms, the unemployment rate declined between 1968 and 1971. Between 1971 and 1973 there was a gradual increase in unemployment from 6.7 percent to 8.1 percent, despite the high rates of external migration and job creation in the social sector. This trend accelerated sharply after 1973 rising to 10.4 percent in 1975. These figures must be cautiously interpreted: they include not only those that are openly unemployed, but also private farmers seeking employment in the social sector and some students.[9] The figures nevertheless reflect the broad trends of open unemployment. Above all, they indicate a revealed preference for social sector employment and thus provide a useful measure of disequilibria in the labor market.

9. Open unemployment in 1975 is estimated to have been about 60 percent of registered unemployment.

Behavioral trends

Despite the structural transformation of the labor market in recent years, the differences and specific changes in participation and activity rates indicate that considerable additional reserves of labor may exist. These differences, particularly evident in the less developed regions, point to a sizable share of the working-age population which either has never sought employment or has withdrawn from the labor force because of the absence of work opportunities and prospects of securing suitable employment. If this segment of the labor supply is taken into account, the magnitude of the employment problem is considerably increased.

The first feature to be noted is the decline in working-age and crude activity rates. Between 1953 and 1971 the working-age activity rate, which is the ratio of the economically active population to the population of working age, declined from 67 percent to 63.7 percent; the crude activity rate declined from 45.6 percent to 43.3 percent. The change in the crude activity rate can be analyzed by breaking down changes of the activity rate into changes caused by shifts in age composition and labor force participation (table 10.6).

Table 10.6. *Effects of Age Composition and Labor Force Participation on Crude Activity Rates, Estimates for 1953–71*

Item	Change in crude activity rates (percent)	Effect of age composition (percentage points)	Effect of labor force participation (percentage points)
Total population			
1953–61	−1.2	−0.7	−0.5
1961–71	−1.1	1.5	−2.6
Male population			
1953–61	−3.0	0.4	−3.4
1961–71	−2.2	2.5	−4.7
Female population			
1953–61	0.3	−1.3	1.6
1961–71	0.1	0.9	−1.1

Source: Economic Institute, "The Determinants of the Labour Force Participation in Yugoslavia" (Belgrade, 1974; processed), table 1.6.

What clearly emerges is the different pattern for the two intercensal periods: 1953–61 and 1961–71. In the first period changes in age composition and in participation rates contributed equally to a decline in the crude activity rate. In the second period the age composition, reflecting the aftermath of the postwar baby boom, had a strong positive effect: participation rates fell sharply and led to the decline of the crude activity rate. The large increase in the size of the working-age population, when about a third of the working-age population already was inactive, may have been important in contributing to the declining participation rate. Although such trends need to be treated with caution, because the nonactive population includes students, housewives, and early retirees, they nevertheless point to considerable and increasing reserves of labor.

The second feature is the difference between regions. The less developed regions had considerably lower crude activity rates than the more developed regions, rates which have been rapidly declining to widen the gap over the 1953–71 period (table 10.7). These differences are particularly apparent in the crude activity rates of females and most pronounced in Kosovo. Furthermore crude activity rates of females declined between 1961 and 1971 in the less developed regions; they continued to rise in the more developed regions. These trends give further support to the hypothesis that the reserves of labor force are considerable, particularly in the less developed regions.

Table 10.7. *Crude Activity Rates, by Region, 1953–71*
(percent)

Region	Male population			Female population			Total population		
	1953	*1961*	*1971*	*1953*	*1961*	*1971*	*1953*	*1961*	*1971*
Less developed regions									
Bosnia-Herzegovina	57.9	54.0	51.3	26.8	24.4	22.7	41.9	38.8	36.7
Kosovo	54.1	50.8	42.7	10.8	17.6	8.4	32.9	34.6	34.0
Macedonia	57.3	54.1	52.7	22.8	23.6	23.4	40.2	39.0	38.3
Montenegro	52.9	48.8	46.1	20.3	20.0	19.9	35.9	34.0	32.7
More developed regions									
Croatia	63.8	60.1	57.9	31.6	33.5	34.0	46.8	46.2	45.5
Serbia	65.4	63.1	63.2	38.5	38.6	40.1	51.7	50.6	51.5
Slovenia	59.8	57.9	56.6	35.0	37.2	40.8	46.7	47.1	48.4
Vojvodina	63.9	62.2	59.7	26.4	25.3	26.5	44.4	43.3	42.7

Source: Same as for table 10.6.

During the second intercensal period, the decline was sharp in participation rates for males 44 years and older. This decline reflected the increase in the number of pensioners from 533,000 in 1966 to 1.1 million in 1971. That increase was mainly the result of special circumstances, notably the encouragement of early retirement. In addition, the effect of the baby boom on the labor market can be clearly seen for the 15–24 age group, which had increasing difficulty in securing employment.[10] Registered unemployment in that group, based on year-end figures, increased from 36 percent of all unemployed in 1961 to 49 percent in 1971 and 53 percent in 1975. Also between 1961 and 1971, those in the 15–24 age group who declared themselves not as housewives, students, or children in the census, but as "other dependents," increased from 28,000 to 159,000.

Structure of demand and labor requirements

Despite a continued rapid increase in GDP after the 1965 reforms, the size of the active resident labor force declined between 1965 and 1975, mainly because of external migration for temporary employment abroad. This led to a considerable decline in the labor-output ratio during that period. Although the labor force grew at an average annual rate of about 0.7 percent between 1965 and 1975, the resident labor force declined at an annual rate of 0.3 percent.

To identify the demand factors behind the change in the resident labor force and to measure their relative influence, a "sources-of-change analysis" of labor use was carried out for the 1966–72 period.[11] In short, the analysis attempts to explain changes in sectoral employment by changes in the level of net final demand, changes in the composition of net final demand, and changes in production technology, which include changes in labor coefficients and input-output coefficients. The indirect employment generated by adjustments of the production of intermediate goods necessitated by each of these factors is attributed to the factor causing the initial change. Thus

10. Employment associations place job-seekers in the greatest need first, such as those with many dependents and those who have waited longest. This practice tends to increase unemployment of the young in a tight labor market.

11. The analytical technique is similar to that discussed in the technical note at the end of chapter eight. The analysis is based on input-output tables for Yugoslavia and described in World Bank, "Yugoslavia: Self-management Socialism and the Challenges of Development," report no. 1615a-YU (a restricted circulation document), 6 vols. (Washington, D.C.: World Bank, 1978; processed), vol. 6.

the effects measured under this approach are total effects: they include the direct and indirect effects of each source of change on employment.

Between 1966 and 1972 total domestic employment declined by 503,000 (table 10.8). The effect of the change in net final demand on employment assumes that there was no change in the technological coefficients and composition of net final demand between 1966 and 1972, but merely a proportional growth in net final demand equal to the observed aggregate growth of net final demand during the same period. Under such circumstances, employment would have increased in all sectors; the total increase would have been about 3.1 million. The discrepancy between this predicted change in employment—based on the assumption of no change in the composition of net final demand and technology—and the actual change can be explained by changes in the composition of demand and production technology. As the figures in table 10.8 show, the contribution of these factors was about equal in the aggregate, but there were significant differences between sectors. The negative technological effect, which reflects increasing labor productivity, was equal to about 20 or 30 percent of the labor force in each of the nonagricultural sectors. In turn, the effect of changes in the composition of net final demand was positive for all sectors except two: forestry and agriculture. For sectors other than agriculture and forestry, the changes in the level and composition of net final demand significantly contributed to increases in sectoral employment; this contribution was partly offset by the reduction in labor requirements caused by technological factors. The result was a net gain in employment in those sectors.

Labor Absorption

The broad structural evolution of employment outlined earlier in this chapter indicated three principal sources of labor absorption in nontraditional activities: the social sector, the private nonagricultural sector, and temporary employment abroad. The principal source of growth in modern employment opportunities has been the social sector. In 1953 that sector employed 1.8 million workers, or 23 percent of the active labor force. By 1975 it employed about 4.6 million workers, or more than 50 percent of the active population. Industry accounted for about 40 percent of employment in

Table 10.8. *Sources of Change in Labor Use, by Sector, 1966–72*

Sector	Change in employment (thousands of workers)	Contribution to change[a] (percent)		
		Level of final demand[b]	Composition of final demand	Production technology[c]
Industry	228	235	47	−183
Agriculture[d]	−1,110	−181	203	78
Forestry[d]	−13	−175	48	227
Construction	97	204	94	−198
Transport and communication	78	149	19	−69
Trade and catering	184	88	78	−66
Handicrafts	32	237	8	−145
Total[d]	−503	−620	378	342

Source: World Bank, "Yugoslavia: Self-management Socialism and the Challenges of Development," vol. 6.

a. The contribution to change is the change in labor use caused by a given effect expressed as a percentage of the actual change. For example, if the technological effect had been neutral, employment in the industrial sector would have been 283 percent of the actual change observed.

b. Final demand is net final demand, which is equal to domestic final demand plus exports minus imports.

c. Production technology includes changes in labor coefficients and input-output coefficients.

d. Because agriculture and forestry registered negative growth in employment, the contributions to change must be cautiously interpreted. The positive signs for the effect of production technology imply that employment was reduced, not increased, as a result of the change in technology.

the social sector in 1975; it was followed by trade and catering with 15 percent and by construction with 12 percent (table 10.9). About 822,000 workers, or 18 percent of workers in the social sector, were employed in government, social services, and banking. The private nonagricultural sector has played a modest role as an absorber of the labor force. Comprehensive data on its size and structure do not exist, but estimates in the social plan for 1976–80 indicate that about 300,000 workers were employed in private nonagricultural activities in 1970. By 1975 the number had risen to 360,000, or 3.9 percent of the labor force. Temporary employment abroad, as indicated earlier, reached a peak of 1.1 million workers in 1973, or 12.2 percent of the labor force. Thus major changes in the conditions governing work abroad have significant repercussions on employment in Yugoslavia.

Table 10.9. *Employment in the Social Sector,*
by Economic Sector, 1975

Sector or branch	Thousands of workers	Percentage of social sector employment
Industry	1,802.1	40.1
Metal products	382.9	8.2
Textiles	315.4	6.8
Food products	168.3	3.6
Wood products	172.1	3.7
Electrical machinery	116.1	2.5
Chemicals	100.9	2.2
Other	610.6	13.1
Agriculture	181.7	4.1
Forestry	66.0	1.3
Construction	484.7	12.5
Transport and communication	360.4	6.8
Trade	622.8	14.8
Handicrafts	132.4	2.2
Public utilities	90.4	0.5
Total	3,869.1	82.3
Government, social services, and banking	822.0	17.7
Total	4,650.2	100.0

Source: *Statistical Bulletin,* no. 1017 (January 1977).

Social sector employment

Most theoretical literature on the self-managed enterprise suggests that the objective function of workers would be to maximize personal income per worker. Consequently Yugoslav enterprises would be expected to opt for high productivity growth and low employment growth. In practice, the opposite is observed. Throughout the postwar period employment in the social sector has grown rapidly in relation to the growth in value added—that is, the elasticities of employment to value added have been high.

The annual growth rate of employment during the 1956–75 period was 3.7 percent: it was 6.2 percent before the 1965 reforms and 3 percent after them. This decline would seem to be consistent with the hypothesis that workers would maximize personal income per worker, particularly given their growing autonomy in decision-making after 1965. But that decline can be explained by other factors. It partly reflects a once-and-for-all adjustment to the 1965 reforms and partly the subsequent decline in the growth rate of the economy, not a change in the capacity of the social sector to generate employment. As already mentioned, the growth of social sector employment stagnated between 1965 and 1968. One objective of the 1965 reforms was to rationalize production methods to increase labor productivity and facilitate a redistribution of income toward personal incomes through higher wages without adversely affecting the competitiveness of Yugoslav commodities. Many workers were encouraged to seek early retirement, and not all of the positions they vacated were filled by new workers. Because this attrition reflects a once-and-for-all adjustment to the inherited production structure, it is best discounted in analyzing the basic underlying trends before and after the reforms. The growth of employment after 1968 nevertheless was considerably below that during 1956–65. The main reason for this is the decline in the growth rate of social sector production. The employment-output elasticity before 1965 and after 1968 was virtually the same at about 0.7.[12] Thus the capacity of the economy to generate employment, if viewed in this simplistic form, seems not to have deteriorated with the reforms. Indeed it compares favorably with that of other countries.[13]

A high elasticity of employment to value added must nevertheless be cautiously interpreted. A high elasticity could, as suggested above, reflect a strategy of high employment growth. Or it could be interpreted as reflecting conscious decisions of enterprises to trade off productivity growth against new work places. Such a tradeoff may be a part of the objective function of Yugoslav enterprises. Given the large unemployment problem, workers often have relatives and

12. The sectoral elasticities shown in appendix table A.34, calculated on the basis of a 29-sector breakdown, are considerably less stable. The aggregate elasticity should be viewed with this instability in mind.

13. For example, the aggregate employment elasticity for all Latin American countries between 1960 and 1969 was 0.6; the sectoral employment elasticity for manufacturing was 0.4. United Nations, Economic Commission for Latin America, *Economic Survey of Latin America, 1968* (New York: United Nations, 1970).

friends seeking work and thus have an interest in ensuring rapid growth of employment opportunities. In addition, communal authorities exert pressure on workers to expand employment opportunities.

Given this tradeoff, low productivity growth does not necessarily indicate poor economic performance. The real effect on aggregate output growth of a strategy of high employment growth depends on such factors as the marginal product of workers in their new occupations, compared with their previous work in the traditional sector. If workers in enterprises seek to maximize family or communal incomes, a strategy of high employment growth would be expected to have a positive effect on aggregate output. Thus, despite low productivity growth, aggregate GDP per capita could increase rapidly, but its distribution under a strategy of high employment growth would differ from that under a strategy of high productivity growth. This tradeoff is likely to be acceptable to workers only if the growth of value added is sufficiently high that, even with a high elasticity of employment to value added, the growth in productivity is adequate to ensure reasonable growth in the real incomes of workers.

The different experience in the more developed and less developed regions lends support to the hypothesis that productivity gains are forgone in the interest of creating additional employment.

The employment-output elasticity in the less developed regions, ranging from 0.94 to 0.86, was consistently higher than in the more developed regions, where elasticities ranged from 0.60 to 0.36 (table 10.10). The outcome is much the same if the total is disaggregated into four major sectors: with few exceptions, the less developed regions tend to exhibit higher elasticities. Given the problem of labor absorption in the less developed regions, a more rapid generation of jobs per unit increase in value added could redress some of the imbalances between regions but only at the expense of the growth in labor productivity. The factors underlying the differences in employment performance of various regions are not clear. In part, the differences may be the result of differences in the output structure, but the greater pressure on the less developed regions to employ workers seems to have been more important. Another factor could be that investment rates were considerably higher in less developed regions, but did not lead to a correspondingly faster increase in output. Higher investment rates could have led to growth in capacity and employment, without the full use of either. To test this hypothesis, elasticities of employment to fixed assets were calculated;

Table 10.10. *Employment Elasticities and Fixed Assets per Employee, by Region, 1969–74*

Region	Elasticity of employment		Elasticity of fixed assets to value added	Fixed assets per employee (thousands of dinars)			
	To value added[a]	To fixed assets		Social sector		Industry	
				1969	1974	1969	1974
Less developed regions							
Bosnia- Herzegovina	0.86	0.64	1.34	112	128	133	151
Kosovo	0.86	0.63	1.37	127	151	178	202
Macedonia	0.94	0.52	1.80	91	120	130	140
Montenegro	0.94	0.66	1.42	153	171	189	201
More developed regions							
Croatia	0.56	0.47	1.19	120	144	112	138
Serbia	0.58	0.42	1.38	95	121	107	138
Slovenia	0.60	0.50	1.20	120	147	116	141
Vojvodina	0.36	0.33	1.09	103	126	105	124
Yugoslavia	0.63	0.48	1.31	110	134	116	142

Source: *Statistical Yearbook of Yugoslavia*, 1976.
a. For 1969–75.

these proved to be uniformly higher for the less developed regions.[14] Thus the employment performance of the less developed regions has been more favorable than that in the more developed regions, but the capital cost per unit of output growth has tended to be somewhat greater.[15] The elasticities nevertheless mask one important

14. Because of the lack of data, these elasticities were based on the levels of employment and fixed asset in 1969 and 1974 and calculated for 1969–74. The elasticities of employment to fixed assets in industry and in the social sector respectively were 0.65 and 0.64 for Bosnia-Herzegovina, 0.80 and 0.66 for Montenegro, 0.41 and 0.47 for Croatia, 0.83 and 0.52 for Macedonia, 0.49 and 0.50 for Slovenia, 0.41 and 0.42 for Serbia, 0.74 and 0.63 for Kosovo, and 0.49 and 0.48 for Vojvodina.

15. If the corresponding implicit elasticities of fixed assets to output are calculated, all ratios are above unity. Furthermore those of the less developed regions are uniformly higher than those of the more developed regions.

feature: the average values of the parameters. If the average capital-labor ratios in various regions are considered, it can be seen that these were uniformly higher in the less developed regions; but with few exceptions the incremental capital-labor ratios are uniformly lower, reflecting the higher elasticity of employment to fixed assets. Thus, although the less developed regions have evolved with a more capital-intensive economic structure, the current trend is toward a reversal of this feature. The corollary of the reversal, however, is unsatisfactory growth of productivity which, in view of the existing differences in productivity, would tend to widen the differences even further.

A second aspect of employment generation is the investment cost for each work place created. Throughout the postwar period there has been a tendency for capital intensity, defined here as fixed assets per employee, to increase. But after the reforms, even allowing for the period of adjustment during 1965–68, there was significant accelera-tion in the growth of fixed assets per employee. That acceleration is evident in figures on the elasticity of employment to fixed assets for the period (see appendix table A.34). An elasticity of less than 1 signifies an increasing capital intensity; a decline in the overall elas-ticity indicates a tendency for capital intensity to increase at a more rapid rate. With few exceptions there was a tendency for capital intensity to grow more rapidly for all sectors after 1965 than before. Part of the acceleration in capital intensity could have been caused by a shift in the structure of production to sectors with higher-than-average capital intensity. To determine the importance of such struc-tural shifts, the capital intensity for 1974 was calculated using 1974 ratios of fixed assets to employees, but with the 1970 relative weights of fixed assets between sectors. The results indicate that the pattern of resource allocation during the period tended to reduce the capital-labor ratio by about 13 percent. Thus there was a near universal tendency after 1968 for capital intensity to increase, a tendency which would have been even more pronounced were it not for a relative shift in the allocation of resources toward sectors with lower-than-average ratios of fixed assets to employees.

The growth of employment in the social sector, if viewed in rela-tion to the growth of output, has thus been fairly impressive. Fur-thermore employment has tended to grow relatively more rapidly in the less developed regions that have been most in need of modern sector work places. This growth in employment has been accom-panied, however, by a rapid increase in the investment cost per work place, a tendency that is likely to be accentuated by the sectoral priorities of the social plan for 1976–80.

Employment in the social sector has had four characteristics. First, the turnover rates have been extremely low, mainly because a worker can be asked to leave his work only under exceptional circumstances.[16] This feature of the system eliminates the adjustment to cyclical fluctuations by changing the size of the work force at given wage rates and replaces it by changing the personal incomes of an unchanged work force. It also reduces the access of the unemployed to social sector jobs and the attractions of other sources of employment, notably the private sector. Second, all contributions paid by enterprises to finance social services are assessed on total personal incomes. Consequently the true cost of labor to the enterprise is considerably higher than the gross earnings of workers. For example, in 1974 such direct contributions were equal to nearly 40 percent of net personal incomes. The high cost of labor in the social sector may thus be important in inducing capital-intensive production. Third, the level of capacity use generally is low. The indications are that capacity use, although notoriously difficult to measure, is about 75 percent, compared with a potential level of 80 to 90 percent. Fourth, the social sector in Yugoslavia is highly concentrated in large enterprises. Given the tendency of such enterprises to opt for capital-intensive techniques of production, increased emphasis on small-scale industry could have a beneficial effect on employment.

Private nonagricultural employment

Comprehensive data on the size and structure of the private nonagricultural sector do not exist. Some understanding of the structure of employment in the sector can nevertheless be obtained by analyzing data on value added. Before 1965 value added in the sector grew by about 4 percent a year; that in the social sector by about 9 percent a year. Immediately after the reforms, however, value added in the private nonagricultural sector grew rapidly: at about 15 percent a year, during 1965–68, compared with 4 percent a year in the

---

16. Data published in the statistical yearbooks indicate that the annual termination of employment, based on monthly averages, is equal to about 1.2 percent of those employed. This rate has been conically declining since 1966.

social sector. The reforms and the lack of social sector employment opportunities thus seem to have had a strong positive effect on the private sector. But its growth rate decelerated to 6 percent a year after 1968. During the 1965–75 period the importance of traditional activities in handicrafts continually declined; that of transport and catering increased. In 1975 handicrafts accounted for 42 percent of the value added in the private nonagricultural sector; woodwork, textiles, and metal processing were most important. Of the remainder of value added, construction accounted for 37 percent, transport for 12 percent, and catering for 10 percent. This breakdown broadly indicates the shares of employment in the various activities.[17]

As would be expected, capital intensity tends to be lower in the private nonagricultural sector than in the social sector. Data on fixed assets per employee in the private sector are not available. But if amortization is taken as a proxy for fixed assets, and national income for employment, a set of indicative figures can be obtained (table 10.11).[18] Although the private nonagricultural sector is about 40 percent less capital-intensive than the social sector, the picture is not uniform.

An additional feature of the private nonagricultural sector is the small size of workshops. In 1974, for example, 198,081 persons were employed in handicrafts; of these, 143,354 were owners. If it is assumed that each workshop has one owner, the average number of workers per establishment would be 1.4; in no subsector does it reach 2. Thus the private handicrafts sector consists principally of owner-operators. The same is likely to be true in catering, tourism, and transport. The sector cannot therefore be compared with the unorganized urban sector which acts as a residual employer of workers leaving the agriculture sector in many less developed countries. Instead it comprises artisans and workers who have returned from abroad and invested their savings in service facilities or vehicles.

17. For example, on the basis of the 1975 estimate of total employment of 359,000 in the private nonagricultural sector, handicrafts accounted for about 57 percent. But if construction handicrafts are classified not as handicrafts but as construction, as they are in data on value added, the ratio drops to 43 percent, which is closer to the share of handicrafts in value added. Similarly the estimated employment in catering is 8.5 percent of the total; the share of catering in value added was 9.6 percent. These figures indicate that shares in value added are a reasonable approximation of shares in employment.

18. The assumption is that earnings are equal in the two sectors. In fact, national income per worker in the private nonagricultural sector and the social sector are similar, the former being somewhat lower.

Table 10.11. *Capital Intensity in the Social
and Private Nonagricultural Sectors, 1975*

Economic sector	Amortization (millions of dinars)		National income (millions of dinars)		Ratio of amortization to national income (percent)	
	Social sector	Private non-agricul-tural sector	Social sector	Private non-agricul-tural sector	Social sector	Private non-agricul-tural sector
Handicrafts	712	287	8,239	7,547	8.6	3.8
Construction	3,635	—	46,343	—	7.8	—
Transport[a]	7,627	398	28,106	1,915	26.0	20.8
Catering and tourism	1,295	135	11,814	1,683	11.0	8.0
Yugoslavia[b]	45,775	1,683	377,731	11,145	12.1	7.4

— Not applicable.
Source: *Statistical Yearbook of Yugoslavia,* 1976.
   a. To make the two sectors more comparable, figures for the social sector include only road transport.
   b. Figures for the private sector exclude construction and agriculture.

Although the rights of the private sector are guaranteed and private enterprises are allowed to employ up to five salaried workers, a number of factors have hampered the development of the sector.[19] First, many individuals are reluctant to work for the private sector because fringe benefits tend to be considerably smaller. Second, private employes have had difficulty in recruiting educated and skilled workers, particularly because job stability has been considerably less in the private sector. Third, with frequent changes in government regulations regarding rights and obligations in the private sector, private owners often take a short-term view and prefer investments with short gestation periods and high profitability. Fourth, in large cities and new developments, there are no sites for setting up workshops. Fifth, the policies for taxation, credit, and foreign exchange have often discriminated against the private sector. The foregoing factors, combined with a generally noncommittal

   19. For the rights of the private sector see *The Constitution of the Socialist Federal Republic of Yugoslavia,* 1974, article 64.

attitude of government toward the sector, have deterred the growth of private initiative in productive activities.

Temporary employment abroad

Of the 1.1 million Yugoslav workers abroad in 1973, it is estimated that 830,000 were in Europe and 270,000 were in other countries.[20] They constituted about 5.2 percent of the population and the equivalent of 26.1 percent of social sector employment. The growth in external migration has in part been a reaction to the general disequilibria in the labor market described earlier in this chapter. Given the limited opportunities for interrepublican migration and the enormous income differences between working in domestic private agriculture and in Western Europe, the rapidly expanding European labor markets provided an increasingly important vent for Yugoslavia's surplus labor.[21] During 1969–73 more than 50 percent of the labor supply was absorbed by migration.[22] But external migration was not limited to workers from the agricultural sector; indeed about 40 percent of those seeking jobs abroad were previously employed in the social sector.

Migration has also had a positive effect on incomes. Sample surveys indicate that about a third of the income of Yugoslav workers abroad was consumed abroad, a third saved abroad, and a third repatriated.[23] The repatriation of incomes to families in Yugoslavia thus helped increase their incomes, reduce income differences, and curb rural-to-urban migration. In addition, by alleviating the pres-

20. See Ivo Baucic, "Some Economic Consequences of Yugoslav External Migration" (Zagreb: University of Zagreb, Center for Migration Studies, 1975; processed), p. 8.
21. For example, the average Yugoslav worker abroad is estimated to have earned $4,500 in 1973; average earnings in private agriculture are estimated to have been about $700. Econometric studies confirm the importance of push and pull factors in the outmigration of Yugoslav workers. For a case study based on quarterly data on Yugoslav workers going to West Germany during 1962–73 see Emmanuel G. Drettakis, *Yugoslav Migration to and from West Germany: 1962–73*, Studies of the Institute of Geography, vol. 13 (Zagreb: University of Zagreb, Center for Migration Studies, 1975).
22. Incremental labor supply is defined as the natural increase in the labor force plus the decline in the agricultural labor force.
23. Because the average product per capita was about $900 in 1973, remittances were fairly close to the average product per worker. And because the marginal product per worker is apt to be lower than the average, benefits through increased incomes can be considerable, even disregarding the two-thirds of income not repatriated. Baucic, "Some Economic Consequences of Yugoslav External Migration," p. 8.

sure on the labor market, migration may also have facilitated a more rapid increase of incomes in Yugoslavia. Workers' remittances increased from 2 percent of Yugoslavia's total foreign exchange earnings in 1965 to about 20 percent in 1975. By alleviating the constraints of foreign exchange and facilitating more rapid growth in the economy, they have thus had important indirect benefits for employment growth in Yugoslavia.

Despite its many apparent benefits to Yugoslavia, external migration has not been without its costs. Given the large increase in the number of Yugoslavs working abroad, those costs have become more noticeable. First, the young, mobile, and best workers usually chose to migrate. Second, about 40 percent of the migrants had previously been employed in the social sector, and many of them were skilled workers. Thus, in addition to the forgone marginal product of the migrating worker, there was the cost of training the unskilled agricultural worker to the level of the social sector worker who migrated.[24] Third, the incidence of migration by region was uneven, in some instances accentuating the regional differences in labor supply and demand (table 10.12). Fourth, workers are often separated for long periods from their families in unfamiliar and at times difficult surroundings. Some workers, having decided to return, face difficulties in integrating with Yugoslav society.[25]

Although precise data on movements of Yugoslav workers do not exist, the available information points to a dramatic shift in market conditions. The most comprehensive estimates, based on data provided by host countries, indicate that the net return of workers was about 80,000 in 1974 and 65,000 in 1975.[26] Table 10.13 shows the number of Yugoslavs who found work abroad through the Yugoslav employment service and the number who have returned and regis-

24. Baucic cites the growing proportion of illiterates among social sector workers in Croatia, the region having the highest rate of external migration, as being indicative of a deteriorating employment structure in Yugoslavia. Illiterates increased from 4.5 percent of social sector employment in 1961 to 6.8 percent in 1970. There is, of course, the reverse side of this phenomenon: Yugoslav workers obtaining skills through their employment abroad and bringing these skills back with them. But the tendency for many returning workers to go into the tourism and transport sectors as owner-operators means that few have been able to use their acquired skills. Baucic, "Some Economic Consequences of Yugoslav External Migration," p. 16.

25. See for example Ivo Baucic, "Social Aspects of External Migration of Workers and the Yugoslav Experience in the Social Protection of Migrants" (Zagreb: University of Zagreb, Center for Migration Studies, 1975; processed).

26. The estimates are those by the Center for Migration Studies at the University of Zagreb.

Table 10.12. *External Migration, by Region, 1971*

Region	Thousands of migrants	Percentage composition	Ratio of migrants to employment in the private sector (percent)
Less developed regions	315	35	28
Bosnia-Herzegovina	196	21	32
Kosovo	33	4	19
Macedonia	76	8	30
Montenegro	10	1	14
More developed regions	597	65	22
Croatia	300	33	42
Serbia	156	17	10
Slovenia	71	8	35
Vojvodina	71	8	22
Yugoslavia	913	100	24

Source: World Bank estimates.

tered with the Yugoslav employment service for employment at home. Because a larger number continue to find jobs at home without the service—as many as 80 percent do not register upon returning—these figures are useful only for showing the underlying trends.

Table 10.13. *Migrants Registered with the Yugoslav Employment Service, 1970–75*
(thousands of workers)

Year	Emigration	Return
1970	125.4	0
1971	81.3	11.1
1972	56.4	10.8
1973	73.4	12.3
1974	10.0	13.4
1975	7.7	19.6

Sources: OECD, "Continuous Reporting System on Migration: Annual Report," various years.

But the dramatic change after 1973 is clear. The number of workers placed abroad by the employment service dropped to 13.6 percent of the 1973 level in 1974 and to about 10 percent in 1975. During the same period the number of migrant job-seekers registered with the service rose rapidly.

Given the demand for the limited number of work places available in host countries, foreign employers concentrated their selection even more on applicants having skills and coming from the more developed regions. Of the migrants securing employment abroad through the employment service, the proportion from the less developed regions declined from 48.8 percent in 1973 to 21.4 percent in 1976; the proportion of unskilled workers declined from 68.5 percent to 26.7 percent over the same period.[27] Most of those able to secure employment abroad were requested by name; thus the employment service had little discretion in placing workers. Returning workers, on the other hand, had worked only for a limited time, were unskilled, and were the least able. It is estimated that about two-thirds of those returning in 1975 went back to the agricultural sector. Because many of these workers were unlikely to have accumulated large savings, they probably added to the ranks of workers seeking social sector employment. An additional feature of the recent developments has been the growing tendency for families to join workers abroad. Although the number of Yugoslav workers in Western Europe declined between 1973 and 1975, the number of dependents increased from 250,000 to 330,000 during the same period. This could indicate a shift toward more permanent settlement in the host countries.

The future prospects for Yugoslavia's migrant labor force are mixed. The recovery in the Western European economies is likely to have a favorable effect. But the host countries are extremely reluctant to increase their dependence on migrant workers because of their concern about accentuating the mounting social problems. Based on official statements made by host countries, the best that can be expected is a gradual decline in number of migrants through attrition, as workers return and are not replaced. In addition, most countries are likely to continue their efforts to facilitate the integration of remaining workers into the social fabric of their countries,

---

27. OECD, "Continuous Reporting System on Migration: Annual Report" (Paris: OECD, Directorate for Social Affairs, Manpower, and Education; processed), various years.

efforts that will further polarize the current situation.[28] The plan foresees a decline of about 250,000 in the number of workers abroad during the 1976–80 period, or 50,000 a year. Workers' remittances are expected to stagnate and decline in real terms and eventually in nominal terms. The reduced importance of remittances will necessitate structural shifts to compensate for their fall. To some extent these changes can be cushioned by attracting the savings held by Yugoslav workers in host countries.[29]

Employment Policy

The social plan for 1976–80 and the long-term perspective plan place considerable emphasis on increasing employment in the social sector and encouraging new forms of nontraditional employment in the private sector. In addition, the plans acknowledge the need to curtail the rate of migration out of the agricultural sector. Although the broad contours of these policies are fairly evident, the specific details to be determined by republics and communes are still being discussed.

Social sector

The principal innovation in employment policy for the social sector is the introduction of social compacts and self-management agreements on employment. Social compacts have been concluded within and among republics, with the executive councils, trade unions, chambers of the economy, and communities of interest for employment as parties. This development has important implications. It is regarded as a means of consciously regulating employment creation and avoiding the uncontrolled growth of employment that would occur if employment were left to the specific inter-

28. In June 1976 the Ministry of Labor of West Germany made it known that the ban on recruitment would be maintained indefinitely and without exception; new procedures were to be adopted for the reintegration of workers in their home countries. France, Switzerland, and the Netherlands made similar statements. Sweden does not have restrictions, but its liberal integration policies favor permanent migration.

29. One figure quoted is $2.6 billion for 1974; even this is likely to be a considerable underestimation. *The Economist*, 17 July 1976, p. 48.

ests of individual enterprises.[30] Social compacts and the self-management agreements concluded by enterprises consider employment creation from a broad national perspective. In addition, the communities of interest for employment are to play an important role in planning employment. With representatives of job-seekers and enterprises in their assemblies, such communities are intended to act as forums for the exchange of information and the coordination of employment policy within and among republics. They will encourage internal migration through special fiscal incentives and take part in the formulation of enterprise plans.

Social compacts offer an opportunity to address two important facets of the employment problem. First, the compacts can directly address the question of a tradeoff between the growth of productivity and employing more workers. This tradeoff can be seen as a distributional tradeoff between the growth of income in the social sector and the use of these increments for creating new jobs. Second, the stipulation of employment targets to enterprises induces them to search for more labor-intensive technologies in their investment programs. If enterprises are obliged to employ more workers than they would otherwise employ, the optimal enterprise strategy would be to choose technology that maximizes output for the given employment target. Indeed, if investment is subject to social compacts, the labor-capital ratio could be predetermined. If that specific factor proportion happens to be at the level that would exist under equilibrium factor prices, and if it can be technologically accommodated, the choice of technology would be optimal.

In addition to the general policy framework outlined here, the plan envisages increased emphasis on small-scale industry in the social sector. This emphasis is seen as a means of developing a labor-intensive sector that can ease the employment problem. That sector could be situated away from industrial centers to ease the heavy investment in housing and urban infrastructure and thus reduce total investment per job created even further. The Socialist Alliance concluded a social compact in May 1976 on the general measures neces-

---

30. "Employment should not be left uncontrolled but should be consciously directed and socially regulated primarily by means of Self-Management Agreements and Social Compacts." Federal Assembly, "Draft Outline of a Common Policy for Long-Term Development in Yugoslavia (until 1985)," p. 75. The social plan expresses the same sentiments. *Social Plan of Yugoslavia: 1976–80*, p. 94.

sary to stimulate small-scale industry. The compact stresses the significance of small-scale industry for the development of Yugoslavia, particularly in complementing industry to eliminate structural bottlenecks, redress regional imbalances, and increase employment opportunities. It acknowledges, despite a clear political position in support of small-scale industry, that few positive results have been achieved. The compact proposes that new initiatives should be taken at the republican and communal levels. It calls for a review of the current situation and problems, continual monitoring by the planning agencies, and a well-defined development program codified in social compacts at the republican level. The compact recommends that measures be introduced in rural areas to support small workshops linked to the agricultural sector and in urban areas to create service facilities linked to manufacturers of motor vehicles, agricultural equipment, and household appliances. Measures providing for legal and material security of workers, particularly in the private sector, are also stressed with particular reference to the pooling of resources through contractual organizations of associated labor (COALS). The compact recommends, in addition, that special measures be taken to provide adequate credit and training facilities and to disseminate information on investment opportunities.

Other measures already in force will be elaborated to facilitate fuller use of existing facilities and an equitable distribution of work opportunities among job-seekers. It is hoped in the course of the plan that capacity use in industry will improve. Furthermore measures will be maintained to limit overtime, supplementary employment outside regular employment, and work by those who have officially retired.

The long-term effect of the new policy measures is difficult to assess. The most powerful instruments for a continued increase in employment will be social compacts and self-management agreements. In 1975 and 1976 these worked effectively to maintain rapid growth in employment in the face of slow output growth. One consequence, however, was the stagnation of labor productivity. This stagnation alone may not be undesirable, as long as workers now employed accept the small increases in productivity and the concomitant low growth in personal incomes as a sacrifice necessary to create additional work opportunities. In 1975 real earnings declined in line with labor productivity. But in 1976 real earnings are estimated to have increased by about 4 percent, even though labor productivity remained unchanged. The pressure to increase earnings in real terms cannot be ignored, particularly because real earnings grew more slowly during 1971–75 than during 1965–70. If the growth of value added is constrained and if an employment target is set and adhered to, there will be a corresponding reduction in the growth of labor productivity. Under these circumstances, there is likely to be pressure for earnings to increase faster than labor productivity, which would lead to inflationary pressure and adversely affect the economy's rate of accumulation. A key factor in the success of employment policy is thus likely to be the achievement of a sufficiently rapid growth rate of value added to facilitate a rise in employment and an increase in real incomes in line with past expectations.

Although the potential of small-scale industry is promising, the effect during 1976–80 is unlikely to be significant. Once the legislation detailing specific measures to encourage small-scale enterprises is passed, there will still be a lag before its application. In addition, it will take time for a list of prospective projects to become available, and even more time for them to become operational. Nevertheless the establishment and support of a small-scale industrial sector is important in the longer run, particularly because it is closely linked to specific measures being introduced to encourage the employment of workers returning from abroad and the development of a productive private nontraditional sector.

Private sector

To encourage the development of the private sector, existing legal provisions for the creation of private sector employment will be strengthened and new legal forms consisting of hybrid private and social entities will be established.

With respect to the first set of measures, a social compact on the development of the private sector is to harmonize and extend existing facilities. Particular attention is expected to be given to providing premises for private workshops, reducing the tax burden, and improving the access to housing and credit. The effectiveness of these measures remains to be seen for three reasons. First, the limit of five on the number of salaried workers in a private enterprise and the high cost of labor will constrain the kinds of activity that can be undertaken. Second, it is not clear to what extent these units will have access to foreign exchange to import necessary inputs. Third, much will depend on the perception by private individuals of prospective changes in policies.

The contractual organization of associated labor (COAL) is seen as an organization that can resolve the dilemma of encouraging private initiative without creating the basis for the growth of large, autonomous private enterprises.[31] In principle, any private individual can create a COAL subject to the approval of the commune, chamber of the economy and the trade union. There is no limit on the number of workers a COAL can employ. But in Slovenia, where COALS were first established, there is an upper limit of ten owners, because each owner's share must be more than 10 percent of the capital. On the basis of the contract creating the COAL, which includes workers as parties, a self-management agreement is concluded to specify in detail the way income is to be shared, the stake of the owners reimbursed, the rights of the workers, and management of the enterprise.

By the end of 1976 some twenty or thirty COALS employing between six and ninety workers had been established in Slovenia. It is too early to evaluate their success. The legal right to management, risk sharing, and unlimited employment is likely to be attractive to private individuals. Furthermore, giving COALS the same rights and access to credits as BOALS, will enable COALS to compete for scarce resources. Moreover a COAL is not likely to carry the same stigma as a purely private entity. But as for any new institutional change, it will take time for COALS to have much effect, particularly because there were few COALS in republics other than Slovenia.

In the agricultural sector new forms of cooperatives among private farmers and new cooperative arrangements between cooperatives and integrated production and processing units in the social sector are to provide equal access to basic inputs and credit. It is expected that these new measures, in addition to the increased share of resources being devoted to the agricultural sector, will rationalize production techniques and enable the more rapid growth of incomes in the private agricultural sector. Although a rise in incomes would help to curb the migration out of the sector, the net effect of the measures is difficult to assess, because rationalization of production through cooperatives may reduce the demand for labor.

Workers temporarily employed abroad

Until 1970 the principal emphasis of policy for Yugoslav workers abroad was to improve their working conditions. By the early 1970s, however, there was growing concern about the number of migrants

31. *The Associated Labour Act*, articles 280–95.

and their structural characteristics—that is, their ages, skills, and origins. Consequently attention was increasingly focused on methods to control the composition of outmigration and to encourage workers to return. Throughout the period attempts were made to encourage the repatriation of workers' savings.

The first comprehensive policy statement in early 1973 documented the need to "make possible a closer link of social funds with the savings of migrant workers and to work out incentives for increasing savings in the home country in order to ensure increased employment through the investment of savings in the development of work organizations."[32] In 1974 a similar position was expressed in a social compact adopted by the republics on the employment of Yugoslav citizens abroad and reaffirmed in a resolution of the tenth congress of the LCY. According to this compact all republics and communes were to initiate programs to stimulate the return of workers and to help them find work. Measures to provide for returnees still are fairly broad in their formulation; concrete programs were to be adopted by republics and communes in 1977.

By 1974, when the recession in Western Europe caused a large return of workers, it became increasingly clear that the primary task was to absorb the growing number of returning workers. The sharp decline in outmigration reduced the significance of measures to control its composition; concurrently the reduced demand severely restricted the ability of employment agencies to place workers. The present policy has the following aspects. First, there is a continuing effort to attract workers' remittances and induce workers to repatriate their large savings abroad: the facilities for opening accounts are liberal; the interest rates on savings accounts denominated in foreign exchange are high; the floating exchange rate and government guarantees also help. Furthermore preferential facilities generally are available for credits in local currency, and some commodities can be purchased at discounts or under favorable customs regulations. Second, there is a growing effort to encourage the channeling of these savings to productive sectors in which new jobs can be created, not to personal consumption and housing construction. To this end, enterprises have been allowed to issue bonds denominated in foreign currency; these bonds often confer special privileges on

32. LCY, "Conclusions of the Presidency of the League of Communists of Yugoslavia; the Presidency of the Socialist Federal Republic of Yugoslavia on the Problem of Employment of Yugoslav Citizens Abroad" (Belgrade, February 1973).

purchasers for obtaining employment in the enterprise. In addition, banks are encouraged to lend counterpart local currency to support new ventures initiated by returning workers, and imports of capital goods by such ventures benefit from special exemptions of customs duties. Third, government has tried to establish bilateral arrangements with recipient countries to secure financial and technical assistance in creating work opportunities for the returnees. Such arrangements have already been made with the Netherlands, which provided 6 million guilders; less formal arrangements exist with West German enterprises. Fourth, new institutional arrangements and the increasing emphasis on private nonagricultural employment widen the scope for workers to invest their funds and to create new work opportunities for themselves and others.

Despite these measures to create new work places with the savings of returning migrants, the success has been limited.[33] This reflects traditional attitudes, the time necessary for all to grasp the new opportunities, and the need for a more coordinated policy, which awaited the conclusion of the republican work programs. There has been a lack of attractive investment programs; banks have been more interested in receiving the deposits of workers than in initiating projects; the chambers of the economy have similarly been inactive in initiating projects. Even for suitable projects, it has not always been easy to secure funds, given the time required for processing documents and delivering imported equipment. Furthermore the returning workers, as already noted, generally are the least skilled and enterprising; they also originate from the least developed regions. In these regions the industrial structure has been concentrated on primary production, and small-scale industry is principally seen to complement the production of final goods. Thus the needs are greatest in regions having the fewest opportunities. Internal migration could alleviate this condition, but cultural barriers and housing shortages pose difficulties.

Population, Active Labor Force, and Employment: 1975–85

The Demographic Research Center in Belgrade has made detailed projections for Yugoslavia's population and active labor force

---

33. There were no hard figures on the jobs created as a result of these measures, but it is unlikely that the number exceeded 2,000 in 1976.

up to 1985.[34] The projections allow for some interrepublican migration based on the assumption that net annual migration between republics will remain fairly stable around the 1961–71 rates. The exceptions are Kosovo, which will have a somewhat larger net outmigration, and Bosnia-Herzegovina, which will have a somewhat smaller net outmigration. For age-specific and sex-specific participation, the projections indicate the following: a continuing decline in rates for both sexes in the 0–14 and 15–24 age groups, though at a lower rate than in the last intercensal period; stable rates for males and some increase for females in the 25–34 and 35–49 age groups; and gradually declining rates for the 50–64 and over-64 age groups. On the whole, the assumptions are conservative. The results of the projections are summarized in appendix table A.33.

Yugoslavia's total population growth rate is expected to decline gradually over the period. The growth rate of the labor force is projected to be slightly lower than that of population during 1976–80, but to fall dramatically during 1980–85. This principally reflects the growing proportion of the population in marginal age groups having declining activity rates. The projections also reflect the varied demographic characteristics of different regions. For 1975–80 the growth in labor force varies from 3.3 percent a year in Kosovo to —0.2 percent a year in Serbia; for 1980–85 the respective figures are 3.4 percent and —0.6 percent. The less developed regions are expected to continue to have larger growth in their labor forces, despite the net migration to the more developed regions (table 10.14).

The figures in table 10.15 show the implications of the natural increase in the labor force for employment opportunities in the social sector. They present the annual increments to the labor force during 1975–80 and 1980–85 and the growth in social sector employment necessary to accommodate these increments. In the more developed regions—Croatia, Serbia, Slovenia, and Vojvodina—the natural increase is small or negligible in relation to any anticipated growth in social sector employment. Thus employment opportunities in these regions must either be filled through transfers from the agricultural sector, where such labor surpluses exist, or through in-

34. Those projections were used in the formulation of the social plan for 1976–80. See Milica Sentic and Dusan Breznik, "Projections of Total and Active Population including Migration," *Stanovnistvo*, vol. 10, nos. 3–4, vol. 11, nos. 1–2 (Belgrade: Institute of Social Sciences, Demographic Research Center, July–December 1972—January–June 1973), pp. 137–74.

Table 10.14. *Growth of Population and Labor Force, 1970–85*
(percent)

Item	Average annual rate of growth		
	1970–75	*1975–80*	*1980–85*
Less developed regions			
Population	1.25	1.26	1.21
Labor force	2.13	1.97	1.60
Male	1.93	1.81	1.48
Female	2.67	2.35	1.92
More developed regions			
Population	0.58	0.55	0.32
Labor force	0.20	0.12	−0.35
Male	0.21	0.05	−0.30
Female	0.18	0.23	−0.43

Source: Appendix table A.33.

creased interrepublican migration, returning migrants, or reduced unemployment. Bosnia-Herzegovina, Montenegro, and Macedonia have high rates of natural increase, but social sector employment is likely to increase even more rapidly and enable some depletion of the agricultural labor force, the employment of returning migrants, or reduced unemployment. Kosovo will continue during this period to have natural increases in the labor force in excess of any reasonable projected growth of employment opportunities in the social sector.

In addition to the natural increase in the labor force, the plan foresees two additional sources of labor supply: a return of 250,000 migrant workers, and a reduction in registered unemployment of 136,000. If these two factors are added to the demographic increase, if the temporary migrants return to the region of origin in the same proportions as the stock of migration in 1971, and if the ranks of unemployed are reduced by the respective shares of regions in total unemployment, the required increase in social sector employment is considerably increased (table 10.16).[35] The opportunities for a continuing decline in the agricultural labor force are likely to be limited

35. The assumptions tend to favor the less developed regions—that is, they understate the problem of labor absorption in those regions. Recent migration trends, as already noted, have generally been heavily biased against the less developed regions.

Table 10.15. *Natural Increase in Labor Force*
and Absorption Requirements, Projections for 1976–85

Region	Increase in labor force (thousands)		Average annual rate of growth in social sector employment necessary to absorb natural increase (percent)	
	1976–80	1980–85	1976–80	1980–85
Less developed regions	208.0	174.9	3.2	2.3
Bosnia-Herzegovina	97.2	61.2	2.8	1.6
Kosovo	52.1	64.8	6.7	6.1
Macedonia	44.9	38.6	2.6	2.0
Montenegro	13.8	10.3	2.6	1.8
More developed regions	69.3	−82.5	0.4	−0.5
Croatia	47.4	−37.1	0.8	−0.6
Serbia	−12.1	−64.7	−0.2	−1.1
Slovenia	10.8	7.5	0.3	0.2
Vojvodina	23.2	11.8	1.0	0.5
Yugoslavia	277.3	92.3	1.2	0.4

Source: Sentic and Bresnik, "Projections of Total and Active Population, including Migration."

in the less developed regions, particularly in Kosovo and Bosnia-Herzegovina. The agricultural labor force in Kosovo is likely to continue to grow, even with fairly optimistic assumptions about the growth in social sector employment and interrepublican migration. In other regions, there are some prospects of a reduction in the agricultural labor force.

According to the plan, employment in the social sector is to grow at 3.5 percent a year; that in the private nonagricultural sector at 5.1 percent a year. The federal plan does not provide any further information, either by sector or region. The planned growth rate for the social sector implies an aggregate employment-output elasticity of 0.47. This would be considerably below the historical elasticity of about 0.7. But given the large structural changes that the plan envisions in favor of more capital-intensive techniques, some change in elasticity can be expected, even if sectoral employment-output elasticities remained unchanged.

Table 10.16. *Planned Return of Migrant Workers,*
Reduced Unemployment, and Absorption Requirements,
by Region, Estimates for 1976–80

| Region | Return-ing mi-grants (thou-sands) | Re-duced unem-ploy-ment (thou-sands) | Average annual rate of growth in social sector employment necessary to absorb increase (percent) | | | | Grow rate soci sect emplo men 1971- (per cent |
			Return-ing mi-grants	Re-duced unem-ploy-ment	Demo-graphic increase	Total	
Less developed regions							
Bosnia-Herzegovina	54	22	1.5	0.6	2.8	4.9	5.5
Kosovo	9	10	1.3	1.4	6.7	9.4	6.7
Macedonia	21	22	1.2	1.3	2.6	5.1	5.3
Montenegro	3	4	0.6	0.8	2.6	4.0	5.3
More developed regions							
Croatia	82	18	1.4	0.3	0.8	2.5	3.7
Serbia	43	42	0.7	0.7	−0.2	1.2	4.0
Slovenia	19	3	0.6	0.1	0.3	1.0	4.4
Vojvodina	19	14	0.8	0.6	1.0	2.4	3.5
Yugoslavia	250	136	1.1	0.6	1.2	2.9	4.4

Note: It is assumed that returning migrants go back to their regions of origin and ⬛ the reduction of unemployment in each region is proportional to the shares of regi⬛ in total unemployment in 1975.
Source: World Bank estimates.

Table 10.17 presents labor-output and capital-labor ratios of the priority sectors and compares these with the average ratios for indus-try and the economy.[36] The average direct labor-output ratio for the priority sectors is about 7 percent lower than the average for

36. The agricultural sector, despite its being a priority sector, has not been included in the analysis. Given the significant effect of the observed structural changes in demand for agricultural produce—from primary to processed prod-ucts—the inclusion of agriculture would have little meaning.

Table 10.17. *Labor-output and Capital-labor Ratios, 1972*

Sector	Direct	Rank	Total	Rank
	Labor-output ratio[a] (workers per million dinars)			
Electricity	5.8	10	10.3	6
Coal	12.9	25	16.4	19
Ferrous metallurgy	4.6	6	10.6	7
Nonferrous metallurgy	4.5	3	9.2	3
Nonmetallic minerals	11.6	23	16.3	18
Chemicals	4.6	4	9.6	4
Shipbuilding	4.9	7	9.9	5
Average for priority industries	5.8	—	n.a.	—
Average for industry	6.8	—	21.3	—
Transport and communications	12.7	24	15.8	16
Average for priority sectors	8.0	—	n.a.	—
Average for economy[c]	8.6	—	18.6	—
	Capital-labor ratio[b] (thousands of dinars per worker)			
Electricity	1,154.1	1	700.9	1
Coal	128.3	8	131.8	8
Ferrous metallurgy	200.4	4	188.5	4
Nonferrous metallurgy	187.5	5	200.1	3
Nonmetallic minerals	87.5	14	107.6	11
Chemicals	163.8	7	170.2	7
Shipbuilding	97.4	13	103.0	12
Average for priority industries	257.1	—	n.a.	—
Average for industry	120.2	—	63.9	—
Transport and communications	208.7	3	188.3	5
Average for priority sectors	235.8	—	n.a.	—
Average for economy[c]	100.7	—	72.3	—

— Not applicable.
n.a. Not available.
Source: Federal Institute of Statistics, *Studies, Analyses, and Reviews,* nos. 80–81 (Belgrade 1976).
a. The lower the rank, the lower the labor-output ratio.
b. The lower the rank, the higher the capital-labor ratio.
c. Excludes agriculture.

the economy, excluding agriculture. To allow for the effect of structural shifts in production toward sectors having low labor-output ratios, the historical employment elasticity was recalculated using sectoral employment elasticities for 1968–74 and the plan vector of gross output targets. The effect is to reduce the elasticity somewhat, but on the basis of historical trends an employment-output elasticity of 0.6 still appears attainable.

Although the effects of the structural changes envisaged in the plan are modest with respect to labor-output ratios, they are substantial for the capital cost per job created. Priority sectors generally rank among the top in capital-labor ratios (see table 10.17). The average direct capital-labor ratio for priority sectors in industry is more than twice the industrial average; the result is much the same for all priority sectors. Thus one significant implication of the current plan's targets is that there will be substantial increases in the cost per job created.

If it is assumed the plan's targets for gross output will be realized, social sector employment could be expected to grow by 4.4 percent a year, based on an elasticity of about 0.6 (table 10.18). This would

Table 10.18. *Employment in the Social Sector,*
Estimates for 1976–80
(percent)

Type of activity	Average annual rate of growth		
	Plan variant	First variant	Third variant
Productive	4.3	3.3	1.6
Nonproductive	5.0	4.5	2.6
Total	4.4	3.5	1.8

Note: The assumptions underlying these variants are described in the text accompanying table 8.14 in chapter eight.
Source: World Bank estimates.

indicate that the assumption in the plan for the growth of employment is conservative. In chapter eight an attempt was made to compare the growth targets in the plan with sectoral growth rates based on historical ICORs and planned investment outlays. If these revised estimates of growth are used, the projected employment growth rate changes considerably. Under the assumptions of the first variant in table 8.14, for which a mechanical extrapolation of growth rates was based on historical ICORs and planned sectoral investment outlays, the growth rate of employment is reduced to 3.5 percent. The principal factor in this decline is the considerably lower projected growth in such sectors as trade, tourism, and construction; another factor is the decline in the economic growth rate. The third variant considers the effect of a 20 percent shortfall in investment outlays over the plan period and assumes that the adjustment is completely borne by the nonpriority sectors. The implications of this scenario are striking. The rate of employment growth plunges to 1.8 percent a year. The target in the plan for employment growth in the social sector thus appears quite realistic as long as the projected growth and investment targets are attained. But if there is a shortfall in investable resources, employment growth will hinge on the way the plan is adjusted. If the binding legal and contractual obligations in priority sectors are strictly followed and if nonpriority sectors are forced to bear the brunt of the adjustment, the effect on employment generation could be unfavorable. Thus if the employment objective is not to be sacrificed, attention must be paid to a balanced reduction of growth targets.

Although the targets for employment growth in the social sector appear attainable if the broad output targets of the plan are satisfied, the planned growth rate for private nonagricultural employment appears to be optimistic. Annual growth in employment of 5.1 percent would imply an employment-output elasticity of about unity, which is considerably higher than the historical rate and would be equivalent to the absence of any productivity growth. An increase in the growth of nonagricultural private employment is likely to occur as a result of the new institutional arrangements and the growing return of migrant workers. But the recent return of migrants has already exhausted work opportunities in certain sectors, notably in catering and road haulage. The new institutional arrangements should encourage private investment in new productive sectors, but the novelty of many arrangements is likely to militate against any sudden and large increase in employment in this sector.

Table 10.19 brings together various elements of labor supply and demand. The incremental labor supply indicates the number of additional job-seekers that would have to be provided with work based on the objectives explicitly enunciated in the plan. Labor absorption indicates the number of additional work places expected to be available. This absorption is based on the plan's assumption for growth in social sector employment and a somewhat reduced growth rate—4 percent, not 5.1 percent—for the private nonagricultural sector. The balance indicates that some depletion of the agricultural labor force would be possible. The 2 percent annual decline would nevertheless be considerably below the 6 percent annual decline between 1970 and 1975. Consequently income differences between the two sectors would narrow only marginally.

Based on the same assumptions, a growth rate of social sector

Table 10.19. *Labor Force Balances, Targets in the Social Plan for 1976–80*
(thousands of workers)

Item	1975	1980	Change 1976–80
Labor force	9,147	9,424	277
Migrants	780	530	250
Unemployment	540	400	140
Incremental labor supply	—	—	667
Social sector	4,667	5,543	876
Private nonagriculture	359	438	78
Total labor absorption	—	—	954
Balance	—	—	−287
Reduction in agricultural labor force (percent)	—	—	2.0

— Not applicable.
Source: Calculated from data supplied by the Federal Institute of Planning.

employment in excess of 2.4 percent would result in demand for labor in excess of the natural increase of the labor force and facilitate a gradual depletion of the agricultural labor force. A growth rate between 1.8 and 2.4 percent would either result in the growth in the agriculture labor force or a sacrifice of the planned objective of reducing the number of unemployed. At a growth rate of less than 1.8 percent, the number of unemployed could increase.

The countrywide evolution of employment is no guide to the development in various regions. Detailed projections of sectoral output are not available for all regions. Thus the effects of structural shifts in the economy cannot be readily ascertained for each region. For indicative purposes, however, the growth of employment can be estimated by assuming that employment elasticities are 50 percent higher in the less developed regions than in the more developed regions. These figures can then be compared with the growth of social sector employment necessary to ensure that the plan's objectives of reduced unemployment, adequate employment opportunities for returning migrants, and the natural increase in the labor force are satisfied. The comparison indicates, given the relatively high assumptions for growth in the plan, that there will be some opportunity for reducing the agricultural labor force in most of the less developed regions (table 10.20). The exception is Kosovo,

Table 10.20. *Growth of Production and Employment in the Social Sector, by Region, Estimates for 1976–80*
(percent)

Region	Average annual rate of growth		Employment requirement[b]
	Social sector production	Social sector employment[a]	
Less developed regions			
Bosnia-Herzegovina	8.5–9.0	7.0	4.9
Kosovo	11.1	8.9	9.4
Macedonia	n.a.	n.a.	5.1
Montenegro	8.3	6.4	4.0
More developed regions			
Croatia	7.0	3.7	2.5
Serbia	7.9	4.2	1.2
Slovenia	n.a.	n.a.	1.0
Vojvodina	n.a.	n.a.	2.4

n.a. Not available.

Sources: Republican five-year plans and World Bank estimates.

a. Based on the assumptions that the elasticity of employment in relation to the growth of value added in the social sector is 0.6 for Yugoslavia and 0.8 for the less developed regions.

b. The annual rate of employment growth in the social sector necessary to ensure the targeted decline in unemployment and to absorb returning migrants and the natural increase in the labor force.

which cannot, even under optimistic assumptions and even if the plan's growth targets are achieved, be expected to absorb the increments to its labor force. The employment situation in other regions may be somewhat less favorable than the foregoing comparison might imply. First, as already indicated, the growth rates for the economy and the regions appear to be somewhat optimistic, given the planned investment outlays. Second, the less developed regions tend to have a relatively high share of basic industries with low labor-output ratios. The emphasis in the plan on these sectors is likely to affect adversely the capacity of the less developed regions to generate employment. In short, if allowances are made for these considerations, the opportunities for migration out of the agricultural sector are likely to be fairly limited, except in Slovenia and Serbia.

Eleven

Regional Disparities

DESPITE YUGOSLAVIA'S EFFORTS since the 1950s to equalize development levels throughout the country, the differences in GMP per
capita between the group of less developed regions and the group
of more developed regions widened until 1970 and barely stabilized
thereafter (table 11.1).[1] The relative positions of Bosnia-Herzegovina
and Kosovo were considerably worse in 1975 than in 1954; those of
all the more developed regions improved during the period. At the
extremes, the spread between Slovenia and Kosovo widened from
4:1 to 6:1. Because of the incidence of transfer payments and parts
of GMP not accruing to households, the differences in household income per capita were narrower; they nevertheless followed the same
pattern. Consequently the differences in GMP per capita should be
regarded as a useful but crude indicator of differences in welfare—
differences that are better reflected in indexes for a variety of social
indicators (table 11.2). In addition, the intraregional differences in
income are considerable in all regions, in some instances extending to
the ratio of 10:1 between communes. Thus some areas in the less
developed regions have reached a level of development similar to
that in most areas of the more developed regions. As the analysis in
this chapter will illustrate, differences in income between urban and
rural areas are at the root of the problem.

The disparities are not the result of stagnation in the less developed regions, but of different growth rates of GMP and population.
The growth of GMP in the less developed regions as a group was only
slightly lower than that in the more developed regions as a group,
with overlapping for various regions (table 11.3). The higher rates

---

1. In accord with the usage adopted throughout this volume, the term *region*
applies to the republics and autonomous provinces.

Table 11.1. *Income per Capita, by Region, 1954–75*

Region	Gross material product per capita[a] (Yugoslavia = 100)				Gross national product per capita[b] (dollars)	Household income per capita (Yugoslavia = 100)
	1954	1964	1970	1975	1975	1973
Less developed regions	71	65	61	62	924	72
Bosnia-Herzegovina	82	69	67	69	1,016	76
Kosovo	48	37	34	33	492	49
Macedonia	69	73	64	69	1,026	78
Montenegro	53	72	78	70	1,035	82
More developed regions	110	118	121	121	1,793	116
Croatia	119	119	125	124	1,840	125
Serbia	84	95	97	92	1,365	100
Slovenia	188	187	193	201	2,979	150
Vojvodina	88	116	110	121	1,790	105
Yugoslavia	100	100	100	100	1,480	100

Sources: GMP per capita from Federal Institute of Statistics, *Statistical Year-book of Yugoslavia*, various issues, and idem, *Index*, 1977, vol. 1; household income per capita calculated from *Statistical Bulletin*, no. 833 (March 1974); GNP per capita from World Bank calculations.
a. Based on current prices.
b. Imputed by applying regional differences in GMP per capita to the national GNP per capita, which was computed according to the method adopted for the World Bank atlases.

of population growth nevertheless diluted the benefits of economic growth: marked differences in the growth of GMP per capita set back all of the less developed regions and widened the absolute income gap between them and the more developed regions. The importance of this demographic parameter is illustrated by the comparison of the empirical differences shown for 1954 and 1975 in table 11.1 with the hypothetical differences that would have resulted for 1975 if the population growth rate in each of the less developed regions had been equal to that observed for the more

Table 11.2. *Basic Social Indicators, by Region, 1975*
(Yugoslavia = 100)

Region	Life expectancy at birth[a] Males	Life expectancy at birth[a] Females	Persons per doctor[b]	Persons per hospital bed[b]	Average area of dwelling per person	Pr por o dw in wi ele tric
Less developed regions						
Bosnia-Herzegovina	98	97	66	75	77	8
Kosovo	99	95	35	48	63	8
Macedonia	100	96	91	91	82	10
Montenegro	104	104	76	130	81	9
More developed regions						
Croatia	100	103	114	118	118	10
Serbia	103	102	120	108	100	10
Slovenia	100	104	133	127	127	10
Vojvodina	101	103	109	101	125	10

Sources: Federal Institute of Statistics, *Statistical Pocket Book of Yugoslavia,* 1977, and *Statistical Yearbook of Yugoslavia,* 1976.

developed regions as a group over the same period.[2] Under this assumption the GMP per capita would have been about 80 percent of the Yugoslav average for Bosnia, Montenegro, and Macedonia, 49 percent for Kosovo, and 77 percent for the less developed regions as a group. In other words the relative worsening for Bosnia and Kosovo would not have occurred, and the position of Montenegro and Macedonia would have significantly improved.[3]

2. Although the assumption is unrealistic because of the actual demographic dynamics, the disregard of repercussions of the growth rate of population on the growth rate of GMP is plausible. In all of the less developed regions the incidence of considerable underemployment and unemployment leads to a marginal product of labor that is close to zero. In addition, the rapid growth rate of population led to high investment and recurrent expenditure for education and health, expenditure which otherwise could have been used for productive investment and raised the growth rate of GMP.

3. These comparisons disregard the repercussions of higher growth rates in the less developed regions on the growth rate of Yugoslavia, which is used as the benchmark for comparison.

Propor- tion of dwell- ings with water and sewer- age	Illiteracy rate[b]			Propor- tion of popula- tion over ten years having secondary or higher education	Per- sons per passen- ger car[b]	Region
	Total	Males	Fe- males			
						Less developed regions
						Bosnia-
68	65	71	63	70	61	Herzegovina
37	48	36	52	46	29	Kosovo
111	83	67	88	76	79	Macedonia
99	90	105	87	94	65	Montenegro
						More developed regions
122	167	159	172	121	114	Croatia
97	85	103	81	103	104	Serbia
133	1,250	667	1,667	144	213	Slovenia
119	167	147	172	111	116	Vojvodina

a. Based on the 1971 census.
b. Inverse ratio.

Dimensions of Regional Disparities

Directly or indirectly, these introductory observations point to four principal factors affecting, in combination, the interregional disparities and the limited success so far of the measures to narrow them: demographic conditions; intraregional disparities; weaknesses of the economic structure of the less developed regions; and institutional weaknesses of the less developed regions.

Demographic conditions

With the exception of Kosovo, the natural growth rates sharply declined (table 11.4). But even in the other three less developed regions they remained two to three times the average of the more developed regions. The birth rates show a similar but less pronounced

Table 11.3. *Growth of Gross Material Product, Population, and Gross Material Product per Capita, by Region, 1966–75*
(percent)

Region	Average annual rate of growth		
	Gross material product	Population	Gross material product per capita
Less developed regions	5.4	1.6	3.5
Bosnia-Herzegovina	5.0	1.3	3.6
Kosovo	6.1	2.7	3.0
Macedonia	6.3	1.5	4.5
Montenegro	5.1	1.1	3.9
More developed regions	5.6	0.6	4.9
Croatia	5.3	0.5	4.8
Serbia	5.4	0.7	4.6
Slovenia	6.8	0.7	6.0
Vojvodina	5.0	0.4	4.6
Yugoslavia	5.6	1.0	4.5

Source: Statistical Yearbook of Yugoslavia, various issues.

pattern. The fertility rates demonstrate the differences of the demographic dynamics most persuasively. Given that a fertility rate of 2.1 roughly corresponds to the replacement level leading to a stable population size in the long run, the figures reveal that the more developed regions as a group dropped below replacement level, that the national average is approaching it, and that three of the four less developed regions are not substantially above replacement level. Natural growth rates, birth rates, and fertility of all more developed regions stabilized in about 1970; the decline in the less developed regions also slowed down markedly at about the same time. In Kosovo, however, where the population continues to grow by almost 3 percent a year and where the fertility rates indicate that the population could more than double in one generation, there is little promise for a significant change of the demographic dynamics. One consequence of those dynamics during the last two decades is this: even if fertility in the less developed regions were to abruptly decline to the replacement level, their total population and working-age population would continue to grow by only slowly declining rates for several decades.

Table 11.4. *Demographic Indicators, by Region, 1950–75*

Region	Rate of natural increase (per 1,000 population)		Birth rate (per 1,000 population)		Fertility rate[a]	
	1950	1975	1950	1975	1956	1975
Less developed regions	25.5	16.3	39.5	24.4	4.6	3.0
Bosnia-Herzegovina	25.1	13.1	38.6	19.1	4.2	2.4
Kosovo	29.1	27.6	46.1	34.6	6.6	5.4
Macedonia	25.6	15.1	40.3	22.5	4.7	2.7
Montenegro	20.7	12.7	30.0	17.7	3.9	2.4
More developed regions	13.5	5.6	26.2	15.6	2.4	1.9
Croatia	12.5	4.4	24.8	14.7	2.5	1.9
Serbia	15.6	6.8	28.0	15.8	2.2	1.9
Slovenia	12.6	7.4	24.4	17.7	2.5	2.1
Vojvodina	11.5	3.3	25.5	14.1	2.3	1.7
Yugoslavia	17.3	9.4	21.0	18.1	3.1	2.3

Sources: Statistical Yearbook of Yugoslavia, 1976 and figures supplied by Federal Institute of Planning.
a. The average number of live births per female of childbearing age.

As would be expected, past demographic dynamics change the interregional distribution of population and result in different regional age structures (table 11.5). The shares of all the less developed regions in total population significantly increased over the period; in addition, the percentages of the population below the age of twenty were substantially higher for the less developed regions in 1974. This difference in age structure, in conjunction with the significantly higher fertility rates, assures that the trend toward a growing share of the less developed regions in total population will continue for several decades. The pattern will aggravate the difficulties (or extend the period) of closing the income differences, even if a somewhat faster rate of GMP growth could be established in the less developed regions. The compound effect of the higher population growth rate and the existing income difference can be illustrated by comparing the extreme cases of Kosovo and Slovenia. Although a $100 rise of the GMP per capita in Slovenia would be associated with an annual rate of GMP growth of about 3 percent, the same rise in Kosovo would require an almost 20 percent GMP growth rate for Kosovo. The high percentage of population under the age of twenty is another problem facing the less developed

Table 11.5. *Distribution of Population, by Region, 1948–75*
(percent)

Region	Share in total population			Population below the age of twenty[a]
	1948	1961	1975	
Less developed regions	30.3	33.0	36.0	45.9
Bosnia-Herzegovina	16.2	17.7	18.6	45.5
Kosovo	4.6	5.2	6.6	52.8
Macedonia	7.2	7.6	8.2	43.0
Montenegro	2.3	2.5	2.6	47.8
More developed regions	69.7	67.0	64.0	31.4
Croatia	23.9	22.4	21.2	31.5
Serbia	26.2	26.0	25.3	31.3
Slovenia	9.1	8.6	8.3	32.9
Vojvodina	10.4	10.0	9.3	30.0
Yugoslavia	100.0	100.0	100.0	36.5

Source: Appendix table A.36 and *Statistical Yearbook of Yugoslavia*, 1976.
a. Figures for 1974.

regions: their working-age population, and their labor force searching for employment in the region, will grow at high rates. Furthermore the generally lower rates of participation in the labor force by the working-age population in all the less developed regions, mainly caused by the low participation rate of women, are likely to increase with social development, and amplify the future growth rates of labor force in those regions.[4]

Intraregional disparities

The interregional differences in GMP per worker in the social sector are, although correlated with GMP per capita, fairly narrow (table 11.6). Thus the income disparities are only to a limited degree explained by interregional differences and must be rooted elsewhere —that is, in the traditional agricultural sector. Interregional differences in the relative size of the modern sector, expressed by the ratio

4. The repercussions of differing demographic structures and behavioral parameters on the problem of employment were discussed in detail in chapter ten.

Table 11.6. *Indexes of Income Differences in the Social Sector, by Region, 1974*
(Yugoslavia = 100)

Region	Gross material product per capita[a]	Gross material product per worker	Gross personal income per worker[b]	Ratio of social sector employment to population (percent)
Less developed regions	63	85	89	15.5
Bosnia-Herzegovina	68	88	92	16.1
Kosovo	34	79	84	9.4
Macedonia	71	81	82	18.4
Montenegro	72	96	95	17.4
More developed regions	121	105	104	24.6
Croatia	124	110	110	24.4
Serbia	95	93	89	21.2
Slovenia	192	120	119	36.5
Vojvodina	121	103	107	23.4
Yugoslavia	100	100	100	21.2

Sources: *Statistical Yearbook of Yugoslavia*, 1976, and *Statistical Bulletin*, no. 833.
a. For total population.
b. For productive activities only.

of social sector employment to population, and the close correlation between this ratio and GMP per capita are more striking. They hint at the importance of intersectoral aspects. In addition, interregional differences of gross personal income per worker in the social sector are even narrower than the interregional differences of GMP per worker, which is equivalent to the average productivity of labor.

These observations lead to some important conclusions. First, within each region there is a wide gulf in productivity and income between the modern social sector and the traditional private sector, which is dominated by agriculture. Second, the differences in the relative size of the two socioeconomic sectors to a large degree determine the interregional disparity; the persistence of these differences prevented a significant narrowing of that disparity. Third, if the ratio of gross personal income per worker to GMP per worker is considered to be an index of the cost of labor per unit of production, the less developed regions would tend to be at a disadvantage with respect to

Table 11.7. *Household Income per Capita, by Region, 1973*
(all Yugoslavia households = 100)

	Household income per capita			
Region	All house-holds	Agri-cultural house-holds	Mixed house-holds	Nonagri-cultural house-holds
Less developed regions	72	58	65	90
Bosnia-Herzegovina	76	61	67	100
Kosovo	49	39	48	61
Macedonia	78	66	73	88
Montenegro	82	58	78	94
More developed regions	116	78	104	140
Croatia	125	85	112	151
Serbia	100	69	86	128
Slovenia	150	106	135	166
Vojvodina	105	87	103	116
Yugoslavia	100	70	89	125

Source: Appendix table A.37.

labor costs, because they have ratios greater than unity. Obviously the income policies in the social sector prohibited the emergence of any comparative advantage of the less developed regions with respect to labor. The policies thus impeded the more rapid expansion of labor-intensive activities in the less developed regions—an expansion which would have somewhat widened the interregional differences in average incomes of the social sector, but simultaneously narrowed the overall income differences by accelerating the transition toward the modern sector.

A comparison of household income per capita in the main socioeconomic sectors brings into focus the distributional significance of intraregional and intersectoral income differences (table 11.7).[5] First, average household income per capita in nonagriculture, which is roughly equivalent to the social sector, generally is about 90 percent

5. Income includes transfer payments and receipts from abroad; the figures thus differ conceptually and absolutely from those shown in table 10.3. The figures on income per capita were derived from survey data on average income per household in eleven categories and the corresponding average sizes of household.

or more of the national average.[6] The clear exception is Kosovo. Average household income per capita also is much larger in non-agriculture than in the other two sectors, in most regions ranging between 150 to 200 percent of that in agriculture. Second, the share of population associated with nonagriculture is directly correlated with GMP per capita, total household income per capita, and the share of social sector employees in population. Third, in each socio-economic sector, the differences in family size and the ratio of active to total number of individuals per household explain to a consider-able degree these differences in household income per capita. Total household incomes scatter over a much narrower range than the per capita figures, which probably tend to exaggerate the interregional differences of the standard of living in each socioeconomic sector. Fourth, in all the less developed regions the average household in-come per capita in agriculture is less than two-thirds of the national average. The shares of agricultural and mixed households are also higher for the less developed regions as a group than for the more developed regions. Thus, although diluted by transfer payments and the large differences of average household size, the income differ-ences largely reflect intersectoral and interregional differences in productivity (table 11.8).

Poverty in Yugoslavia is relative, not absolute, and its incidence is basically rural. For food consumption the household survey data show adequate caloric and a fairly high level of protein intake for all Yugoslavia, though lower levels for the lower income groups.[7] The institutional setup for financing and supplying social services provides access to education to all levels for all income groups and for comprehensive medical insurance coverage for almost the entire population. The system of social security and welfare also provides some compensation to the unemployed and contributions to the needy. A significant share of financial transfers for investment is for the construction of social infrastructure in the less developed regions; budgetary grants support recurrent expenditure on social services in the poorer communities. Nevertheless there clearly is evidence of relative poverty, localized by region and socioeco-nomic sector.

---

6. The correspondence is approximate. It is probable that a large number of households in the mixed category also received some income from the social sector from some members of the household.

7. Milan Petrovic, "Changes in the National Diet, 1963–73," *Yugoslav Sur-vey*, vol. 17, no. 2 (May 1976), pp. 83–96.

Table 11.8. *Characteristics of Households,*
by Region, 1973

Region	Average number of members in household	Number of active members	Percentage of population in nonagri- culture
Less developed regions	4.9	1.9	36
Bosnia-Herzegovina	4.6	1.9	33
Kosovo	7.1	2.2	32
Macedonia	4.8	2.0	43
Montenegro	4.1	1.6	45
More developed regions	3.5	1.9	47
Croatia	3.4	1.8	47
Serbia	3.7	2.0	50
Slovenia	3.4	2.0	58
Vojvodina	3.1	1.6	48
Yugoslavia	3.9	1.9	44

Source: Statistical Bulletin, no. 833.

The lower income groups—those with per capita household income less than half the country average, or less than about $300 in
1973 prices and exchange rates—were largely concentrated in the
less developed regions, especially Kosovo where they accounted for
two-thirds of the population (table 11.9).[8] The proportion of population below the national average was at least 80 percent in each
less developed region; in Kosovo it was 100 percent. For the more
developed regions about a third of the population in Serbia and
Vojvodina had a per capita income above the national average; that
proportion was more than 50 percent in Croatia and 85 percent in
Slovenia. The highest income groups—those with per capita household incomes more than 50 percent above the national average—also
accounted for a fifth of the population in Croatia and a third of that
in Slovenia.

8. Studies of the distribution of income indicate a Gini coefficient of 0.23 for
Yugoslavia and a Theil index of 0.11. World Bank, "Yugoslavia: Self-management Socialism and the Challenges of Development," report no. 1615a-YU
(a restricted circulation document), 6 vols. (Washington, D.C.: World Bank,
1978), vol.4, pp. 365–69.

Table 11.9. *Distribution of Households, by Region and Household Income per Capita, 1973*

	Percentage of households			
Region	*Less than 50 percent of the Yugoslav average income*[a]	*50–100 percent of the Yugoslav average income*	*100–150 percent of the Yugoslav average income*	*More than 150 percent of the Yugoslav average income*
Less developed regions				
Bosnia-Herzegovina	33	53	10	4
Kosovo	66	34	0	0
Macedonia	33	47	12	8
Montenegro	11	75	11	3
More developed regions				
Croatia	1	46	33	20
Serbia	12	56	20	12
Slovenia	0	15	53	32
Vojvodina	7	61	24	8
Yugoslavia	11	57	22	10

Sources: Appendix table A.38 and *Statistical Bulletin*, no. 833.

a. Households with household income per capita that is equal to or less than that for the third lowest of eleven income groups at the national level.

Two factors, mentioned before, must nevertheless be kept in mind. First, per capita differences exaggerate differences of living standards because of the differences in household size and the economies of size associated with large households. Second, the distribution of the three socioeconomic categories over the four income groups is very uneven: the nonagricultural population constitutes much of the two top income groups; the agricultural and mixed populations constitute much of the two bottom groups in the less developed regions, but extend into the middle-income group in the more developed regions. In Kosovo, for example, where about 28 percent of the population is in agriculture, about 75 percent of households in the agricultural sector were in the bottom income group.

Weakness of the economic structure
in the less developed regions

Of the many parameters that can be used to assess the economic structure of regions, five are examined here:

- The output-capital ratio, which is the inverse of the capital-output ratio and measured by the ratio of GMP to fixed assets.
- The labor-capital ratio, which is measured by the ratio of workers to fixed assets.
- The index of unit labor costs, a measure of productivity proxied by the ratio of the index of gross personal income per worker to that of GMP per worker.
- The accumulation rate, which is measured by the ratio to fixed assets of depreciation plus allocations to enterprise funds (undistributed profits).
- The capital stock per capita, which is measured by the fixed assets per inhabitant.

By most of these standards, the economic structure of the less developed regions is demonstrably weaker than that in more developed regions. The figures in table 11.10 bring out a number of

Table 11.10. *Structural and Operational Coefficients*
for Productive Activities in the Social Sector, by Region, 1974
(Yugoslavia = 100)

Region	Output-capital ratio	Labor-capital ratio	Unit labor cost	Accumulation rate	Capital stock per capita
Less developed regions	87	102	105	74	71
Bosnia-Herzegovina	95	104	105	74	73
Kosovo	70	88	106	48	44
Macedonia	91	111	101	70	78
Montenegro	71	78	96	108	102
More developed regions	104	99	96	111	116
Croatia	102	93	100	108	124
Serbia	102	111	96	92	89
Slovenia	109	91	98	145	192
Vojvodina	107	105	104	110	103

Source: *Statistical Bulletin*, no. 954 (December 1975).

important features. First, in all less developed regions the efficiency of using the existing fixed assets is significantly below that of all more developed regions. Second, despite the importance of the integration of the labor force with the modern sector in reducing the income differences within and between regions, capital intensity is higher—that is, employment per unit of fixed assets is lower—in Montenegro and Kosovo than in any of the more developed regions; only in Macedonia is labor intensity significantly above the national average. Third, in three of the four less developed regions the per unit labor cost tends to be above the national average, indicating the absence of any comparative advantage for labor-intensive activities. Fourth, in all the less developed regions except Montenegro, the accumulation generated per unit of fixed assets is less than three-quarters of the national average; in Kosovo it is less than half the national average. This performance reflects two features: the level of personal incomes in these regions is maintained at the expense of accumulation for reinvestment; without substantial transfers of investment resources, the differences in accumulation capacity would tend to increase differences in the availability of fixed assets and the income differences between regions, even if the rates of population growth were equal. The great interregional differences in demographic dynamics amplify this tendency, particularly in Kosovo. Fifth, only in Montenegro is the endowment with capital stock in the modern sector, measured by fixed assets per capita, close to the national average; in the other less developed regions, particularly in Kosovo, it is far below average.

These features, striking as they are, do not give the complete picture. The regions also differ greatly with respect to the composition of the modern economic sector. The five economic coefficients tend to follow the same pattern as that for the total, although somewhat less conspicuously, for all major sectors and branches in each region. In sum, the modern sector of the less developed regions compares unfavorably with that of the more developed regions because of two interlocked reasons: they have lower efficiency across the board, and their overall structure is biased toward less efficient activities.[9]

9. The importance of these two reasons is highlighted by the illustrative inversion of the sector and branch coefficients applied to the structures of Slovenia and Kosovo in chapter eight. It was found that inverting those coefficients makes little difference for the gross profit rates.

Causes of Regional Disparities

Before the turn of the century, the spillover of rapid industrialization from central Europe laid the foundation of modern industrial development in Slovenia and Croatia. The less developed regions nevertheless remained, with the exception of a few enclaves, in the backwater of development until after the Second World War. This lag in the initiation of modern economic development is reflected in large interregional differences in accumulated technical and managerial know-how. Such differences between countries would normally be neutralized by the mechanism of exchange rates or be corrected by temporary measures to protect infant industries until they establish the basis for international competitiveness. These options naturally are not open to the regions of Yugoslavia; moreover they would contradict the principle of the unity of the Yugoslav market. These conditions, together with the interregional leveling of the structure of personal income in the social sector and the historically determined limitations to labor mobility, make all but impossible any reduction of income differences by automatic mechanisms based on comparative advantage. They also constrain the scope for remedial policies.

In the unified Yugoslav market the less developed regions face the problem of their distance from the economic centers of the country. The disadvantages associated with this distance are amplified by the deficiencies of the physical infrastructure, particularly in intraregional and interregional systems for transport and communication. These deficiencies, in turn, have forced the less developed regions to allocate a higher proportion of their investment resources to the development of infrastructure which, for a number of reasons, does not yield quick and direct returns. Furthermore the mountainous topography of all the less developed regions and the great intraregional differences in population density tend to make the development of an adequate network of infrastructure extremely costly.

There also are stark differences in economic and social infrastructure. Economic infrastructure comprises such services as trade, banking, and repair and maintenance; it supports efficient economic development. If these services are insufficiently developed, as they are in the less developed regions, the repercussions on economic efficiency, although impossible to quantify, probably are severe.

For social infrastructure—such as quality and access to education and health facilities, housing, administration, cultural services, and facilities for health and education—the repercussions on development are less direct, only in part measurable, but probably no less severe. These deficiencies lead to the diversion of a large share of available investment resources from productive investment. As the deficiencies become conspicuous, they tend to induce the most mobile and best educated segment of the population to move from the deprived countryside of the less developed regions to urban centers, particularly those in the more developed regions. The resultant gap in critical skills naturally impedes economic development in the less developed regions.

The preoccupation of the less developed regions with the development of basic industries—such as mining and metallurgy, electric power generation, pulp and paper products, and basic chemicals—and the greater emphasis of more developed regions on processing industries have also contributed to the differences in their respective levels of development. What have been the considerations underlying that preoccupation? First, the physical availability of natural resources was on occasion perceived to be sufficient indication of the economic feasibility of their use. Second, it frequently was felt in each region that the only sound development strategy would be to begin by developing the indigenous raw materials and that development would then automatically progress downstream. Third, given the shortage of well-educated and experienced skilled manpower, the choice of basic industries was seen to be logical because those industries require less skill per unit of investment and incorporate a higher degree of the required know-how in imported equipment. Fourth, given the competition in the domestic market and the scarcity of production design and marketing know-how, the development of basic industries was seen to be easier and less risky. Fifth, access to relatively inexpensive credits and the tendency for high labor costs per unit of output tended to create a bias in financial analyses toward capital-intensive basic industries.

There is, in addition, some circumstantial evidence that the intersectoral terms of trade were unfavorable for the production of such raw materials as ores, coal, and lumber and such intermediate goods as electric power, metallurgy, and semifinished products—activities which have a relatively strong position in the economic structure of the less developed regions. That evidence is frequently referred to in Yugoslavia, but not supported by the available statistical data. If and to the degree this claim is borne out by the facts, it would have

resulted in a transfer of benefits, and ultimately of implicit subsidies, from the producing less developed regions to the consuming
more developed regions.

There were few tangible incentives to established enterprises in
the more developed regions for any voluntary transfer of investment resources, technical know-how, or entire activities to the less
developed regions. This lack is to a large degree a result of the self-
management principle. Despite the need and scope for greater investment in all regions, workers are motivated in their decisions on
investment by loyalty to their own organization and to their own
community or region. Moreover they generally had little to gain
from such transfers, which were inherently risky because of the high
labor costs, at least through the initial stages, and the claims to the
surplus generated subordinate to other claims to generated income.
The unilateral cessation of operations by a subsidiary could not be
prevented.[10] Although the evidence is scarce, it probably is fair to
conclude that the limited transfers which occurred were the result of
one or both of two conditions: the initiating enterprise lacked
resources of its own and had only the choice between no investment
or investment in the less developed regions, usually financed by resources of the less developed regions; the initiating enterprise was
the sole market outlet for the initiated venture, enabling it to reap
substantial indirect benefits by securing a totally dependent source
of supply.

Measures to Redress Regional Disparities

Considerations of solidarity, as well as the recognition that progress toward redressing interregional disparities was imperative for
political reasons, led in the 1950s to sizable transfers of investment
resources from the federal General Investment Fund and to grants
from the federal budget to the less developed regions. When the
General Investment Fund was discontinued in 1965, two new
schemes for transferring funds replaced it: the Federal Fund and
budgetary grants. Because repayment obligations to the General
Investment Fund and the Federal Fund up to 1970 were eventually
waived, all contributions earlier than that year in effect were grants
to the less developed regions.

10. The law on associated labor, with its emphasis on the joint pooling of
resources, should reduce some of these concerns over time.

In 1971 the two transfer schemes were, after some changes, legally formalized for the five-year plan period, 1971–75. The Federal Fund collected from each region 1.94 percent of GMP of the social sector, in compulsory loans from enterprises. These resources were earmarked for loans to the less developed regions for their productive investment at highly concessionary terms: an interest rate of 4 percent (3 percent for Kosovo), a grace period of three years, and a maturity of eighteen years (twenty-one years for Kosovo). The use of these resources was exclusively decided by the less developed region receiving them and administered by its designated regional commercial bank. Of the funds collected, 5 percent was directly set aside for Kosovo; the remainder was allocated according to the shares shown in table 11.11. Budgetary transfers were earmarked for social services, with investment and current expenditure exclusively decided by the region receiving them; they were to be equal to 0.83 percent of Yugoslavia's GMP and were directly provided from the federal budget in accord with specified shares (see table 11.11).

Table 11.11. *Distribution of Transfers to the Less Developed Regions, Prescriptions for 1971–75*
(percent)

	Federal fund	Budget transfers
Bosnia-Herzegovina	34	40.15
Kosovo	30	31.25
Macedonia	24	18.30
Montenegro	12	10.30

Source: Figures supplied by the Federal Institute of Planning.

The actual amounts of transfers can be estimated by applying the formulas for the collection and distribution of resources to national accounts data for 1974 (table 11.12).[11] Although the transfers were equal to about 10 percent of the GMP of the less developed regions, the effect varied greatly. In Kosovo, for example, they were equivalent to more than a third of its social product, a figure that highlights the economic situation this region would suffer without the support of the Yugoslav community. About 60 percent of the trans-

11. Yugoslav sources report that actual transfers closely approximated those prescribed by law. The principal cause for deviations apparently was the ex ante determination of contributions in the absence of GMP figures, which only became available after a considerable lag.

Table 11.12. *Transfers to the Less Developed Regions, 1974*

Region	Transfers in relation to gross material product (percent)	Transfers per capita (dollars)
Less developed regions	9.3	71
Bosnia-Herzegovina	5.1	43
Kosovo	34.5	144
Macedonia	7.4	64
Montenegro	12.9	112

Note: Transfers are net of the contributions of recipient regions to the Federal Fund.
Source: Statistical Yearbook of Yugoslavia, 1976.

fers were credits ultimately to be repaid. But the low interest rates and favorable terms, when compared with regular credits, imply that the grant element has been very large. By assuming an interest rate of 12 percent, the most frequently mentioned rate for normal long-term enterprise borrowing, and discounting the debt service payments under the repayment terms for the recipient regions, the grant equivalent in the federal fund loans was more than 60 percent for Kosovo in 1974; for the other three less developed regions it was more than 50 percent.[12] Although the underlying considerations of solidarity and increased equity justify such transfers, the figures raise some questions about the rationale for the distribution. For example, the figures for the transfers to Bosnia-Herzegovina appear small in relation to its GMP per capita, which is about the same as that for Montenegro and Macedonia. The disparity becomes all the more apposite when it is considered that Bosnia-Herzegovina was increasingly falling behind the Yugoslav average, while Montenegro and Macedonia clearly were catching up.[13] The transfers constitute a considerable burden for the more developed regions. In 1974 they amounted to 2.7 percent of the combined GMP of the more developed regions. For Federal Fund resources—which have to be paid from

12. Because of the high rates of inflation in recent years, the grant element is even higher than the figures cited.
13. The considerations for the distribution of resources of the Federal Fund to the less developed regions include, in addition to GMP per capita, their capacity for accumulation, access to foreign borrowing, and capital coefficients.

enterprise surpluses and commensurately reduce their investment and eventually their potential for growth—the transfers are equivalent to about 10 percent of their investment volume.

The effect of these transfers in relation to the investment of the paying and receiving regions comes out even more strongly by focusing on their impact on investment rather than GMP (table 11.13). Because of the transfers, the investment rate of the less

Table 11.13. *Investment and Transfers, by Region, 1974*

Region	Share of investment in GMP (percent)	Share of Federal Fund in productive investment in the social sector (percent)	Productive investment in the social sector per capita (Yugoslavia = 100)	Productive investment in fixed assets in the social sector per capita (Yugoslavia = 100)
Less developed regions	38	24	84	71
Bosnia-Herzegovina	39	11	89	73
Kosovo	51	72	62	44
Macedonia	28	27	71	78
Montenegro	47	27	136	102
More developed regions	27	−10	109	116
Croatia	25	−11	106	124
Serbia	25	−11	79	89
Slovenia	32	−9	208	192
Vojvodina	26	−9	111	103
Yugoslavia	29	0	100	100

Source: *Statistical Yearbook of Yugoslavia*, 1976.

developed regions generally is much higher than that of the more developed regions; in Montenegro and Kosovo it hovers around an astonishing 50 percent.[14] This observation raises another important question: Given such high rates of investment and given the institutional causes of the regional disparities already discussed, is there

14. The investment rate in relation to GNP, which is about 10 percent higher than national GMP, would be somewhat lower.

not the distinct possibility of some problems of absorptive capacity in two, if not three, of the less developed regions? As the concept of absorptive capacity is generally perceived, it does not constitute an absolute limit to the volume of possible investment. What it does imply, however, is this: because of the swamping of limited administrative and managerial capacity, investment at the margin is bound to be less efficient per unit of investment than if it were at lower investment rates. The much lower average accumulation capacity per unit of invested fixed assets for the less developed regions strongly suggests that the marginal rates would be even more diverse (see table 11.12). This may be an underlying reason for the lower efficiency of the less developed regions, and it points to the loss of some growth by the entire country. Some Yugoslav statements appear to concede, at least indirectly, the validity of such a hypothesis by placing heavy emphasis on the dynamic long-term effects of these transfers. That is to say, some waste of investment resources may be inevitable in the short and medium terms. But the price is considered to be worth paying, even on strictly economic grounds, because the resources would enable the less developed regions to improve their efficiency in the long term to a higher level than the more advanced regions enjoy today.

The figures relating the size of transfers to investment in the less developed regions and more developed regions highlight four additional features (see table 11.13). First, without the Federal Fund transfers, the investment program of the social sector in Kosovo would be only about a quarter of its present size; in Montenegro and Macedonia, the programs would be about three-quarters of their present level. Second, despite the importance of Federal Fund resources in financing the investment program for productive activities, investment per capita still falls significantly behind the Yugoslav average in all the less developed regions except Montenegro. Third, the comparison of investment per capita and the availability of fixed assets per capita is particularly disturbing. Even under the assumption of equal average and incremental capital-output ratios in all regions, the figures suggest that the differences in relation to the more developed regions would tend to widen for all the less developed regions except Montenegro. Moreover the problems of catching up are more severe than the figures suggest: both the incremental capital-output ratios and the capital-output ratios tend to be higher in the less developed regions; and the differences in demographic dynamics work to the disadvantage of the less developed regions. Fourth, the more developed regions are a heterogenous aggregate by any standard. Croatia, Slovenia, and Vojvodina have a built-in growth momentum which tends, despite the transfers, to propel them further and further ahead of the country average. Serbia, however, carries a comparable burden in the transfer of resources to the less developed regions, despite its less favorable position in GMP per capita. It may well continue to linger at or below the country average.

The purpose of the Federal Fund is to channel resources that enterprises would not otherwise make available to the less developed regions. Three conditions militate against voluntary transfers: the decentralized political structure leads to compartmentalized "financial markets"; financial returns tend to be lower, and risks higher, in the less developed regions; the decisionmaking of self-managed enterprises strongly leans toward the use of accumulation by the generating enterprise or in its commune or republic. Consequently, if the less developed regions are to have the chance to establish competitive economic positions at comparable levels of personal income, they need some form of subsidy. This subsidy, the grant element referred to earlier, nevertheless has two negative features. First, the subsidy is distributed in proportion to the funds borrowed at preferential terms. Thus the subsidy has no link to the basic cause of lower efficiency: the lower productivity of labor because of the lack of accumulated know-how. Second, this method for distributing the subsidy could—if and when considerations of financial profitability affect the choice or design of projects—lead to a bias toward projects that are more capital-intensive and largely financed by preferential credits. Ultimately the method may have repercussions on the emerging pattern of allocation. Given these features, established enterprises could be tempted to propose projects that would enable them to pass on much of the incorporated subsidy to the personal incomes of their workers. That would reduce the number of ultimate recipients, increase the income subsidy per recipient, and reduce the capacity of the less developed regions to generate employment with given resources. Such a subsidy to personal incomes, already reflected in the comparatively high labor costs and the low accumulation rates shown in table 11.10, may be inevitable and in principle economically justifiable as a means of relieving the problems of infant industries. But the actual mechanism of distribution to final recipients probably is economically and socially less than optimal. The reason is that the same subsidy could, without any loss to society, be directly distributed to personal incomes, directly reducing the unit labor costs of deserving enterprises, and designed to increase employment.[15]

Other measures intended to reduce regional disparities include reduced import duties, preferential access to foreign exchange, selective credits by the national bank system, preferential participation in institutional borrowing abroad, and tax preferences to foreign partners in joint ventures. Compared with interregional transfers, their effect has probably been marginal.

Targets and Measures of the Social Plan for 1976–80

The targets in the social plan for regional growth of GMP, given the economic growth rate of 6.9 percent for the economy and the deviations in the growth of regions, are as follows. From a base of Din113.2 billion in 1975, the GMP in the less developed regions is to grow at 8.2 percent a year during the plan period (table 11.14). Based on official population estimates for 1975 and 1980, this growth would raise GMP per capita in the less developed regions from 62.4 percent of the Yugoslav average to 64.3 percent. The GMP in the more developed regions is to grow at 6.7 percent a year during 1976–80 from a base of Din503.1 billion in 1975; their GMP per capita is to remain constant at 121.2 percent of the Yugoslav average. The plan thus foresees only a marginal decline in the income differences between the less developed and more developed regions. The main reason is that high rates of population growth dilute the effects of higher rates of GMP growth for the less developed regions, just as in the past.[16]

Transfer schemes are to continue in slightly modified form. The resources of the Federal Fund were increased from 1.94 percent of the GMP of the social sector to 1.97 percent. Of this total, about 10 percent is first allocated to Kosovo; the balance is to be distributed

15. Such a turnaround in the subsidy scheme could run counter to strongly engrained views and to legal provisions for the use of resources in the Federal Fund.

16. Unless the demographic parameter markedly changes, substantial income differences will persist well into the future. The illustrative example in the section on regional differences in chapter five indicated that the differences in income between regions are unlikely to narrow substantially during the rest of this century (see pp. 105–06).

among the four less developed regions as in the 1971–75 period (see table 11.11). The changes in terms have been marginal; they eliminate the need for budgetary funding of any difference between the borrowing and lending terms. The interest rate is 4.167 percent; the grace period still is three years; and the repayment period is fourteen years. As in the past, the Federal Fund does not participate in allocative decisions; it only monitors the collection and distribution of resources. Transfers to the less developed regions from the federal budget have been raised from the equivalent of 0.83 percent of GMP to 0.93 percent, with the additional 0.10 percent shared by Kosovo (0.07 percent) and Montenegro (0.03 percent). The remainder is being distributed on the same basis as that for the past plan period (see table 11.14).

There is growing recognition that the provision of financial resources, although necessary to narrow the disparities, is not a suffi-

Table 11.14. *Gross Material Product, by Region, 1975
and Targets in the Social Plan for 1976–80*

Region	Gross material product in 1975 (billions of dinars)	Gross material product per capita in 1975 (Yugoslavia = 100)	Average annual rate of GMP growth for 1976–80 (percent)	Gross material product per capita in 1980 (Yugoslavia = 100)
Less developed regions	113.2	62.4	8.2	64.3
Bosnia-Herzegovina	64.3	68.6	8.2[a]	71.7
Kosovo	11.0	33.2	9.5	34.2
Macedonia	28.7	69.3	8.0	70.9
Montenegro	9.2	69.9	8.3	73.1
More developed regions	389.9	121.2	6.7	121.2
Croatia	132.1	124.3	6.5	124.3
Serbia	117.2	92.2	7.0	93.6
Slovenia	84.3	201.3	6.1	195.3
Vojvodina	56.3	121.0	7.1	125.5
Yugoslavia	503.1	100.0	6.9	100.0

Sources: *Statistical Yearbook of Yugoslavia,* 1976; *Index,* 1977, vol. 1; figures supplied by the Federal Institute of Planning; and *Social Plan of Yugoslavia, 1976–80.*
a. The targeted rate is between 8 and 8.5 percent.

cient condition, unless it is extended beyond politically sustainable and economically rational levels. As a result, special attention is being given to the transfer of technical and managerial know-how in conjunction with financial resources. This new emphasis has led to an important, though limited, departure from previous Federal Fund procedures: the joint pooling of resources by enterprises in the more developed and less developed regions can now count for up to 20 percent of the obligatory contributions of the more developed regions. Because the parties to such interenterprise arrangements share risks and benefits, the self-interest of contributing enterprises, which usually are well established, is injected into the arrangement. That self-interest is likely to induce them to make their know-how available more readily than in the past and to prevent wasteful allocative decisions. Questions remain about the rationale for limiting these transfers to any specific percentage.[17]

In addition, the establishment of reproduction entities, in which development programs and investment resources are pooled by vertically linked enterprises, is expected to have a positive effect on the less developed regions in all activities for which they have the raw materials. To the degree that interregional entities materialize, they would lead to a flow of investment resources to the less developed regions over and above the resources channeled through the Federal Fund. They would also mobilize the self-interest of enterprises in the more developed regions in sharing the know-how that the less developed regions now lack.

Supplementary measures

Although the continuation of transfer schemes and the new departures will have effects in the right direction, three broad measures could reinforce Yugoslavia's efforts to reduce regional disparities: restructuring the interregional division of labor, revamping the system of relative prices, and encouraging population movements

---

17. It was not clear at the time of writing whether the figure of 20 percent would apply to enterprises or regions—that is, whether the accountable amount for each contributing enterprise would be 20 percent of its obligations to the Federal Fund, or whether enterprises could account up to 100 percent of their total obligation against joint pooling until a regional average of 20 percent were reached. In the first case the provision would be too small to have much effect. In the second case there would be little justification for imposing any limit, particularly if the arrangements prove to be as beneficial to the parties as is hoped.

to the more developed regions. They are only now beginning to be mentioned in public discussions and official documents.

INTERREGIONAL DIVISION OF LABOR. According to the prevailing view in Yugoslavia, interregional disparities are to disappear in time as the result of higher growth rates in the less developed regions and presumably in every sector and branch. This view overlooks two interrelated aspects. First, given the low growth rate of the working-age population and its high participation rate, Slovenia probably has already exceeded full employment for its indigenous labor force, if temporary immigrants from other regions, temporary migrants abroad, and unemployment are considered. Its labor force is likely to stabilize in the long run. For the same reasons, large parts of the other more developed regions will probably approach that stage over the next decade. Unless compensated for by large-scale migration from the less developed regions, this stabilization of the labor force will reduce the growth rates possible in these regions, compel them to follow a more capital-intensive growth path, or do both concurrently.[18]

Second, there is no a priori reason for the desirability of achieving high and uniform (or even positive) growth rates in every sector and branch of the economy in every region. In fact, if the economy of a particular region approaches full employment after absorbing its rural underemployment and returning migrants, it should gradually shift its development toward activities in which it can maximize growth. This shift would inevitably result in negative growth rates in some activities and in the gradual redirection of their financial assets and their labor forces toward other activities. That is to say, it would be to the long-term advantage of a developed region to plan for such a restructuring and in effect to vacate certain fields of activity. In Yugoslavia, this would mean systematically drawing down some of the most labor-intensive activities in the more developed regions and making available the know-how, resources, and vacated market shares to less developed regions likely to suffer a persistent lack of employment opportunities for a rapidly growing labor force. Such a shift in the interregional division of labor would be tantamount to what is considered internationally to be to the long-term benefit of all countries.

---

18. Large-scale migration, discussed below in the subsection on population movements, is not considered here.

Such rearrangements of the interregional division of labor would probably have to be initiated and propelled by the regions that vacate activities and markets. Naturally the repercussions could be severe, at least in the short term. Activities constituting part of the heritage of economic development of the regions would decline. Enterprises would have to contract or diversify into new activities at potentially considerable social and financial costs to their workers and communes. Passing on know-how would also be costly, given the transfer procedures required for training and temporarily exchanging staff in key skills. For such a reorientation of the interregional division of labor to be viable, there would have to be some kind of fund for "adjustment assistance" in the more developed regions or at the federal level—a fund that would mitigate the short-term social and economic costs of affected individuals and communities. Because the reorientation would be to the ultimate benefit of the less developed regions as well, such adjustment assistance could be construed as a contribution to redressing regional disparities.

RELATIVE PRICES. An indicated earlier, some of the sectors and branches that show low returns (low gross accumulation rates) in every region are strongly represented in most less developed regions. Thus the position of the less developed regions could be improved if relative prices were changed in favor of these sectors and activities.[19] Three strong arguments nevertheless suggest that such a policy could introduce new problems if it were pursued without further investigation into its ramifications.

First, there apparently is no direct statistical evidence of a distortion of Yugoslav internal relative prices in relation to international relative prices. Some of the circumstantial evidence frequently cited in Yugoslavia for the existence of such distortions is not convincing: for example, the incidence of price controls does not prove that distortions between controlled and uncontrolled prices are grave; nor does it prove that distortions always discriminate against the early stages of production. Moreover some of the evidence appears to be a biased generalization of special cases by the parties directly affected. Second, a pattern of domestic relative prices differing more than moderately from that of international relative prices could have dangerous repercussions. For example, if the domestic prices for

---

19. Just as for the interregional division of labor, the analogy to developments in the international sphere is evident for changes in relative prices.

intermediate steel goods were substantially raised above international prices, this action would affect the cost structure of the downstream processing industries, such as shipbuilding, and possibly erode their international competitiveness. Third, the low accumulation rates of some activities, caused by low but internationally comparable relative prices, can simply indicate that these activities are not internationally competitive in Yugoslavia, at least in the short term. Unless a clear case can be established in favor of dynamic benefits, either for the activity or for the economy, an increase of relative prices could perpetuate a pattern that should not have been established in the first place.

POPULATION MOVEMENTS. In parts of the more developed regions, the pool of unabsorbed indigenous labor is already exhausted or will be exhausted in a few years, given their demographic conditions and state of development. Some of the less developed regions are likely to continue to have a severe problem of labor absorption for many years, or even decades. The conclusion alluded to earlier about reorienting the interregional division of labor can be turned around. Rather than have production facilities move to the labor force seeking employment, labor could be moved to areas that are gradually running out of the labor force in a quantity sufficient to maintain their growth momentum. In this regard, the ten-year plan devotes a chapter to population policy.[20] In addition to citing the need for family planning in some parts of the less developed regions, the chapter stresses the need for some stepped-up internal migration. Such migration would increase the growth potential of the country and immediately relieve the unemployment problem in areas where it is most severe. Furthermore such migration would reduce the diluting effect of rapid population growth on incomes in the less developed regions, particularly if the migrating workers were accompanied by their dependents.

On closer examination, however, several factors make this route less easy in practice than it might appear in theory. First, for a variety of social and economic reasons, temporary interregional migration, patterned after temporary migration abroad, appears to be undesirable for sending and receiving regions for the same reasons that temporary international migration is viewed to be undesirable:

---

20. Federal Assembly, "Draft Outline of a Common Policy for Long-Term Development of Yugoslavia (until 1985)," *Yugoslav Survey*, vol. 16, no. 4 (November 1975), pp. 19–90.

the separation of families, the living conditions of migrants in enclaves, and the inability or unwillingness of migrants to integrate with an alien cultural environment. Second, permanent migration including all dependents of workers would appear in the long term to be the only viable form of movement of labor force. But the ethnic, cultural, and linguistic differences between regions could impede the social integration of migrants if that integration were left to chance. Alternatively, successful programs of integration could be costly for the regions receiving migrants. Third, the young, well-educated, and highly motivated persons would probably be most eager to migrate. Their migration could deplete the human resources of the less developed regions and make it even more difficult for these regions to overcome their institutional weaknesses. There is no easy solution to this problem, particularly because migrants having such qualities would be the ones most welcome and most likely to integrate with the cultured milieu of the receiving region. Moreover the constitutional principle of free movement excludes the possibility of subjecting interregional migration to a system of discretionary admission or exclusion.

Summary assessment

As the empirical evidence suggests and the targets of the five-year plan imply, any sizable reduction of interregional income differences will be slow and expensive, even under optimistic assumptions. For the less developed regions the gradual reduction of income disparities might be accompanied by an extended period of rising unemployment. The working-age population in the less developed regions will continue to grow by fairly high rates. The participation rates of the working-age population, particularly for women, are rising because of new expectations and cultural patterns induced by development. Massive transfers of resources will thus continue to be necessary well beyond the current plan period. But massive transfers are not—as now is increasingly acknowledged—a panacea. The returns from any further relative increase of transfers could in some instances be diminishing because of the problems associated with absorptive capacity. Moreover the analysis in this chapter has shown that neither the sacrifices these transfers entail for the more developed regions nor the benefits they bring to the less developed regions appear to be equitable.

Gradually closing the regional disparities to dimensions that are socially and politically acceptable will probably require more than administrative transfers of resources. This now is the thinking in Yugoslavia. It will require innovative schemes to induce voluntary transfers of resources and associated technological know-how.[21] It will also require a gradual reorientation of the interregional division of labor, some changes in the system of relative prices, and the initiation of sizable population movements. Such additional programs do not provide easy, quick, or inexpensive solutions. Nor do they promise scope for more than gradual improvement over those obtainable by simply transferring resources. But unless there is a determined extension of efforts beyond the confines of past measures, the problem of regional disparities could defy resolution.

---

21. This requirement for voluntary transfers of resources and know-how underlies the emphasis on integration and the concept of the reproduction entity, which integrates producers in interlinked production processes in the various regions.

Appendix

Social and Economic Statistics

THE ANNUAL YEARBOOKS published by the Federal Institute of Statistics—under the title *Statisticki Godisnjak SFRJ*—and the annual reports and quarterly economic bulletins published by the National Bank of Yugoslavia are the principal sources in Yugoslavia for social and economic statistics. Occasional publications of the Federal Institute of Statistics—under the series titles *Statisticki Bilten (Statistical Bulletin)* and *Studije, analize i prikazi (Sudies, Analyses, and Reviews)*—are useful sources for statistics on specific subjects.

A.1. Composition and Growth of Gross Material Product, by Sector, 1966–75

A.2. Indexes of the Cost of Living, by Category of Expenditure, 1966–75

A.3. Indexes of Average Net Personal Receipts, by Productive and Nonproductive Activities, 1966–75

A.4. Holdings of Money Supply, by Sector, 1966–75

A.5. Budgetary and Extrabudgetary Receipts, 1966–75

A.6. Gross Savings, Financial Savings, and Gross Investment, by Sector, 1961–65, 1966–70, and 1971–75

A.7. Credits of Banks, by Term and Sector, Annual Increases for 1970–75 and Year-end Position in 1975

A.8. Financial Assets, by Sector and Type of Asset, Year-end Position in 1970 and 1975

A.9. Gross Material Product of Enterprises in the Social Sector, 1966–75

A.10. Investment and Financial Savings of Households, 1966–75

A.11. Industrial Origin of Gross Domestic Product in Constant 1972 Prices, 1966–75

A.12. Sources and Uses of Gross Domestic Product in Current Prices, 1966–75

A.13. Sources and Uses of Gross Domestic Product in Constant 1972 Prices, 1966–75

A.14. Composition of Investment in Fixed Assets, by Sector, 1962–74

A.15. Average and Incremental Capital-Output and Capital-Labor Ratios in Constant 1966 Prices for Productive Activities in the Social Sector, 1952–74

A.16. Investment in Fixed Assets, by Type of Activity and Sector, 1971–75 and Projections in the Social Plan for 1976–80

A.17. Balance of Payments, 1966–76

A.18. Balance of Current Account, 1967–75

A.19. Indexes of the Balance of Trade, 1956, 1961, and 1966–76

A.20. Structure of Trade by Destination, 1956, 1961, and 1966–76

A.21. Structure of Exports, by End Use, 1954, 1960, and 1966–76

A.22. Structure of Imports, by End Use, 1954, 1960, and 1966–76

A.23. Structure of Exports, by Sector and Branch, 1956, 1965, and 1975

A.24. Import Content of Production, by Sector and Branch, 1966, 1968, 1970, and 1972

A.25. Ratio of Imports to Domestic Supply, by Sector and Branch, Selected Years, 1962–75

A.26. Foreign Investment, by Sector and Branch, January 31, 1974

A.27. Labor Force, by Category of Employment, 1961 and 1966–75

A.28. Labor Force, by Category of Employment and Region, 1971

A.29. Employment in the Social Sector, by Type of Activity and Economic Sector and Branch, Selected Years, 1966–75

A.30. Growth of Employment, Value Added, Productivity, and Real Earnings, 1965–76

A.31. Gross Income, Active Labor Force, and Income per Worker in Private Agriculture, Selected Years, 1966–75

A.32. Remittances and Foreign Exchange Deposits by Yugoslav Workers Abroad, 1964–75

A.33. Population and Active Labor Force, by Region and Sex, 1975, 1980, and 1985

A.34. Elasticities of Employment to Gross Output and Fixed Assets in the Social Sector, by Sector and Branch, 1956–65 and 1968–74

A.35. Elasticity of Employment to Value Added in the Social Sector in Constant 1972 Prices, by Region, 1969–75

Table A.1. Composition and Growth of Gross Material Product, by Sector, 1966–75

Item or sector	1966	1967	1968	1969	1970	1971	1972	1973	1974	1975[a]
Gross material product (billions of dinars)										
Total economy	99.0	101.6	105.7	116.6	123.7	134.6	140.8	147.9	161.1	167.1
Industry	34.1	34.3	36.7	41.0	45.1	50.1	53.6	56.4	62.8	66.0
Agriculture and forestry	26.1	26.2	25.3	27.7	26.3	28.3	27.9	30.3	32.6	31.7
Other	38.8	41.1	43.7	47.9	51.3	56.2	59.3	61.2	65.7	69.4
Index of growth (1966 = 100)										
Total economy	100.0	102.6	106.8	117.8	125.0	136.0	142.2	149.4	162.7	168.7
Industry	100.0	100.6	107.6	120.2	132.3	146.9	157.2	165.4	184.2	193.6
Agriculture and forestry	100.0	100.4	96.9	106.1	100.8	108.4	106.9	116.1	124.9	121.6
Other	100.0	105.9	112.6	123.5	132.2	144.9	152.8	157.7	169.3	178.8
Annual rate of growth (percent)										
Total economy	8.6	2.6	4.0	10.3	6.1	8.8	4.6	5.0	8.9	3.7
Industry	4.6	0.6	7.0	11.7	10.0	11.1	7.0	5.2	11.4	5.1
Agriculture and forestry	17.6	0.4	−3.4	9.5	−5.0	7.6	1.4	8.6	7.6	−2.7
Other	6.3	5.9	6.3	9.6	7.1	9.6	5.5	3.2	7.4	5.6
Share of gross material product (percent)										
Industry	34.4	33.8	34.7	35.2	36.5	37.2	38.1	38.1	39.0	39.5
Agriculture and forestry	26.4	25.8	23.9	23.8	21.3	21.0	19.8	20.5	20.2	19.0
Other	39.2	40.5	41.3	41.1	41.5	41.8	42.1	41.4	40.8	41.5

Note: All figures are in 1966 prices and calculated according to the establishment principle.
Source: Federal Institute of Statistics, Statistical Yearbook of Yugoslavia 1975, 1976, and 1977.

Table A.2. Indexes of the Cost of Living, by Category of Expenditure, 1966–75
(1974 = 100)

Category of expenditure	1966	1967	1968	1969	1970	1971	1972	1973	1974	1975
Food	40	41	42	46	51	59	71	86	100	124
Tobacco and drinks	40	44	45	48	52	61	73	86	100	135
Clothing	37	41	43	47	52	58	67	81	100	122
Rent	36	44	53	63	66	68	74	85	100	122
Fuel and electricity	34	34	35	35	40	50	60	72	100	132
Furniture	41	44	45	48	53	60	68	79	100	130
Hygiene and health	36	43	44	46	50	57	65	72	100	121
Recreation	35	40	44	47	53	62	67	79	100	128
Transport and communications	38	41	44	46	49	58	69	80	100	114
Goods	39	41	42	45	50	58	69	82	100	124
Services	36	42	48	54	58	66	72	84	100	125
Total	38	41	43	46	51	59	69	83	100	124

Source: Statistical Yearbook of Yugoslavia, 1976.

Table A.3. Indexes of Average Net Personal Receipts, by Productive and Nonproductive Activities, 1966–75
(1974 = 100)

Index or type of activity	1966	1967	1968	1969	1970	1971	1972	1973	1974	1975
Nominal average net personal receipts	28	32	35	40	47	58	68	78	100	124
Productive activities	27	31	34	40	47	57	67	78	100	123
Nonproductive activities	29	34	36	42	49	60	70	78	100	126
Real average net personal receipts	74	78	81	87	92	98	99	94	100	99
Productive activities	71	76	79	87	92	97	97	94	100	99
Nonproductive activities	76	83	84	91	96	102	101	94	100	101

Source: Statistical Yearbook of Yugoslavia, 1976.

Table A.4. Holdings of Money Supply, by Sector, 1966–75
(millions of dinars)

Sector	1966	1967	1968	1969	1970	1971	1972	1973	1974	1975
Total money supply[a]	23,185	21,895	27,603	30,828	38,454	43,266	60,541	82,083	103,437	137,085
Socialist enterprises	7,815	5,777	7,077	6,745	7,462	8,117	12,983	22,793	27,687	46,207
Federation	457	403	860	579	1,264	1,027	1,808	1,429	1,485	2,531
Other sociopolitical communities	1,064	981	2,123	2,883	3,367	3,863	5,446	8,532	12,381	11,219
Investment loan funds	814	808	445	430	1,836	814	1,251	2,170	1,738	3,269
Other social sector organizations	3,504	3,860	4,325	5,552	6,739	8,805	10,326	12,859	17,786	23,800
Households	7,097	8,123	9,789	12,262	15,409	18,706	23,956	29,537	35,726	42,591
Rest of the world	442	560	664	101	103	119	228	229	369	366
Float	1,992	1,383	2,320	2,276	2,274	1,815	4,543	4,534	6,265	7,102

Sources: National Bank of Yugoslavia, Annual Report, various years.
a. Currency, demand deposits, and float.

Table A.5. *Budgetary and Extrabudgetary Receipts, 1966–75*
(billions of dinars)

Item	1966	1967	1968	1969	1970	1971	1972	1973	1974	1975
Budgetary receipts	15.52	17.37	19.98	22.92	29.95	35.10	43.80	54.75	66.00	81.21
Income taxes	4.11	5.18	5.33	5.21	6.05	5.51	7.00	9.32	8.89	10.97
Turnover taxes	7.52	8.69	10.21	12.44	15.82	19.56	24.71	30.64	35.66	43.10
Stamp duties	0.41	0.60	0.58	0.74	1.62	1.04	1.07	1.26	1.32	1.64
Custom duties	1.85	2.41	3.32	4.33	5.69	8.48	10.18	12.68	18.71	23.45
Other	1.63	0.49	0.54	0.23	0.77	0.51	0.84	0.85	1.43	2.05
Receipts of communities of interest	13.73	14.44	17.02	20.85	26.00	32.30	38.95	43.29	69.74	100.20
Education[a]	2.80	3.65	4.26	5.38	6.84	8.22	9.05	8.70	15.19	22.10
Health[b]	n.a.	n.a.	n.a.	n.a.	6.60	8.61	10.94	12.56	20.36	26.85
Pension[b]	10.93	10.79	11.23	13.53	10.37	12.91	15.74	17.27	25.35	32.16
Child welfare[b]	n.a.	n.a.	1.24	1.56	1.71	1.99	2.51	3.11	4.82	6.30
Unemployment[b]	n.a.	n.a.	0.29	0.37	0.48	0.57	0.72	0.73	1.04	1.25
Other	0.00	0.00	0.00	0.00	0.00	0.00	0.00	0.92	2.98	11.54

Receipts of special funds	5.85	6.39	6.90	7.54	8.16	8.52	11.83	13.50	17.28	20.61
Interest of funds of productive activities	2.35	3.00	3.33	3.40	3.31	3.16	5.07	4.79	5.79	8.04
Funds for the reconstruction of Skopje and Basanska Krajina	1.00	0.97	0.94	0.97	0.92	0.83	0.98	1.21	1.53	1.81
Joint reserve of enterprises	0.90	0.60	0.42	0.47	0.65	0.73	1.10	1.43	1.49	2.16
Public roads	0.19	0.72	1.12	1.26	1.53	1.82	2.22	2.62	2.82	3.15
Water	0.22	0.27	0.27	0.30	0.30	0.31	0.34	0.46	0.60	0.48
Other[c]	1.19	0.83	0.82	1.14	1.45	1.67	2.12	2.99	5.05	4.97
Gross material product	99.10	103.70	112.00	131.90	157.20	204.10	245.40	306.30	407.20	497.80
Total receipts	35.10	38.20	43.90	51.31	64.11	75.92	94.58	111.54	153.02	202.02

n.a. Not applicable.

Sources: *Statistical Yearbook of Yugoslavia*, various years.

a. Until 1971 contributions for education were classified under budgetary receipts. The subsequent reclassification along functional lines therefore conceals the relative decline in budgetary receipts.

b. Subsumes social security and social welfare, including the contributions for health insurance and pensions in 1966–69 and those for child welfare and unemployment in 1966–67.

c. Includes contributions to solidarity funds for housing, rent subsidies, local self-contributions, and other.

Table A.6. Gross Savings, Financial Savings, and Gross Investment, by Sector, 1961–65, 1966–70, and 1971–75
(billions of dinars)

Sector	1961–65			1966–70			1971–75		
	Gross savings	Gross investment	Financial savings	Gross savings	Gross investment	Financial savings	Gross savings	Gross investment	Financial savings
Socialist enterprises	52.0	83.5	−31.5	110.7	161.9	−51.2	334.9	452.4	−117.5
Federation	−10.6	1.9	−12.5	−4.7	0.9	−5.6	−32.0	6.0	−38.0
Other sociopolitical communities	9.2	9.4	−0.2	12.8	9.9	2.9	28.2	28.8	−0.6
Other social sector organizations	11.5	6.7	4.8	17.9	11.6	6.3	66.8	42.8	24.0
Investment loan funds	29.7	0.0	29.7	33.4	0.0	33.4	22.9	0.0	22.9
Households	10.4	8.2	2.2	57.4	39.2	18.2	202.5	119.8	82.7
Unclassified	4.8	0.0	4.8	−10.8	0.0	−10.8	1.3	0.0	1.3
Rest of the world	2.7	0.0	2.7	6.8	0.0	6.8	25.2	0.0	25.2
Total	109.7	109.7	0.0	223.5	223.5	0.0	649.8	649.8	0.0

Note: Because transactions are recorded on a payments basis in the flow-of-funds accounts, figures for gross savings and investment, as well as their sectoral breakdown, somewhat differ from those in national accounts and other statistical sources in which investments are recorded on a realization basis. Investment figures also refer to both gross investment in fixed assets and investment in working assets (inventories), which significantly increased in later periods. In addition, because of adjustments for inventory overvaluation in other tables, the figures in those tables, especially for enterprises, somewhat differ from the figures here.

Sources: NBY, *Annual Report*, various years; NBY, *Quarterly Economic Bulletin*, July 1975 and July 1976.

Table A.7. *Credits of Banks, by Term and Sector, Annual Increases for 1970–75 and Year-end Position in 1975*

Term or sector	Annual increase (billions of dinars)						Position at year-end, 1975	
	1970	1971[a]	1972	1973	1974	1975	Billions of dinars	Percentage composition
Total credits[b]	31.8	37.8	36.4	43.3	68.6	96.8	456.8	100.0
Socialist enterprises	24.7	25.5	29.1	34.0	52.6	74.0	350.9	76.8
Federation	0.7	7.4	1.9	0.8	6.4	10.2	41.3	9.0
Other social sector organizations	2.2	2.5	3.6	4.8	2.4	2.4	25.9	5.7
Households	4.2	2.4	1.8	3.7	7.2	10.2	38.7	8.5
Short-term credits	10.8	10.7	12.1	26.6	26.4	38.5	138.3	100.0
Socialist enterprises	8.2	9.7	11.8	24.8	21.5	28.0	114.1	82.5
Federation	0.1	0.6	0.5	−0.2	0.3	3.7	4.2	3.0
Other social sector organizations	0.4	0.4	0.5	0.3	0.3	0.5	1.3	1.0
Households	2.0	0.0	−0.7	1.7	4.3	6.3	18.7	13.5
Long-term credits	21.0	27.1	24.3	16.7	42.2	58.3	318.5	100.0
Socialist enterprises	16.4	15.8	17.4	9.2	31.1	46.0	236.8	74.4
Federation	0.6	6.9	1.4	1.0	6.1	6.4	37.1	11.7
Other social sector organizations	1.8	2.1	3.1	4.5	2.1	2.0	24.6	7.7
Households	2.2	2.4	2.4	2.0	2.9	3.9	20.0	6.2

Sources: National Bank of Yugoslavia, *Annual Report*, various years.
a. Excludes the conversion of Din14.5 billion from short-term to long-term credits in 1971.
b. Includes foreign exchange credits granted to enterprises and, since 1974, the resources transferred to enterprises and socio-political communities for their permanent use.

Table A.8. *Financial Assets, by Sector and Type of Asset,*
Year-end Position in 1970 and 1975

	Billions of dinars		Percentage composition	
Sector or type of asset	1970	1975	1970	1975
Nonfinancial sectors				
Money	35.8	134.1	6.5	9.7
Currency	15.0	41.9	2.7	3.0
Demand deposits	20.8	92.2	3.8	6.7
Other deposits	68.7	208.4	12.6	15.0
Sight deposits	13.7	49.0	2.5	3.5
Restricted deposits	17.9	31.4	3.3	2.3
Time deposits	26.0	57.3	4.8	4.1
Foreign exchange deposits with domestic banks	7.6	56.8	1.4	4.1
Foreign exchange deposits with foreign banks	3.5	13.9	0.6	1.0
Securities	1.9	8.4	0.3	0.6
Government	1.3	4.8	0.2	0.3
Banks	0.6	3.6	0.1	0.3
Contributions to bank funds	9.1	13.8	1.7	1.0
Credits for the sale of goods	110.9	265.9	20.3	19.2
Credits granted by nonfinancial sector	0.9	29.1	0.2	2.1
Other transactions and unclassified	7.9	38.0	1.4	2.7
Total	235.2	697.7	43.0	50.3
Financial sector				
Credits of banks	198.4	487.2	36.3	35.1
Investment loan funds	28.6	44.1	5.2	3.2
Foreign assets	11.9	53.8	2.2	3.9
Other[a]	101.0	149.1	18.5	10.7
Total	311.3	690.1	57.0	49.7
Financial and nonfinancial sectors	546.5	1,387.8	100.0	100.0
Foreign sector	43.3	126.7	n.a.	n.a.
All sectors	589.8	1,514.5	n.a.	n.a.

n.a. Not applicable.

Sources: Figures for 1975 from NBY, *Quarterly Economic Bulletin*, July 1976; figures for 1970 calculated from figures for 1975 and data on annual changes supplied by NBY.

a. Includes money, deposits, contributions to bank funds, and other relations between financial organizations.

Table A.9. Gross Material Product of Enterprises in the Social Sector, 1966–75
(percentage of GMP)

Item	1966	1967	1968	1969	1970	1971	1972	1973	1974	1975[a]
Gross material product	100.0	100.0	100.0	100.0	100.0	100.0	100.0	100.0	100.0	100.0
Depreciation[b]	8.6	10.7	10.8	10.8	10.5	10.2	11.3	11.6	12.2	10.8
Net product	91.4	89.3	89.2	89.2	89.5	89.8	88.7	88.4	87.8	89.2
Fiscal and parafiscal contributions	36.2	37.9	38.1	42.5	41.2	37.8	38.9	40.0	38.7	39.0
Net personal income	34.8	35.7	35.9	36.5	37.1	36.5	36.0	34.6	33.6	34.5
Allocation to funds	20.3	15.7	15.1	10.2	11.3	15.5	13.8	13.8	15.4	15.7
Net enterprise income[c]	63.8	62.1	61.8	57.6	58.8	62.2	61.1	60.0	61.3	61.0
Gross personal income	51.6	51.7	52.1	52.8	52.9	51.0	50.4	48.1	46.1	47.1
Gross savings[d]	28.9	26.4	25.9	21.0	21.8	25.7	25.1	25.4	27.6	26.5
Adjustment for inventory overvaluation[e]	−5.7	−0.9	−1.1	−5.0	−7.7	−8.5	−7.1	−9.6	−13.6	−8.2
Adjusted gross savings	24.6	25.5	25.1	16.1	15.2	18.8	19.4	17.5	16.3	20.1
Gross material product (billions of dinars)	76.2	80.1	89.7	105.4	128.3	168.9	203.4	249.7	341.1	426.5

Sources: Statistical Yearbook of Yugoslavia, various years; and World Bank adjustments (see note e).
a. Preliminary figures.
b. Equivalent to gross value added.
c. Depreciation plus net personal income and allocation to funds.
d. Depreciation plus allocation to funds.
e. In Yugoslav statistics inventories are valued at year-end prices, which under the conditions of inflation and stockpiling in the first half of the 1970s inflated the value of investment in working assets (inventories) and consequently the figures for total savings and investment. The adjustment made by World Bank staff essentially corrects the inventory valuation by taking into account the difference between year-end and mid-year prices.

Table A.10. Investment and Financial Savings of Households, 1966–75
(billions of dinars)

Item	1966	1967	1968	1969	1970	1971	1972	1973	1974	1975
Current receipts	56.33	64.84	73.78	89.36	110.08	146.25	176.70	224.92	288.82	367.22
Current expenditures	48.26	55.50	63.78	75.23	94.36	121.50	147.33	186.32	242.83	303.39
Gross savings	8.07	9.34	10.00	14.13	15.72	24.75	29.37	38.60	46.00	63.83
Investment	3.11	6.30	8.59	9.80	11.37	13.30	16.30	22.00	29.20	39.00
Fixed assets	2.44	5.50	7.20	8.20	9.55	11.00	13.70	18.50	24.00	32.00
Changes in stocks	0.66	0.80	1.39	1.60	1.82	2.30	2.60	3.50	5.20	7.00
Financial savings[a]	4.97	3.04	1.40	4.33	4.35	11.45	13.07	16.60	16.79	24.83
Money	1.74	0.96	1.60	2.39	3.07	3.17	5.10	5.48	6.04	7.36
Other liquid assets	1.83	1.03	1.35	2.21	2.30	2.65	2.30	4.41	6.29	9.63
Nonliquid assets	0.37	0.38	0.86	1.04	1.58	1.95	1.74	2.60	3.80	4.97
Short-term credits	0.50	−0.23	−2.48	−1.49	−2.80	−0.80	0.86	−1.36	−7.07	−6.96
Long- and medium-term credits	−0.36	−0.54	−1.05	−0.89	−2.39	−2.44	−2.45	−1.96	−2.90	−3.87
Short-term foreign exchange transactions[b]	0.88	0.97	1.00	0.62	1.86	4.44	3.20	4.92	6.56	8.03
Long-term foreign exchange transactions	...	...	0.12	0.45	0.72	2.48	2.31	2.52	4.07	5.66

... Zero or negligible.
Sources: NBY, Annual Report, various years; and NBY, Quarterly Economic Bulletin, various issues.
a. The difference between gross savings and physical investment.
b. Includes estimated private holdings of foreign exchange with foreign banks.

Table A.11. *Industrial Origin of Gross Domestic Product in Constant 1972 Prices, 1966–75* (millions of dinars)

Sector	1966	1967	1968	1969	1970	1971	1972	1973	1974	1975
Agriculture and forestry	40,268	39,874	38,545	41,980	39,636	42,219	41,355	44,961	47,487	46,329
Mining	5,560	5,331	5,374	5,619	6,184	6,885	6,860	7,248	7,862	8,296
Manufacturing	40,334	39,921	42,011	46,327	49,787	54,782	58,877	62,662	70,244	74,537
Construction	20,745	22,261	23,891	26,048	28,444	28,822	29,888	29,350	31,140	34,566
Electricity, gas, and water	3,869	4,173	4,521	5,153	5,620	6,291	6,891	7,243	8,231	8,143
Transport and communications	12,602	13,726	14,577	15,768	17,184	18,664	19,254	20,556	22,684	23,374
Trade	16,929	17,755	18,817	21,041	23,158	25,668	27,193	28,109	30,099	30,128
Financial institutions	2,902	3,017	3,178	3,646	3,804	4,288	4,846	5,403	5,245	67,888
Ownership of dwellings	1,334	1,396	1,663	1,844	1,981	2,175	2,300	2,494	2,484	
Public administration	9,065	9,308	9,979	10,421	10,503	11,241	11,757	12,469	16,218	
Other services	20,610	21,500	25,046	31,338	31,946	35,887	39,377	37,169	39,477	
Gross domestic product at factor cost	174,218	178,262	187,602	209,185	218,247	236,922	248,598	257,664	281,171	293,261

Source: World Bank estimates based on figures supplied by the Federal Institute of Statistics.

Table A.12. *Sources and Uses of Gross Domestic Product in Current Prices, 1966–75*
(millions of dinars)

Source or use	1966	1967	1968	1969	1970
Total consumption[a]	76,888	84,185	93,627	107,893	125,745
Private[a]	59,281	64,078	70,627	81,839	95,261
General government	17,607	20,107	23,000	26,054	30,484
Gross domestic investment	30,716	35,283	38,044	43,049	55,523
Gross fixed investment	26,616	30,283	35,044	41,049	51,723
Change in stocks	4,100	5,000	3,000	2,000	3,800
Net exports of goods and nonfactor services	−1,100	−1,700	−2,600	−3,375	−9,150
Exports of goods and nonfactor services	20,988	22,213	22,988	26,675	31,100
Imports of goods and nonfactor services	22,088	23,913	25,588	30,050	40,250
Gross domestic product at market prices	106,504	117,768	129,071	147,567	172,118
Net factor income	663	675	1,038	2,013	4,738
Gross national product at market prices	107,167	118,443	130,109	149,580	176,856
Net indirect taxes	7,136	9,040	10,513	11,693	14,577
Gross national product at factor cost	100,031	109,403	119,596	137,887	162,279
Capital consumption allowances	8,370	9,845	12,041	14,238	16,644
Net national income	91,661	99,558	107,555	123,649	145,635
Domestic savings	29,616	33,583	35,444	39,674	46,373
National savings	30,279	34,258	36,482	41,687	51,111

n.a. Not available.
Source: World Bank estimates based on figures supplied by the Federal Institute of Statistics.
a. Calculated as a residual.

1971	1972	1973	1974	1975	Source or use
162,272	200,985	249,809	339,527	403,025	Total consumption[a]
125,586	155,695	197,067	265,227	305,111	Private[a]
36,686	45,290	52,742	74,300	97,914	General government
					Gross domestic
72,351	74,507	93,224	128,800	177,587	investment
					Gross fixed
64,651	74,107	85,324	117,400	163,287	investment
7,700	400	7,900	11,400	14,300	Change in stocks
					Net exports of goods
					and nonfactor
−13,612	−6,630	−13,469	−42,027	−42,647	services
					Exports of goods
					and nonfactor
42,032	58,208	70,066	90,640	109,654	services
					Imports of goods
					and nonfactor
55,644	64,838	83,535	132,667	152,301	services
					Gross domestic
					product at
221,011	268,862	329,564	426,300	537,965	market prices
8,541	13,634	19,718	22,644	24,688	Net factor income
					Gross national
					product at
229,552	282,496	349,282	448,944	562,653	market prices
19,251	20,264	21,045	45,790	66,800	Net indirect taxes
					Gross national
					product at
210,301	262,232	328,237	403,154	495,853	factor cost
					Capital consump-
21,180	27,979	36,290	50,840	n.a.	tion allowances
189,121	234,253	291,947	352,314	n.a.	Net national income
58,739	67,877	79,755	86,773	134,940	Domestic savings
67,280	81,511	99,473	109,417	159,628	National savings

Table A.13. *Sources and Uses of Gross Domestic Product in Constant 1972 Prices, 1966–75*
(millions of dinars)

Source or use	1966	1967	1968	1969	1970
Total consumption[a]	131,793	137,374	148,291	169,813	178,663
Private[a]	93,847	99,861	108,011	129,167	136,904
General government	37,946	37,513	40,280	40,646	41,759
Gross domestic investment	56,926	58,578	59,862	61,624	72,359
Gross fixed investment	50,058	50,826	55,323	58,807	67,346
Change in stocks	6,868	7,752	4,539	2,817	5,013
Net exports of goods and nonfactor services	−1,870	−2,890	−3,927	−4,411	−12,631
Exports of goods and nonfactor services	35,680	37,762	39,573	44,241	47,524
Imports of goods and nonfactor services	37,550	40,652	43,500	48,652	60,155
Gross domestic product at market prices	186,849	193,062	204,226	227,026	238,391
Net factor income	829	844	1,298	2,382	5,212
Gross national product at market prices	187,678	193,906	205,524	229,408	243,603
Net indirect taxes	12,631	14,800	16,624	17,841	20,144
Gross national product at factor cost	175,047	179,106	188,900	211,567	223,459

n.a. Not available.
Source: World Bank estimates based on figures supplied by the Federal Institute of Statistics.
a. Calculated as a residual.

1971	1972	1973	1974	1975	Source or use
194,634	200,985	203,775	244,924	249,846	Total consumption[a]
151,976	155,695	157,469	195,325	n.a.	Private[a]
42,658	45,290	46,306	49,599	n.a.	General government
80,679	74,507	82,821	89,855	97,163	Gross domestic investment
71,839	74,107	76,017	82,787	90,238	Gross fixed investment
8,840	400	6,804	7,068	6,925	Change in stocks
−15,910	−6,630	−11,271	−19,701	−18,598	Net exports of goods and nonfactor services
51,366	58,208	61,829	61,287	62,337	Exports of goods and nonfactor services
67,276	64,838	73,100	80,988	80,935	Imports of goods and nonfactor services
259,403	268,862	275,325	315,078	328,411	Gross domestic product at market prices
9,038	13,634	16,570	13,044	13,513	Net factor income
268,441	282,496	291,895	328,122	341,924	Gross national product at market prices
22,481	20,264	17,661	33,907	35,150	Net indirect taxes
245,960	262,232	274,234	294,215	306,774	Gross national product at factor cost

Table A.14. *Composition of Investment in Fixed Assets, by Sector, 1962–74*
(percent)

Category of investment or sector	1962	1963	1964	1965	1966	1967
Productive investment	64.3	63.4	64.2	60.1	64.3	72.4
Social sector	62.2	61.1	62.2	56.0	60.5	68.0
Private sector	2.1	2.3	1.9	4.1	3.9	4.4
Nonproductive investment	35.6	36.5	35.8	39.9	35.7	27.6
Social sector	28.4	29.1	28.0	29.1	22.0	12.9
Private sector	7.2	7.5	7.9	10.8	13.6	14.8
Social sector	90.6	90.2	90.2	85.1	82.5	80.9
Private sector	9.4	9.8	9.8	14.9	17.5	19.1
Housing and communal services	30.0	30.6	29.4	33.6	27.0	23.4
Construction work	54.0	53.2	54.2	55.7	54.9	54.2
Own resources of enterprises	n.a.	n.a.	n.a.	n.a.	n.a.	50.7
Ratio of investment to gross material product	35.3	34.6	33.4	27.4	26.9	29.2
Ratio of investment to gross national product	30.9	30.7	31.5	26.0	24.7	25.7

n.a. Not available.
Note: Figures are in current prices, except those for housing and communal services during 1962–68, which are calculated from data in constant prices.
Sources: Statistical Yearbook of Yugoslavia, various years; World Bank estimates of GNP.

1968	1969	1970	1971	1972	1973	1974	Category of investment or sector
72.2	73.1	70.2	70.7	68.2	67.3	67.8	Productive investment
67.9	69.2	66.3	66.0	63.3	59.4	61.1	Social sector
4.3	4.0	3.9	4.7	4.9	7.9	6.7	Private sector
27.8	26.9	29.8	29.3	31.8	32.7	32.2	Nonproductive investment
13.3	12.7	15.0	13.4	15.0	14.7	14.9	Social sector
14.5	14.1	14.8	15.9	16.8	17.9	17.3	Private sector
81.1	81.9	81.3	79.4	78.2	74.2	76.0	Social sector
18.8	18.1	18.7	20.6	21.8	25.8	24.0	Private sector
21.9	20.1	21.8	21.1	25.1	23.4	22.4	Housing and communal services
55.4	55.3	58.1	58.2	58.4	55.3	55.0	Construction work
51.3	50.6	50.2	53.0	53.5	55.6	56.3	Own resources of enterprises
31.3	31.1	32.9	31.6	30.1	27.9	28.8	Ratio of investment to gross material product
27.0	27.6	28.9	28.8	26.2	24.2	27.1	Ratio of investment to gross national product

Table A.15. *Average and Incremental Capital-Output and Capital-Labor Ratios in Constant 1966 Prices for Productive Activities in the Social Sector, 1952–74*

Year	Fixed assets (billions of dinars)	Employment[a] (thousands of workers)	Gross material product[a] (billions of dinars)	Investment[a] (billions of dinars)	Average capital-labor ratio[b] (thousands of dinars)	Average capital-output ratio[c]	Average productivity[d]	Incremental capital-labor ratio[e] (thousands of dinars)	Incremental capital-output ratio[f]	Incremental capital-labor ratio[g] (thousands of dinars)	Incremental capital-output ratio[g]
1952	55.76	1,439	22.20	n.a.	38,749	2.51	15,425	n.a.	n.a.	n.a.	n.a.
1953	59.51	1,495	22.82	7.43	39,806	2.61	15,261	n.a.	n.a.	n.a.	n.a.
1954	62.24	1,634	24.79	7.81	38,010	2.51	15,171	26.98	1.90	132.7	7.81
1955	68.66	1,740	26.21	8.13	39,459	2.62	15,063	25.75	1.92	56.2	3.96
1956	75.19	1,842	28.80	7.97	40,819	2.61	15,636	62.94	2.48	76.7	5.73
1957	83.03	1,928	31.42	8.15	43,065	2.64	16,294	75.93	2.49	78.1	3.08
1958	90.88	2,069	35.81	8.59	43,924	2.54	17,306	55.60	1.79	94.8	3.11
1959	96.92	2,234	40.52	9.75	43,384	2.39	18,137	47.58	1.67	60.9	1.96
1960	105.23	2,432	45.61	11.19	43,268	2.31	18,754	30.51	1.19	51.9	2.07
1961	115.94	2,596	49.95	12.56	44,661	2.32	19,239	50.67	1.92	56.5	2.20

Year											
1962	128.80	2,711	54.91	13.47	47,510	2.35	20,253	75.42	2.15	76.6	2.89
1963	140.34	2,813	61.26	14.17	49,889	2.29	21,778	126.08	2.03	117.1	2.72
1964	151.86	2,907	67.43	15.57	52,239	2.25	23,115	122.77	1.87	138.9	2.23
1965	165.44	2,952	72.46	15.84	56,043	2.28	24,547	256.00	2.29	165.6	2.52
1966	178.44	2,924	75.44	16.88	61,025	2.37	25,801	—h	4.54	352.0	3.15
1967	190.33	2,887	79.11	17.63	65,926	2.41	27,403	—h	3.54	—h	5.66
1968	204.37	2,919	84.20	20.17	70,013	2.43	28,844	371.56	2.36	—h	4.80
1969	223.38	2,997	91.20	22.15	74,534	2.45	30,431	180.00	2.01	630.3	3.96
1970	241.86	3,123	99.93	24.52	77,444	2.42	31,999	150.87	2.18	284.0	3.16
1971	266.36	3,258	107.81	26.84	81,755	2.47	33,091	133.19	2.28	194.6	2.81
1972	285.53	3,378	114.68	28.63	84,526	2.49	33,948	204.17	3.57	198.8	3.41
1973	308.59	3,505	122.12	29.70	88,042	2.53	34,842	150.94	2.58	238.6	4.17
1974	331.22	3,653	129.37	31.28	90,670	2.56	35,414	155.81	3.18	233.6	3.99

n.a. Not available.
Sources: Calculated from Statistical Yearbook of Yugoslavia, various years.
a. Three-year moving averages.
b. Fixed assets per worker.
c. Ratio of fixed assets to GMP.
d. GMP per worker.
e. Calculated from changes in capital stock.
f. Calculated from changes in capital stock with a one-year lag.
g. Calculated from gross investment with a one-year lag.
h. Because employment declined, the ratio is infinite.

Table A.16. *Investment in Fixed Assets, by Type of Activity and Sector, 1971–75 and Projections in the Social Plan for 1976–80*
(percent)

Type of activity or sector	Composition				Average annual rate of growth, 1971–75	Investment in 1980 (1976 = 100)
	1975	1980	1971–75	1976–80		
Productive activities						
Social sector	91.6	93.0	92.6	92.8	8.5	150
Industry	51.6	50.7	47.2	50.7	10.0	161
Energy	n.a.	n.a.	8.4	13.5	19.3	241
Basic metals	n.a.	n.a.	8.6	6.6	2.7	114
Basic chemistry	n.a.	n.a.	1.7	4.3	30.0	371
Other	n.a.	n.a.	25.7	18.6	1.7	109
Agriculture and forestry	9.5	9.9	9.6	9.5	8.3	149
Construction	4.2	2.8	3.2	3.0	6.7	138
Transport and communications	16.8	17.6	18.5	17.6	7.4	143

			billions of dinars in 1975 prices			
Trade and tourism	8.4	7.7	12.1	8.2	0.4	102
Handicraft	2.1	1.4	1.7	1.6	7.4	143
Undistributed	—	3.5	—	2.0	—	—
Private sector	7.4	7.0	7.4	7.4	8.4	150
Nonproductive activities						
Housing	72.6	73.0	71.1	72.8	7.9	146
Social sector	30.6	31.5	30.4	31.6	8.3	149
Private sector	40.3	41.6	40.7	41.2	7.6	145
Other social sector	27.4	27.0	28.9	27.2	6.1	135
Total investment	156	231	674	994	8.1	147
Productive activities	95	142	405	608	8.5	150
Nonproductive activities	62	89	270	386	7.4	143

— Not applicable.
n.a. Not available.
Note: Figures may not reconcile because of rounding.
Source: Federal Institute of Planning, "Analytical Basis for the Documents of the Social Plan of Yugoslavia for the Period 1976–1980: Development Indicators and Main Balances" (Belgrade, 1976; processed).

Table A.17. *Balance of Payments, 1966–76*
(millions of dollars)

Item	1966	1967	1968	1969	1970	1971	1972	1973	1974	1975	1976[a]
Merchandise exports	1,220	1,252	1,264	1,475	1,679	1,814	2,237	2,853	3,805	4,072	4,878
Merchandise imports	1,575	1,707	1,797	2,134	2,874	3,253	3,227	4,511	7,542	7,697	7,367
Trade balance	−355	−455	−533	−659	−1,195	−1,439	−990	−1,658	−3,737	−3,625	−2,489
Tourism and travel receipts	117	150	189	241	275	360	462	630	699	768	800
Other nonfactor service receipts	342	375	386	418	534	636	725	880	1,192	1,467	n.a.
Tourism and travel expenses	−35	−52	−53	−73	−129	−220	−244	−250	−295	−435	−530
Other nonfactor service expenses	−155	−154	−179	−197	−216	−247	−357	−363	−500	−628	n.a.
Nonfactor service balance	267	319	343	389	463	495	586	897	1,095	1,172	1,184
Resource balance	−86	−136	−189	−271	−731	−944	−404	−761	−2,641	−2,453	−1,405

Interest payments	−76	−75	−85	−102	−128	−147	−165	−222	−285	−337	−350
Workers' remittances	64	89	122	206	440	652	889	1,301	1,511	1,575	1,728
Other factor services (net)[b]	65	40	46	57	79	81	99	146	231	183	177
Current account balance	−33	−82	−106	−110	−340	−358	419	464	−1,184	−1,032	150
Medium- and long-term loans											
Disbursements[c]	279	334	390	517	636	857	943	1,170	1,426	1,850	1,700
Repayments	−178	−173	−219	−239	−335	−504	−570	−686	−814	−930	800
Net disbursements	101	161	171	278	301	353	373	484	612	920	900
Capital transactions[d]	−101	−144	−22	−246	−51	−104	−117	−255	134	−68	−133
Use of reserves	−33	−65	43	−78	90	109	−675	−663	438	180	−917
Memo item: total official reserves	115	80	132	253	140	212	731	1,338	1,147	871	2,049

n.a. Not available.
Source: Vinod Dubey and others, *Yugoslavia: Development with Decentralization* (Washington, D.C.: Johns Hopkins University Press for the World Bank, 1975); and figures supplied by NBY.
a. Preliminary figures.
b. Includes current transfers.
c. Includes direct foreign investment.
d. Covers errors and omissions, net export credits, short-term loans, International Monetary Fund account, and national bank and commercial bank credits.

Table A.18. *Balance of Current Account, 1967–75*
(millions of dollars)

Destination or item	1967	1968	1969	1970	1971	1972	1973	1974	1975
Convertible-currency area									
Merchandise exports	715	738	922	1,033	1,053	1,381	1,895	2,380	2,555
Merchandise imports	1,147	1,208	1,500	2,133	2,329	2,343	3,350	5,790	6,145
Trade balance	−432	−470	−578	−1,100	−1,276	−962	−1,455	−3,410	−3,590
Service exports[a]	n.a.	n.a.	n.a.	1,151	1,567	1,981	2,835	3,398	3,678
Service imports	n.a.	n.a.	n.a.	425	573	708	844	1,000	1,340
Service balance	300	346	490	726	994	1,273	1,991	2,398	2,338
Current account balance	−132	−124	−88	−374	−282	311	536	−1,012	−1,252
Bilateral-clearing area									
Merchandise exports	537	426	553	646	761	856	958	1,425	1,517
Merchandise imports	570	589	634	741	924	890	1,161	1,752	1,552
Trade balance	−37	163	−81	−95	−163	−34	−203	−327	−35
Service exports[a]	n.a.	n.a.	n.a.	177	178	181	166	235	315
Service imports	n.a.	n.a.	n.a.	−49	−91	−51	−35	−80	−60
Service balance	83	181	60	128	87	130	131	155	255
Current account balance	50	18	−21	33	−76	96	−72	−172	220

n.a. Not available.
Source: NBY, *Annual Report*, various years; and figures supplied by NBY.
a. Include net positive transfers.

Table A.19. Indexes of the Balance of Trade, 1956, 1961, and 1966–76

Year	Gross material product[a]	Volume		Prices		Barter terms of trade[b]	Nominal exports[e]	Import capacity[d]
		Exports	Imports	Exports	Imports			
1956	100	100	100	100	100	100	100	100
1961	162	172	188	102	102	100	177	174
1966	231	296	278	128	120	107	413	344
1967	236	301	301	128	120	107	442	368
1968	244	310	316	126	121	104	465	384
1969	268	347	357	131	127	103	555	437
1970	283	363	445	143	137	104	695	507
1971	306	375	486	149	142	105	824	580
1972	319	440	456	154	150	106	1,021	681
1973	335	470	531	190	180	106	1,360	1,360
1974	363	474	608	250	263	95	1,777	655
1975	375	465	590	273	276	99	1,890	685
1976[a]	390	535	549	276	278	100	2,264	814

Source: Statistical Yearbook of Yugoslavia, 1976.
a. In 1972 prices.
b. $[(PE_t/PM_t)/(PE_0/PM_0)] \times 100$.
c. $NE_t = $ Export volume index $\times$ export price index (computed from absolute values).
d. $NE_t/(PM_t/PM_0)$.
e. Preliminary estimates.

Table A.20. Structure of Trade by Destination, 1956, 1961, and 1966–76
(percent)

	1956	1961	1966	1967	1968	1969	1970	1971	1972	1973	1974	1975	1976[a]
Exports													
OECD countries	65	53	48	52	52	56	56	53	57	56	47	36	42
EEC countries	41	39	32	34	33	38	39	36	36	36	27	23	27
Italy	14	12	14	18	14	15	15	12	14	16	11	9	12
Federal Republic of Germany	15	10	9	8	10	11	12	12	12	11	10	8	9
United States	6	6	6	6	7	6	5	6	7	8	8	7	7
Centrally planned economies	23	32	37	36	34	31	33	37	36	34	41	47	42
Soviet Union	13	9	16	17	16	14	14	15	15	14	18	25	23
Less developed countries	12	15	15	12	14	13	11	10	7	10	12	17	16
Imports													
OECD countries	66	71	56	63	64	65	69	66	65	63	61	61	55
EEC countries	30	41	32	44	44	45	46	44	44	42	40	41	39
Italy	9	15	11	13	15	15	13	12	12	12	12	11	10
Federal Republic of Germany	10	16	10	17	18	18	20	19	19	19	18	19	17
United States	27	20	13	7	5	4	6	6	6	4	5	5	5
Centrally planned economies	23	19	32	27	27	24	21	24	25	25	23	25	29
Soviet Union	15	4	9	10	11	8	8	9	9	9	10	10	14
Less developed countries	11	10	12	10	9	11	10	10	10	12	16	14	16

Sources: OECD, Statistics of Foreign Trade, Series B, various years; Federal Institute of Statistics, Yugoslavia 1945–1964

Table A.21. Structure of Exports, by End Use, 1954, 1960, and 1966–76
(percent)

End use	1954	1960	1966	1967	1968	1969	1970	1971	1972	1973	1974	1975	1976
Raw materials and semimanufactures	57.1	45.6	43.0	48.1	49.8	52.6	52.4	49.8	50.6	53.1	59.8	53.0	53.1
Raw materials and semiprocessed goods	52.1	37.0	29.0	33.9	35.7	37.3	36.2	33.3	33.5	35.8	42.6	34.4	33.2
Fuels	2.6	1.3	2.1	2.1	1.2	1.3	1.4	1.3	0.9	1.0	1.4	0.9	1.2
Semimanufactures	2.4	7.3	11.9	12.1	12.9	14.0	14.8	15.2	16.2	16.3	15.8	17.7	18.7
Capital goods	2.7	9.7	18.3	14.1	15.5	13.9	14.4	14.9	14.1	13.6	13.5	17.0	16.9
Agricultural machinery	...	0.3	1.6	1.4	1.2	0.8	0.7	0.6	0.6	0.3	0.3	0.3	0.6
Electrical motors and equipment	0.2	0.9	2.0	2.3	2.6	2.3	2.2	1.8	1.9	1.8	2.1	2.2	2.2
Transport equipment	2.3	5.9	11.3	7.0	8.8	7.9	9.0	8.5	8.4	8.5	7.6	9.4	8.2
Other	0.2	2.6	3.4	3.4	2.9	2.9	2.5	4.0	3.2	3.0	3.5	5.1	5.9
Consumer goods	40.2	44.7	38.7	37.8	34.7	33.5	33.2	35.3	35.3	33.3	26.7	30.0	30.0
Food	29.7	28.9	18.3	15.7	12.0	12.0	11.5	11.5	11.4	11.1	6.3	6.8	6.9
Beverages and tobacco	4.3	4.7	3.8	4.0	3.3	2.8	3.4	3.4	2.6	2.1	2.1	2.5	2.4
Clothing and footwear	0.2	2.6	7.6	9.8	9.9	9.1	8.4	9.3	10.4	8.7	7.7	9.5	9.4
Textiles[a]	2.2	2.9	2.9	2.9	3.1	3.0	2.5	2.6	2.6	2.9	2.3	2.5	3.0
Other	3.8	5.6	6.1	5.4	6.3	6.6	7.5	8.5	8.3	8.5	8.3	8.7	8.3
Total	100.0	100.0	100.0	100.0	100.0	100.0	100.0	100.0	100.0	100.0	100.0	100.0	100.0

... Zero or negligible.
Sources: Statistical Yearbook of Yugoslavia, various years.
a. Excludes clothing.

Table A.22. *Structure of Imports, by End Use, 1954, 1960, and 1966–76* (percent)

End use	1954	1960	1966	1967	1968	1969	1970	1971	1972	1973	1974	1975	1976
Raw materials and semimanufactures	51.9	56.8	57.5	57.2	56.9	60.2	63.2	63.7	63.2	62.2	69.7	65.6	63.7
Raw materials and semiprocessed goods	33.0	35.5	38.0	36.7	35.6	38.7	40.5	40.4	40.2	38.0	41.0	36.7	33.1
Fuels	9.1	5.5	5.2	5.0	5.5	4.8	4.8	5.9	5.5	7.9	12.6	12.2	14.6
Semimanufactures	9.8	15.8	14.3	15.5	15.8	16.7	17.9	17.6	17.5	16.3	16.1	16.7	16.0
Capital goods	22.2	28.5	21.8	21.7	24.9	22.3	21.4	21.0	21.3	22.3	17.4	24.5	23.9
Agricultural machinery	0.2	2.9	1.0	1.3	1.1	0.9	1.1	1.2	1.3	1.2	1.3	1.5	1.2
Electrical motors and equipment	2.8	2.7	2.2	2.1	2.5	2.7	2.3	2.2	2.2	1.9	1.6	2.3	2.7
Transport equipment	1.7	5.2	4.8	4.4	4.5	3.6	4.8	2.3	2.3	5.5	3.6	4.0	2.9
Other	17.5	17.7	13.8	13.9	16.8	15.1	13.2	15.3	15.5	13.7	10.9	16.7	17.1
Consumer goods	25.9	14.7	20.7	21.1	18.2	17.5	15.4	15.3	15.5	15.5	12.9	9.9	12.4
Food	23.8	8.1	12.8	8.9	4.7	4.5	4.1	5.3	6.4	7.5	5.9	3.5	6.8
Textiles[a]	0.1	2.2	3.2	3.7	4.6	4.1	3.3	2.2	3.0	2.3	2.0	1.9	1.5
Other	2.0	4.4	4.7	8.5	8.9	8.9	8.0	7.8	6.1	5.7	5.0	4.5	4.1
Total	100.0	100.0	100.0	100.0	100.0	100.0	100.0	100.0	100.0	100.0	100.0	100.0	100.0

Sources: Statistical Yearbook of Yugoslavia, various years.
a. Includes clothing and footwear.

Table A.23. *Structure of Exports, by Sector and Branch,*
1956, 1965, and 1975
(percent)

Sector or branch	1956	1965	1975
Total	100.0	100.0	100.0
Agriculture and forestry	29.4	18.8	9.0
Industry	70.6	81.2	91.0
Electrical power	0.1	...	0.1
Coal	0.8	...	0.2
Petroleum	0.7	0.9	0.5
Ferrous metallurgy	6.1	1.9	3.3
Nonferrous metallurgy	14.9	9.4	11.2
Nonmetallic mineral products	3.4	3.0	2.3
Metal products	2.5	15.0	18.3
Shipbuilding	1.9	7.2	7.5
Electrical equipment	1.7	5.7	8.5
Chemicals	3.3	5.0	10.3
Building materials	0.2	0.2	0.1
Wood products	13.4	8.8	6.6
Paper and paper products	1.0	1.7	1.4
Textiles	5.1	8.4	8.8
Leather and leather products	2.0	3.9	5.9
Rubber and rubber products	0.1	0.3	1.2
Food processing	4.3	6.3	2.6
Printing	...	0.3	0.4
Tobacco processing	6.0	3.2	1.8
Other	3.1	...	...

... Zero or negligible.
Sources: *Statistical Yearbook of Yugoslavia*, various years.

Table A.24. *Import Content of Production, by Sector and Branch,* *1966, 1968, 1970, and 1972*
(percent)

| Sector or branch | Total import content | | | | Direct import content, | Indirect import content, |
	1966	1968	1970	1972	1972	1972
Electric power	5.4	5.7	5.6	7.8	2.0	5.8
Coal	15.3	15.2	15.8	19.4	15.4	4.0
Petroleum	33.3	34.2	39.2	38.6	28.8	9.8
Ferrous metallurgy	22.9	23.2	27.3	28.4	17.5	10.8
Nonferrous metallurgy	21.4	26.5	37.9	39.0	26.4	12.6
Nonmetallic mineral products	9.8	12.3	14.3	16.8	9.4	7.4
Metal products	18.5	18.0	25.7	27.8	17.4	10.4
Shipbuilding	31.6	30.9	37.9	41.3	32.8	8.5
Electrical equipment	21.7	22.3	28.8	31.8	20.1	11.7
Chemicals	26.4	29.8	34.6	36.8	25.0	11.8
Building materials	7.6	7.8	10.5	13.5	6.0	7.5
Wood products	9.6	12.0	16.8	16.9	9.9	7.1
Paper and paper products	13.3	16.0	26.8	23.2	12.5	10.7
Textiles	27.7	29.1	29.8	30.7	19.1	11.6
Leather and leather products	23.7	24.0	37.0	30.0	17.8	12.2
Rubber and rubber products	39.2	31.0	35.7	39.6	31.5	8.1
Food processing	10.3	13.2	13.3	15.3	8.0	7.3
Printing	6.1	10.5	15.0	15.5	8.2	7.3
Tobacco processing	6.3	7.8	13.5	12.1	5.1	7.0
Films	7.5	9.3	17.5	17.1	13.9	3.2
Miscellaneous manufacturing	15.3	17.2	23.0	27.1	19.2	7.9
Agriculture	3.7	4.9	4.9	6.3	1.5	4.8
Forestry	2.0	1.9	2.7	2.8	0.9	1.9
Construction	6.4	7.1	9.8	10.1	2.5	7.6
Transport and communications	14.8	14.1	15.7	17.5	13.2	4.3
Trade and tourism	1.3	1.4	1.6	1.8	0.3	1.5
Handicrafts	10.0	9.7	11.0	12.0	3.4	8.6
Public relations	4.7	5.0	6.7	7.2	2.1	5.1

Sources: Figures for 1966, 1968, 1970, and 1972 were respectively calculated from Federal Institute of Statistics, *Studies, Analyses, and Reviews,* nos. 50 (Belgrade, 1970), 57 (Belgrade, 1971), 71 (Belgrade, 1975), and 80–81 (Belgrade, 1976).

Table A.25. *Ratio of Imports to Domestic Supply,
by Sector and Branch, Selected Years, 1962–75*
(percent)

Sector or branch	1962	1966	1968	1970	1972	1975
Electric power	...	0.8	1.1	0.9	0.2	0.8
Coal	13.3	13.1	11.8	13.9	16.4	20.0
Petroleum	22.5	28.0	30.7	30.9	29.7	33.8
Ferrous metallurgy	15.7	22.9	18.3	32.9	30.2	23.2
Nonferrous metallurgy	6.2	9.4	13.3	26.4	32.1	12.7
Nonmetallic mineral products	15.9	22.1	24.5	27.3	29.0	19.6
Metal products	28.1	28.7	35.1	36.2	36.3	27.1
Shipbuilding	7.4	15.1	16.5	15.9	5.7	16.1
Electrical equipment	16.6	19.4	20.7	21.6	20.1	17.9
Chemicals	26.7	26.4	27.5	28.2	29.7	26.0
Building materials	0.1	3.0	3.4	8.9	6.5	0.5
Wood products	0.6	1.3	2.2	5.2	4.7	3.5
Paper and paper products	5.5	6.0	10.8	18.8	12.6	13.1
Textiles	7.8	8.6	11.0	11.0	10.7	10.4
Leather and leather products	0.4	0.8	5.9	10.0	5.8	4.8
Rubber and rubber products	12.7	27.5	27.2	24.3	29.0	20.1
Food processing	8.0	6.5	6.5	7.0	8.7	5.4
Printing	2.0	3.1	3.9	2.1	2.1	2.6
Tobacco processing	3.4	1.3	0.7	2.7	3.1	0.9
Films	3.4	3.8	3.6	6.1	5.1	12.4
Agriculture	9.4	9.2	6.0	5.8	7.3	3.9
Forestry	0.9	2.9	3.0	7.8	7.8	10.7

... Zero or negligible.
Sources: Figures for 1975 calculated from *Statistical Yearbook of Yugoslavia,
1976*; all others from *Studies, Analyses, and Reviews*, nos. 50, 57, 71, and 80–81.

Table A.26. Foreign Investment, by Sector and Branch, January 31, 1974

Sector or branch	Number of contracts	Investment by Yugoslav partner	Investment by foreign partner (millions of dollars)	Total investment	Share of foreign partner (percent)	Composition of foreign investment (percent)
Petroleum	1	5.4	5.2	10.7	49.0	3.8
Ferrous metallurgy	4	239.6	5.3	244.8	2.2	3.8
Nonferrous metallurgy	2	31.4	3.4	34.7	9.7	2.5
Nonmetallic mineral products	4	9.2	4.6	13.8	33.6	3.4
Metal products	31	194.3	63.4	257.7	24.6	46.2
Electrical equipment	11	50.4	8.3	58.7	14.1	6.0
Chemicals	17	46.7	21.4	68.1	31.5	15.6
Building materials	3	0.5	0.3	0.8	37.0	0.2
Wood products	1	8.6	1.8	10.3	17.0	1.3
Paper and paper products	5	34.7	6.5	41.2	15.8	4.7
Textiles	4	1.2	1.2	2.4	49.3	0.9
Rubber and rubber products	4	21.2	10.5	31.7	33.0	7.6
Food processing	3	7.0	1.1	8.1	13.4	0.8
Printing	1	0.1	0.1	0.3	49.0	0.1
Tobacco processing	1	0.2	0.1	0.3	40.0	0.1
Agriculture	1	0.2	0.2	0.3	49.0	0.1
Construction	1	6.5	2.8	9.4	30.1	2.0
Trade and tourism	3	7.4	1.2	8.6	13.5	0.8
Total	97	664.6	137.3	801.9	17.1	100.0

Note: Figures may not reconcile because of rounding.
Source: OECD, Foreign Investment in Yugoslavia (Paris: OECD, 1974).

Table A.27. Labor Force, by Category of Employment, 1961 and 1966–75
(thousands of workers)

Employment category	1961	1966	1967	1968	1969	1970	1971	1972	1973	1974	1975
Social sector	3,170	3,500	3,466	3,485	3,622	3,756	3,966	4,130	4,222	4,421	4,650
Private agriculture	4,755	4,420	4,473	4,368	4,095	3,816	3,545	3,350	3,145	2,997	2,914
Private nonagriculture	230	260	269	280	290	301	310	322	334	346	359
Resident active labor force	8,155	8,180	8,208	8,133	8,007	7,873	7,821	7,802	7,701	7,764	7,923
Migrant workers	n.a.	275	296	401	572	783	913	1,020	1,100	1,050	900
Migrant workers in Europe	70	210	220	230	430	550	660	760	830	790	780
Active labor force	8,225	8,455	8,504	8,534	8,579	8,656	8,734	8,822	8,801	8,814	8,823
Unemployed[a]	115	155	161	187	198	192	175	189	229	269	324
Labor force	8,340	8,610	8,665	8,721	8,777	8,848	8,909	9,011	9,030	9,083	9,147

n.a. Not available.
Sources: Social sector employment from Statistical Yearbook of Yugoslavia, various years; private agricultural and nonagricultural employment from estimates by the World Bank; migrant workers from estimates by the Federal Secretariat for Employment; migrant workers in Europe from estimates by the Center for Migration Studies in Zagreb; labor force from Milica Sentic and Dusan Breznik, "Projeckcije ukupnog i aktivnog stanovnistva Jugoslavije sa migracionom komponentom [Projections of the Total and Active Population of Yugoslavia, including Migration]," Stanovnistvo [Population], vol. 10, nos. 3–4, vol. 11, nos. 1–2 (July–December 1972—January–June 1973), pp. 137–76.
a. Estimated as being 60 percent of the workers registered as unemployed.

Table A.28. *Labor Force, by Category of Employment and Region, 1971*
(thousands of workers)

Employment category	Bosnia-Herzegovina	Kosovo	Macedonia	Montenegro	Croatia	Serbia	Slovenia	Vojvodina	Total
Social sector	539	103	270	89	974	1,015	553	423	3,966
Private agriculture[a]	577	164	238	67	634	1,424	151	293	3,545
Private nonagriculture[b]	44	9	14	4	86	67	54	32	310
Resident active labor force	1,160	276	522	160	1,694	2,506	758	748	7,821
Migrant workers[b]	196	33	76	10	300	156	71	71	913
Active labor force	1,355	309	598	170	1,994	2,662	829	819	8,734
Unemployed[c]	19	14	34	3	25	52	9	16	175
Labor force	1,374	323	632	173	2,019	2,714	838	835	8,909

Sources: Same as for table A.27.
a. Determined as a residual.
b. Regional allocation based on total population in the census.
c. Estimated as being 60 percent of the workers registered as unemployed.

Table A.29. *Employment in the Social Sector, by Type of Activity and Economic Sector and Branch, Selected Years, 1966–75*

Type of activity, sector, or branch	1966	1968	1970	1971	1972	1973	1974	1975
Productive activities	2,907.6	2,882.4	3,103.9	3,283.2	3,416.2	3,480.0	3,641.4	3,828.2
Industry and mining	1,425.3	1,395.1	1,507.9	1,591.4	1,653.6	1,708.6	1,777.9	1,866.3
Electric power	35.0	37.4	40.2	42.6	45.3	46.0	48.0	54.9
Coal	78.3	65.0	56.8	55.8	58.6	54.1	55.1	59.8
Petroleum	8.5	9.4	10.8	12.0	13.0	13.9	14.1	15.0
Ferrous metallurgy	43.3	39.9	39.9	50.7	53.0	54.0	55.1	55.8
Nonferrous metallurgy	42.4	43.0	44.7	47.9	46.6	49.2	49.0	49.4
Nonmetallic mineral products	45.4	43.7	46.6	47.3	49.2	50.4	49.8	51.9
Metal products	273.6	265.9	306.6	323.2	334.3	343.8	361.9	382.9
Shipbuilding	20.6	20.5	22.4	23.2	23.7	24.2	25.1	25.0
Electrical equipment	73.5	74.4	87.9	91.8	96.6	103.3	110.1	116.1
Chemicals	67.7	70.9	80.6	85.8	91.4	93.2	96.4	100.9
Building materials	72.3	71.9	76.8	76.5	77.6	79.4	82.6	84.9
Wood products	145.7	135.0	142.5	149.8	154.2	158.3	162.0	172.1

(*Table continues on the following page*)

Table A.29 (*continued*)

Type of activity, sector, or branch	1966	1968	1970	1971	1972	1973	1974	1975
Paper and paper products	26.5	26.6	29.5	32.1	31.9	31.5	35.0	35.2
Textiles	230.4	230.6	245.3	257.9	273.5	286.6	298.0	315.4
Leather and leather products	49.9	50.0	53.5	57.6	62.8	65.5	68.1	71.1
Rubber and rubber products	14.9	16.3	18.2	19.4	20.7	21.9	23.5	22.7
Food processing	125.6	123.7	133.9	142.9	145.4	155.1	164.1	168.3
Printing	42.0	44.4	47.0	49.7	51.0	52.1	53.7	57.1
Tobacco processing	19.5	16.6	15.3	15.3	15.6	16.4	16.2	17.1
Other	10.1	10.5	9.2	10.0	9.0	9.6	9.3	10.8
Agriculture	238.0	207.9	188.7	185.9	196.0	183.8	187.9	192.7
Forestry	73.1	63.1	58.6	60.1	59.9	58.9	60.4	59.6
Construction	433.7	454.3	498.5	526.7	533.6	516.4	544.6	581.3
Transport and communications	253.1	247.5	269.5	285.0	290.5	294.8	309.9	315.4
Trade and catering	412.6	444.0	501.8	549.5	593.1	619.9	654.6	689.0
Handicrafts	56.9	53.7	60.0	65.6	70.9	78.1	84.6	102.3
Other	14.9	16.8	18.9	18.9	18.6	19.5	21.5	21.6
Nonproductive activities	592.0	603.0	652.0	683.0	714.0	742.0	780.0	822.0
Total	3,499.6	3,485.4	3,755.9	3,966.2	4,130.0	4,222.0	4,421.4	4,650.2

Sources: Federal Institute of Statistics, *Statistical Bulletin*, nos. 744 (October 1972), 767 (January 1973), 773 (February 1973), 830 (December 1973), 889 (December 1974), 954 (December 1975), and 1017 (January 1977).

Table A.30. *Growth of Employment, Value Added,
Productivity, and Real Earnings, 1965–76*
(percent)

Year or period	Employment	Annual rate of real growth		
		Value added	Productivity	Real earnings
1965	1.5	3.6	2.1	2.3
1966	−2.2	5.3	7.5	12.4
1967	−0.6	2.4	3.0	5.4
1968	0.1	5.3	5.2	3.8
1969	3.3	9.6	6.3	7.4
1970	3.9	7.8	3.9	5.7
1971	4.8	9.1	4.3	6.5
1972	4.4	5.0	0.6	1.0
1973	2.3	4.3	2.0	−5.1
1974	4.8	9.5	4.7	6.4
1975	5.4	4.0	−1.4	−1.0
1976[a]	4.0	4.0	0.0	4.0
1965–70	1.0	6.1	5.1	6.9
1970–75	4.3	6.4	2.1	1.5

Source: Statistical Yearbook of Yugoslavia, 1976.
a. Estimates.

Table A.31. *Gross Income, Active Labor Force, and Income per Worker in Private Agriculture, Selected Years, 1966–75*

	Gross income (millions of dinars)		Active labor force (thousands of workers)	Average annual income per worker (dinars)		Cost of living index (1966 = 100)	Average annual agricultural income per worker (1966 dinars)
Year	Agricultural activities	Agricultural and non-agricultural activities		Agricultural activities	Agricultural and non-agricultural activities		
1966	15,046	17,044	4,420	3,400	3,860	100	3,400
1968	14,063	16,155	4,368	3,220	3,700	112	2,880
1970	18,011	20,519	3,816	4,720	5,380	131	3,600
1971	21,150	24,376	3,545	5,970	6,880	151	3,950
1972	25,995	29,887	3,350	7,760	8,920	174	4,460
1973	32,729	37,483	3,145	10,410	11,920	207	5,030
1974	40,800	47,026	2,997	13,610	15,690	260	5,230
1975	45,699	53,274	2,914	15,683	18,282	329	4,767

Sources: Figures supplied by the Federal Institute of Statistics, and World Bank estimates of the active labor force in agriculture.

Table A.32. *Remittances and Foreign Exchange Deposits by Yugoslav Workers Abroad, 1964–75*

Year	Yugoslav workers abroad	Yugoslav workers in Western Europe	Remittances (millions of dollars)	Remittances per worker abroad (dollars)	Foreign exchange deposits held in Yugoslavia (millions of dollars)
1964	138,000	115,000	31	225	n.a.
1965	174,000	140,000	32	184	n.a.
1966	275,000	210,000	64	233	38
1967	296,000	220,000	89	301	57
1968	401,000	230,000	122	304	80
1969	572,000	430,000	206	360	134
1970	783,000	550,000	441	563	269
1971	913,000	660,000	652	714	528
1972	1,020,000	760,000	868	851	746
1973	1,100,000	830,000	1,310	1,191	1,129
1974	1,050,000	790,000	1,512	1,440	1,512
1975	900,000	780,000[a]	1,575	1,750	2,063

n.a. Not available.

Sources: Workers abroad from estimates by the Federal Secretariat for Employment; workers in Western Europe from estimates by the Center for Migration Studies in Zagreb; remittances and foreign exchange deposits from figures supplied by NBY.

a. Interpolated from a year-end estimate of 770,000.

Table A.33. *Population and Active Labor Force,*
by Region and Sex, 1975, 1980, and 1985

Region or sex	Population (thousands of persons)			Average annual percentage rate of change[a]		
	1975	1980	1985	1970–75	1975–80	1980–85
Bosnia-Herzegovina	3,865.3	4,030.6	4,197.3	0.86	0.84	0.81
Male	1,896.6	1,982.8	2,070.7			
Female	1,968.6	2,047.8	2,126.6			
Kosovo	1,356.6	1,522.6	1,707.2	2.26	2.34	2.32
Male	695.4	781.1	876.4			
Female	661.2	741.4	830.8			
Macedonia	1,752.7	1,882.1	2,005.2	1.51	1.43	1.28
Male	888.3	953.8	1,015.9			
Female	864.4	928.3	989.3			
Montenegro	544.1	568.1	591.2	0.78	0.87	0.80
Male	267.2	279.8	292.1			
Female	276.9	288.3	299.0			
Croatia	4,501.6	4,595.1	4,678.9	0.41	0.41	0.36
Male	2,179.3	2,231.3	2,281.2			
Female	2,322.3	2,363.8	2,397.7			
Serbia	5,417.9	5,592.3	5,726.4	0.72	0.64	0.48
Male	2,673.4	2,763.8	2,833.8			
Female	2,744.4	2,828.5	2,892.6			
Slovenia	1,781.4	1,845.7	1,907.8	0.71	0.71	0.66
Male	863.9	898.1	932.8			
Female	917.5	947.5	975.0			
Vojvodina	1,998.0	2,044.6	2,082.3	0.51	0.46	0.37
Male	974.6	998.7	1,019.0			
Female	1,023.5	1,045.9	1,063.3			
Yugoslavia	21,217.5	22,081.1	22,896.4	0.82	0.80	0.73
Male	10,438.6	10,889.4	11,322.0			
Female	10,779.0	11,191.6	11,574.4			

Note: Migration is taken into account.
Source: Sentic and Breznik, "Projections of the Total and Active Population of Yugoslavia, including Migration."
a. Rates for males and females were not calculated because of their near equivalence with rates for republics.

Active labor force (thousands of persons)			Average annual percentage rate of change			
1975	1980	1985	1970–75	1975–80	1980–85	Region or sex
1,456.6	1,553.8	1,615.0	1.49	1.30	0.78	Bosnia-Herzegovina
991.8	1,052.2	1,091.1	1.33	1.19	0.73	Male
464.7	501.6	523.9	1.84	1.54	0.87	Female
357.9	410.0	474.9	2.55	2.76	2.98	Kosovo
293.3	323.9	361.3	1.82	2.01	2.21	Male
64.6	86.1	113.6	6.34	5.91	5.70	Female
671.9	716.8	755.3	1.54	1.30	1.05	Macedonia
467.0	495.9	520.3	1.42	1.21	0.97	Male
204.9	220.8	235.0	1.83	1.51	1.25	Female
184.6	198.4	208.6	1.55	1.45	1.00	Montenegro
126.9	136.0	142.1	1.41	1.40	0.88	Male
57.6	62.4	66.5	1.79	1.61	1.28	Female
2,041.6	2,089.0	2,051.9	0.29	0.46	−0.36	Croatia
1,254.8	1,264.7	1,253.5	0.26	0.16	−0.18	Male
786.8	824.3	798.4	0.33	0.94	−0.64	Female
2,726.9	2,714.8	2,650.1	0.13	−0.09	−0.48	Serbia
1,653.1	1,652.6	1,616.8	0.20	−0.01	−0.44	Male
1,073.8	1,062.3	1,033.4	0.01	−0.22	−0.55	Female
848.3	859.1	866.6	0.31	0.25	0.17	Slovenia
482.8	492.0	498.6	0.46	0.38	0.27	Male
365.6	367.2	368.0	0.12	0.09	0.04	Female
859.9	882.1	893.9	0.70	0.51	0.27	Vojvodina
581.0	589.8	589.5	0.49	0.30	−0.01	Male
277.9	292.3	304.3	1.16	1.02	0.81	Female
9,146.8	9,424.0	9,516.3	0.67	0.60	0.20	Yugoslavia
5,850.7	6,007.1	6,073.2	0.65	0.53	0.22	Male
3,296.0	3,417.0	3,443.1	0.69	0.72	0.15	Female

Table A.34. *Elasticities of Employment to Gross Output and Fixed Assets in the Social Sector, by Sector and Branch, 1956–65 and 1968–74*

| Sector or branch | Employment to gross output | | | |
| | 1956–65 | | 1968–74 | |
	Elasticity	R^2	Elasticity	R^2
Industry	0.54	0.99	0.49	0.99
Electric power	0.50	0.93	0.41	0.99
Coal	−0.28	0.57	−0.67	0.48
Petroleum	0.27	0.66	0.80	0.94
Ferrous metallurgy	0.34	0.88	0.71	0.83
Nonferrous metallurgy	0.15	0.76	0.29	0.74
Nonmetallic mineral products	0.47	0.94	0.29	0.88
Metal products	0.63	0.99	0.57	0.99
Shipbuilding	0.32	0.61	0.52	0.61
Electrical equipment	0.64	0.99	0.60	0.96
Chemicals	0.54	0.99	0.38	0.99
Building materials	0.37	0.79	0.25	0.91
Wood products	0.56	0.98	0.40	0.97
Paper and paper products	0.49	0.96	0.51	0.86
Textiles	0.75	0.99	0.65	0.99
Leather and leather products	0.65	0.99	0.96	0.97
Rubber and rubber products	0.68	0.95	0.60	0.97
Food processing	0.72	0.97	0.56	0.97
Printing	0.95	0.97	0.53	0.88
Tobacco processing	0.52	0.59	0.13[a]	−0.01
Construction	0.50	0.97	0.75	0.94
Transport and communication	0.63	0.98	0.48	0.95
Trade and catering	n.a.	n.a.	n.a.	n.a.
Handicrafts	n.a.	n.a.	n.a.	n.a.

n.a. Not available.
Sources: Statistical Yearbook of Yugoslavia, various years.

| | Employment to fixed assets | | | |
| | 1956–65 | | 1968–74 | |
Sector or branch	Elasticity	R^2	Elasticity	R^2
Industry	0.65	0.97	0.50	0.99
Electric power	0.61	0.93	0.52	0.98
Coal	−0.19	0.58	−0.54[a]	0.73
Petroleum	0.54	0.74	0.64	0.81
Ferrous metallurgy	0.38	0.82	1.05	0.82
Nonferrous metallurgy	0.14	0.68	0.25	0.72
Nonmetallic mineral products	0.81	0.90	0.28	0.88
Metal products	0.92	0.94	0.52	0.89
Shipbuilding	0.81	0.79	0.46	0.89
Electrical equipment	1.15	0.97	0.63	0.98
Chemicals	0.75	0.96	0.67	0.98
Building materials	0.46	0.65	0.21	0.86
Wood products	0.84	0.94	0.31	0.98
Paper and paper products	0.49	0.96	0.60	0.88
Textiles	0.74	0.94	0.49	0.99
Leather and leather products	0.76	0.95	0.49	0.98
Rubber and rubber products	n.a.	n.a.	0.61	0.99
Food processing	0.86	0.96	0.56	0.96
Printing	0.82	0.81	0.44	˙0.88
Tobacco processing	n.a.	n.a.	−0.02[a]	−0.19
Construction	0.36	0.77	0.25	0.83
Transport and communication	1.09	0.98	0.57	0.96
Trade and catering	0.53	0.92	0.54	0.97
Handicrafts	0.22	0.67	0.90	0.99

a. Not statistically significant at the 95 percent level of confidence.

Table A.35. Elasticity of Employment to Value Added in the Social Sector in Constant 1972 Prices, by Region, 1969–75

Region	Industry		Construction		Transport and communication		Trade and catering		Total[a]	
	Elasticity	R²	Elasticity	R²	Elasticity	R²	Elasticity	R²	Elasticity	R²
Bosnia-Herzegovina	0.76	0.99	1.55	0.98	0.29	0.52	1.19	0.95	0.86	0.99
Kosovo	0.84	0.99	0.58	0.81	0.86	0.94	1.34	0.95	0.86	0.99
Macedonia	0.90	0.96	0.96[b]	−0.15	0.83	0.95	1.3	0.93	0.94	0.98
Montenegro	1.1	0.67	0.42[b]	0.07	0.1[b]	...	0.90	0.99	0.94	0.91
Croatia	0.48	0.98	0.58	0.69	0.53	0.94	1.0	0.97	0.56	0.97
Serbia	0.43	0.99	0.44	0.41	0.71	0.95	1.1	0.96	0.58	0.97
Slovenia	0.51	0.99	0.53	0.96	0.60	0.99	1.0	0.97	0.60	0.99
Vojvodina	0.50	0.97	0.37	0.44	0.19	0.44	0.55	0.92	0.36	0.91
Yugoslavia	0.56	0.99	0.75	0.94	0.54	0.97	1.02	0.97	0.63	0.99

... Zero or negligible.
Sources: Statistical Yearbook of Yugoslavia, various years.
a. Total for productive activities.
b. Not statistically significant at the 95 percent level of confidence.

Table A.36. Population and Average Annual Rate of Increase, by Region, 1948, 1961, 1971, and 1975

Region	Thousands of persons				Percentage composition				Average annual increase per thousand persons		
	1948	1961	1971	1975	1948	1961	1971	1975	1948–61	1961–71	1971–75
Less developed regions	4,827	6,120	7,167	7,696	30.3	33.3	35.0	36.0	18.4	15.9	16.9
Bosnia-Herzegovina	2,564	3,278	3,746	3,977	16.2	17.7	18.3	18.6	19.1	13.4	14.4
Kosovo	733	964	1,244	1,405	4.6	5.2	6.1	6.6	21.3	25.8	28.6
Macedonia	1,153	1,406	1,406	1,756	7.2	7.6	8.0	8.2	15.4	15.9	15.1
Montenegro	377	472	530	558	2.3	2.5	2.6	2.6	17.4	11.7	12.3
More developed regions	11,015	12,430	13,356	13,656	69.7	67.0	65.0	64.0	9.3	7.2	5.4
Croatia	3,780	4,160	4,426	4,509	23.9	22.4	21.6	21.1	7.4	6.2	4.4
Serbia	4,154	4,823	5,250	5,393	26.2	26.0	25.6	25.3	11.6	8.5	6.6
Slovenia	1,440	1,592	1,727	1,778	9.1	8.6	8.4	8.3	7.8	8.2	6.9
Vojvodina	1,641	1,855	1,953	1,976	10.4	10.0	9.5	9.3	9.5	5.2	3.1
Yugoslavia	15,842	18,550	20,523	21,352	100.0	100.0	100.0	100.0	12.2	10.2	9.5

Note: Figures for 1975 are based on projections; all other figures are from census data.
Sources: Statistical Yearbook of Yugoslavia, 1975 and 1976.

Table A.37. *Household Income per Capita, by Region, 1973*

Region	All households		Agricultural households		Mixed agricultural and nonagricultural households		Nonagricultural households	
	Thousands of persons	Dinars per capita	Thousands of persons	Dinars per capita	Thousands of persons	Dinars per capita	Thousands of persons	Dinars per capita
Less developed regions	7,716	7,243	2,030	5,811	2,925	6,552	2,774	9,005
Bosnia-Herzegovina	4,007	7,643	1,096	6,104	1,615	6,735	1,319	10,028
Kosovo	1,394	4,967	392	3,892	552	4,780	443	6,154
Macedonia	1,809	7,835	459	8,752	562	7,329	783	8,824
Montenegro	506	8,224	83	5,795	196	7,805	229	9,458
More developed regions	13,915	11,612	2,923	7,883	4,350	10,456	6,569	14,066
Croatia	4,634	12,579	822	8,503	1,641	11,244	2,192	15,160
Serbia	5,546	10,040	1,457	6,928	1,619	8,596	2,798	12,872
Slovenia	1,805	15,060	180	10,630	568	13,567	1,047	16,642
Vojvodina	1,930	10,581	464	8,716	557	10,370	932	11,670
Yugoslavia	21,561	10,052	4,928	7,034	7,220	8,904	9,394	12,549

Note: Totals and subtotals may not reconcile because of rounding errors in data on family size.
Source: Federal Institute of Statistics, *Statistical Bulletin,* no. 833 (March 1974).

Table A.38. *Distribution of Household Income per Member of Household, for Eleven Groups of Equal Frequency, by Region, 1973*
(dinars)

Region	Average income per member of household[a]										
	1	2	3	4	5	6	7	8	9	10	11
Yugoslavia	2,581 (0.9)	4,647 (3.5)	5,390 (11.4)	6,176 (22.2)	6,912 (34.6)	8,484 (57.0)	10,761 (73.1)	12,892 (83.9)	15,499 (89.9)	17,300 (93.8)	22,201 (99.3)
Bosnia-Herzegovina	2,113 (0.9)	3,220 (5.2)	4,074 (13.4)	4,902 (26.6)	5,872 (40.9)	6,926 (67.5)	9,287 (82.2)	10,845 (90.4)	14,290 (94.8)	15,771 (97.2)	17,909 (98.0)
Kosovo	1,802 (0.7)	2,294 (5.1)	2,756 (15.5)	3,499 (29.4)	4,089 (40.4)	4,886 (60.8)	5,537 (74.2)	6,654 (74.2)	7,204 (89.6)	7,230 (93.5)	8,548 (99.8)
Macedonia	2,352 (0.5)	3,431 (3.1)	3,778 (13.8)	4,809 (27.9)	5,600 (43.6)	7,517 (63.7)	8,855 (78.9)	16,230 (88.3)	11,217 (91.9)	18,414 (93.2)	20,009 (99.6)
Montenegro	2,937 (0.8)	5,725 (4.1)	5,395 (10.7)	5,661 (22.7)	5,977 (38.0)	7,377 (69.3)	9,418 (84.0)	11,586 (91.6)	13,244 (96.5)	16,212 (97.7)	21,533 (100.9)
Croatia	3,325 (0.6)	7,117 (3.5)	7,585 (8.4)	8,044 (15.4)	8,675 (25.7)	10,045 (47.4)	12,170 (65.5)	14,153 (78.6)	17,030 (87.3)	18,418 (92.7)	26,929 (99.5)
Serbia	3,176 (0.9)	4,928 (4.5)	5,383 (12.3)	6,377 (24.8)	7,271 (37.8)	8,877 (60.1)	10,996 (75.3)	13,522 (85.7)	16,051 (91.1)	17,910 (94.8)	21,109 (99.4)
Slovenia	3,604 (0.3)	6,691 (1.8)	10,003 (4.3)	11,022 (9.1)	10,445 (15.2)	10,865 (31.6)	12,625 (52.1)	15,223 (68.6)	16,637 (79.2)	19,418 (86.3)	25,517 (99.6)
Vojvodina	2,429 (2.3)	5,657 (7.6)	7,165 (15.5)	7,445 (27.6)	7,740 (41.2)	9,600 (65.5)	11,693 (82.2)	15,094 (92.2)	18,287 (95.8)	19,393 (99.0)	32,432 (101.4)

Source: Statistical Bulletin, no. 833.
a. Cumulative percentages of the population, shown in parentheses, do not reconcile because of sampling and rounding errors.

Table A.39. Federal Fund and Federal Budget Transfers, by Region, 1974

Region	Federal budget trans- fers	Contri- butions to Federal Fund (billions of dinars)	Receipts from Federal Fund Gross	Receipts from Federal Fund Net	Ratio of transfers and net receipts to GMP (per- cent)	Trans- fers and net receipts per capita (dinars)	Ratio of net receipts to invest- ment[a]	Ratio of total invest- ment to GMP[b] (percent)	Productive investment in the social sector Per capita (dinars)	Productive investment in the social sector Percent- age of Yugoslav average
Less developed regions	3,380	1,465	6,618	5,153	9.3	1,127	23.5	38.3	2,836	84
Bosnia- Herzegovina	1,357	824	2,146	1,322	5.2	683	11.1	39.3	3,022	89
Kosovo	1,056	132	2,200c	2,068	34.5	2,287	71.7	51.0	2,112	62
Macedonia	619	383	1,515	1,132	7.4	1,012	27.0	28.2	2,420	71
Montenegro	348	126	757	631	12.9	1,774	27.3	47.3	4,605	136
More devel- oped regions	—	5,153	—	—	—	—	−10.2	26.8	3,702	109
Croatia	—	1,780	—	—	—	—	−11.1	25.4	3,582	106
Serbia	—	1,528	—	—	—	—	−10.7	25.4	2,672	79
Slovenia	—	1,152	—	—	—	—	−9.2	31.8	7,069	208
Vojvodina	—	693	—	—	—	—	−9.4	25.8	3,756	111
Yugoslavia	—	6,618	—	—	—	—	—	29.4	3,392	100

— Not applicable.
Source: Calculated by the World Bank on the basis of published GMP data and legal provisions for mobilization on allocation, expressed as percentages of GMP.
a. Investment here refers to investment in productive activities in the social sector.
b. Total investment was disaggregated by region on the basis of each region's share in investment in productive activities in th

Glossary

Administrative socialism. A socialist system in which the economy is controlled in all its aspects by the centralized government or its administrative agencies and in which minor and short-run decisions are, at best, delegated to ENTERPRISES. It is largely identical with what frequently is referred to in Yugoslavia as STATE CAPITALISM.

Alienation. The Marxian term to characterize what in the Yugoslav perception is manifest when the WORKERS control neither the MEANS OF PRODUCTION with which they work, nor the results of their work, including the distribution of INCOME (between WORKERS and ENTERPRISE FUNDS and among WORKERS) and the allocation of undistributed parts of income for specific investment purposes. According to this concept ALIENATION prevails under capitalism as well as ADMINISTRATIVE SOCIALISM.

Anonymous financial capital. The Yugoslav term to characterize a situation in which large blocks of the socially owned financial assets are de jure or de facto controlled by BANKS, which use this control to control the fate of an ECONOMIC ORGANIZATION indebted to them.

Associated bank. See BANK.

Association. The Yugoslav term for consultative bodies formed along the lines of industrial branches within a region—that is, within a province, a republic, or the federation. All ENTERPRISES are, by law, members of an association.

Association of labor. A Yugoslav term used in two overlapping meanings: as a broad, generic term synonymous with SELF-MANAGEMENT socialism; in a narrow sense to characterize the relations of workers within a BOAL.

Association of labor and resources. See POOLING OF LABOR AND RESOURCES and POOLING OF RESOURCES.

Bank. Under the Yugoslav legal system banks are neither BOALS nor ENTERPRISES, but WORK COMMUNITIES. There are two principal practical differences associated with this status: first, all decisions by banks are made not by the WORKERS of the bank, but by their members, the depositing or borrowing ECONOMIC ORGANIZATIONS that jointly carry the liability for all bank obligations; second, banks do not accumulate financial assets from INCOME, nor are they expected to generate INCOME for their members.

With the promulgation of the new law on banking, business banks are replaced by a three-layer banking system. Internal banks operate within an ENTERPRISE or COMPOSITE ORGANIZATION OF ASSOCIATED LABOR; their main function is to administer POOLING OF LABOR AND RESOURCES and POOLING OF RESOURCES among member BOALS or ENTERPRISES. Basic banks are all-purpose banks largely carrying over the activities of the former business banks. Associated banks specialize in such areas as foreign trade and investment in particular sectors.

Basic bank. See BANK.

Basic proportions. The Yugoslav term used in connection with SOCIAL PLANNING. It refers to such broad macroeconomic categories as investment ratios and sectoral shares in GMP.

Basic organization of associated labor (BOAL). The BOAL is the basic unit in which the ASSOCIATION OF LABOR takes place. The locus of all economic decisionmaking, the BOAL is an autonomous legal entity having its own INCOME statement and balance sheet. Within an ENTERPRISE the BOAL is the smallest distinguishable technological entity producing a marketed or marketable output.

BOAL. See BASIC ORGANIZATION OF ASSOCIATED LABOR.

Business bank. See BANK.

Business community. See ORGANIZATION OF ASSOCIATED LABOR.

Chamber of the economy. All ASSOCIATIONS of a province, republic, or the federation constitute a chamber of the economy. It is not only a consultative body; it also has certain quasi-legislative functions, insofar as it prepares and signs SOCIAL COMPACTS with SOCIO-POLITICAL COMMUNITIES and trade unions on behalf of consenting members (ENTERPRISES).

COAL. See CONTRACTUAL ORGANIZATION OF ASSOCIATED LABOR.

Collective consumption. The Yugoslav term for consumption financed not from personal income but from the pool of social income. At the microeconomic level it includes housing funds, holiday facilities, and family allowances financed from ENTERPRISE INCOME. At the macroeconomic level it includes health and education services provided by COMMUNITIES OF INTEREST.

Commune. The basic unit of decisionmaking in the sociopolitical sphere; its counterpart in the economic sphere is the BOAL.

Community for planning and business cooperation. See ORGANIZATION OF ASSOCIATED LABOR.

Community of interest. The Yugoslav term for an organization comprising both users and suppliers of particular services; in most instances the users and suppliers are themselves organizations of one form or another. The community of interest regulates all matters concerning short-term and long-term supply and demand, including investment credits. It thus transcends both the market mechanism and the state as regulators. Communities of interest are obligatory for education, health, science, and culture; they are increasingly being used in areas governed by increasing returns to scale and monopoly, such as railways, public utilities, and electric power generation and distribution.

Given the principle of DECENTRALIZATION, a community of interest is organized on the smallest regional scale possible under particular circumstances. Because of the explicit exclusion of any concept of market, the transactions between members of the community of interest are referred to as FREE EXCHANGES OF LABOR, although the flows usually are goods and services in one direction and monetary compensation in the other.

Composite organization of associated labor. The Yugoslav term for an organization in which several ENTERPRISES have agreed to collaborate in accord with a SELF-MANAGEMENT AGREEMENT. That agreement generally covers the POOLING OF LABOR AND RESOURCES or the POOLING OF RESOURCES. An ENTERPRISE can be a member of several composite organizations.

Contractual organization of associated labor (COAL). The Yugoslav term for a particular organizational form in which individual private owners of MEANS OF PRODUCTION agree among each other on the POOLING OF LABOR AND RESOURCES. The COAL is considered to be a transitional phase from private enterprise to associated labor.

Decentralization. Under the prevailing Yugoslav usage, and in this report, the term applies to the process of rearranging political and general economic decisionmaking power to the lowest level of

SOCIOPOLITICAL COMMUNITY in which such decisions can reasonably be made. The term is also used in a broader sense that encompasses DESTATIZATION and is close to the use of the term common in other socialist countries.

Delegate system. The Yugoslav term to denote the particular form of citizen or WORKER participation under SELF-MANAGEMENT. Delegates are elected at the level of the smallest unit within a COMMUNE or BOAL and in turn elect delegates at the next broader level, and so on. Delegates have strictly limited terms. They do not give up their prior status as WORKERS; they must solicit the views of their constituency on any important issues on which they will vote; they can be recalled at any time if the constituency decides that its views or interests are not being adequately represented.

Democratic centralism. The Leninist principle characterizing the relations between party members and the party. In the Yugoslav interpretation it denotes the unrestricted discussion of options before the LCY adopts a firm position on a particular issue and the unwavering duty of the members to act in accord with the position once it is adopted.

Destatization. Synonymous with deetatization, the Yugoslav term for curtailing the role of the state administration in all economic matters for which SELF-MANAGEMENT arrangements can be designed.

Economic organizations. The Yugoslav shorthand term for such an ORGANIZATION OF ASSOCIATED LABOR as a BOAL, ENTERPRISE, or COMPOSITE ORGANIZATION OF ASSOCIATED LABOR.

Enterprise. The direct translation from the Serbo-Croatian would be "work organization." Most enterprises comprise several BOALS as their principal units; an enterprise is constituted by a SELF-MANAGEMENT AGREEMENT between BOALS. The stronger and more permanent identity of BOALS is evidenced by the right of BOALS to separate from the enterprise under certain conditions and either constitute themselves as individual enterprises or join another one.

Enterprise fund. Strictly speaking, ENTERPRISE funds are the funds of constituent BOALS. Three funds are commonly distinguished: a business fund, which is roughly equivalent to equity; a reserve fund to provide some financial support in the event of adverse business results; a common consumption fund for investment in housing and holiday facilities or for credits for private housing construction.

Federal Fund. The complete Serbo-Croatian name is the Federal Fund for Financing the Accelerated Development of the Less Developed Republics and the Autonomous Province of Kosovo. It collects mandatory loans from ENTERPRISES and transfers them in accord with a SOCIAL COMPACT to the less developed regions, which are responsible for the allocation to ENTERPRISES.

Free exchange of labor. See COMMUNITY OF INTEREST.

General consumption. The Yugoslav national accounts term for budgetary expenditure on administration and defense and subsidies to COMMUNITIES OF INTEREST for education, health, and pensions over and above regular expenditure, which is included under COLLECTIVE CONSUMPTION.

General Investment Fund. This was a federal investment fund which collected revenues from ENTERPRISES and received budget allocations; it then allocated these resources as credits or grants to particular ENTERPRISES. In the course of DECENTRALIZATION and DESTATIZ\TION, it was abolished before the economic reforms of 1965 and ts resources and responsibilities were transferrd to ENTERPRISES and BANKS.

GMP. See GROSS MATERIAL PRODUCT.

Gross material product. A national accounts concept used in all socialist countries to measure the output of goods and services. It is equivalent to the GDP of what are called "productive activities," disregarding the "nonproductive activities." The nonproductive activities do not generate "value" as defined by classical economics; they comprise administration, health, education, culture, defense, banking, and housing as the main components. According to the same concept, such economic variables as investment and employment distinguish between the productive and nonproductive.

Group ownership. The Yugoslav term for ENTERPRISE behavior geared to the maximization of the benefit of the present collective of WORKERS, who de facto appropriate the social property they use in the process. Group ownership now is strongly rejected as a corruption of socialism, a corruption that establishes monopoly rents for a privileged class of workers and does away with the socialist principle of solidarity. The conventional western theory of the Yugoslav-type firm, as propounded by Ward, Vanek, Domar, Mead, and others, is in fact a theory of group ownership.

Income. The Yugoslav term for the net income—after costs, depreciation, and taxes and contributions to COMMUNITIES OF INTEREST

—of a BOAL or ENTERPRISE before distribution to the personal INCOME of WORKERS and allocation to ENTERPRISE FUNDS.

Integration. The Yugoslav term denoting the establishment of permanent links, including mergers, between independent ENTERPRISES. Legally this can take the form of a COMPOSITE ORGANIZATION OF ASSOCIATED LABOR, BUSINESS COMMUNITY, or COMMUNITY FOR PLANNING AND BUSINESS COOPERATION established by specific SELF-MANAGEMENT AGREEMENTS on collaboration that does not establish a new legal entity (see REPRODUCTION ENTITY).

Internal bank. See BANK.

Joint pooling. The self-financing of investment with income and risk shared by participating BOALS and ENTERPRISES. See POOLING OF LABOR AND RESOURCES and POOLING OF RESOURCES.

Labor cost. In the Yugoslav accounting concepts focusing on INCOME, there are, strictly speaking, no labor costs because WORKERS do not receive contractual wages but some portion of the residual INCOME of the BOAL or ENTERPRISE. Labor cost is used as shorthand in this report for the sum of gross personal INCOMES of WORKERS and various contributions paid directly by the organization for services provided by a COMMUNITY OF INTEREST.

Market socialism. A particular theoretical model mostly associated with Lange and Lerner, its major proponents. It combines public ownership of MEANS OF PRODUCTION and central planning with enterprise decisionmaking on the basis of conventional marginal theorems. The term often was somewhat loosely applied to the Yugoslav system after 1965, but now has largely fallen out of favor.

Means of production. The common Marxian term for fixed and working assets.

Nonpriority activity. See PRIORITY ACTIVITY.

Nonproductive activity. See GROSS MATERIAL PRODUCT.

Organization of associated labor. The Yugoslav generic term for all legal entities that function by the ASSOCIATION OF LABOR, such entities as BOALS, ENTERPRISES, and COMPOSITE ORGANIZATIONS OF ASSOCIATED LABOR.

Past labor. Marxian term for capital used in connection with income distribution. It is based on the classical labor theory of value, which considers labor to be the only factor of production.

Personal income. See INCOME and WORKER.

Planning. See SELF-MANAGEMENT PLANNING and SOCIAL PLANNING.

Pooling of labor and resources. ENTERPRISES are constituted by BOALS under SELF-MANAGEMENT AGREEMENTS on the pooling of labor and resources. COMPOSITE ORGANIZATIONS OF ASSOCIATED LABOR and some less frequently used organizational arrangements between ENTERPRISES are established in the same way. Once the pooling of labor and resources is established, the members agree on the sharing of income and risk.

Pooling of resources. Financial links between BOALS and ENTERPRISES are established by SELF-MANAGEMENT AGREEMENTS on the pooling of resources. Such agreements regulate the conditions under which one organization temporarily makes financial resources available to another. The arrangement can be a traditional medium-term or long-term credit arrangement. It more frequently and increasingly implies the sharing of income and risk under JOINT POOLING.

Priority activity. An economic activity singled out in the SOCIAL PLAN of a SOCIOPOLITICAL COMMUNITY as being of special importance. Through SOCIAL COMPACTS priority activities have a higher degree of coordination and stronger commitments for implementation in the planning of affected ENTERPRISES than nonpriority activities. They also have the first claim to resources in the financing of investment programs and projects.

Productive activity. See GROSS MATERIAL PRODUCT.

Profit rate. The term used in this report to denote the rate at which an investable surplus is generated by BOALS and ENTERPRISES. The gross profit rate is depreciation plus additions to ENTERPRISE FUNDS, expressed as a percentage of the price-adjusted and depreciated value of fixed assets.

Reproduction entity. The Yugoslav term for a group of independent ENTERPRISES that are vertically linked and have concluded SELF-MANAGEMENT AGREEMENTS on collaboration, frequently including the POOLING OF RESOURCES. The reproduction entity does not constitute a legal entity.

Self-management. The Yugoslav term, akin to direct democracy, indicating that decisionmaking power is the exclusive prerogative of individuals who have to carry out decisions or are directly affected by them. Self-management excludes decisionmaking by elected representatives, who are legally autonomous throughout their term. Workers' self-management pertains to ECONOMIC ORGANIZATIONS.

Self-management agreement. A specific form of contract concluded among individuals—for example, on the ASSOCIATION OF LABOR within a BOAL—or among social sector organizations—for example, the POOLING OF LABOR AND RESOURCES among BOALS within an ENTERPRISE. The time horizon of such agreements extends over a five-year plan period or longer. Although reversible, they are normally expected to establish a permanent relationship.

Self-management planning. The Yugoslav term for planning conducted within and among ECONOMIC ORGANIZATIONS.

Sharing of income and risk. See POOLING OF LABOR AND RESOURCES and POOLING OF RESOURCES.

Social compact. The Yugoslav term for a specific form of contract concluded among SOCIOPOLITICAL COMMUNITIES or between SOCIO-POLITICAL COMMUNITIES and CHAMBERS OF THE ECONOMY on behalf of ENTERPRISES, trade unions, or both. They regulate such broad policy matters as BASIC PROPORTIONS, distributing ENTERPRISE INCOME, and allocating foreign exchange. Their main purpose is to regulate issues in a way consistent with the principle of SELF-MANAGEMENT, issues which in most countries are managed by the government or its agencies. In practice social compacts have the force of law for all signatories and for all nondissenting members (ENTERPRISES) of ASSOCIATIONS.

Socialist commodity production. The term "commodity" dates back to Marx and denotes reproducible goods manufactured with the input of labor for exchange at the market. Socialist commodity production is a common Marxian term referring to commodity production under socialism—that is, under a system of public ownership of the MEANS OF PRODUCTION and planning. In the special way the term was interpreted by Boris Kidric, it provided the basis for the Yugoslav route to socialism, with emphasis on DE-CENTRALIZATION and DESTATIZATION.

Social planning. The Yugoslav term for planning by SOCIOPOLITICAL COMMUNITIES.

Sociopolitical community. The Yugoslav term for a territorial unit having political and administrative functions. Sociopolitical communities comprise the federation, the republics and provinces, and the communes.

Sociopolitical organization. The Yugoslav term embracing the following organizations: the League of Communists of Yugoslavia (LCY), the Socialist Alliance, the Confederation of Trade Unions, the Veterans Federation, and the Union of Socialist Youth.

Solidarity fund. The Yugoslav term for a joint reserve fund established by all ENTERPRISES within the territory of a SOCIOPOLITICAL COMMUNITY. Its resources support ENTERPRISES that have exhausted their reserve funds (see ENTERPRISE FUND).

Stabilization. The Yugoslav term, adopted in this report as well, referring to action for correcting a variety of disequilibrium phenomena, such as inflation, balance-of-payment deficits, and physical shortages of inputs and outputs.

State capitalism. The term commonly used in Yugoslavia with a derogatory connotation to denote a political system in which the state owns the MEANS OF PRODUCTION and controls the economic process in such a way that the difference from private capitalism is reduced to formal ownership. The term essentially is identical with ADMINISTRATIVE SOCIALISM, which carries a less polemical connotation.

State planning. Planning under a system of ADMINISTRATIVE SOCIALISM or STATE CAPITALISM. The central administration carries out planning, which determines the targets for peripheral state organs and ENTERPRISES.

Statism. Synonymous with etatism, the term is applied in Yugoslavia to STATE CAPITALISM and ADMINISTRATIVE SOCIALISM.

Structural imbalances. The Yugoslav term characterizing the incidence of a variety of economic phenomena, including overly heavy import reliance, overly heavy dependence on volatile export markets, and capacity constraints in the production of raw materials and intermediate goods and excess capacity in the production of final goods.

Surplus product. A Marxian concept based on the classical labor theory of value. It denotes the fact that WORKERS do not receive the full value (net value added) of the output produced and that the retained surplus value—or expropriated labor time—is appropriated by the private owners of the MEANS OF PRODUCTION in a capitalist order or by society under socialism.

Surplus value. See SURPLUS PRODUCT.

Unity of the Yugoslav market. The Yugoslav term for the legal exclusion of restrictive business practices related to territorial considerations.

Work community. The Yugoslav term for an organizational unit that carries out special services—such as administration, planning, accounting, banking, and research and development—for a number of BOALS or ENTERPRISES. They carry out these services in exchange for compensation of incurred costs, including personal income.

Worker. In this report the term applies to all persons employed in the social sector and all wage earners in the private sector. Workers in social sector organizations do not receive contractual wages but a portion of the residual INCOME of the organization as their personal INCOME. In Yugoslavia usage, the self-employed in the private sector are referred to as "working people."

Working people. See WORKER.

Work organization. See ENTERPRISE.

Index

The full range of World Bank publications, both free and for sale, is described in the *Catalog of World Bank Publications*, and of the continuing research program of the World Bank, in *World Bank Research Program: Abstracts of Current Studies*. The most recent edition of each is available without charge from:

PUBLICATIONS UNIT
THE WORLD BANK
1818 H STREET, N.W.
WASHINGTON, D.C. 20433
U.S.A.